Capitalism Contested

Capitalism Contested

The New Deal and Its Legacies

Edited by

Romain Huret,
Nelson Lichtenstein,

and

Jean-Christian Vinel

PENN

UNIVERSITY OF PENNSYLVANIA PRESS

PHILADELPHIA

Published by
University of Pennsylvania Press
Philadelphia, Pennsylvania 19104-4112
www.upenn.edu/pennpress

Printed in the United States of America on acid-free paper
10 9 8 7 6 5 4 3 2 1

Library of Congress Cataloging-in-Publication Data
Names: Huret, Romain, editor. | Lichtenstein, Nelson, editor. |
Vinel, Jean-Christian, editor.
Title: Capitalism contested : the New Deal and its legacies / edited by
Romain Huret, Nelson Lichtenstein, and Jean-Christian Vinel.
Description: Philadelphia : University of Pennsylvania Press, [2020] |
Includes bibliographical references and index.
Identifiers: LCCN 2020010042 | ISBN 978-0-8122-5262-0 (hardcover)
Subjects: LCSH: New Deal, 1933–1939. | Capitalism—United States—
History—20th century. | Capitalism—United States—History—
21st century. | United States—Economic policy—20th century. |
United States—Economic policy—21st century. | United States—
Economic conditions—20th century. | United States—Economic
conditions—21st century. | United States—Politics and
government—20th century. | United States—Politics and government—
21st century.
Classification: LCC E806 .C325 2020 | DDC 973.917—dc23
LC record available at https://lccn.loc.gov/2020010042

CONTENTS

The New Deal: A Lost Golden Age?

Romain Huret, Nelson Lichtenstein, and Jean-Christian Vinel

In the historical narrative that prevails in the early twenty-first century, the New Deal years are positioned between two equally despised Gilded Ages, the first in the late nineteenth century, which inspired Mark Twain's witty phrase, and the second characterized by the new world of Walmart, globalization, and right-wing populism in which we currently live. What defines these two ages is an important and increasing level of inequality legitimized by powerful ideologies—namely, Social Darwinism at the end of the nineteenth century and neoliberalism today. In stark contrast, the era of the New Deal was first and foremost an attempt to put an end to inequality in U.S. society. In the historical *longue durée*, it appears today as a kind of golden age when policymakers and citizens sought to devise solutions to two major questions—labor on one side, social on the other—that stood at the heart of the U.S. political economy during the twentieth century.[1]

The increasing prominence of this reading of U.S. history owes much to the French economist Thomas Piketty's *Capital in the Twenty-First Century* and the U-shaped curve that has come to summarize his research.[2] With an impressive set of data, Piketty highlights the failure of an idea popularized during the Cold War by the National Bureau of Economic Research (NBER) economist Simon Kuznets.[3] Taking note of the reduction in income inequality from 1913 to 1948, Kuznets, an anticommunist émigré born in Russia, predicted that the United States had entered a new phase in its economic history, as a growing number of individuals reaped the benefits of growth and the share of the national income held by the richest individuals continued decreasing.[4] Kuznets's bell-shaped curve, which traced the relationship between growth and inequality, typified the optimism of the liberal consensus of the time on questions of political economy. Much like industrial pluralists who believed that collective bargaining had ended the class struggle in the United States, Kuznets suggested that inequality as an attribute of U.S. society was fading.[5]

Piketty's U-shaped curve traces the fall and rise of income inequality and shows that Kuznets's hypothesis—now a vanished dream—was too optimistic even in the 1950s.[6] With its emphasis on taxes and inheritance, Piketty's work offers an additional dimension to the work of historians and sociologists who have traced the rise and decline of labor unions as a key to the political economy that sustained the more cohesive class structure of the United States in the postwar era. Indeed, Piketty's story correlates well with the rise and fall of union membership density, which follows a symmetrically opposite curve.[7] Piketty has hardly been alone in his rediscovery of the exceptional period that coincides with the so-called New Deal order. Taken up by both pundits and scholars since the early years of the twenty-first century and famously advertised in Paul Krugman's *New York Times* article, "For Richer," in 2002, this statistical investigation of inequality gradually helped produce a new narrative in which the New Deal order is highlighted as a period of decreasing inequality, with the years between the 1930s and the 1970s becoming an exceptional "great compression." The publication of *Capital*, then, was a political moment that crystallized mounting fears and tensions about the state and sustainability of U.S. democracy and thus exposed as a fallacy the notion that Americans ignore or tolerate high levels of economic inequality.

In fact, from the end of the Cold War to the financial collapse of 2008, from the presidency of Barack Obama to that of Donald Trump, U.S. political culture has been in a state of both polarization and flux. The labor question seems very much back on the political and social agenda, even if it has been put there by right-wing populists seeking to dismantle all that is left of New Deal social provision and regulation. But whatever the partisan context, the return of Gilded Age levels of income inequality in a globalized world of capitalist instability and working-class multiculturalism has returned bedrock economic issues involving jobs, income, and security to the center of U.S. politics. Notably, in the first years of the Obama presidency, two prominent political sociologists called their survey of his first term "Reaching for a New New Deal."[8]

Such zeitgeist animates this collective book. We argue that Piketty's *Capital*—inasmuch as it enables historians to assess once again the period that opened up after the Great Depression—marked the passing of a historiographical moment.[9] Kuznets's theory, indeed, was very much in tune with the end of reform that underwrote the concept of the "New Deal order" as Steven Fraser and Gary Gerstle defined it in their famous 1989 book. Over the past fifteen years, as we note below, many historians have sought to move beyond this framework because they have found the concept too limited. Yet the return of a discussion of economic inequality has breathed new life into the concept of the New Deal order, this time as a political construct used to criticize the rise of neoliberalism—that is, the attempt to insert the principles of classical liberalism into modern governance—and its social consequences. This in turn has gone hand in hand with a more positive reading of the importance and consequence of the New Deal, a macrohistorical event that Ira Katznelson has compared to the French Revolution in *Fear Itself*.[10]

Our book, *Capitalism Contested*, is thus premised on the notion that we are today at an important historiographical juncture in the political history of the twentieth century, with questions of economic power, class relations, and political economy occupying a prominent position. Our current predicament—the high incidence of social inequality and poverty, the inescapable class dimension of many aspects of the lives of Americans from housing to education, working conditions, and health care—is deeply anchored in the history of the New Deal order. The moment is ripe, we believe, to revisit it, as both a concept and a historical phenomenon.

Revisiting the New Deal Order

For all the statistical allure of the "great compression," our argument that the New Deal order remains a useful concept for thinking about change and continuity in U.S. political, social, and economic history certainly requires elaboration. All historical concepts have a life cycle, and some might contend that the New Deal order has been so thoroughly discussed and challenged since 1989 that it has already lost most of its explanatory power.[11]

Measures of inequality were conspicuously absent from Fraser and Gerstle's volume, originally published in 1989. Rather, their purpose was to provide a chronology based on the concept of electoral realignment and an analysis of the ideological structures that sustained this order from the 1932 election until the Reaganite breakthrough in 1980. The New Deal electoral coalition, they explained, was the mainstay of an order that was defined by "an ideological character, a moral perspective, and a set of political relationships among policy elites, interest groups, and electoral constituencies that decidedly shaped American political life for forty years." But they did not aim to lament the end of a great past. The articles contained in that collection emphasized New Deal reformism as moderate and limited. It was merely a lost opportunity rather than a lost golden age. As a whole, the collection faulted liberals for failing in the 1960s to prevent the disintegration of the order they had created.[12]

In the decades since the publication of that book, scholars have uncovered the racial and gender dynamics at work in the making of New Deal social provisions, suggesting the tensions were so strong that the New Deal order was fragmented and fragile from the beginning. Many women were excluded from the Wagner Act, the Social Security Act, and the Fair Labor Standards Act. Although drafted in gender-neutral terms, these laws used a definition of "employee" that limited security to full-time workers, thus excluding part-time, hospital, educational, and agricultural workers. Almost all government workers were excluded from coverage by federal labor laws, and many retail and clerical workers were unable to secure benefits under the Social Security Act. Domestic service, the largest source of employment for women in the United States before 1940, was excluded from employment legislation by both Congress and state legislatures in the first decades of the twentieth century. Southern congressmen were not the only culprits; middle-class Progressive activists in the North who supported labor reform for men and children contended that domestic service was a fundamentally different activity that did not deserve coverage by the New Deal statutes. The New Deal social wage was thus only available to about one-fifth of all women, and the rest were consigned to a dependent status by a "maternalist ideal" that did not construe them as legitimate breadwinners; their dependency was "succored," in Gwendolyn Mink's apt phrase, by programs of assistance.[13]

Historians have not simply shifted the social basis of New Deal provisions from electoral constituencies to the male breadwinner household. They have also revealed the extent to which the New Deal order presumed white citizenship. Racial issues proved equally vexing to the early New Dealers, in the unions and in terms of social policy. Occupations that heavily employed blacks, including agriculture and the service trades, were excluded from coverage by key New Deal statutes. This decision reflected the power of southern congressmen, whose defense of segregation became the warp and woof of New Deal social provision. Yet Southerners were not alone in shaping a white New Deal—indeed, the New Deal political economy contained many obstacles to black economic advancement. In the North and South, African Americans faced a combination of local and federal policies, labor union rules, municipal machines, and social practices that turned the quest for security into a racialized pattern of insiders and outsiders. Reviewing a host of local struggles that developed in response to this institutionalized exclusion, historians such as Martha Biondi, Robert Self, Rhonda Williams, Matthew Countryman, Paul Jones, Jacqueline Hall, Gordon Mantler, and Thomas Sugrue have shown that a long civil rights movement was embedded within the shifting trajectory of the liberal state from the1930s to the 1970s.[14] Rooted in the popular front and the civil rights unionism that developed in the 1940s, this movement had an important social democratic potential that transcended the formal rights-oriented color blindness on which the traditional historiography of the civil rights movement had focused. The March on Washington "for Jobs and Freedom" and the debates over the mid-1960s Freedom Budget were illustrative of this potential. Yet the policy impasse at the federal level ensured that it was mostly in local struggles for equal opportunity in employment and housing in the North and West that the movement advanced its agenda, even if, notably, these struggles failed to effect the transformation of the urban political economy that would have been necessary to prevent the white suburbanization that led to the urban crisis.[15]

Equally important in the long history and outcome of these struggles against entrenched white economic power was the evolution of the law and the bifurcation of the labor and civil rights impulses into two different legal venues. As the legal historians Reuel Schiller and Sophia Lee have shown, because postwar liberals failed to promote an economic egalitarianism that would also sustain African Americans' quest for racial justice in the workplace, the labor movement and the civil rights movement increasingly relied on separate and conflicting legal mechanisms—labor law on the one hand and an emerging civil rights legal discourse on the other—that often turned trade unions and their erstwhile civil rights allies into increasingly embittered rivals.[16]

Our book does not challenge these fundamental insights. Rather, we argue that the New Deal order has been a continually evolving construct that remains the key to understanding twentieth-century political, social, and economic history. The New Deal order was a product of a particular set of political institutions, social movements, ideological propensities, and legislative initiatives that gave shape and substance to this mid-twentieth-century reform impulse. Bringing back these structural forces seems crucial to making sense of the New Deal order, especially in the field of political economy.

Bringing Back Political Economy

As the study of both domestic and global capitalism has become an increasingly compelling focus of historical inquiry, it is apparent that the rise of New Deal reformism was predicated on and shaped by the particular character of the capitalist economy it sought to reshape. Three features of that economy are notable. First, as scholars of nineteenth- and early twentieth-century U.S. capitalism, including Jonathan Levy, Andrew Wender Cohen, Scott Nelson, Edward Balleisen, Jeffrey Sklansky, and Richard White, have demonstrated, corruption, instability, inequality, ethnic conflict, and partisanship were deeply embedded within U.S. entrepreneurial culture.[17] The corporation, as a legal and organizational construct, remained a highly contested form of economic enterprise.[18] Unresolved too was the capacity of the state to use either the Federal Reserve or other regulatory instruments to ameliorate the business cycle, curb unemployment, and increase working-class incomes. Both the money question and the labor question were as yet unresolved at the dawn of the New Deal impulse.

Second, the New Deal proved efficacious because it coincided with that epoch in U.S. history when the American economy was continental in scope yet insular in relation to that of other countries. Foreign trade and finance were relatively unimportant. This made Keynesian tools of economic governance highly effective: these included countercyclical fiscal policy, monetary stability, state support for collective bargaining, and regulatory policies designed to boost consumption.[19] As the economic historians Robert Collins and Robert Gordon have demonstrated, productivity growth—and economic growth more generally—was uniquely high, even when the transition from an economic regime based on heavy industry to a more consumer-oriented one helped make the Great Depression truly great, an argument first advanced by the historians Michael Bernstein and Colin Gordon.[20]

Finally, a notable feature of New Deal political economy was the centrality of the vertically integrated, multidivisional corporation to the politics and regulatory statecraft of that era. As Philip Scranton, Howell Harris, and other business historians have demonstrated, smaller, proprietary firms remained important and dynamic features of the industrial landscape before and during the New Deal era.[21] But the giant industrial corporation, often with a mass production technology at its heart, captured the imagination of the New Deal generation. Both Alfred Chandler and John Kenneth Galbraith made these bureaucratically structured institutions central to their understanding of the U.S. economy.[22] Likewise, Adolf Berle, Gardiner Means, and Peter Drucker, not to mention Franklin Roosevelt himself, saw the democratization, if not the breakup, of these enterprises as central to any reform of U.S. capitalism. And, as Joshua Freeman demonstrates in *Behemoth: A History of the Factory in the Making of the Modern World*, the fact that such companies were also identified with gigantic production complexes employing tens of thousands of proletarians proved ideologically attractive to reformers of the Left as well as those advocating the industrial status quo. From Alfred Sloan to Walter Reuther, and from Thomas Watson to Philip Murray, the effort to regulate and democratize the giant corporation remained a much-contested terrain of struggle during the New Deal era.[23] All this would become enormously consequential when U.S. corporations encountered a more challenging economic environment, a product of both greater competition from abroad and financialization at home.

Although the first generation of New Deal historians were well aware of the ideological and economic headwinds faced by this effort to reform U.S. capitalism, scholars writing in the twenty-first century have demonstrated the breadth, depth, and ideological diversity of those hostile to the Rooseveltian project in particular and to social democracy more generally. Intellectual historians have been particularly important to this project. In *Transcending Capitalism: Visions of a New Society in Modern American Thought*, Howard Brick explored how reformist intellectuals of the interwar era sought to decenter the market and the profit motive in their effort to imagine a postcapitalist society that enhanced and advanced New Deal principles of social welfare and corporate regulation. But that project encountered furious resistance among those who considered virtually any effort to manage U.S. capitalism a subversion of a free society. Jennifer Burns, Angus Burgin, and Nancy MacLean have explored the work of a highly influential set of anti–New Deal and procapitalist intellectuals, and Kim Philips-Fein and Lawrence Glickman have demonstrated the degree to which businessmen and politicians have sustained and contributed to this increasingly powerful anti–New Deal discourse.[24]

More important than ideology, however, in tracing the rise of opposition to the New Deal and its increasing efficacy in the 1970s and afterward, have been the concrete struggles between labor and management and among capitalists who have sought to escape or thwart the regulatory structures erected by a generation of New Dealers. The 1940s and 1950s were exceptionally prosperous, but that good fortune hardly tempered corporate hostility to the New Deal state and the trade union movement that had flourished under its wing. Writing in the early 1980s, Howell Harris demonstrated that the corporate "right to manage" proved a banner under which a business mobilization against labor took place, and more recently Mark Wilson has shown that despite nearly guaranteed sales and profits, big business found the political economy that governed the World War II production effort far too intrusive. Jennifer Klein has shown during this same era that business hostility to the expansion of the New Deal welfare state was also based on a fear of labor militancy and the growth of state power and legitimacy. And in their studies of regionally based businessmen and politicians, Elizabeth Shermer and Shane Hamilton have demonstrated that powerful elites, especially in the South and West, have sought to escape the New Deal regulatory state in the name of economic development. This same highly politicized and culturally resonant impulse helped corporations like Walmart and Lone Star Steel, and the many enterprise migrants from North to South, generate a business culture and political environment that was allergic to the thrust of the entire New Deal idea. By the 1970s, corporations and politicians hostile to any limitation on the market were increasingly active in U.S. politics.[25]

The business counteroffensive against the whole structure of New Deal regulation took place not just on an ideological, geographical, or cultural plane, but in terms of the very structure of enterprise and employment. By the 1970s and 1980s, the managerial quest for "shareholder value" proved a spur to a radical reorganization of many businesses. Instead of scope and scale, managers now sought a radical focus on just the core operations and values of the enterprise. Global supply chains replaced vertically integrated production; "fissured" employment enabled management to rely on the market to discipline labor; meanwhile, new forms of contracted and temporary labor began to eviscerate the traditional employee-employer relationship and the New Deal regulations and protections associated with that framework.[26]

The progressivity of the New Deal–era tax regime has also proved a highly partisan issue that has increasingly tilted toward the interests of capital. In the 1980s historians such as Mark Leff argued that Rooseveltian "soak the rich" taxation rhetoric was but a symbolic effort designed to appease the forces of democracy. But in more recent decades a new generation of scholars has revisited the tax policy of that era to demonstrate that New Dealers invented one of the most ambitious forms of progressive taxation, a fiscal state that emerged, as the legal scholar Ajay Mehrotra has shown, at the end of Reconstruction and took its full shape during World War II. It was both broadly based and highly progressive. Conservatives had, of course, attacked this tax structure in the 1930s, but mobilization against it made headway only in the 1970s and afterward when those hostile to the political economy of the New Deal took advantage of the stagflation and productivity decline characteristic of that decade to deploy a set of supply-side slogans and initiatives that could make the evisceration of progressive taxation appeal to millions of Americans and not just a tiny circle of rich white men.[27]

All this amounted to what we today call "neoliberalism." In his contribution to the original *Rise and Fall of the Fall of the New Order*, Ira Katznelson noted that one of the hallmarks of that order was the disappearance of sustained discussion investigating the relationship between the social and the economic. He asked "whether a 'third way' could be found to maximize the chances for prosperity *and* liberty in the post-depression, post-war world." Ideologically totalizing viewpoints exemplified by books such as Karl Polanyi's *Great Transformation* or Friedrich Hayek's the *Road to Serfdom*, Katznelson explained, had given way to a moderate Keynesianism that relegated questions of political economy to specialists who studied the national economy in isolation from the social and political dynamics characteristic of the society as a whole.[28] More recent scholarship, however, has shown that the search for the "third way" did not stop in the 1940s. In fact, Hayek stood at the center of an international intellectual community that never accepted Polanyi's famous double transformation. Angus Burgin, Philip Mirowski and Dieter Plehwe, Jean Solchany, and Daniel Stedman Jones have uncovered much of that story.[29] Starting in 1938 with the Colloque Walter Lippman held in Paris and then moving forward—thanks to lavish business funding directed toward the Mont Pèlerin Society and the Chicago School of economists after 1948—this generation of libertarian economists worked to make a case for their vision of a disembedded market as the source of human freedom and market principles as a mode of social organization.

To be sure, this neoliberalism never quite achieved either unanimity or hegemony. First, there were important differences of opinion between members of the group (between Europeans and Americans on the status of labor unions; and between the Virginia School's James Buchanan and Gordon Tullock and Chicago's Milton Friedman on the relationship between the free market and democracy). Second, neoliberal prescriptions, which ranged from monetarism to the privatization of social protections, including health care and education, remained heavily influenced and constrained by the institutional and political characteristics of each national context.[30] Nevertheless, by the 1980s and 1990s there was no denying the influence of neoliberal ideas on both the left- and the right sides of the political spectrum, in the United States and the United Kingdom certainly, but also in Sweden and other traditionally social democratic European polities.[31] In this respect the 1970s were indeed a "pivotal decade," as Judith Stein has noted. Against the backdrop of a crisis that frayed the Keynesian consensus, policymakers created the political and social framework that engendered austerity at home, the increasing financialization of much economic activity, and the emergence of a global trading system that eroded U.S. manufacturing.[32]

A Structural and *Longue Durée* Framework

In assessing the influence of neoliberalism on the New Deal, however, it is important to see that order in the *longue durée* of U.S. governance. In this respect, the literature on U.S. political development is most valuable. Historians working in this field have successfully challenged the notion that the U.S. state was weak in the nineteenth century. By adopting a more capacious definition of state activism, they have uncovered previously unseen forms of public governance. Such an approach expands the continuity and rupture of the New Deal order both chronologically and thematically.[33] Similarly, it would be wrong to conclude that the 1980s and Republican victories at the polls in that decade and later ushered in a period during which—under the sway of increasingly powerful neoliberal ideas—the state was thoroughly removed from U.S. society and its economy, turning the United States into a homogeneously "Right Nation," to use the title of a well-known volume.[34]

Although there is no denying the importance of the political changes that have been wrought since the presidency of Ronald Reagan, some of which have struck at the heart of the ideal of security that was the "moral imperative" of the New Deal order, we nevertheless need a more complex perspective that takes into account the long-term influence of liberal reform. Here again, the work done by scholars of U.S. political development is important. As Stephen Skowronek has argued, "The conservative turn did as much to expose the legacy of liberalism as it did to displace it." Far from erasing the structures erected by liberal reformers from the institutional landscape, conservatives have had to work with them and through them to produce conservative results. Their ability to do so has been constrained by the U.S. electorate's preferences, which do not mirror the ideological logic of neoliberal treatises, but also by the fact that liberal reform has not simply built state power, it has empowered entrenched interest groups to vie for influence over the formulation and implementation of key state policies. All in all, the liberal state has shaped conservatism as much as conservatism has transformed it.[35]

Although U.S. liberalism has certainly not regained the credibility and dominance it had during the 1930s and 1940s, and although the coalition that sustained that midcentury, labor-oriented polity is gone, we argue that the neoliberal assault on the New Deal order has fallen far short of its grandest expectations both in the Reaganite 1980s and during subsequent conservative presidencies. Despite a Supreme Court that toys with Lochner-era jurisprudence, the fiscal and regulatory powers of the federal government remain extensive, and the "culture wars" have been largely won by Progressives. Furthermore, key pillars of the U.S. welfare state, including federal guarantees covering retirement security and health insurance have either been preserved or enhanced, at least through the end of the Obama presidency.

Although the U.S. Right can take satisfaction in the virtual destruction of the labor movement and the legal framework that once sustained it, in the end, no political order exhibiting the potent "ideological character and moral perspective" that Steve Fraser and Gary Gerstle identified with the New Deal has successfully arisen in its stead. Rather, a struggle over the fate of that order has gone a long way toward maintaining the ideological breach that has divided Left from Right during the past century and the partisan line that has divided most Republicans from most Democrats during that same era. We suggest, then, that the New Deal order remains a very effective framework to make sense of U.S. political history and the transformation of U.S. political economy in the years since 1929. The essays assembled here therefore offer a historicized analysis of the degree to which that political, economic, and ideological order persists and the ways in which it has been transcended or even overthrown. These essays pay great attention not only to those ideas and social forces hostile to the New Deal but also to the contradictions and debilities that were present at the inauguration or became inherent in this liberal impulse during the last half of the twentieth century. The unifying theme among the essays consists not in their subject matter—politics, political economy, social thought, and legal scholarship are all well-represented—but in a historical quest to assess the transformation and fate of an economic and policy order nearly a century after its creation.

*   *   *

The book is organized into three parts. Part I, "The Political Economy of New Deal Reformism," probes the ideological meaning and policy framework that both sustained and subverted the New Deal order. In Chapter 1, K. Sabeel Rahman emphasizes the technocratic managerialism that stood at the heart of so many aspects of the New Deal regulatory state, contrasting this effort to make markets work in a more efficient manner with the more democratic and radical Progressivism of theorists and practitioners such as Louis Brandeis and John Dewey a generation before. Both Brandeis and Dewey had put forth a more expansive and radical vision of democracy that directly confronted both the concentrated economic power inherent in corporate capital and the inequalities generated by untamed market forces. The New Deal achieved many of these Progressive policy aspirations, but the New Dealers' emphasis on what Rahman calls the "neutral goals of growth and welfare," led them to narrow down the role of economic experts to the efficient management of the market, thus opening the door to the rise of a neoliberalism that mobilized popular hostility to governmental power and expertise on grounds of inefficiency and interest capture. Much of the brittleness of the New Deal political economy, Rahman argues, is rooted in the New Dealers' decision to move away from attempts to find democratic solutions to questions of class and inequality in the modern economy.

In Chapter 2, Timothy Shenk discusses the emergence in the early twentieth century of the idea of a national economy that sustains Rahman's critique of New Deal technocratic politics. In the Progressive era and before, the idea that it was the responsibility of the federal government to measure and then enhance overall economic growth was foreign to both progressives and reactionaries. The very concept of an integrated, interdependent national economy simply did not exist. New Deal economists and statisticians helped create that understanding of how the world works, but in the process an emphasis on economic growth and full employment helped narrow the meaning of U.S. liberalism and relegitimize the giant corporation, whose power and purpose now seemed less salient than the sheer job-creating growth of an entity like General Motors or General Electric.

Jason Scott Smith (Chapter 3) and Samir Sonti (Chapter 4) offer a set of more favorable understandings of the New Deal impulse that stand in marked contrast to the technocratic critique put forward by Rahman and Shenk. In his essay, Smith celebrates the mixed economy that he identifies as key to the New Deal's highly successful state-sponsored economic development characteristic of the 1930s and 1940s. Economic growth was "spectacular" during these decades, but, argues Smith, it did not displace the effort to "reform" U.S. capitalism as Alan Brinkley argued in his contribution to the 1989 volume edited by Fraser and Gerstle. There was far more continuity between the early years of the New Deal, including the era of the corporatist National Industrial Recovery Administration, and the experience of World War II and after, when the enormous growth and transformation of the economy—and the rise of living standards for black, brown, and white—represented a triumph of American liberalism.

Like Smith, Samir Sonti argues that not all aspects of New Deal–era Keynesianism were obstacles to a more thoroughgoing reform of U.S. capitalism. Sonti identifies a strand of New Deal statecraft he labels "institutional Keynesianism." Emerging out of the Department of Agriculture, where figures like Mordecai Ezekiel, Gardiner Means, and Donald Montgomery sought to reverse deflationary pressures, this cohort of policymakers and intellectuals came to see the persistent inflationary pressures that bedeviled postwar America as a product of oligopolistic corporate power, especially in key industries such as steel and automobiles, which "administered" prices by managerial fiat. The demand for full employment by Keynesians of this institutional orientation did not represent a retreat from a program of structural intervention in favor of the politics of growth, argues Sonti. Instead, their program, whose influence continued well beyond the 1930s, was designed to achieve a national social democracy that began with the radical reorganization and regulation of the farm economy and then sustained working-class purchasing power by integrating the otherwise segmented urban and rural political economies.

In Part II of our book, "New Deal Headwinds: Contestation and Resistance," four authors interrogate the structural forces that helped dismantle the New Deal order. In Chapter 5, Karen Tani argues that New Deal welfare programs did not replicate the paternalism of earlier eras. Instead they created a set of "rights" that welfare recipients used both to their own advantage and to that of those New Dealers charged with advancing a robust welfare state. Although the decentralization of New Deal welfare programs, which gave a larger role to states and localities, has often facilitated racist and sexist administrative welfare regimes, Tani shows that during the most dynamic phases of the early New Deal, the lack of local and state capacity meant that local officials had to structure their program in line with mandates from Washington. In Chapter 6, in parallel fashion, Elizabeth Tandy Shermer examines the fate of another government program, considering the origins of the contemporary student debt crisis, which now burdens college graduates with more than a trillion dollars in outstanding financial obligations. Shermer shows that because of the racial and religious divides that fractured postsecondary education, as well as the elitism of many private colleges and universities, New Deal efforts to expand higher education were distorted and constrained. Offering aid and loans to individual students, rather than institutions, proved a dysfunctional compromise that increasingly put the burden of higher education finance on hard-pressed families, while encouraging tuition hikes, the growth of for-profit institutions, and a fragmentation of the country's system of higher education.

Conservative ideology and practice constitute the subject of two additional chapters in this part of our book. In a discussion of the historical background to California's Proposition 13 and other property tax limitation laws at the state level, Isaac William Martin (Chapter 7) reaches back to the late nineteenth century and the era of the New Deal to demonstrate that such tax "revolts" are nothing new, but represent a favorite strategy of those elements of the population, both plebian and elite, hostile to government regulatory initiatives. Neoliberal ideology had little to do with the actual origins of Proposition 13 and other tax limitation initiatives of the 1970s: rather, deep structural flaws in the New Deal order, which left state and local governments fiscally responsible for a growing burden of welfare services and infrastructure expenditures, stoked the resentments of middle-class homeowners whose taxes had jumped as the nominal value of their property ballooned in an era of stagflation and fiscal crisis. A victory of the antitax Right was not inevitable: labor and the Democrats had their own tax-relief plans for hard-pressed homeowners. But a combination of happenstance and hard work enabled veteran conservatives like Howard Jarvis to champion this discontent and thereby constitutionalize an utterly regressive and austerity-generating tax regime that has hobbled the New Deal order for more than four decades.

In Chapter 8, on the influence of the libertarian Koch brothers' network on U.S. politics and social policy, Nancy MacLean also demonstrates the interplay between ideology and organizational power, the latter abundantly fueled by tens of millions of Koch dollars. Milton Friedman and the Chicago School of economic theorists effectively made the argument that business and the market had to be freed from the hand of the state in order for capitalist liberty to flourish, whereas James Buchanan and his Virginia School of economic and political thought put equal emphasis on the fettering of democracy itself, a project powerfully advanced in the twenty-first century by the billionaire Koch brothers and their like-minded confederates. MacLean's on-the-ground analysis of how the Koch network funded a regiment of politicians, academics, and operatives goes a long way toward explaining how, at a moment in 2008 and 2009, when financial capitalism had so clearly demonstrated its failures, a powerful, right-wing movement arose that rapidly deployed an effective set of state-level policy initiatives designed to eviscerate the labor movement, block the implementation of the Affordable Care Act, and entrench Republican Party rule in a fashion that subverted democratic norms.

Part III of this book, "Capital and Labor at the Twilight of the New Deal," analyzes economic structures that shape political debates and articulate social tensions. In Chapter 9, Nelson Lichtenstein explains how and why New Dealers once thought that the giant, centralized, vertically integrated corporation stood close to the heart of their social imagination, as an object of both scorn and reform. But in recent decades corporate management has deployed an extensive set of legal and organizational innovations to disaggregate the corporation and "fissure" the workplace, thus giving capital an enormous legal, financial, and managerial advantage in the governance of the supply chains that are today the sinews of global trade and production. In Chapter 10, Margaret O'Mara examines a particular variant of corporate America, the people and companies of the modern technology industry and its command-and-control center in Silicon Valley. She offers a critical deconstruction of the high-tech executives and professionals who see themselves as "disrupters" of traditional industries, markets, and state institutions. Early success in Silicon Valley was highly dependent on the Cold War state, but the same forces that destabilized the business and labor constituencies of the New Deal order in the 1970s also opened up avenues for small, agile new businesses that could quickly globalize supply chains, slash labor costs, and generate an antiunion, contingent-employment regime.

In Chapter 11, William P. Jones turns to the world of labor to examine the history of public employment unionism. He argues that although such unions were once subject to intense hostility because of their left-wing character in the 1930s and 1940s, the reemergence of state and local public employee unionism in the 1960s constituted a victory for both labor and the New Deal that partially compensated for the failure of unions to organize the South. But the success of such unionism could not stand in isolation from the larger conservative assault on the New Deal order, evidenced most recently in judicial decisions undermining the organizational and financial strength of public-sector unionism. Finally, in Chapter 12, Kate Andrias confronts this new labor relations regime, delineating the erosion of the legal structures sustaining a potent union movement, and also identifying the sources of a new legal regime that might sustain a different kind of unionism, one more attuned to the needs of workers and the characteristics of workplaces in today's economy. Inspired by the "Fight for $15" movement and other such low-wage, industrywide insurgencies, this new framework moves labor law away from the individual worksite and the traditional employer/employee dyad while claiming a greater role for unions in formulating public employment policy and, indeed, the direction of the entire political economy.

PART I

The Political Economy of
New Deal Reformism

CHAPTER 1

Transcending the New Deal Idea of the State

Managerialism, Neoliberalism, and Democracy

K. Sabeel Rahman

On January 20, 2017, Donald Trump was inaugurated as the forty-fifth president of the United States. Trump's rise fueled and encapsulated a particularly brazen vision of right-wing populism, fusing exclusionary racial resentment and appeals to white nationalism and identity, with the deregulatory antigovernment zeal of the modern conservative movement. Trump's ascendance represented a stunning repudiation of the core tenets of twentieth-century liberalism: its faith in government and its commitment to a broadly inclusive membership and an expansive vision for social and economic citizenship. Along with a Republican-dominated Congress, the incoming Trump administration was poised to dismantle the policies of the Obama administration—and of the longer-term legacy of the New Deal, from financial regulations to the social safety net to labor rights and more. The whiplash of this political transition, following the efforts of President Barack Obama (who himself came into office with a transformative mandate to revive government and address economic inequities in the aftermath of the 2008 financial crisis) to update, revive, and deepen the New Deal legacy in areas like health care, financial reform, labor rights, and more, raises the question of what happened to this legacy. A growing and rich literature explores the rise of movement conservatism and right-wing populism driving the politics of the Right.[1] But to understand the transformations of the present, we must also look inward to the failures and limitations within late twentieth-century and early twenty-first-century liberalism itself.

In their classic 1989 volume, *The Rise and Fall of the New Deal Order*, Steve Fraser and Gary Gerstle assembled essays tracing the ways in which the New Deal transformed and ultimately narrowed the scope of twentieth-century economic liberalism.[2] The idea of a New Deal order has been problematized in various ways since then: the origins of New Deal policies rooted in the Progressive and Populist eras preceding Franklin Roosevelt's election; diagnosing the racialized and gendered limitations of the New Deal; and documenting the many cross-currents and tensions within the New Deal itself.[3] Nevertheless, nearly thirty years later, Fraser and Gerstle's volume provides a starting point for assessing the limitations of contemporary liberalism.

In this chapter, I suggest that the brittleness of contemporary liberalism is largely a product of its reliance on a particular conception of political economy rooted in a specific strand of New Deal statecraft: specifically, a managerial, technocratic idea of the state.[4] This "managerial" view of political economy is characterized by two presumptions: first, that the purposes of state action are to optimize the functioning of an otherwise desirable and efficient free market; and second, that these purposes should be achieved through the use of expert, technocratic regulators operating apart from the ordinary ebbs and flows of democratic politics. Managerial political economy represents one (but not the only) strand of New Deal, and pre–New Deal progressive political thought, but arguably played an out-sized role in shaping liberal law, policy, and discourse. The debates over political economy in the Obama administration are indicative of this managerial vision. Consider the financial regulation debate, for example. Despite the widespread popular discontent with Wall Street, financial elites, and economic inequality following the 2008 crash, the Obama administration cast the problem of finance not as one of deeper democratic mobilization or economic transformation, but rather as a project of filling "gaps and weaknesses in the supervision and regulation of financial firms," to be accomplished by expanding the resources, authorities, and insulation of expert federal regulators.[5] This managerial view was codified in the administration's financial reform bill and its effort to address the problem of "systemic risk" and too-big-to-fail financial firms.[6] The Obama financial reform package was emblematic of a broader pattern of technocratic, managerial economic policy in which mainstream contemporary liberalism largely *de*politicized fundamental conflicts over economic power and economic equity, casting problems of financial and corporate power and economic inequality as matters of market optimization to be addressed by neutral, efficiency-enhancing expert regulators.[7]

Although this managerial vision of political economy seeks to ground the legitimacy of the liberal state—and its efforts to manage the vicissitudes of capitalism—on the efficacy and neutrality of government by experts, it remains troublingly vulnerable to neoliberal critique. If the liberal project is premised on optimizing the market through technocratic expertise, as soon as the market can be shown to be self-regulating, and the efficacy and accountability of expertise called into question, this idea of the state crumbles. Anxieties about expertise, capture, and regulatory failure are not just conservative fictions; they are real—as is the need to get beyond a vision of regulation that is limited solely to market management and optimization. Furthermore, managerialism displaces more democratic visions of political economy that, in their appeal to bottom-up mobilization, participation, and power-building, and their thick moral commitment to social and economic inclusion, provide a very different foundation for the legitimacy and force of liberalism. In the financial reform context, for example, a variety of political actors, thinkers, and scholars espoused a very different response, using the crisis to call for a more democratic mobilization of citizens and communities, geared toward an attack on the economic and political power of finance and corporate concentration.[8]

The challenge of twenty-first-century liberalism, therefore, is not to re-create, but rather to transcend this managerialist legacy of the New Deal idea of the state. Indeed, there is another tradition of U.S. liberalism that provides the starting point for such an alternative: not the technocratic, managerialist New Deal vision, but a more radical democratic account of the state articulated by the preceding generation of populists, progressives, and labor republicans. In this rival, "democratic" vision of political economy, the purpose of the state was not merely to manage the market but to structurally transform the economy in an egalitarian direction by checking excesses of private power and economic domination.[9] Furthermore, these thinkers argued that such economic transformation depended in part on a grassroots democratic vision of reform politics, which needed mobilization and participation to drive economic transformation. This tradition informed some alternative strands of early New Deal reform and has periodically resurfaced in reform politics over the course of the past century. This is the tradition that contemporary liberalism must recover.

Managerialism and the New Deal Idea of the State

The New Deal radically transformed not only the U.S. economy but also underlying conceptions of the modern state. In the Progressive Era stretching from the late nineteenth to the early twentieth century (roughly 1880–1920), the upheavals of industrial capitalism generated a rich intellectual critique of economic power. These ideas and the reform movements they inspired animated much of early New Deal politics. But although the New Deal built on and in many ways codified earlier Progressive Era critiques of industrial capitalism and aspirations for more mobilized, democratic politics, by the mid-twentieth century, New Deal statecraft had transformed to emphasize a particular strand of technocratic, managerial governance that would later prove a problematic foundation for late-century liberalism.

Confronted by new, powerful corporate entities—from railroad monopolies, trusts like Standard Oil, and financial elites like J. P. Morgan—as well as recurring financial panics, industrialization, and widespread dislocation, a disparate set of Progressive Era thinkers and reformers turned to ideas of democracy as part of their critique of industrial capitalism, and their emerging vision of the modern state.[10] The focus for many thinkers and reformers was the problem of private power and the need for democratic government to hold private actors accountable. In the words of the legal reformer and later Supreme Court Justice Louis Brandeis, the new mega-corporations of the industrial age enjoyed profits while paying less-than-subsistence wages, creating a disparity in political power that was akin to slavery, which made workers "absolutely subject" to the will of the corporation.[11] Labor republicans developed a similar critique of "wage slavery" as driven by the arbitrary power of bosses and owners to interfere with workers, whether through outright harassment or the routinized processes of hierarchical, authoritarian, workplace order.[12]

The problem of corporate power was not just one of "bigness" and monopoly; it was a more generalized problem of private actors channeling a degree of influence and power that made them akin to sovereign states, yet lacking in any of the checks and balances imposed on republican governments. Louis Jaffe argued that private trade groups and corporations created *law* by generating standard practices and customs: in effect, for Jaffe, "The state has relinquished to the individual the 'sovereign' function of laying down the rules which govern society."[13] As Guido Marx, a Stanford University professor of mechanical engineering and leading voice among progressive-minded academics, wrote in the *Nation* in 1931, the grant of corporate charter was, in effect, "an alienation of sovereignty" that improperly conveyed to private elites the power to tax and to control access to those goods through their control over production, pricing, and distribution.[14] The problem with such private power was not just its arbitrary authority over workers and consumers but also the ways in which the nominal "privateness" of firms obscured these exercises of power and made them more difficult to contest and hold accountable in comparison to the public debates over state laws and policies.[15] If corporations had state-like coercive powers, they would have to be subjected to the kinds of democratic checks and accountability to ensure that such power served the public, not private, good.

This Progressive Era critique of capitalism extended to the problem of power not only in its corporate form but also in the form of the more diffused structure of the market system itself. During the early decades of the twentieth century, the legal realist movement, a collection of legal and economist academics, came to view the market not as a natural force, but as a human-made system arising from the aggregation of individual transactions and bargains that themselves were shaped by background conditions of property, contract, and tort law. These transactions were shaped by background disparities of bargaining power and influence. The "market" rates for wages or prices—and the distribution of income itself—were therefore not "natural," but rather a product of the "relative power of coercion which the different members of the community can exert against one another."[16] This critique of market capitalism—that the market was not a domain of efficient binary transactions but rather one suffused with coercion, disparities of power, and fundamentally the product of background laws and policy judgments affected the distribution of such power—also shaped the thought of institutional economists like John Commons and Richard Ely, in addition to lawyers like Brandeis and philosophers like John Dewey.[17] Because the coercive powers of private individuals themselves derived from state-sanctioned structures of property and contract rights, these distributions were products of human action—and therefore open to reform. As with the critique of concentrated private power, this critique of the market system opened up space for state action to respond. The blurring of the distinction between state power and private power was vital to enabling more open policy interventions aimed at economic ills such as income inequality or low wages.[18]

This critique of capitalism motivated a turn to state action and regulation as a counterweight to private and market power. As Bill Novak argues, during the late nineteenth century, these Progressive Era reformers constructed new regulatory institutions at the state, local, and federal levels to manage problems like monopoly power, railroads, and social welfare conditions, serving as a precursor to the New Deal state.[19] But there remained an underlying tension between different understandings of *how* such state institutions ought to be constituted and directed. Progressive Era reformers were very much enamored of the newfound power of social science and technical expertise to serve the public interest. But at the same time, many reformers also saw the state in quintessentially democratic terms, as an arena for giving voice to, empowering, and catalyzing bottom-up movements, organizations, and associations.

In the midst of the Great Depression, Franklin Roosevelt drew readily on these Progressive Era ideas in campaigning for office and for the New Deal itself. Roosevelt denounced "the ruthless manipulation of professional gamblers" for the stock market crash.[20] He rejected appeals to liberty that were used to attack economic regulation: "I do not believe that in the name of that sacred word a few powerful interests should be permitted to make industrial cannon fodder of the lives of half the population of the United States."[21] Government, for Roosevelt, was "not a thing apart," but "a democratic expression of organized self-help," a tradition running from the founding to the frontier, and to the New Deal itself.[22]

The early New Deal can be understood as the deployment of new forms of managerial expertise and capacity to fulfill older progressive aspirations for contesting corporate power, promoting social welfare, and developing a thicker form of social and economic citizenship. The flurry of financial and banking regulation in the early New Deal, for example, successfully dismantled concentrated financial power that was the central villain for Progressive reformers like Brandeis. These New Dealers sought the creation of expert regulatory bodies and initiatives: separating commercial and investment banking through the Glass–Steagall Act, imposing transparency requirements through the newly created Securities and Exchange Commission (SEC), and expanding Federal Reserve regulations on depository fees and activities.[23] These financial and securities reform initiatives followed Brandeisian ideas in counteracting concentrated financial and corporate power.[24]

These regulatory initiatives were at first complementary to efforts to expand the democratic power of citizens and workers. Early New Deal efforts at economic planning from 1933–1936 experimented with direct citizen involvement in the planning process, through local advisory boards.[25] Louis Jaffe himself went on to serve as a lawyer for the National Labor Relations Board and the Agricultural Adjustment Administration, and called for a shift to "group administration," in which regulation would formalize and equalize the participation of interest groups to ensure a truly inclusive process rather than passively absorbing input from only the most powerful individuals and groups.[26] The Wagner Act not only acted as a "Magna Carta" for labor rights and economic security but also helped institutionalize countervailing worker power.[27] The corporatism of the early New Deal empowered labor as a significant actor bargaining directly with peak employers, from the National Industrial Recovery Act to wartime planning bodies such as the War Labor Board and the Office of Price Administration (OPA). Similarly, Progressive Era thinkers had often emphasized the importance of empowering workers and consumers as a political force to check the excesses of corporations, a language picked up by early New Deal reformers seeking consumer mobilization as a way to check businesses and enhance consumer protections.[28] Grassroots organizations such as the National Consumers League and consumer cooperatives found themselves in positions of political and policy influence through New Deal organizations like the Consumer Advisory Board of the National Recovery Administration, or the Office of Consumer Counsel in the Agricultural Adjustment Administration. This strategy of consumer empowerment also extended into the wartime state, as the OPA deliberately engaged with deep grassroots mobilization to enforce and extend economic regulations in a form of "state building from the bottom up."[29]

Yet these state-building efforts created tensions between more bottom-up and top-down conceptions of economic governance. As Timothy Shenk (Chapter 2) and Samir Sonti (Chapter 4) argue in their contributions to this volume, this was a period during which New Deal technocrats began to construct the idea of a macroeconomy that could be managed, measured, and optimized—and in so doing, developed a conception of economic policy that began a shift away from the Progressive Era focus on economic power and democratic mobilization. Corporate law reformers like Adolf Berle and Gardiner Means shared the Progressive Era critique of private power as a kind of unchecked quasi-sovereign threat to the public, but later came to disagree over whether the public interest would be better protected by corporate managers, or by democratizing the corporation internally to better represent a more diverse array of shareholders empowered to control management.[30] For many New Dealers like Raymond Moley, FDR's antitrust adviser, managerial oversight was a better route to assuring the public good, a pragmatic evolution away "from the nostalgic philosophy of the trust busters."[31] Such managerialism enabled the deployment of expertise and knowledge but would also harness the efficiencies and powers of big business to promote economic growth and optimal market functioning. Indeed, although Progressive Era discourses critiquing concentrated power as a threat to democracy remained, they were increasingly marginalized—and even taken up by critics of New Deal economic regulation. Even signature New Deal achievements like the Glass–Steagall Act were increasingly framed by New Dealers in terms of promoting economic efficiency, rather than remedying disparities of economic power.[32]

By the late New Deal after 1937, the earlier democratic, mobilizational, corporatist impulses had faded.[33] The participation of bottom-up movements of workers and consumers was increasingly depoliticized, as citizens were downgraded from active drivers of governance to passive beneficiaries.[34] Similarly, the labor movement was also chastened, by a combination of active suppression through changes in labor law (such as the passage of the Taft–Hartley Act) and the related decline of interunion solidarity and collaboration.[35] Some unions opted for shorter-term gains of collective bargaining rights with particular firms, moving away from support for more radical and structural restraints on corporate and private power.[36]

Thus, as Alan Brinkley argued in his classic 1989 essay, during the New Deal ideas of the state shifted as policymakers sought to achieve familiar economic goals, such as regulation of monopolies, through resort to more centralized technocratic policymaking, rather than decentralized and participatory democratic alternatives. By the late 1930s, New Dealers were "coming to a common vision of government—a vision of capable, committed administrators who would seize control of state institutions, invigorate them, expand their powers when necessary, and make them permanent actors in the workings of the marketplace."[37] This managerial vision of the state had two related dimensions. First, as a matter of substantive goals, the purpose of the state was ultimately to optimize the efficient functioning of the complex modern economy. This understanding of purpose represented a significant departure from more radical, structural accounts of economic regulation to redistribute wealth, constrain corporate power, and the like. Second, the method by which the state was to achieve these goals depended primarily on the technocratic expertise of administrators and regulators that would realize the public interest through a combination of public-minded expertise and presidential oversight. This "administrative ideology" of the New Deal conceived of the state as a fundamentally technocratic, managerial project that pursued the public interest through a combination of expertise, insulation from politics, and coordination under a strong executive.[38]

The managerial vision of government is best exemplified by James Landis. One of the central architects of the New Deal, a protégé of Felix Frankfurter and former clerk for the Supreme Court Justice Louis Brandeis, Landis was already a leading young law professor when he helped design the newly minted SEC, which he would later chair. In a famous address in 1938, Landis defended the New Deal regulatory state as a much-needed revolution in governance.[39] In a complex modern economy, growth and market efficiency could only come through the judicious oversight of regulatory agencies, staffed by specialized experts capable of making policy on the substantive merits rather than according to the dictates of interest group politics or the archaic limits of legal doctrine. Agencies could make more effective public policy by drawing on specialized expertise, and could do so more rapidly than legislatures or courts. Accountability would be assured not by legal formalism or elections but rather by the publicity of agency policies,[40] the professionalism and expertise of regulators, and their independence from political pressure.[41] "The administrative process is, in essence," argued Landis, "our generation's answer to the inadequacy of the judicial and legislative process."[42]

The emergence of administrative law during the 1930s and 1940s helped codify and institutionalize this managerial idea of the state.[43] Initially, the New Deal expansions of regulatory authority were met by stiff opposition, particularly from the legal elite. The earliest debates pitted unapologetic defenders of technocratic governance by New Dealers like James Landis against legalists like Roscoe Pound and the American Bar Association who feared the reach of regulatory institutions that existed apart from the constitutional schema of separated adjudicatory, legislative, and executive functions—and therefore seemed to threaten unaccountable and illiberal state power.[44] In the 1930s, the Supreme Court echoed these concerns, striking down the National Industrial Recovery Act, and seemingly limiting the scope of regulatory powers to make rules and adjudicate disputes.[45] But by the late 1930s the Landis-style theory of insulated regulatory expertise had been effectively endorsed by the Supreme Court.[46] The battles over early New Deal agencies ultimately led to the institutionalization of legal norms and lawyers themselves as mechanisms to legitimate administrative authority, for example, through the absorption of quasi-judicial standards for providing evidence on the record justifying agency actions.[47] The 1946 Administrative Procedure Act consolidated this acceptance of the New Deal state. FDR vetoed the stricter Walter–Logan bill, which sought tighter limits on federal regulatory power to resist the threat of totalitarianism,[48] but seemed to Roosevelt to unduly limit the scope for expertise and undermine insulation from special interest pressures.[49] These legal norms and procedures did restrain agency powers, but they did not fundamentally challenge or restructure them; rather, they helped ratify and legitimate the managerial ethos, now blessed by familiar norms in the rule of law.

Landis's account thus represents one particular strain of New Deal statecraft, which came to shape mid- and late-century conceptions of political economy. This shift in the justifications for state action away from a moralized vision of economic justice or critique of private power toward a focus on optimizing growth and market function also represented a search for a more morally neutral, uncontroversial foundation for state action, particularly in the face of Cold War fears of totalitarianism.[50] Growth and welfarist policies seeking to compensate individuals for market failures rather than addressing structural disparities of economic power and opportunity represented an effort to ground the growing economic role of the state on a relatively uncontroversial vision of economic progress.[51]

The managerialist vision of the state—focused on correcting market failures through technocratic expertise—thus has its roots in the New Deal. This is not to suggest that the New Deal was by any means monolithic in its approach to governance, or hegemonic. But by midcentury, this managerial conception was well established. The problem with this account of the state, however, is that it rests the value and legitimacy of economic regulation on thin grounds. The goal is simply to make the market work better, through technocratic oversight and expertise. Once morally neutral goals of growth and welfare are seen as better served through another mechanism—such as deregulated, competitive markets—and once experts themselves are seen as less reliable and more corruptible, the foundations for this idea of the state crumble. This vulnerability is embedded in the managerial vision, and came to the fore over the course of the late twentieth-century rise of neoliberalism.

Managerialism in the Face of Neoliberalism

Although the term *neoliberalism* can be difficult to define, there was a discernible shift in the late twentieth century from the New Deal–era faith in government, expertise, and macroeconomic management, to a stance that is more critical of government economic regulation and more solicitous of the benefits of free markets, privatization, and business interests.[52] This shift from a New Deal idea of the state to a neoliberal one in which the state was seen as more minimalist, getting out of the way of self-correcting and growth-enhancing free market innovation and competition, was driven by conceptual changes that undercut the core of the New Deal argument for a governmental role in the modern economy.

First, intellectual developments in midcentury social science during the 1950s and 1960s challenged the New Deal faith in expertise. Economics and political science were increasingly shaped by theoretical developments that challenged the idea that collective democratic politics could in fact generate rational decisions in light of the diversity of preferences and difficulties of aggregation. The Nobel laureate Kenneth Arrow outlined this critique in his "impossibility theorem," and although Arrow himself viewed the problem of preference aggregation as applying to both democratic and market-based mechanisms, the argument became the foundation for a concerted intellectual attack on the rationality and efficacy of government decision making.[53] James Buchanan and Gordon Tullock of the University of Virginia built on Arrow's findings to recast politics as a marketplace for self-interested parties to maximize their individual utilities, leading to transactions between policymakers seeking support and interest groups seeking favorable treatment from the state.[54] This kind of political transaction created a skepticism toward the very idea of the common good as illusory at best or as a gateway to state tyranny at worst.[55] Other scholars argued that the democratic public itself was irrational: either because it was cost-effective for individual voters to remain ignorant or uninvolved in the political process or because this ignorance and demobilization magnified the likelihood that special interests would successfully "capture" state institutions, using them to further their own private interests rather than the public good.[56]

These intellectual currents established the ideas of free-riding, rent-seeking, and interest group capture as mainstays of the social science and broader public discourse. The public interest, according to these views, was illusory, and governmental failure endemic. The natural implication seemed to suggest that the public good could be best served by deregulating large segments of the economy, removing the danger of interest or capture altogether.[57] This theory of political power as a matter of economistic and self-interested transactions supplanted rival theories of collective and cultural power. In contrast to the Left's growing focus on culture and consciousness as domains of power, or the previous generation of social scientists who examined the power of institutional, economic, and political structures, this economistic notion of power seemed more objective, simple, and tractable.[58] Indeed, public-choice theory purported to be more than conjecture; it also appeared to have empirical backing through case studies of governmental corruption and capture.[59] Although many of these empirical foundations were themselves shaky as a matter of scholarship,[60] the overall intellectual framework proved persuasive. As Edward Purcell notes, in this new science of politics, "objectivism and skepticism concerning democracy went together," as public-choice theories and their empirical foundations "appeared to confirm the arguments of those who claimed popular government did not and could not work."[61]

The second development during this time undermined the managerial idea of the state from the other direction, by bolstering faith in the market as a self-regulating system. In contrast to the corruption, inefficiency, and illiberalism of regulation, markets increasingly came to be viewed as exemplifying ideals of freedom, choice, and reason. Furthermore, as self-equilibrating systems, they seemed more effective and adaptable to a complex modern economy.[62] The work of Milton Friedman and the revival of the work of Friedrich Hayek are emblematic in this turn to markets as seemingly more efficient aggregators of information and allocators of resources. In financial economics, for example, the efficient markets hypothesis became central, suggesting that well-functioning financial markets would optimally price assets according to risk, and therefore allocate social resources most effectively. These academic accounts combined with the growing profitability of the financial sector to help drive a new generation of financial market advocates and practitioners.[63] Meanwhile, scholarship in law and economics changed prevailing accounts of the corporation, from an artificial entity that posed a risk of arbitrary, unaccountable power of the sort that triggered concern among Progressive and New Deal reformers, to simply an efficient mode of organization, driven by the need to optimize production in the face of transaction costs. The rise of the shareholder theory of the firm suggested that existing financial markets would be sufficient to discipline and hold accountable corporate power, by making managers accountable to the imperatives of shareholder value.[64]

Third, business interests and conservative philanthropists helped bankroll and gradually popularize these critiques.[65] By focusing not on electoral politics, but rather on the production of ideas, policy analysis, and public intellectuals, this growing conservative movement helped build the intellectual foundations for the deregulatory turn.[66] As one historian notes, "The think tanks, radio stations, magazines, and intellectual organizations that were funded by business contributions during the 1950s helped to form the infrastructure for the rise of the conservative movement." From Hayek's Mont Pelerin Society to conservative journals like the *National Review*, and to more scholarly institutions like the Olin Foundation and the Heritage Foundation, "all of these organizations relied on the contribution of businessmen, and all of them sought to encourage businessmen to do what they could to fight the power" of the New Deal state, and its primary political constituents including labor unions.[67] With these conceptual foundations in place, the conservative movement could shift to more explicit policy advocacy, through organizations like the Chamber of Commerce, which, by the 1970s, commenced a systematic lobbying effort aimed at promoting deregulation in defense of the "free enterprise system."[68]

Finally, these intellectual and political developments also linked together this valorization of markets and this hostility to the federal government with the growing backlash against the civil rights movement, and the efforts to resist racial integration. As Nancy MacLean has argued in her work and in this volume (Chapter 8), neoliberal conceptions—from the Virginia School critiques of democratic capture to the celebration of markets—were part of a larger intellectual project to undercut a federal government increasingly associated with a powerful commitment to racial equity and desegregation.[69] Landmark civil rights achievements like the Supreme Court's *Brown v. Board of Education* (1954) ruling, committing the federal government to desegregating public schools, and the eventual passage of the Civil Rights Act (1964) effectively adapted and expanded the New Deal conception of a powerful federal bureaucracy to the cause of racial equality.[70] The political backlash against this push for racial inclusion provided an especially powerful motivation for the philanthropic donors and business interests behind the attack on the New Deal order, stitching together free market, antigovernment, and anti–civil rights constituencies on the political Right.

The political implications of these conceptual shifts seemed clear: in place of the muscular faith of New Dealers in the capacity of expert regulators to promote the public good, postwar social science seemed to suggest— scientifically, no less—that regulation was instead highly suspect, prone to capture, and inefficiency. Landis himself, by 1960 when he authored a special report on regulatory reform for the White House, saw the regulatory state as broken by inefficiency and threatened by the risk of interest group capture.[71] This "high politics" intellectual critique of the state was paralleled by a "vernacular politics" that, through business interests and conservative donors, helped drive a political attack on civil rights and economic inclusion as examples of growing federal overreach. These critiques forced defenders of the idea of economic regulation to engage in successive waves of reform aimed at defusing these growing anxieties about the power of the emerging regulatory state. But what is surprising about the response to neoliberalism in the 1990s and onward is the degree to which scholarship and policy discourse alike both *absorbed* the neoliberal critique and, at the same time, *doubled-down* on a New Deal–style technocratic form of governance, albeit in an even more chastened and limited form.

Scholars of the regulatory state themselves became increasingly skeptical of the desirability of New Deal–style regulation, seeming to accept the basic premises of the neoliberal critique. Thus, even defenders of the regulatory state after the 1980s began to speak in terms of minimizing the costs of regulation, of narrowing the purpose of state action to closing market failures, and of employing greater cooperative measures between regulation, on the one hand, and more efficient and less coercive market mechanisms, on the other. This "new Chicago School" of regulation shared with the old Chicago school of Milton Friedman an awareness of the social and economic costs of regulation, but sought to rescue the technocratic ideal of welfare-enhancing public policy by developing new tools for expert regulators themselves.[72] These regulators thus increasingly turned to measures such as cost-benefit analysis to provide objective proof and legitimation for the social value of regulations,[73] while reforming regulatory policies to allow for more deregulation, market-based regulation, and self-regulation where possible.[74]

This new vision of regulation would make it more efficient, flexible, and cost-effective—and ultimately, more minimalist and market-friendly.[75]

This willful skepticism even among defenders of the modern regulatory state influenced the thought and practice of judges, policymakers, and practitioners aimed at deregulation.[76] At the same time, this shift effectively circled back once again to the same New Deal managerialist mentality of relying on the professionalism and expertise of the regulators themselves to protect against the dangers of interest group capture, and ensure effective policymaking.[77] This attempt to restore technocracy was a more chastened, constrained vision of expert governance—a technocratic state that, in place of the self-confident mastery of Landis, was bound by the requirements of cost-benefit analysis, transparency, and oversight by the democratically elected executive. But by limiting itself to operating within a familiar managerial ethos, this effort to restore faith in regulation did little to address the central challenge of capture and ineffectiveness of the regulators.

This doubling-down on the managerial idea of the state manifests in contemporary policy and legal debates about regulation, but these efforts are ultimately unable to overcome the limitations of managerial conceptions of governance. First, much modern judicial review of administrative agency action involves "expertise-forcing"—an attempt by courts to ensure that agencies base their policies on scientific expertise, free from outside political pressures from the White House or political appointees.[78] The continued use of executive branch review of agency regulations similarly disciplines agencies to use cost-benefit analysis and technocratic expertise to justify the value and efficacy of regulation.[79] But such expertise-forcing can just as easily operate to undermine the role of the state as it can to support it. Efforts to discipline agencies to incentivize their acting on the basis of technocratic expertise more often than not serve as a cloak for ideologically driven disputes between overseers—whether the courts or executive branch officials—and regulators.[80] In the financial regulation context, for example, as agencies deregulated New Deal–era constraints on the financial sector in the 1980s and 1990s, courts often deferred to this work in legal challenges, citing agency expertise.[81] More recent efforts to expand regulation under the Dodd–Frank financial reform statute have been hobbled by courts striking down agency actions on the grounds that they lacked sufficient foundations in expert knowledge—despite the apparent presence of agency fact-finding and explicit congressional commands to implement the regulations.[82]

Second, the other major current in contemporary administrative law is to ground the legitimacy of regulatory action in terms of deference to political branches. Regulators deserve deference not because they are expert but because they are executing the will of a democratically elected president. This oversight view has a wide following in contemporary administrative law, articulated in the scholarship of the professor and now-Justice Elena Kagan and employed by judges like Chief Justice John Roberts.[83] In a 2010 case,[84] Roberts argued that defenses of the modern administrative state seeking to preserve its insulation and expertise overlook the importance of binding regulatory action to the political will of the people: "One can have a government that functions without being ruled by functionaries, and a government that benefits from expertise without being ruled by experts. Our Constitution was adopted to enable the people to govern themselves, through their elected leaders. The growth of the Executive Branch, which now wields vast power and touches almost every aspect of daily life, heightens the concern that it may slip from the Executive's control, and thus from that of the people."[85]

This appeal to presidentialism also has a New Deal pedigree, evoking the vitality and legitimacy of a muscular, unitary executive that acts on behalf of the public as a whole. And despite its rhetoric of democratic accountability, this appeal to presidential oversight also accomplishes less than it appears. The simple fact is that neither Congress nor the executive directly controls every regulatory agency or initiative; the scope of regulation is just too vast. In practice, presidential oversight of regulatory agencies operates either in the managerial vein—for example, by improving the coordination of regulatory agencies, incentivizing cost-benefit analysis, and enhancing the flow of information to regulators[86]—or as an assertion of political control over the bureaucracy, subject to the same concerns of capture, corruption, or unaccountability.

These two strategies of political oversight and expertise-forcing have shaped modern liberal attempts to restore the efficacy and legitimacy of economic regulation. The 2010 Dodd–Frank financial reform bill is emblematic of the Obama-era effort to revive faith in expertise.[87] Much of the bill revolved around the creation of the Financial Stability Oversight Council, a centralized, super-regulatory body housed in the Federal Reserve Board and chaired by the treasury secretary, who is directly accountable to the president. Other provisions sought to promote greater coordination between agencies, and to channel greater resources into research, technical expertise, or data collection.

The act also imposed other expertise-forcing checks, such as statutory requirements for cost-benefit analysis, congressional audits of agencies, and the use of agency inspectors general.[88] Yet the persistent attacks on Obama-era economic regulation underscores how little these conceptions of expertise or political oversight address deeper concerns about both the substantive goals of regulation and the accountability of regulators.

Reconstructing a Democratic Idea of the State

If managerialism, despite its occasional successes, remains so limited—vulnerable to neoliberal critique and co-option, dissociated from more thickly egalitarian transformative visions and grassroots democratic social movements—what is the alternative? Alongside the emergence and decline of managerial political economy we can see a rival counternarrative of a more democratic idea of the state. From the more radical subset of populist, progressive, and labor republican thinkers from the era of industrialization a century ago running through to the present, this rival conception of governance contrasts with managerialism. Unlike managerialism, this democratic political economy sees the purposes of state action not in the seemingly neutral task of optimizing growth or markets, but in the more thickly egalitarian aspiration for inclusive economic and social citizenship, in opposition to unaccountable concentrations of social, economic, and political power. This concern with power in turn pairs with a view of the state not as a vehicle for technocratic expertise, but rather as a facilitator of *democratic* empowerment of citizens—and through them, accountability of both private and public actors.

Consider the thought of the philosopher John Dewey. Like other antidomination critics of industrial capitalism, Dewey saw the problem of economic governance not as a matter of growth or market management, but as fundamentally an issue of disparities of political power. The task of reform was not merely to defend markets in the name of liberty but rather to recognize the market system as simply one configuration of power and to seek a "more equal and equitable balance of powers that will enhance and multiplied the effective liberties of the mass of individuals."[89] This more equitable economic system would in turn require the participation of citizens in the day-to-day business of governance. Although Dewey agreed with other Progressive Era reformers that professional expertise was needed to develop effective public policies, he argued that such expertise had to be integrated with democratic engagement. Such participation was crucial to keeping policymakers themselves accountable, for "no government by experts in which the masses do not have the chance to inform the experts will be anything but an oligarchy in the interests of a few."[90] Rather, through greater educative public discourse and more regular forms of citizen participation in governance, lay citizens could become more effective participants in self-rule over time. A truly democratic state thus demanded institutional innovation beyond a reliance on mere elections and parties: as Dewey argued, there was "no sanctity" to such received "devices" of democratic institutions.[91]

Louis Brandeis, similarly, paired his critique of corporate and monopoly power with a faith in participatory democratic action—whether through labor unions or through local-level democracy—to realize a thick conception of economic citizenship and well-being and to assure countervailing power against economic domination.[92] Like Dewey, Brandeis saw an important role for expertise, but despite his admiration of the new techniques of expertise and "scientific management," Brandeis routinely argued for the linking of labor representatives alongside expert policymakers in the making of trade, antitrust, and workplace regulations.[93] For example, in the 1932 case of *Liggett v. Lee*, the Supreme Court struck down a Florida tax designed to limit the spread of newly emerging chain stores such as A&P as fundamentally irrational, but Brandeis's famous dissent argued in favor of upholding the Florida law.[94] Brandeis defended the statute as part of a broader resistance against economic domination and private power.[95] Furthermore, the long-term goal of preventing domination could only emerge through specifically democratic politics. "Only through participation by the many in the responsibilities and determinations of business can Americans secure the moral and intellectual development which is essential to the maintenance of liberty," wrote Brandeis.[96]

These democratic aspirations also animated many on-the-ground political movements and actors. Radical labor republicans sought to transform workplace relations in egalitarian and participatory terms, and saw a close relationship between labor organizing on the one hand and state action on the other to realize these aspirations.[97] Progressive and populist reformers alike mobilized to promote greater democratic participation. The National Direct Legislation League, for example, educated and organized state activists pushing reforms that established direct democratic processes at the state level such as ballot referenda, also endorsed by the People's Party and

Progressive Party activists in state legislatures. Many of these reformers similarly railed against the courts as an entrenched oligarchy, forming the centerpiece of Senator Robert LaFollette's 1924 run for the presidency.[98] This was also the era that saw the expansion of urban democracy through the Home Rule movement and the City Beautiful movement.[99] It must be noted that these movements, despite their democratic aspirations, were still marred by a tacit or explicit commitment to racialized limits on the scope of this empowered democratic public. Yet, there were also important efforts to organize a more inclusive, multiracial coalition advancing a critique of economic power and a push for more radically participatory democracy built along lines of racial inclusion. These cross-racial democratizing coalitions had limited success in the early twentieth century, from the violent suppression of fusion coalitions among black and white populists, to the (partial) successes of the CIO serving as a multiracial working-class movement that acted as the left flank of the New Deal, planting the seeds for the long-term linking of civil rights and economic populism within the Democratic Party.[100]

This democratic idea of the state continued to animate periods of creative reform among activists seeking a more compelling moral vision of economic governance and attempting to address anxieties about the efficacy and accountability of expertise. It also animated grassroots social movements on the Left that sought to better integrate racial and gender equity into these visions for a democratized economic order. For example, in the 1960s and 1970s, as concerns about regulatory capture grew, administrative law briefly flirted with a similar idea of expanded interest representation as a way to restore bureaucratic legitimacy through expanded statutory participation rights and doctrines of due process and standing—reforms that came about in part as a result of the mobilization around the civil rights and welfare rights movements.[101] At about the same time, the War on Poverty represented a radical effort to democratize economic governance: although much of the program focused on specific initiatives such as job training, work-study, and access to legal services, the radicalism of the program lay in its attempt to fund and catalyze community organizations to represent the voices of the poor, particularly among communities of color, more directly in state and local policymaking. Although this "maximum feasible participation" mandate was quickly attacked and dismantled by bureaucrats who saw the mobilization of civil rights and community-based groups as a threat to their power, for the brief time of its operation, the War on Poverty arguably created major footholds and points of leverage for the poor in the modern state, and in some cases dramatically shifted policies around investment, lending, and local economic development.[102]

In the last twenty years, the appeal of a broadened participatory approach to economic governance has resurfaced again, in modified forms. Several scholars have suggested a return to the interest representation idea, for example, by calling for "regulatory public defenders" who would help identify and act on behalf of underrepresented groups.[103] Others have looked to the administrative process as a possible arena for greater participatory governance and problem-solving, engaging all stakeholders to work alongside experts to collectively and collaboratively devise public policies.[104] These policies would be provisional and experimental, in a Deweyan sense, iterated and adapted over time. Such participation would also provide multiple forms of accountability of regulators and private actors alike to citizens, while facilitating greater responsiveness through more fluid and adaptable regulation.[105] The rise of the open government movement offers additional technological tools for enabling participation and civic engagement in the regulatory process.[106] Twenty-first-century movements for racial justice have begun calling for greater democratic participatory institutions, from budgeting to campaign finance reform.[107]

Transcending the New Deal Idea of the State

The managerialist idea of the state—focused on the neutral task of optimizing markets and growth through technocratic governance—originated with a particular strand of New Deal political economy and continues to operate as a kind of default starting point for contemporary debates about liberalism and economic governance. For liberals responding to the 2008 financial crisis and the ensuing Great Recession, this ideal of technocratic management kept resurfacing as a template for governance reform and public policy. But for conservative critics of economic regulation, this ideal remains deeply flawed, as ineffectual and corrupt in comparison to self-regulating markets. This neoliberal deconstruction of the New Deal state remains powerful both as a critique of economic regulation and as an implicit repudiation of the idea that a powerful central state ought to deploy its coercive powers in the service of economic and racial inclusion. The brazen reassertion of right-wing populism, starting with the rise of Trump and Trumpism in 2016, represents a particularly chilling vision of this politics that fuses this distrust of elites with racially exclusionary conceptions of U.S. identity, and a governing agenda that remains committed not to economic populism but rather to the dismantling of regulation in the service of big business interests. The surge of this conservative vision and its weaponization by Trumpist politicians underscores the moral brittleness of the New Deal (and managerial) vision of statecraft.

But the alternative democratic idea of the state suggests a different foundation for modern economic governance. First, the goal of government on this view is not just to optimize the market, a purpose that, under neoliberal criticisms, may be better served by markets themselves. Rather, it is to address fundamentally moral aspirations for economic opportunity and equality against the threat of private power and structural economic domination. This purpose almost by definition cannot be met by "self-regulating" markets, for the starting point is a recognition of the ways in which market society creates and magnifies the moral harms of domination. No matter how morally controversial these ends might be, they are substantive, not neutral, and thus they provide a more robust and mobilizing aspiration for reform politics. Second, this democratic idea of the state views governance as a necessarily democratic, participatory process in which expertise is embedded in a broader process of citizen mobilization, advocacy, participation, and accountability. This aspect also necessarily requires a turn to politics, not markets, as a means of collective decision making, but has embedded in it a response to the concerns about the relative lack of knowledge or accountability among regulators themselves.

The existence of these proposals and opportunities suggests that the democratic idea of the state is not just a matter of historical or theoretical interest; it is a very real possibility. It is also a necessity. Regardless of the outcome of a Trump administration, much of the New Deal order is now in tatters, eroded by a combination of technological and structural change, deliberate dismantling under a neoliberal critique, and further collapse in the face of right-populist and corporate counterreaction. Given the pitched battles about the purposes and mechanisms of the modern state in this New Gilded Age, there is as great a need as ever for an alternative to either managerial or neoliberal accounts of the state. The democratic vision suggested by Progressive Era thinkers like Dewey and Brandeis and echoed by radicals—running from nineteenth century labor republicans through civil and welfare rights advocates of the 1960s—offers a compelling alternative vision of government oriented not just toward growth and market management but to combating domination and expanding economic empowerment. It is equally important that this vision sees government not as the province of experts to whom we delegate authority to rule but rather as a forum and process through which we the people are empowered to have a voice in the day-to-day decisions of government. This democratic ethos is very different from the managerialist inclinations of New Deal–style liberalism, and has within it the resources to address the latent concerns about government effectiveness and accountability that help animate the neoliberal critique.

How might such a democratic state be realized? The brief critique and recovery discussed above suggest at least two important, related, elements. First, the democratic alternative was lost in part because of the ascendance of managerial and neoliberal conceptions of the state among political elites; but it also suffered from the decline and fragmentation of bottom-up worker and community-based movements for radical reform rooted in a multiracial working class—an echo of the managerial and neoliberal transformations of the state itself. Labor's erosion and decline in the mid- and late twentieth century has been well documented, as has the shift away from federated, grassroots movement organization to professionalized policy and a legal organizational ecosystem. Yet the moments in which democratic political economy has thrived have depended in large part on the efforts of organic social movements in pushing a more egalitarian and participatory vision of governance that fused values of democracy, economic justice, and racial equity.

Second, these democratic aspirations depend crucially on an institutional structure that can respond in ways that deepen democratic agency, shifting political power by creating institutionalized hooks and levers through which grassroots movements can continue to exercise power against economic and political elites in a durable way. It is through this dynamic interaction between movements from below and state institutional structures from above that democratic governance is made real. Indeed, the rise of new left social movements in today's era of economic inequality and revived right-wing populism are experimenting with precisely this confluence of reform strategies. This is one way to understand the renewed vitality and influence of social movements like the Movement for Black Lives focused on structural racial injustice and increasingly shaping progressive policy concepts to address underlying racial and economic inequities. This impulse also animates, as Kate Andrias notes in her contribution to this volume (Chapter 12), the rise of "alt-labor" worker movements operating outside of conventional labor union and Wagner Act structures. Similar themes are echoed in the emergence of intersectional and cross-community movement organizing in opposition to the Trump administration—from the North Carolina–based Poor People's Campaign to the coalition of resistance groups looking to link together shared commitments around racial justice, immigrant rights, economic inequality, and democracy reform.

Finally, the democratic idea of the state also suggests a way forward for scholarship as well. The regulatory state has never been in actuality the top-down, expert-driven image projected by the New Deal or modern liberals. As scholars of "bureaucratic politics" highlight, the bureaucracy is a key site in which diverse interest groups, ideologies, and social movements operate and clash to produce norms, policies, and institutions over time.[108] The flip side is that electoral and party politics do not exhaust the terrain of the battles that construct and constitute modern governance in the aggregate. The ways in which law, policy, and institutions emerge come largely from struggles that occur outside the arena of "high politics": national elections, Congress, or the two-party system. Rather, it is the micropolitics of regulation, of local government, of grassroots clashes between civil society, interest groups, and policymakers that constitute the daily realities of governance. We must therefore deepen our understanding of the way democratic politics currently operates on the ground—and in the process, help chart a pathway toward a more democratic idea of the modern state.

CHAPTER 2

Inventing the American Economy

Timothy Shenk

In the fall of 2011, Barack Obama decided that he would go to Kansas. His approval ratings were underwater, pundits were chattering about a presidency that had lost its way, and disillusioned former supporters were asking what had happened to hope and change. Obama saw his trip as a chance to restart the conversation. He would deliver a speech, a wide-ranging reflection on U.S. politics of the kind that had turned him into a celebrity at the 2004 Democratic National Convention. One subject loomed in his mind, and in the title of the address, published by the White House under the heading, "Remarks by the President on the Economy in Osawatomie, Kansas."[1]

Obama and his team chose the location of his speech with care. Almost a century earlier, Theodore Roosevelt (TR) had outlined his vision of a "New Nationalism" in Osawatomie.[2] Obama cited TR repeatedly in his talk, casting himself as the inheritor of the progressive tradition embodied by Roosevelt. As Obama explained it, Roosevelt had charted a path between extremes in a country grappling with the challenges of industrialization. "He praised what the titans of industry had done to create jobs and grow the economy," Obama said, but also "understood the free market only works when there are rules of the road that ensure competition is fair and open and honest."[3]

Now Americans had reached another crossroads. Arguing that Republicans offered a "brand of 'you're on your own' economics," the president insisted that only Democrats would create "an economy that's built to last." Marrying this proposition to a favorite theme of another President Roosevelt, Obama linked economic progress with the recognition of interdependence: "Rebuilding this economy based on fair play, a fair shot, and a fair share," he said, "will require all of us to see that we have a stake in each other's success." A vibrant democracy and an expanding economy—this was the progressive vision Obama promised to revive.[4]

It was not, however, what Roosevelt had spoken about in Osawatomie. Early in his speech, TR connected "the triumph of a real democracy" with "an economic system under which each man shall be guaranteed the opportunity to show the best that there is in him," but that was the last time he mentioned anything like "the economy."[5] Instead, he focused on more pressing matters. An outraged *New York Times* editorial summarized Roosevelt's "various schemes," which included putting "all corporations under federal regulation . . . reaching out the federal hand on all the vast natural resources of the land," and "intervention regarding sanitation and home life."[6] Like the former president, the *Times* felt no need to mention the economy.

There is a puzzle here. Why did Roosevelt's address include just one glancing mention of the "economic system"? And why did Obama think that his predecessor's speech had focused on "the economy"?

The short answer is that in Roosevelt's lifetime the idea of the economy as Americans would come to understand it had not attained anything like its later ubiquity.[7] The longer answer begins by recognizing that the entrance of the economy into the public debate was part of a much larger shift that created a new kind of politics with a different vocabulary, different goals, different tools, and a different kind of policymaker than anything that existed a century ago.

Libraries could be filled with histories of the twentieth century focused on the clash of ideologies in an age of extremes. There would be a special section in that library for books chronicling the rise and fall of the New Deal order. Examining the conceptual history of the economy clarifies the profound consequences of the journey from the age of Roosevelt to the age of Reagan. But it also fits into a developing body of scholarship that emphasizes continuities running across the period, and challenges accounts that depict the twentieth century as a battle between a clearly defined Left and Right.[8]

The economy became the terrain upon which political debate was fought because it seemed as if it was big enough to accommodate any goal: conservatives could defend it in the name of private enterprise, Leftists could seek to direct it toward the public good, and the overwhelming majority of Americans could agree that a growing economy benefited the country as a whole. Technocrats had an array of tools for managing its performance, business leaders took comfort in macroeconomic stability, and voters could use it as a yardstick for measuring the performance of their elected representatives. Everybody, it seemed, had something to gain from taking the economy seriously.

But the economy's capaciousness was deceptive. The rise of a politics centered on the economy was based on a particular set of assumptions that converged at a specific moment—assumptions that are increasingly dubious, and a moment that is receding farther into the past. To decide where we might want to go next, however, we first have to reckon with the road that brought us here.

*   *   *

"In order that we may clearly understand each other," wrote the railroad magnate Stuyvesant Fish in 1906, "permit me to define the word Economy."[9] According to Fish, "Economy" referred to the system of rules for managing an undertaking. The undertaking could be almost any collective endeavor, from a family to a government. Whatever the organization, Fish thought it should be managed economically, which meant extracting the most output from a given set of inputs. As the British civil servant and economist Henry Higgs explained it, economy "in its true sense" stood for "the wise management, husbandry, or administration of resources." This was the definition of the term used by the Commission on Economy and Efficiency appointed by William Howard Taft in 1910 to explore ways the government could, in Taft's words, conduct its "business with maximum dispatch."[10]

Alongside this narrow definition of economy, there was a hazily conceived notion of "prosperity," whose history was as old as the United States itself. When Alexander Hamilton was making the case for a national bank and public debt in 1781, he conjured the vision of a future in which "industry is increased, commodities are multiplied, agriculture and manufacturers flourish, and herein consist the true wealth and prosperity of a state."[11] Six years later, the Anti-Federalist Agrippa used the same language to argue against the Constitution Hamilton helped design, arguing that in a time of "general prosperity" there was no need to rashly adopt a new government.[12]

As U.S. politics democratized over the next half century, prosperity became a campaign issue. In 1835 Democrats argued that Andrew Jackson's record as president justified electing his chosen successor, Martin Van Buren, by asking about the country, "When was it ever more, if indeed so prosperous? When was public or private credit more stable? Prices so high? The people so happy?"[13] Those questions became decidedly inconvenient for Democrats after the Panic of 1837, and in 1840 Whigs successfully campaigned on a platform they summarized as "Harrison and Prosperity or Van Buren and Ruin."[14]

While politicians scrambled for electoral advantage, self-styled political economists dwelled on loftier subjects. Claiming to have uncovered laws that not even the most powerful monarch could defy, political economists drew attention to an economic logic they applied to subjects ranging from money and trade to agriculture and population. Economic reasoning could be applied to particular situations, the word "economic" could be attached to a variety of objects or practices, and over time references to larger "economic systems" became more frequent. But the central ambition of political economy was to uncover the laws of the marketplace, not to determine the workings of the economy.

Markets did not exist in an abstract sphere untethered from everyday life. Voicing a common sentiment, one early political economist insisted that "economic science" was "nothing but the application of natural order to the government of societies."[15] According to John Stuart Mill's popular survey, the science of political economy was devoted to studying "the economical phenomena of society."[16] His usage of "society" was deliberate. "We can never either understand in theory or command in practice the condition of a society in any one respect," he believed, "without taking into consideration its condition in all other respects."[17] That focus was still obvious to careful readers early in the twentieth century. As Thorstein Veblen remarked in 1901: "The point of view from which the early, and even the later, classical economists discussed economic life was that of 'the society' taken as a collective whole and conceived as an organic unit."[18]

Political economists were not the only figures concerned with society. The belief that society existed prior to the state, that it obeyed its own internally generated rules, and that these rules could be discovered by rational investigation was an obsession of the age.[19] "Upon this point all speculative politicians will agree," John Adams remarked in 1776, "the happiness of society is the end of government."[20] *Commercial society* was the term Adam Smith used to describe his area of inquiry in *The Wealth of Nations*; *civil society* was the phrase used by that close reader of Smith, G.W. F. Hegel. Alexis de Tocqueville, characteristically, was the most evocative. "Society is all pervasive," he observed. "The individual takes the trouble to be born; for the rest, society takes him in its arms like a nurse."[21] Society and the individual—here, in this couplet, was the essence of a novel, distinctly liberal, way of thinking about collective life.

The social and the economic remained master categories of analysis for political economy—and, later, economics—until well into the twentieth century. This union can be seen most clearly in textbooks, which read to contemporary eyes like an awkward union of primitive microeconomics and historical sociology. By the 1920s, a typical introductory economics textbook could include, in addition to discussions of supply and demand, chapters on "the economics of railroad transportation," "industrial monopoly and its control," "population," "immigration," "problems of the working day," "the organized labor movement," and, often by way of conclusion, "socialism."[22] Missing from this collection was any discussion of "the economy."

There were, however, occasional references to the deceptively familiar term *national economy*. The German economist Friedrich List had popularized the concept in 1841 with his enormously influential, *National Systems of Political Economy*. According to List, "national economy" was equivalent to "state administration"—that is, the set of policies that managed economic transactions within a nation.[23] This is, essentially, a synonym for economic nationalism. To practice national economy meant looking out for domestic economic interests, rather than subordinating them to the demands of global marketplaces: think of raising tariffs to keep out foreign goods, rather than lowering taxes to combat a recession; think Alexander Hamilton, not John Maynard Keynes.

By the end of the nineteenth century, German economists were discussing another collection of terms that seem like obvious precursors to the economy, if not outright synonyms—for instance, *Volkswirtschaft*, and *Weltwirtschaft*. Today we would render these as national economy and world economy. At the time, however, the choice was not so clear. In 1893 a political scientist complained "that the English language contains no generally accepted word to describe the conscious activity of human beings in the joint satisfaction of their individual desires" and suggested that "economy" might be an acceptable translation for what the Germans called "*Wirtschaft*."[24] Before deploying the concept, he felt compelled to ascertain *Wirtschaft*'s "constituent elements"—"first, the surface of the earth, with its annuity of heat, light, air and moisture, and second, the human beings who inhabit this surface"—and then moved to an explication of Socrates on the duality of human nature and the essence of the self.[25]

Almost invariably in this period, "economy" appeared as the second item in a pair: for instance, village economy, town economy, slave economy, capitalist economy, planned economy, market economy, national economy, world economy, and money economy. In these formulations, an economy was not a natural feature of collective life. It was something that had to be created through the extension of commerce and subsequent remaking of state and society. "The economic life of a politically organized independent people," a textbook published in 1889 observed, "is often called a *national economy*," but no such economy could be said to exist without "independent political unity" and "an independent state." As late as 1936, the Rockefeller Foundation could organize a conference dedicated to exploring whether the nations of the world possessed enough "organic unity" to "warran[t] the conclusion that there is such a thing as a 'world economy'" or if there was "nothing more than a physical aggregate of unrelated and disjointed forces."[26]

While economists debated the existence of the economy, one object dominated public debate: society. Talk of society was ubiquitous, including in economics. Alfred Marshall's celebrated *Principles of Economics* also defined its subject as the study of "the economic aspects" of "social life."[27] An 1888 textbook from Richard Ely, one of the most influential of a rising generation of U.S. economists, described political economy as a "branch of sociology" devoted to maximizing "the welfare of society."[28] "Humanity is now 'society,'" maintained Ely's younger colleague Allyn Young, who added that society was "the concrete reality, of which the individual is a mere abstraction."[29] Even the mathematically inclined Irving Fisher believed that economics was "only one branch of a greater subject,—Sociology," or, as he elsewhere phrased it "Societology."[30] This is why early discussions of the various economies— town economy, national economy, world economy, and so on—had such a thickly social character. Society provided the unifying framework for economic inquiry, as it had done for more than a century.

Outside the narrow world of academic economics, this was, as Daniel Rodgers has termed it, "an age of social politics," a more ambitious version of the well-regulated society that William Novak has shown was central to the ambitions of politicians at the state and local level in the nineteenth century.[31] "Society is looking itself over, in our day, from top to bottom," Woodrow Wilson announced in a speech he delivered two years before his election to the presidency.[32] The country's industrial capacity had reached levels Americans just a few decades earlier could not have imagined, but so had tensions between labor and capital. "The economic power of society," he explained, had become focused in corporations, each of which constituted "an economic society, a little economic State" that existed in uneasy relation to the national state.[33] That transformation had brought economic concerns to the fore of national politics, replacing the political issues that Wilson said had occupied earlier generations. "The life of the nation" no longer revolved around "questions of governmental structure or of the distribution of governmental powers. It centers upon economic questions, questions of the very structure and operation of society itself."[34] According to Wilson, the stakes were as high as could be imagined: society itself hung in the balance.

Economic concerns featured prominently in the politics of society, but, as with Progressive politics as a whole, there was almost too much to think about. A profusion of concepts offered a variety of competing diagnoses, each of which could provide larger meaning for local problems. Financial panics, industrial depressions, and business cycles were familiar notions, but they were explicitly limited in their scope. For example, Wesley Mitchell, the era's leading business-cycle theorist, believed that agriculture fell outside the purview of his research. As Mitchell explained it, his analysis was confined "to a certain type of business enterprise."[35] Agriculture moved to its own rhythms, and should not be lumped together with the business world. Even speaking of a coherent "business world" was misleading. Mitchell saw modern business as a "maze of interacting processes" always looping into itself. "A real chart of one business cycle," he concluded, "would be a hopelessly complex tangle of hundreds of curves."[36]

"A hopelessly complex tangle": it was a fitting description of what more than a hundred years of economic inquiry had resulted in. But that was about to change.

*   *   *

Economy and prosperity, market and society, business cycles and money flows: out of this jumble emerged the new concept of the economy. For experts, the economy was a circular flow linking production and consumption through the constant cycling of money; for the public, the economy could be seen as a totalizing entity that operated by its own logics and was set apart from state and society. The economy could be measured through statistics, modeled by economists, and managed by the government. To borrow a useful bit of jargon from science studies, it had become a sociotechnical object. But it had also become a subject of political debate that both public figures

Figure 2.1. References to "the American economy" in the *New York Times,* 1900–1980. On the uses of surveys like the Ngram Viewer, see Jean-Baptiste Michel, Yuan Kui Shen, Aviva Presser Aiden et al., "Quantitative Analysis of Culture Using Millions of Digitized Books," *Science* 331, no. 6014 (January 2011): 176–182.

and average citizens felt demanded their attention. The economy was defined by this dual character. It was conceptually fuzzy and technically precise— large enough to contain the anxieties of voters who regularly listed it as their most important concern, but small enough to fit inside a report from the Council of Economic Advisers (established, revealingly, in 1946).

With this understanding of the concept in mind, the economy became the subject of endless conversation in the midcentury United States—in stump speeches, newspaper headlines, radio broadcasts, and television specials. The phrase "economy as a whole" did not appear in the *American Economic Review,* the discipline's leading journal, until 1930.[37] Then, suddenly, talk of the economy was everywhere.

Measurements of more limited archives, like the record of references to "the American economy" in the *New York Times,* provide one way of tracking this shift.

Political rhetoric offers yet another way of gauging the transformation. Consider State of the Union addresses. Before the 1920s, presidents did not consider the economy in their annual messages to Congress. During the worst years of the Depression, Franklin Roosevelt made only occasional references

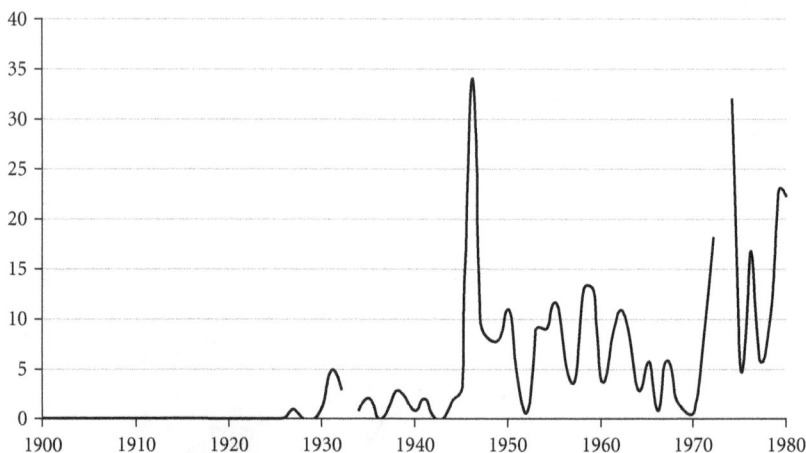

Figure 2.2. References to the economy and its cognates in State of the Union messages, 1900–1980.

to the subject. The economy's breakthrough took place in 1946, when Harry Truman explained that "the growing responsibility of modern government to foster economic expansion" had made it necessary "to formulate and determine the Government program in the light of national economic conditions as a whole." By the time Bill Clinton took office almost half a century later, what had seemed noteworthy to Truman now appeared natural. "For all the many tasks that require our attention," he said in his 1993 State of the Union, "I believe tonight one calls on us to focus, to unite, and to act. And that is our economy. For more than anything else, our task tonight as Americans is to make our economy thrive again."[38]

This was not just a matter of rhetorical presentation. Politicians had become covinced that their careers were bound up with the economy's trajectory. John Kennedy was assasinated on November 22, 1963. On November 23, Lyndon Johnson had his first meeting with the head of the Council of Economic Advisers.[39] Soon, his administration was taken over by the campaign to achieve one of Kennedy's great unfinished tasks: passing the first tax cut in U.S. history designed to stimulate the economy. During Johnson's presidential campaign a year later, the Democratic Party platform described the "expansion of the American economy" as "the national purpose."[40]

What is most striking, looking at aggregate measurements of the economy's usage over time, is how quickly the change occurred. Time and again, these charts depict a virtually nonexistent concept rocketing upward in just a few years.

This same phenomenon can also be seen at the level of individual thinkers. In 1935 Walter Lippmann argued that since the onset of the Depression, guaranteeing the economic security of its population had become "the central task of government." According to Lippmann, this belief reflected "the fundamental assumption of the whole period since 1929"—namely, "that we have a national economy and not a mere aggregation of individual enterprises."[41] He used "national economy" by itself here, but elsewhere he regularly attached (often with italics) the phrase "*as a whole*," an emphasis that revealed the novelty of the concept.[42] The basic assumptions of government had changed, and his language had to keep up.

Lippmann repeatedly insisted on the revolutionary character of this turn toward the economy. He could have made the point by citing his own work. Lippmann published his first book in 1913, just a few years after graduating from Harvard, and he followed it up with a sequel one year later. Both volumes—*A Preface to Politics* and *Drift and Mastery*—contain just a handful of references to economy, all of which borrow from older senses of the term: a passing allusion to the transition "from the old mercantilist economy to the capitalistic economics of the nineteenth century,"[43] for example, or a brief mention of "the economy of trusts" that had developed in the United States.[44] Much more important to his politics was the idea of society. "We have been taught to think of society as a body," he lamented in 1927. "We have had foisted upon us by various great propagative movements the notion of a mythical entity called Society."[45]

Not even the World's Fair was immune to the eruption of economy talk. At the 1904 World's Fair in St. Louis a "Palace of Education and Social Economy" featured exhibits on a host of subjects, including " "Public Health," "Municipal Improvement," "Co-operative Institutions," "Organization of Industrial Workers," and "State Regulation of Industry and Labor."[46] Here was the intellectual world of Progressive politics condensed into an exhibit, an overflowing surplus of ideas with no clear ranking of priorities, united chiefly by an urgent desire to grapple with the transition to what would later be known as industrial capitalism.

Jump forward sixty years to the 1964 New York World's Fair, where the "Hall of Free Enterprise" promised a display that would be "the first time the totality of a free economy has ever been put together in simple, visual form." The focus of the exhibit was a computer programmed to answer visitor's questions. "There is a kind of oracular infallibility to this machine that makes it more impressive than a live pundit," observed the *New Republic*. "A group of awe-stricken visitors punched it and read replies. What it said must be so, they seemed to feel, because after all a machine is unbiased and impartial."[47] Here was the intellectual world of technocratic liberalism, condensed into an exhibit, where disinterested expertise offered the hope of doing away with the obsolete ideological conflicts. As John Kennedy put it in 1962, "What is at stake in our economic decisions today is not some grand warfare of rival ideologies which will sweep the country with passion but the practical management of a modern economy."[48]

Policymakers were acutely aware of the transformation that had taken place. In 1965, Kermit Gordon—a member of Kennedy's Council of Economic Advisers and, later, director of the Bureau of the Budget—told the House Committee on Appropriations that just thirty years earlier policymakers "didn't give any consideration to what the effect of that policy would be on the economy." According to Gordon, they simply didn't know any better. Luckily, times had changed. "With the great improvements that have taken place in the intervening years in economic statistics and general economic understanding, we are all more aware of the relationship between budget actions and the nation's economic health," he explained.[49]

Intellectuals could see the shift, too. Five years before Gordon's testimony, Daniel Bell marveled in the *End of Ideology* at the shortsightedness of earlier academics and policymakers. "What is amazing, in retrospect," he wrote, "is that while the commitment to a politically managed economy could have been foreseen, we were quite badly deficient in organizing our economic thinking for it."[50] The need to maintain full employment and guard against the threat of a second Great Depression had turned managing the economy into a political necessity. Meanwhile, the radically expanded size of the federal government—from 3.6 percent of gross domestic product (GDP) in 1930 to 14.2 percent in 1950—had made it inevitable that the government would exert a decisive influence over the economy, whether politicians recognized it or not.[51] Despite all this, Bell noted, the Department of Commerce did not produce national income estimates until 1936; there were no official measurements of the gross national product until 1942; and they were not brought together in a major government analysis until Franklin Roosevelt's budget message of 1945.

Statistics and budgets were only part of the story. The deepest account came from the political theorist Sheldon Wolin. Writing in 1981, Wolin argued that a "quiet revolution" had taken place in the past fifty years: "'The economy' has emerged in the public consciousness as a sharply outlined, autonomous entity, the theater in which the destiny and meaning of the society will be worked out. Relegated to secondary importance are the main notions through which the society once understood its identity, notions such as 'democracy,' 'republic,' 'the Constitution,' and 'the nation' whose meaning was essentially political."[52] For Wolin (born in 1922), as for Gordon (born in 1916) and Bell (born in 1919), there was something personal about this shift: it had taken place within their lifetimes.

A remarkable transformation had taken place in just a few decades. Specialists in the new field of macroeconomics replaced vague references to prosperity, poverty, and the cost of living with a precise vocabulary of economic growth, unemployment, and inflation rates. Whereas earlier economic debates had tended to focus on long-term questions like tariffs, antitrust, or the gold standard, the politics of the economy concentrated on the short run, promising that the right mix of monetary and fiscal policy could ensure sustained growth. But the economy also existed over a much longer time horizon. It was transhistorical, an all-but-inevitable feature of collective life. The question was not whether the economy existed, but what kind of economy a given group had created. It could be local, national, or global. Whatever the scale, it could not be escaped.[53]

* * *

How did this happen? It is a complex answer that can be usefully simplified by focusing on three changes that took place in the first half of the twentieth century. Think of it as a story of three M's. The economy could be *measured*, via statistics like national income accounts, which the United States government, like a handful of other governments, began regularly producing during the Great Depression. It could be *modeled* using the mathematics that became the lingua franca of economics in the middle of the century, replacing looser styles of verbal reasoning that had earlier dominated the discipline. And it could be *managed* through fiscal and monetary policies implemented by an ensemble of institutions at the federal level, made possible in the United States by institutions like the Federal Reserve and passage of a national income tax. Not just an abstract "economic system," the economy was an object whose fluctuations could, with the appropriate policies, be controlled.

How the economy emerged is only part of the story. The deeper question is why it occurred in the first place. For convenience, the factors contributing to the economy's appearance can be divided into two camps: economic and political.

On the economic side, it helps to begin by noting the short history of economic growth. Persistent rates of economic growth over extended lengths of time were not a part of the human experience before the eighteenth century, when a slow but steady uptick became a norm in the United States and parts of Europe. The real breakthrough, however, occurred in the 1870s, the dawning of what the economist Robert Gordon has termed a "special century" of economic growth in the United States that exceeded anything that prevailed before or since.[54] Calculations of national income could be, and were, dismissed as objects of merely academic curiosity when it was assumed that the total would stay roughly the same year after year. In a world of fluctuating economic growth rates, on the other hand, annual differences of a percent or two could have profound consequences.

The routinization of economic growth was tied up with other, more tangible economic transformations. The second half of the nineteenth century witnessed the creation of a single national marketplace thanks to innovations like the telegraph and the railroad. The making of a national market was both cause and consequence of what Alfred Chandler called a "managerial revolution" that brought the modern corporation into being.[55] With fewer firms to count, leviathan corporations simplified the task of economic calculation. Household production and self-employment waned, turning wage labor into an increasingly prevalent mode of life, once again making it easier to gather data. The Federal Reserve helped bring order to a crazy-quilt system of rival currencies, and the obligation to file income taxes made economic tabulation into an annual ritual for a rising number of Americans.[56] As corporations increased in size, more and more Americans began working for wages. These wage earners discovered that their economic fortunes were now chained to the fluctuations of the business cycle.

This brings up the politics of the economy. The double blow of the Great Depression and the Cold War left an abiding fear among political elites that a crisis of the kind the United States had survived in the 1930s might be fatal if repeated. Focusing on the economy also solved an electoral problem for midcentury America's dominant political party, the Democrats, who were eager to find a cause that could hold their increasingly divided coalition together. Whatever their other differences, segregationists and civil rights activists both favored a growing economy. So did liberals who worried about whether the government could afford to maintain the welfare state at home while leading a global crusade against communism. Politicians of both parties soon learned to identify their odds of reelection with the economy's fortunes, a conclusion validated by political scientists researching the connection between economic and electoral performance.[57] Economic growth rates offered a scorecard in the Cold War, a seemingly neutral way of measuring the achievements of rival powers.[58] Focusing on the economy also gave coherence to policymaking. The details were complex, the data partial, and the tools limited, but the ideal could still bring consistency to a process always threatening to lurch out of control. In the prospect of unity, there even lay the hope of moving beyond politics altogether, replacing squabbling politicians with disinterested technocrats.[59]

By the 1950s, corporate managers and government bureaucrats could both agree on the importance of a properly managed economy. If the government could ensure full employment and maximum economic growth, then it could take a lighter hand with General Electric and AT&T. Managing the economy, in short, allowed Americans to reconcile democracy with the modern corporation—a union that had appeared by no means certain during the violent protests of the Gilded Age, or at the nadir of the Depression.

So far, this account has put politics on one side and economics on the other. That divide is, of course, far too simple. What about, for instance, taxation? Before the introduction of the income tax, most of the federal government's funding came from customs duties, with another third provided by taxes on alcohol and tobacco. By 1920 the income tax supplied two-thirds of the budget, linking the financing of the U.S. state to the fluctuations of national income, and providing an important incentive for the government to monitor the fluctuations of the economy as a whole.[60]

Then there is the question of monetary policy. Americans today assume that inflation will continue along at a slow but steady rate. That was not the case before the twentieth century, and for good reason. The price level in the United States in 1900 was around the same as it had been in 1800.[61] The breakdown of the gold standard and the rise of managed currencies made possible both sustained inflation and the aggressive oversight of the money

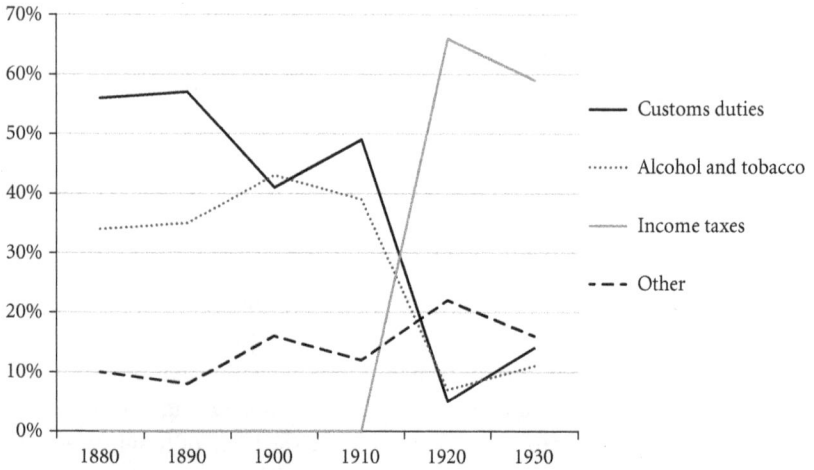

Figure 2.3. Sources of U.S. federal budget, 1880–1930.

supply provided by the Federal Reserve (a role the Fed's founders did not envision for the body when it was established in 1913).[62]

Or consider the experts who were supposed to guide institutions like the Fed. At the turn of the twentieth century, the only person employed by the federal government with the title of economist was an "economic orni-thologist."[63] By World War II, that number had ballooned to five thousand. Despite an initial retreat in peacetime, when economists returned to the acad-emy, by the 1970s the total was back at wartime levels, where it has stayed ever since. These economists were supplied by a rapidly expanding network of research universities, nonprofit entities that benefited from both increased government support and the backing of major corporations.[64]

Let us take stock of the argument so far. The immediate cause behind the proliferation of talk around the economy in the early decades of the twenti-eth century was that, for the first time, the economy became an object that could be measured by national income accounts, modeled by economists, and managed through fiscal and monetary policy. But stepping back brings a much larger history into focus. This history ties together subjects ranging from the emergence of modern economic growth and the making of the mod-ern corporation to the self-interest of politicians seeking reelection and the need for Cold War Democrats to hold together their fractious coalition. Though complex in its particulars, the core of this account is simple. The sec-ond half of the nineteenth century created an economic problem that would be solved politically in the first half of the twentieth century by committing the government to managing the economy.

* * *

Why does any of this matter? To begin with, there is the simple desire for accuracy. Historians have supplied genealogies for many of the modern world's foundational categories, including class, sexuality, race, gender, human rights, and modernity itself. The best of this scholarship has reckoned with both the long conceptual histories of the subjects under investigation and the possibility for radical change.[65] It is past time for historians of the United States to give the economy similar consideration.

Taking this history into account has important consequences for how scholars understand the past century. Part of the challenge to standard accounts is methodological. Following the economy's ascent forces us to move across the divides that too often separate economic, social, political, intellectual, and cultural history.[66] Changing methodologies yields a different vantage point on the century as a whole. Blending these methods produces a kind of synthesis, but one that cuts across customary narratives.

Consider, for example, the unlikely legacy of Wesley Mitchell. A former student of John Dewey and Thorstein Veblen, Mitchell devoted his life to fusing the legacy of these two influences. They came together in the founding of the National Bureau of Economic Research, or NBER, founded in 1920 with Mitchell as its intellectual leader. Like Mitchell, the NBER was devoted to revising economic theory so that it better captured the realities of economic life. During his time at the NBER, Mitchell had two great students. One, Simon Kuznets, pioneered the development of national-income accounting and conducted pathbreaking studies of economic inequality.[67] If Kuznets carried on the tradition in academic research, Arthur Burns took up the mantle in policymaking, serving first as head of the Council of Economic Advisers under Dwight Eisenhower and later as chairman of the Federal Reserve. (He was, revealingly, the first Fed chair to hold a doctorate in economics.) Before any of that happened, Burns succeeded Mitchell as research director at the NBER.[68]

At the NBER, Burns encouraged a protégé of his own. While a graduate student at Columbia, where he was studying under Mitchell, Burns helped make ends meet by lecturing undergraduates at Rutgers. There he met a young Milton Friedman, who had arrived at Rutgers planning to become an actuary, but who, under Burns's influence, graduated an aspiring economist.[69] Friedman split his graduate career between the University of Chicago and Columbia, where he also worked with Mitchell. That connection helped secure him a post at the NBER, a valuable opportunity in the midst of the Depression. There, Friedman served as a research assistant for Kuznets, who ultimately coauthored the younger man's dissertation.

With his doctorate in hand, Friedman embarked on an extraordinarily successful career, but his affiliation with the NBER was not done yet. In 1950 Burns asked Friedman to study the influence of the money supply on business cycles, enlisting his former student in a project that dated back to the bureau's founding. Thirteen years later, Burns's request led to the publication of the book for which Friedman is best known among economists. Weighing in at more than eight hundred pages, *A Monetary History of the United States, 1867–1960* did more than any other work to make Friedman's views on macroeconomics acceptable to the rest of his profession—and, eventually, to politicians, central bankers, and the general public.[70] (Ben Bernanke, for one, credits it with sparking his interest in monetary theory.)[71] It was an NBER book through and through: published under the NBER's auspices, based on data produced by NBER investigations, and coauthored with Anna Schwartz, an NBER staffer. There is a thread running from John Dewey to Milton Friedman, and it goes through Wesley Mitchell.

The economy is the favorite child of a distinct period in the history of U.S. democracy: not the social politics that flourished a century ago, but the technocratic politics that came to define the boundaries of the possible.[72] It is the product of a distinct kind of world—a world of behemoth corporations and commodified production, where a federal government overflowing with trained experts was mandated by law to maintain economic growth. The economy is the name Americans used to make sense of this world after it became exceedingly difficult to imagine that life had ever been, or could ever be, otherwise.

CHAPTER 3

The Triumph of the Mixed Economy

The New Deal Order, Keynes, and the Genius of American Liberalism

Jason Scott Smith

What was New Deal liberalism? At its core, I argue, Franklin D. Roosevelt's program was a political response to the economic disaster of the Great Depression. Eschewing the extremes of free-market capitalism, on the one hand, and statist control of every aspect of economic relations, on the other, the New Deal expanded the power of the federal government in order to stabilize the capitalist system. In so doing, the New Deal created an approach to government–economic relations that transcended FDR's presidency and underwrote what Gary Gerstle and Steve Fraser termed a "New Deal Order" that stretched until 1980.[1]

This essay makes three claims. First, the "mixed economy" created under the auspices of the New Deal lacked intellectual coherence. Second, despite (or perhaps because of) this state of affairs, the New Deal's mixed economy worked tremendously well: it generated extraordinary rates of gross domestic product (GDP) growth during the Great Depression and cut mass unemployment in half during the first four years of Franklin Roosevelt's presidency, it ultimately put an end to the Depression's more than ten-year economic collapse and achieved full employment during World War II, and it set the institutional and intellectual foundations in place for an extraordinary multidecade period of economic prosperity after the war. Third, I argue that historians, since the 1960s, have generally elided or ignored the success of the New Deal's contribution to economic policymaking, creating a situation where the tangible achievements forged by liberal statecraft have, for all practical purposes, dropped out of our history books. (Conventional wisdom still maintains that it was World War II that ended the Great Depression, not the New Deal.) To support these claims, I trace what I call "the triumph" of the New Deal's mixed economy from the Depression through World War II and on into the postwar years.

What defined the New Deal's mixed economy? The program created by Franklin Roosevelt's many advisers and supporters stressed the federal government's responsibility for stimulating economic growth and ameliorating unemployment. In this sense, the New Deal built on a wide range of previous public policies, intervening in the economy and underscoring what one historian once declared of nineteenth-century U.S. government, that "King Laissez Faire" was "not only dead; the hallowed report of his reign had all been a mistake." As many scholars have pointed out, "free-market capitalism" in the United States had long relied on a range of public policies that explicitly promoted economic activity, including the funding of public-works construction ("internal improvements"), the maintenance of public authority over the country's currency, a system of protectionist tariffs, the federal postal system, publicly chartered limited liability corporations, and a bankruptcy code that encouraged entrepreneurial activity, to name but several.[2] In direct response to the failures of the market economy during the Great Depression, the New Deal instituted a variety of programs that built on and surpassed previous policy measures: New Dealers attempted to drive down mass unemployment, stimulate consumer spending, encourage business activity, raise the wages of workers (and encourage them to unionize), restore investor confidence in the country's capital markets and depositor confidence in the country's banking system, create a social safety net (through unemployment insurance and social security), raise farm incomes, regulate industries such as trucking, airlines, and interstate electric and gas utilities, and generate employment through the building of a wide range of socially useful public-works projects, including roads, bridges, hydroelectric dams, and airports, among others. As Jordan Schwarz has argued, we might readily consider the New Deal, when viewed as a whole, as "a massive governmental recapitalization for purposes of economic development," one that "sought to create long-term markets by building an infrastructure in undeveloped regions."[3]

The New Deal's mixed economy, as outlined above, did not spring from the mind of a single individual and, given the contradictory nature of its various policy measures, appears from an intellectual point of view as messy or incoherent. Indeed, as Alan Brinkley pointed out in his famous essay "The New Deal and the Idea of the State," his contribution to Steve Fraser and Gary Gerstle's *The Rise and Fall of the New Deal Order, 1930–1980*, many New Dealers were themselves not sure what, if anything, provided a "theory" that justified the New Deal's many interventions in the economy. As Brinkley points out, when the Yale economist Alvin Hansen was asked in 1940 if the New Deal was based on sound economic principles, he responded, "I really do not know what the basic principle of the New Deal is." Hansen elaborated, "I know from my experience in the government that there are as many conflicting opinions among the people in Washington under this administration as we have in the country at large."[4]

Even before President Franklin Roosevelt's first one hundred days in office came to an end, Americans struggled to comprehend the nature and limits of what Fraser and Gerstle have termed "the New Deal order."[5] Historians have argued whether the New Deal was truly "America's Third Revolution," or is it better viewed as a "halfway revolution" that left much undone?[6] Whether portrayed as a new departure in the trajectory of a reforming impulse that stretched back to William Jennings Bryan, or as a high point in a generation's rendezvous with destiny, the New Deal was initially viewed by historians as a fundamentally liberal and progressive political event.[7]

This reading, however, has been qualified by a variety of scholars who have, in different ways, presented the New Deal as a historical moment that signaled the end of reform (including, most notably, Brinkley himself).[8] Whereas the older work of liberal historians, such as Arthur Schlesinger Jr., viewed the period as the "Age of Roosevelt," dominated by the dashing president who soaked the rich and mobilized the state against economic royalists on behalf of the "forgotten man," the work of subsequent scholars has been much more skeptical.[9] Mark Leff, for example, observes that high federal income-tax rates enacted by the New Dealers did not actually generate much revenue and served mainly as a smoke screen to distract the public from the heavy sales taxes levied by the New Deal on consumers.[10] The new regulations enacted by the state, Colin Gordon has claimed, in fact reflected the interests of business.[11] Whereas earlier historians believed that organized labor had at last found its "Magna Charta" in New Deal labor law, scholars such as Christopher Tomlins have asserted that this guarantee of collective bargaining functioned merely as a sham, as a "counterfeit liberty."[12]

The skepticism of Brinkley and other historians can be traced back to William E. Leuchtenburg's influential 1963 synthesis, *Franklin D. Roosevelt and the New Deal*. In much the same way that Schlesinger's *Age of Roosevelt* determined the boundaries of debate for an earlier generation of historians, Leuchtenburg's book was a turning point in our understanding of the legacy of the New Deal. Leuchtenburg, like Schlesinger, approached the New Deal from a sympathetic, liberal perspective. Departing from the untempered optimism of earlier interpretations, however, Leuchtenburg advanced what the historian James T. Patterson has termed a "cautiously positive interpretation of Roosevelt," paying more attention to the limits of the New Deal, its multiyear inability to solve the puzzle of the Depression, its failure to restructure the economic order, and its mixed record on racial equality. As Leuchtenburg himself put it, the New Deal's approach to the economy "left many problems unsolved and even created some new ones," adding, "It never demonstrated that it could achieve prosperity in peacetime."[13]

Leuchtenburg's judicious, evenhanded synthesis foreshadowed the subsequent revisionist efforts of New Left scholars such as Howard Zinn and Barton Bernstein.[14] In the introductory essay to his 1966 document anthology, *New Deal Thought*, Zinn revisits the New Deal years not to bury them but instead to find a usable past that could speak to the concerns of intellectuals in the 1960s. Zinn begins this reexamination with the definition of New Deal ideology provided by Richard Hofstadter in *Age of Reform*. Hofstadter had argued that the works of the New Deal antitrust expert Thurman Arnold epitomized the essence of the New Deal, for in them, Hofstadter wrote, "we find a sharp and sustained attack upon ideologies, rational principles, and moralism in politics. We find, in short, the theoretical equivalent of FDR's opportunistic virtuosity in practical politics—a theory that attacks theories."[15] Zinn presses this definition of New Deal ideology further than Hofstadter, pointing out the darker consequences of emphasizing method over substance and focusing on the suffering of millions of people who, in his words, "still awaited a genuine 'new deal.'"[16] Zinn acknowledges the New Deal's accomplishments, but he sees liberalism's potential for achieving real reforms as falling victim to Roosevelt's "experimental, shifting, and opportunistic" temperament.[17] Zinn is less than generous in his overall assessment of the New Deal, arguing that the "TVA [Tennessee Valley Authority], a brief golden period of federal theater, a thin spread of public housing, and a public works program called into play only at times of desperation, represented the New Deal's ideological and emotional limits in the creation of public enterprise."[18]

Other revisionist accounts of the New Deal came to similar conclusions. Relying on the assumptions that underwrite most "corporate liberal" interpretations of U.S. history, the historian Barton Bernstein argued that "the liberal reforms of the New Deal did not transform the American system; they conserved and protected American capitalism, occasionally by absorbing parts of threatening programs."[19] Because the New Deal's achievements were ultimately so limited, in Bernstein's view, the people who joined the New Deal political coalition were evidence of "one of the crueler ironies of liberal politics, that the marginal men trapped in hopelessness were seduced by rhetoric, by the style and movement, by the symbolism of efforts seldom reaching beyond words."[20] To the extent that the New Deal achieved anything, in Bernstein's view, it served to create a sort of false consciousness, capable only of duping the masses into voting for FDR.

Alan Brinkley offered a more nuanced assessment of the New Deal than New Leftists such as Zinn and Bernstein, but his story is one, like theirs, that reinforces the tendency of scholars to overlook the New Deal's economic achievements. Brinkley nests changes in liberal policymaking during the 1930s and 1940s within an explicit narrative of declension and failure. During the early years of the New Deal, Brinkley argues, Roosevelt and his advisers were open to pursuing a structural "critique of modern capitalism," one that would directly confront and constrain corporate power in the economy. By the end of World War II, however, this critique was "largely gone, or at least so attenuated as to be of little more than rhetorical significance. In its place was a set of liberal ideas essentially reconciled to the existing structure of the economy and committed to using the state to compensate for capitalism's inevitable flaws—a philosophy that signaled, implicitly at least, a resolution of some of the most divisive political controversies of the industrial era." This shift in priorities for New Deal liberals—from the structural reform of U.S. capitalism itself to "the idea that the state could manage the economy without managing the institutions of the economy"—constitutes, for Brinkley, the "end of reform." As he put it, by the end of World War II, "when liberals spoke now of government's responsibility to protect the health of the industrial world, they defined that responsibility less as a commitment to restructure the economy than as an effort to stabilize it and help it to grow. They were no longer much concerned about controlling or punishing 'plutocrats' and 'economic royalists,' an impulse central to New Deal rhetoric in the mid-1930s. Instead, they spoke of their commitment to providing a healthy environment in which the corporate world could flourish and in which the economy could sustain 'full employment.'"[21]

On closer scrutiny, a number of turns in Brinkley's argument appear problematic: it is unclear exactly how the programs of the early New Deal, in particular the industrial codes of competition enacted and enforced by the National Recovery Administration (NRA) (1933–1935), constituted an attempt to bring about deep "structural" reform of U.S. capitalism, to use the state, as Brinkley argues, to directly challenge corporate behavior. As Ellis Hawley pointed out in the 1960s, and as Andrew Wender Cohen reminded us in the 2000s, the NRA in fact constituted a failed attempt to suspend antitrust laws and institute cartels in a range of U.S. industries, an undertaking that drew on New Era–style "associationalism" and served to dramatically reinforce the power of big business at the expense of smaller firms, labor, and consumers. As one contemporary observer put it, the NRA's intervention in the economy resembled a "bargain between business leaders on the one hand and businessmen in the guise of government officials on the other." The NRA, in short, hardly constitutes an impressive test case for the ability of "New Deal reform" to offer a deep structural critique of the power of corporate capitalism.[22]

Turning from the early New Deal to the heart of Brinkley's account—FDR's embrace of deficit spending in the 1937–1938 "Roosevelt Recession" and the nation's mobilization for World War II—we are offered a brilliant intellectual history of the New Deal, but one that misses the broader context of the political economy of the 1930s and 1940s. For example, key policy measures, such as the Housing Act of 1937 and the Fair Labor Standards Act of 1938, policies that might represent the continuation, rather than the end, of a kind of liberal reform that challenged corporate power, are entirely absent from Brinkley's narrative. Instead, we are presented with a lively history of the New Deal that focuses on what liberals and their allies thought about the political fortunes of American liberalism. Indeed, as the historian Thomas McCraw points out (in a largely sympathetic and insightful review of *The End of Reform*), Brinkley's history "is a lot stronger on politics than on economics" because he "relies too heavily on the tendentious economic ideas of forties journalists such as Dwight Macdonald, Richard Strout, and I. F. Stone and too little on evaluations by economists and economic historians." McCraw observes that *The End of Reform*'s chapter on war mobilization "focuses on what liberals *thought* and how dispirited they were not to be running the whole show" during World War II. Brinkley "thereby turns the economic bang of the war and postwar years, the strongest performance the world had ever seen, into a political whimper." The economic achievements of the New Deal's mixed economy are too impressive for historians to continue to ignore in such a fashion.[23]

If we turn, as McCraw suggests, to the work of economists and economic historians, what can they tell us about the mixed economy during the Great Depression? The economist Christina Romer, in an important and much-cited essay published three years after the appearance of Fraser and Gerstle's *Rise and Fall of the New Deal Order*, points out that during FDR's first four years in office, "real GNP [gross national product] in the United States grew at an average rate of over 8 percent per year; between 1938 and 1941 [i.e., before U.S. entry into World War II] it grew over 10 percent per year." Romer rightly terms these rates of growth "spectacular," overturning arguments advanced by a range of economists (from E. Cary Brown, to Milton Friedman and Anna Schwartz, to Ben Bernanke, to Brad De Long and Lawrence Summers) that had generally minimized the role played by New Deal policies in stimulating economic recovery. Romer instead points to the impact that the influx of gold and other foreign investment had on the U.S. economy, an influx that stemmed from economic and political instability in Europe and from the Roosevelt administration's 1934 decision to uncouple the dollar from the gold standard and inflate the country's currency, a mixture of factors that Romer describes as "due partly to historical accident and partly to policy." Barry Eichengreen offers a slightly more pessimistic assessment of New Deal policymaking than does Romer, asserting that "devaluation may have freed the Fed and the Roosevelt administration of their golden fetters, but they failed to take full advantage of their liberty." That said, the effect of this cross-border movement of capital on the U.S. economy was, to again quote Romer, "spectacular." As the economic historian Alex Field has argued, although the 1930s were years of economic depression they were also a period marked not only by the growth that Romer identified but also by tremendous advances in total factor productivity and organizational innovation, advances funded by private research and development spending and by the New Deal's commitment to building the infrastructure necessary for a truly national market.[24]

Other policy measures of the early New Deal likewise contributed to restoring stability and underwriting economic growth during the Depression. The New Deal saved the country's failing banking system and insured depositor bank accounts through the Federal Deposit Insurance Corporation.

The New Deal regulated the country's capital markets through the creation of the Securities and Exchange Commission. New Dealers slowly began to spend $3.3 billion on public-works construction, an enormous amount of investment relative to the size of the federal government and the size of the U.S. economy. This 1933 appropriation constituted just over 165 percent of federal revenues that year, or 5.9 percent of the country's gross domestic product. Although the Public Works Administration (PWA), under the direction of the interior secretary Harold Ickes, spent these funds too slowly and cautiously to have a swift influence on the unemployment rate, the short-lived Civil Works Administration (during the winter of 1933–1934) and Harry Hopkins's Works Progress Administration (WPA) (1935–1943) reinforced the New Deal's tremendous and widespread commitment to public-works construction.

Relying on private contractors, the PWA deployed its funds in all but three of the country's 3,071 counties while helping to pay for projects like the Tennessee Valley Authority and Boulder Dam. Created in 1935, the WPA did lighter construction work and avoided private contracting. Its initial appropriation of $4.88 billion was about 135 percent of the federal government's revenues in 1935, or about 6.7 percent of GDP in that year. Although primarily intended as a vast relief effort for employing the unskilled, the WPA built an impressive range of projects, including over 480 airports, 78,000 bridges, and nearly 40,000 public buildings. During the Great Depression, the payrolls of the PWA and the WPA were among the biggest in the country, easily dwarfing those of the largest private enterprises. In carrying out their mandates, the two programs integrated a multitude of municipal construction experts, members of the Army Corps of Engineers, and civil engineers into the national state.[25]

During the war, federal spending priorities expanded in both scale and scope. If federal spending during the Great Depression focused on public-works projects, during wartime it focused on defense, reaching a staggering 40 percent of GDP. (In 1938, by contrast, federal spending was only 8 percent of GDP.) Public spending on such an enormous scale finally brought economic recovery within sight. Indeed, the economic boom brought on by mobilizing the U.S. economy and putting it on a wartime footing served to deliver, in full, on the promise of the New Deal's mixed economy during the Depression: full employment (unemployment dropped to 3.1 percent in 1943, to 1.77 percent in 1944, and to 1.23 percent—a record low—in 1944), a higher standard of living for Americans, and a substantial increase in farm income.

These were just three of the many economic achievements wrought by massive federal spending during wartime. The income gap between the rich and poor, which had decreased during the Great Depression, narrowed even more dramatically during World War II: between 1941 and 1945, the poorest 40 percent of U.S. families saw their incomes begin to turn upward. The passage of the Servicemen's Readjustment Act—popularly known as the G.I. Bill—in 1944 guaranteed the country's veterans one year of unemployment payments following the end of their term of service, along with access and funding for higher education, vocational training, and loans for buying homes and starting businesses.

Whereas federal spending became a huge presence in the country's economy during wartime, relative to what it had been during the Great Depression, FDR's approach to administration in both cases remained quite similar. To figure out how to best mobilize the nation for wartime production, Roosevelt and the New Dealers relied on a range of bureaucratic organizations, often with overlapping areas of responsibility, in an attempt to arrive at a pragmatic balance between centralized policymaking and decentralized decision making. In war, as during the Depression, New Dealers used public authority, often in an ad hoc fashion, to structure the private market.

FDR set the tone for what would be required of the country in May 1940, following the fall of France to Nazi Germany, when he declared that the United States would need to produce 50,000 military aircraft each year to adequately defend itself and supply allied nations. (Between 1919 and 1929, the country had manufactured a total of just 13,500 of these airplanes.) Although critics scoffed at such an apparently unrealistic figure, the United States subsequently produced 26,000 military aircraft in 1941; in 1942, 48,000; in 1943, 86,000; in 1944, 96,000; and in 1945, 50,000. This production miracle was a product of the New Deal's mixed economy, in this case using government authority to maximize the productive capacity of U.S. labor and business. To produce military supplies and goods in sufficient volume, the federal government relied on the private marketplace, leaning particularly on the skills and capacities contained in large industrial corporations. Thirty percent of the $175 billion in defense-related contracts awarded between June 1940 and September 1944 went to just ten companies, including General Motors, Ford, United Aircraft, Bethlehem Steel, Chrysler, and General Electric. As a result, cities and regions like Detroit, Los Angeles, and the San Francisco Bay Area became key sites in the arsenal of production, with the aircraft industry and shipbuilding main areas of focus. The U.S. West, in particular, benefited from defense spending, with its growth skyrocketing during the war. By 1943, for example, the aircraft industry was responsible for 40 percent of the manufacturing jobs in Los Angeles, and the city trailed only Detroit in its productive output. The population of the entire state of California exploded during the war, growing by one-third, with people pouring into cities like San Francisco (which grew 29 percent) and San Diego (which grew by 46 percent).[26]

Perhaps the most famous domestic undertaking during the war, the top-secret effort to build an atomic bomb, illustrates the widespread effect of large-scale federal investment and the ways the war effort capitalized on the mixed economy constructed by the New Deal in the 1930s. The Manhattan Project relied directly on the electricity generated by the TVA for its uranium enrichment process at Oak Ridge, Tennessee, and leveraged the New Deal's investment in the country's infrastructure in many of its activities, both major and minor. For example, some of the scientists and their families at work in Los Alamos, New Mexico, were housed in buildings that had originally been constructed by the Civilian Conservation Corps at the nearby Bandelier National Monument. Henry Kaiser took his firm's experience building dams for the PWA and put its logistical and engineering capacities to work assembling cargo ships for the war effort in record-setting fashion. The army engineer Brehon Somervell built on his experience running the WPA in New York City, where he supervised the building of projects such as LaGuardia Airport, when he was promoted to brigadier general and put in charge of the Quartermaster Corps. During the war, Somervell directed the construction of a variety of military installations, including the Pentagon.

The return of economic activity and the virtual elimination of unemployment during the war served to bring about two of the most important aims of the New Deal's mixed economy. As one reformer observed in 1943, in view of these wartime achievements, "the honest-minded liberal will admit that the common man is getting a better break than ever he did under the New Deal."[27] Business hiring and private investment returned with a vengeance during the 1940s, but the wartime economy also held improved news for consumers and workers. The federal government's Office of Price Administration marked the culmination of New Deal efforts to include consumers within the polity, serving to tamp down inflation and ration consumer goods. Organized labor benefited during the war as well. Labor leaders took a "no strike" pledge in return for government and business agreeing to arbitration procedures that brought increased wages, benefits, and maintenance of membership clauses to labor agreements. Women poured into the workforce, particularly in the aircraft industry. African Americans embraced the "Double-V" campaign, arguing that victory abroad must go hand in hand with victory over racist oppression at home. Pressing for a fair share in the return of prosperity, A. Philip Randolph and other African American leaders extracted FDR's commitment to create a Fair Employment Practices Committee, in return calling off plans for a massive "March on Washington" to demand economic justice.

The validation that the New Deal's mixed economy received during the crucible of wartime served also to validate the ideas of the English economist John Maynard Keynes, who had published his classic work, *The General Theory of Employment, Interest and Money*, in 1936. A veritable army of young economists, acquainted with Keynes's insight about the importance of deficit spending to fight downturns in the business cycle, flocked to Washington, DC, and applied Keynes's ideas in their work. The New Deal's programs were originally intended to address the economic crisis of the 1930s, but the intellectual scaffolding for these efforts was not widely recognized—or even developed—until after World War II, with the widespread adoption of Keynesian theory in managing modern economies. Whereas the New Deal did indeed fail to end mass unemployment during the Great Depression, post–World War II economists across the political spectrum finally recognized that the stimulus provided by wartime mobilization and massive amounts of federal spending served to validate the policy measures originally implemented under the New Deal's mixed economy.[28]

* * *

During the Great Depression, unchecked market capitalism had led to the collapse of the global economy. In the United States, the New Deal made it clear to all that the federal government would not witness such a situation while doing nothing. As Stuart Chase wrote in 1942, "Adam Smith may heave in his grave . . . but no nation in this dangerous world of 1942 is meekly going bankrupt because some textbooks say it ought to. . . . Put your book away, my friend. The books which will explain the new world we are entering have not been written."[29] New institutions, a social safety net, and a commitment to rescuing capitalism, taken together, created a new way of conceiving of the relationship between the government and the market. This way of thinking was subsequently exported to the international stage. Indeed, many elements of the New Deal's mixed economy traveled overseas after World War II. These reform impulses were transmitted by multinational corporations, which took their experience working for the federal government during the Great Depression and applied it in foreign markets. They were also present at Bretton Woods, New Hampshire, as New Dealers, scarred by the economic collapse of the 1930s and the devastation of World War II, worked with colleagues from other countries to create postwar institutions like the International Monetary Fund (IMF), the International Bank for Reconstruction and Development (World Bank), and the General Agreement on Tariffs and Trade (GATT), injecting stability into the global economy. As these ideas and institutions shaped the economies and societies of other countries, they were often subsequently imported back into the United States, usually with little knowledge of their real origins.[30]

In short, domestic efforts undertaken by the federal government to support economic development during the 1930s and 1940s, which witnessed the southern and western regions of the United States becoming home to military bases, an expanded highway network, and new and improved airports, did not stop at the country's borders after World War II. Abroad, postwar efforts such as the Marshall Plan, the reconstruction of Japan, and projects such as the Pan-American Highway in Latin America began to carry the New Dealers' vision of economic development overseas, fostering the idea that economic growth could follow from publicly funded improvements in infrastructure and government regulation of markets. Politicians, policymakers, and multinational corporations drew on this intellectual tradition of planning. For example, Lyndon Johnson's vision of exporting Keynesian-style economic development to Southeast Asia (by replicating the Tennessee Valley Authority on the Mekong Delta) reflected the powerful legacy of the New Deal for postwar liberals who were struggling to reconcile foreign and domestic policy goals. This struggle helped to transform New Deal liberalism, as the imperatives of Cold War anticommunism increasingly shaped the ideas and objectives of U.S. politicians, businesspeople, and labor leaders.[31]

Overseas, of course, New Deal–style regulations and institutions often found a mixed reception, as local elites, business, and labor organizations modified (or rejected outright) various elements of U.S. capitalism. These differing power relationships shaped the range of possible actions for U.S. politicians, as well as for multinational construction firms such as Bechtel, Morrison-Knudsen, and Brown & Root (a longtime subsidiary of Halliburton). U.S. politicians and corporations, however, did not work diligently to spread

U.S. ideas about human rights around the globe. Rather, they were at times selective with respect to the countries they chose as multilateral partners, often working with dictatorial and repressive regimes in embarking on a fierce Cold War with the Soviet Union for the ideological affections of the rest of the planet. Marshall Plan aid, for example, functioned at times as a kind of subsidy that allowed Western European countries to fund wars and conflicts with their colonial possessions, thwarting their desires for independence and self-determination.[32] In other words, after 1945 U.S. government and business aimed to enact portions of the New Deal for only part of the world, an arrangement that at times boiled down to increasing access to foreign markets for U.S. firms and supporting political and economic stability in strategically important countries. Following World War II, New Deal liberalism built a postwar global economy that was decidedly friendly to multinational corporations in order to halt the spread of communism. That said, postwar liberalism, in focusing on using public resources and regulating the activities of private capitalism, managed to foster impressive rates of economic growth (particularly in the United States, Western Europe, and Japan) and to intervene powerfully in the economies and societies of other countries. However, these achievements were often accomplished at the expense of more progressive ideas about deploying public authority to address concerns about social justice, human rights, and the distribution of wealth.

The central idea underlying much of the New Deal's mixed economy was that of state-sponsored economic development. In deploying this idea, New Dealers were, at once, empirical, flexible, inconsistent, and boldly experimental. They embraced precedent when it served their purposes and abandoned it when it did not. They brought new forms of social and economic expertise into the U.S. state, as lawyers, economists, civil engineers, and social workers became part of the federal bureaucracy on a new scale. These professions reshaped U.S. statecraft in the last half of the twentieth century. The scale and scope of the New Deal's spending during the Great Depression (two-thirds of the New Deal's funds went toward building public-works projects) secured the foundations for a national market in the postwar years. The New Deal's investment in infrastructure spurred dramatic advances in economic productivity, improving the country's transportation networks, expanding domestic military bases and facilities, and drawing up the blueprints for a national highway system. This public investment also foreshadowed the rise of the Sunbelt. It was no accident that the developing West and, to a lesser extent, the underdeveloped South, welcomed the arrival of federal dollars in their regions. While investing for the future, the New Deal's public-works programs created millions of jobs—both direct employment at the construction site and indirect employment, thanks to the multiplier effect of public spending. In public-works spending, the New Deal gave U.S. politicians—both Democrats and Republicans—a policy tool that would be used to influence overseas development, from the onset of the Cold War, through the Vietnam War, and continuing to today. As the economist Albert Hirschman observed, "These filial connections of Keynesian ideas with the economics of growth and development had a remarkable consequence." He continued, "A body of thought that was conceived in the Depression and was designed to deal with the problems of unemployment and stagnation has come to be intimately and deservedly associated with *les trente glorieuses*—the glorious thirty post–World War II years—that is, with the most sustained and dynamic period of economic expansion in human history, both in the economically advanced and in many of the less developed countries."[33]

The welfare state built by the New Deal, like its public-works spending, illustrated the federal government's assumption of the power to intervene in the economy. Measures like social security, unemployment insurance, and public-works employment functioned to ameliorate the harsh effects of the Depression, helping to smooth out the business cycle. The 1946 Employment Act, with its creation of the Council of Economic Advisers, enshrined into law the principle that the federal government could and should act vigorously to prevent future depressions. While historians like Brinkley have viewed the 1946 act as having been eviscerated by business groups and left "so filled with qualifications and ambiguities that it was almost meaningless," others, such as Michael Bernstein, have recognized the act's importance as a landmark of public policy, a product of the New Deal's mixed economy.[34]

As politicians, journalists, scholars, and concerned citizens attempt to make sense of the financial collapse of 2008 and the ensuing Great Recession, it seems that many have forgotten the achievements wrought by the New Deal to counter the Great Depression. Still others eagerly consume attempts to rehabilitate the public policies of Warren Harding, Calvin Coolidge, and Herbert Hoover, books and articles produced by a veritable army of right-wing journalists and quasi-historians.[35]

Mainstream historians also bear some blame for this state of collective amnesia regarding the New Deal's mixed economy. Since the 1960s, the profession has rendered a consistently pessimistic judgment on the New Deal's failure with respect to economic policy. "Within the one inescapable context of the thirties—the need for economic growth—the New Deal was a short-run failure," writes Paul Conkin. "It has become commonplace to point out that the New Deal, despite its variety of economic ministrations, failed to 'cure' the Great Depression," echoes Joseph Huthmacher. This judgment continues to warp historical interpretations offered to the general public and to university students. The New Deal, argues David Kennedy, "fell pathetically short of achieving full economic recovery." For Mary Beth Norton and her colleagues, it was "World War II, not the New Deal" that "reinvigorated the American economy."[36]

This one-note verdict misses a great deal. With the exception of the 1937–1938 recession—when FDR followed conservative orthodoxy and cut public spending—every year of the New Deal witnessed increases in the country's GDP averaging between 8 percent per year (between 1933 and 1937) and 10 percent per year (between 1938 and 1941), coupled with decreasing unemployment. As Christina Romer has judged, "These rates of growth are spectacular, even for an economy pulling out of a severe depression." When FDR took office, unemployment as a percentage of the civilian labor force stood at 20.9 percent (as a proportion of the civilian private nonfarm labor force, unemployment had hit 30.02 percent). By 1937, four years of New Deal policies had cut unemployment in the civilian labor force in half, down to 9.18 percent. Viewed as a proportion of the civilian private nonfarm labor force, unemployment had been cut by the New Deal by almost two-thirds, down to 13.25 percent. The economic stimulus provided by the renewed public spending associated with wartime mobilization drove unemployment down further, to historic lows. By 1944, eleven years after FDR's first inauguration, unemployment in the civilian labor force was 1.23 percent, and only slightly higher—1.69 percent—as a share of the civilian private nonfarm labor force. The GDP of the United States grew at an average rate of 3 percent per capita every year between 1940 and 1973. Thanks to the policies inaugurated by the New Deal, the United States began to recover from the disastrous economic mismanagement of Herbert Hoover and started an unprecedented run of economic growth. With the dramatic federal investment associated with the New Deal and World War II, a generation of Americans witnessed the power of the New Deal's mixed economy to bring about economic growth and virtually eliminate mass unemployment. With the regulations put in place by the New Deal, this same generation recognized the necessity of government to a functioning and thriving economy.

The wide gap between the robust legacies of the New Deal's mixed economy and the comparatively impoverished discussions of our present moment stands to remind us that the way we write and use our history matters a great deal. To argue that the New Deal's mixed economy marked the end of the reform impulse in American liberalism misses its extraordinary performance during the Great Depression, World War II, and afterward. For much of the twentieth century, in fact, the New Deal's mixed economy represented a triumph of American liberalism.

CHAPTER 4

The Strange Career of Institutional Keynesianism

Samir Sonti

Thanks in large part to the demonstrated failure of twenty-first-century capitalism to meet the most basic needs of a growing share of the U.S. population, the New Deal is back in fashion. Leading progressives in the Democratic Party have proposed a Green New Deal that would deploy significant federal investment to begin addressing the twin economic and ecological crises affecting countries the world over. Increasing numbers of elected officials have expressed support for an overhaul of the health-care industry that would eliminate private insurers and establish a public, single-payer system. Financial sector firms and tech giants have come under intensive scrutiny, with calls to regulate, dismember, or restructure them now found well within the mainstream. And perhaps most important, workers have begun taking action, with a revived labor militancy spreading from educators to service workers to journalists and beyond.

For historians, this presents an opportunity to revisit the question of what happened to the original New Deal. Answers have been provided at least since the Reagan years, and they are all over the map. But on one point most scholars tend to agree. The Keynesian consensus that emerged out of the 1930s and 1940s took the structure of the corporate economy as a given and did not attempt to transform it. Above all, New Deal liberalism was directed toward stabilizing that system, not replacing it. Measures to increase consumer purchasing power could serve this end, so a basic welfare state and workplace regulations were logical and indeed progressive reforms. Yet most of these benefits accrued to a certain type of worker—one employed in manufacturing, most likely white, and almost certainly male. The smokestack industries in which they worked offered a decent wage for a time, but postwar liberals did little to prevent their employers from shutting down and moving in search of cheaper labor, let alone to require them to pay for the long-term damage their addition to carbon would cause. Moreover, Keynesianism was not just doomed from an environmental perspective: it was also incapable of weathering the economic crises it was destined to confront. The 1970s crisis of stagflation—when inflation and recession occurred at once—represented a structural conjuncture that this growth liberalism was ill-equipped to handle. Stimuli that would boost demand added inflationary pressure, while contractionary policy aimed at stabilizing the price level prolonged the stagnation. Into this void the neoliberals strode, and we have been living in the world they made ever since.[1]

But was there only ever one Keynesianism? This essay contends that the midcentury liberal imagination was shaped by more than just growth economics; instead it explores the history of an alternative Keynesian tradition that I call Institutional Keynesianism.[2] In the 1930s and 1940s the figures that I characterize as Institutional Keynesians were often called reds, radicals, planners, or New Dealers, but whatever the contemporary label they melded an older, institutional economics concerned with history, structure, and power with Keynesian insights about purchasing-power–driven growth. The tradition was born, of all places, in the New Deal Department of Agriculture, where a cohort of left-liberal intellectuals and activists grappled with the problem of stagnation and the chronic imbalances between the agricultural and industrial sectors. In the process, they developed a powerful analysis that began with a case for direct intervention in corporate decision making and ended, by the late 1930s, with a call for planning for maximum production and even full employment. These were some of the first calls for "full employment," and they came from the U.S. Department of Agriculture (USDA).[3]

The Institutional Keynesians' demand for full employment did not represent a retreat from a program of structural intervention in favor of the politics of growth. It was instead a practical strategy designed to achieve their ultimate objective: a national social democracy that integrated the otherwise segmented urban and rural political economies. In their eyes, working people in the cities and the countryside shared a common fate—laboring and living under the undemocratic authority of a corporate power that determined the incomes they would earn, if any, and the prices they would pay.[4] Challenging this reality required striking at the heart of corporate capitalism itself—that is, questioning how wages, prices, and profits were set. The way to do that, the Institutional Keynesians in time realized, was through planning an economy that guaranteed *all* urban workers a job that provided sufficient income to enable them to afford the things they needed. This included, most of all, food—which they hoped would come from agricultural workers who produced a diversified array of crops through sound land-use practices and who were in turn well-enough compensated to enjoy a dignified living. In other words, full employment and planning, industrial and agricultural reform, were all part of the same struggle. Understanding what the Institutional Keynesians stood for and the challenges they confronted may help to inform perspectives on what it will take to achieve an economically just and environmentally sustainable progressive agenda today.

The Birth of Institutional Keynesianism

By the time Roosevelt took office, one issue preoccupied everyone concerned with agricultural policy: deflation. Through the 1920s and into the 1930s, commodity prices had tumbled, a painful rerun of the long downturn of the late nineteenth century that culminated in the rise and fall of Populism. To the big growers who controlled the top seats at the Agricultural Adjustment Administration (AAA), the source of the problem as well as its solution were relatively simple. Overproduction of food and fiber had resulted in surpluses, so the way forward was to cut supply and thereby raise market prices. Led by George Peek, who left his post as head of the Moline Plow Company to enter the Roosevelt administration, the AAA incentivized production restraint by offering large landowners subsidies in exchange for their agreement to comply with quotas set by the federal government. On one level, the program was a great success—agricultural prices did stabilize, and they soon began to rise. But recovery came at a cost. Tenant farmers, sharecroppers, and other landless farm workers whose services were no longer needed faced unemployment, eviction, or worse. As the National Farmers Union (NFU) president John Simpson put it, during the 1930s the only things in overproduction were "empty stomachs and bare backs."[5]

One of the most powerful challenges to the worldview held by George Peek and his allies came from the Institutional Keynesians within the Department of Agriculture itself. They proposed a much different interpretation of the crisis, one that led them to an alternative policy framework for responding to it: a system of comprehensive economic planning that would confront corporate power and thereby reconcile the structural imbalance between production and consumption. By the end of the 1930s, they were calling for "maximum production" and "full employment" with "low prices and high wages." This, the Institutional Keynesians well understood, could only be achieved through direct, structural intervention into every aspect of the economy—from investment and production decisions to pricing and profit levels.

The bleak economic conditions in the U.S. countryside had led agricultural economists to grapple with the issue of stagnation before the Depression drew the attention of the rest of the profession. The Department of Agriculture played an important role in encouraging this process. The Bureau of Agricultural Economics (BAE), established in 1922 by Secretary Henry C. Wallace, along with the USDA Graduate School, provided a home to a cohort of quantitatively informed institutional economists like Mordecai Ezekiel and Louis Bean. Ezekiel, who had established himself as one of the world's leading statisticians with his 1930 publication of *Methods of Correlation Analysis*, spent most of the 1920s at the BAE. Together with Bean and others at the BAE, Ezekiel's work investigated how structural imbalances between agriculture and industry affected production, prices, and purchasing power. By the early 1930s, he was anticipating Keynes's insights, calling for deficit spending on a robust public-works agenda. Appointed economic adviser to Henry A. Wallace in 1933, Ezekiel would become a leading Institutional Keynesian in the department throughout the New Deal. His 1939 book, *Jobs for All*, was among the first extensive arguments for planning for a full employment policy.[6]

In 1922 Secretary Henry C. Wallace had also established a Bureau of Home Economics (BHE) with the objective of helping households navigate the welter of new consumer goods they confronted in the marketplace. The field of home economics paralleled agricultural economics: it emerged through the USDA; it gained a foothold among progressive intellectuals in universities and in many places became established as its own department; and its practitioners were mainly concerned with the relationship between agriculture and the rest of the economy. From 1923 until 1943, the BHE was led by Louise Stanley, a 1911 Yale PhD in biochemistry and a member of the Department of Home Economics faculty at the University of Missouri. At the BHE, Stanley hired more female professionals than any other federal agency, and as Carolyn Goldstein has shown, their "approach to the home would prove to be wide ranging, covering issues of production, distribution, and consumption of foods, clothing, and household equipment."[7] During the New Deal, BHE staffers used their positions as spokespersons for housewives as an opportunity to articulate underconsumptionist and planning arguments that aligned with those that Ezekiel and others were promoting at the BAE. The mere presence of women, however, would not change the fact that virtually all New Dealers thought about production and consumption in terms of the family wage. And the women in the BHE were not exactly a representative sample. Still, if by the end of the twentieth century just about everyone had come to see home economics as an artifact of a bygone era, in the 1930s the profession played a progressive function.

To complement the underconsumptionist thinkers in the BAE and BHE, Undersecretary of Agriculture Rexford Tugwell and Wallace recruited Gardiner Means to join Ezekiel in the Office of the Economic Adviser. Fresh off his 1932 publication, with Adolf Berle, of *The Modern Corporation and Private Property*, Means set about uncovering the causes of the agricultural-industrial disparities and resultant weakness of purchasing power. His conclusion, subsequently published by the Senate as *Industrial Prices and Their Relative Inflexibility*, introduced a principle that would remain central to the Institutional Keynesian tradition for going forward: the theory of administered prices. Whereas economic orthodoxy held that prices were constantly "made in the market as the result of the interaction of buyers and sellers," Means thought administered prices were "rigid, at least for a period of time, and sales (and usually production) fluctuate with the demand at the rigid price."[8] The implied peril was grave—in the face of low demand, administered prices may remain stable or even rise while production falls. These were conditions that could result in simultaneous stagnation and price inflation.[9] And Means showed how industries with high levels of concentration had behaved just that way during the depths of the Depression. But the practice, he admitted, was not necessarily pernicious. It stemmed from the "shift from market to administrative coordination of economic activity," one that "made possible tremendous increases in the efficiency of industrial production" but that also "by its nature destroyed the free market and disrupted the operations of the law of supply and demand in a great many industries and for the economy as a whole."[10] As a result, Means observed, "a major part of American economic activity" occurred not in response to the market, but at the will of those "great administrative units—our great corporations."[11]

The Senate published *Industrial Prices* in 1935, just as the Supreme Court struck down the National Recovery Administration (NRA) and appeared poised to do the same to the AAA. With the centerpieces of the New Deal tottering and the Depression grinding into its fifth year, popular sentiment toward big business hit a nadir, a turn to which Berle and Means's own book, *The Modern Corporation*, had contributed at least in part. The so-called Roosevelt Recession, which began in 1937 and had by 1938 erased most of the gains achieved by the early New Deal, only added to the widespread frustration. Roosevelt responded by establishing the Temporary National Economic Committee (TNEC), a body that for the next three years would study and issue reports on corporate power in a number of industries, becoming the most extensive federal inquiry on that question to date. Scholars have with some cause characterized the TNEC as a last gasp of the New Deal antitrust impulse. Certain old-school populists were behind its creation, such as the Wyoming senator Joseph O'Mahoney, and its investigations dovetailed with Assistant Attorney General for Antitrust Thurmond Arnold's crusading efforts around the same time.[12] But the principal inspiration for the TNEC was Means's administered price thesis, and, as he had stressed all along, "administered pricing should not be confused with monopoly. . . . Few realize the extent to which it would be necessary to pulverize industry," he observed, nor appreciate "the loss of efficiency which it would entail," to break up the great corporations.[13] To Means, the only solution was to plan. He would spend the rest of the decade at another center of the New Deal planning impulse, the National Resources Committee, which later became the National Resources Planning Board, trying to do just that.[14]

Together, Ezekiel, Stanley, Means, and others in the USDA presented a set of ideas that would serve as the foundation of Institutional Keynesian politics and thought until the end of the 1930s. The crisis was one of underconsumption, and underconsumption resulted from gross imbalances of power. Economic planning, which involved direct intervention in corporate production and pricing decisions along with significant income redistribution, was the only way out of chronic stagnation. But changing political and economic conditions over the course of the decade altered the way these figures thought about the most effective route to that promised land. Struggles they and their allies waged in the immediate years to come led them to experiment with a new way of advocating for planning—one that involved calling for maximum production and full employment, even before the economic miracles achieved during World War II had brought those terms into the mainstream. This was not growth economics displacing planning or structural reform, but rather a political calculation by planners to use the compelling logic of full employment to their advantage.

Institutionalism Keynesianism in Action

The most interesting thing about the New Deal USDA was not that it provided a home to heterodox thinkers like Means, Ezekiel, and Stanley, but that it had administrative divisions chock full of radicals ready to organize around those ideas. The Legal Division of the AAA, which was led by Jerome Frank and staffed by card-carrying Communists like Lee Pressman, Nathaniel Witt, and Alger Hiss—along with other left-liberals like Leon Keyserling—was arguably the reddest entity ever in the federal government. Their laudable efforts on behalf of the Southern Tenant Farmers' Union (STFU) in 1935, which ultimately resulted in Henry A. Wallace's decision to fire a number of them, has been taken by many historians to mark the end of an extraordinary if idealistic phase in the New Deal USDA. But the Legal Division's pro-STFU campaign was only their most visible challenge to the powerful interests that ran the AAA.[15]

Take Lee Pressman, who after his time with the federal government went on to serve as general counsel of the CIO, before being removed from that position in the infamous Taft–Hartley purges that engulfed the labor movement.[16] For the first six months of the AAA's existence, Pressman oversaw the drafting of marketing agreements with large processors, and during that time he had repeatedly feuded with Peek over the character and scope of those contracts. The issue that, as Pressman saw it, "led to the most bitter disputes within the AAA," was whether or not the government had the authority and the right to access corporate processors' account books and records so as to ensure that, as middlemen, they did not accumulate excessive profits at the expense of consumers. Such transparency, Pressman argued, was a most reasonable concession in exchange for the immunity from antitrust prosecution the processors enjoyed, and he went on to insist that this issue more than any other would determine whether the AAA would actually seek "to regulate, or whether the government would merely be a cat's paw for the processors."[17]

The men who ran the big processing concerns felt otherwise. Internal financial data—on capital outlays, costs, profits—must, for long-term competitive purposes, remain confidential, they held, and in any event the government had no constitutional right to encroach on this most dearly held prerogative. The sanctity of private property itself was at stake. George Peek, a representative of those big farm leaders who Tugwell had accused of being "owned body and soul by the processors," tended to agree. Peek would act, as he himself put it, "with as little interference with established institutions and methods—indeed with as little administration of any kind as is consistent with the fixed purpose of the law; namely, to raise farm prices."[18] Pressman felt his removal from the AAA was owing above all to his insistence on just the kind of interference with established institutions and methods that Peek sought to avoid.

Another, less well-remembered site of organizing within the AAA was the Office of the Consumers' Counsel. In a decision he would later regret, Peek had established the Consumers' Counsel in June 1933 at the behest of Wallace, who was himself urged on by Ezekiel and Tugwell. Given that the AAA provided "for adequate representation of the producer and the distributor and processor," Wallace wrote to Peek, the department's ability "to justify our decisions before Congress and other political groups" will require showing "that we have given equal interest to consumers' interests."[19] The secretary, in other words, acknowledged a glaring weakness in the entire agricultural program—that higher prices for farm commodities, if simply passed on by processors and distributors, meant an increasing cost of living for already hard-pressed consumers.

At the recommendation of the BAE official Louis Bean, Wallace tapped Frederic Howe to serve as head of the Consumers' Counsel.[20] Howe was a veteran Progressive—he had earned his doctorate at Johns Hopkins in 1892, cut his teeth at the famous Goodrich Settlement House in Cleveland, and authored a number of books on reform causes. George Peek, for his part, felt that he "had been seriously bitten by some kind of pink bug and had accumulated a hazy half radical, half uplifter set of views and attitudes." Howe "was against the profit system and was all for abolishing it," he continued, "without, however, exactly knowing what he wanted to put in its place." Still, Peek had to admit, Howe's views spread through the AAA "like an epidemic," and to many of the young reformers this sixty-six-year-old stood as a towering figure of the ascendant U.S. liberalism.[21] Joining Howe was Gardner "Pat"

Jackson, a crusading journalist whom Lee Pressman and Nathaniel Witt had recruited "to get in the show and help remake the world." The wealthy son of a Colorado mining executive, Jackson attributed his progressive politics to a "terrible resistance to the social privilege concept into which the accident of birth brought me."[22] Howe and Jackson were joined by Thomas Blaisdell, a Columbia University economist who Tugwell had brought to Washington, and Mary Taylor, a seasoned progressive journalist who edited the office's publication, *Consumers Guide*.[23] Later they added Donald Montgomery, who studied economics at the University of Wisconsin and who would later go on to serve as a senior adviser to Walter Reuther in the United Automobile Workers. The team had considerable intellectual firepower.

They also had real institutional capacity. A defining feature of the AAA Consumers' Counsel, in contrast to the three other New Deal consumers' agencies, was its status as an administrative unit with paid staff as opposed to an advisory committee composed of subject matter experts.[24] What was more, they had influential internal allies among the Legal Division's left-leaning attorneys. As Jackson remembered, "in actual practice, from the very start, the consumers' counsel's office and the general counsel's office collaborated with great intimacy and always took the same positions." The Consumers' Counsel therefore, in Blaisdell's words, "became the focus for internal Agricultural Department conflicts between the traditional conservative elements whose thinking represented the larger, successful farmers and those with a more social outlook who were regarded as liberals or radicals."[25]

And along with Pressman and others in the Legal Division, the Consumers' Counsel officials understood that advancing that social outlook would require the capacity to keep the corporate beneficiaries of AAA policy—the processors and distributors—in line. To do so they would need access to those firms' books and records, authority that Howe understood would serve as "a kind of Damocles sword hanging over the processors." Because "he will not know how closely we follow his accounts," Howe noted in the summer of 1933, "he will be operating with a daily concern for his standing with the third party to the agreement, which is the Government."[26] Secretary Wallace was just as clear on the issue. The federal government "will have to insist on a complete look at the books," he averred before the Special Industrial Recovery Board in the fall of 1933, "because of the fact that capitalism, as I see it, inevitably takes out too much in the way of profits and does not pay out enough for labor and agriculture."[27] Expressing such an idea in the abstract was one thing. Accomplishing it in practice was another.

From Consumption to Production:
The Case of "Nature's Perfect Food"

Some of the most contentious battles over the Institutional Keynesians' regulatory objectives occurred with respect to what nutritional experts had come to call "nature's perfect food"—milk. This was in part owing to the peculiar, regional political economy of the dairy industry, which lent local activists more opportunities to challenge entrenched interests than was the case in a national showdown with, say, the cotton aristocrats.[28] The tensions became apparent in 1933, during the drafting of the first AAA milk code in Chicago. Jerome Frank and the AAA Legal Division had succeeded in inserting a books and records transparency clause in the potentially precedent setting Chicago milk deal, but months later they had yet to receive satisfactory data.[29] In advance of public hearings on the agreement that fall, Mary Taylor initiated a campaign in the pages of the *Consumers Guide* that railed against the rising cost of milk, placing the blame squarely on the powerful milk dealers and encouraging readers to attend and speak their mind when "The New Deal Comes to Town."[30] The three thousand Chicagoans in attendance reportedly erupted in deafening applause when the cochair of the hearing announced his intention to pry these records out of the milkmen whether they liked it or not.[31]

The political stakes of dairy only grew with time. In 1937, milk prices in New York were galloping and Mayor Fiorella La Guardia made the issue a centerpiece of his reelection campaign. La Guardia called for a municipally owned milk distribution system to serve as a "yardstick" for regulation of the private sector that would eliminate "the wide gap between the amount the [milk] trust pays the farmer and the price it extorts from the consumer."[32] The AAA Consumers' Counsel did everything they could to promote the idea. In the *Consumers Guide*, Mary Taylor publicized the findings of a study of the Milwaukee milk distribution system that concluded: "A publicly owned system of milk distribution in Milwaukee could sell milk to the consumer for 2 cents per quart less than the present prices and could pay farmers 21 cents more a hundredweight for their milk."[33] Donald Montgomery, then the head of the Consumers' Counsel, even appeared at an event of the Milk

Consumers Protective Committee, an umbrella group composed of some forty activist consumer organizations, hosted by the Transport Workers union to explore further the idea of municipal ownership.[34]

None of this went unnoticed by corporate America. In the spring of 1939, Archie Wright, head of the CIO-backed Dairy Farmers Union (DFU), reported learning from reliable sources that the chairman of General Electric (GE), Owen D. Young, "was preparing to finance [a] Central Sales Committee"— with support from GE, U.S. Steel, International Harvester, and General Motors—to serve as "a more closely controlled milk-shed-wide front organization." And as a DFU attorney suggested to Montgomery, "this same source might well be supplying the funds for other reactionary farm organization committees."[35] The largest corporations in the United States were not actively organizing themselves and committing material resources simply to protect the profit margins of milk distributors like Borden Dairy by some few percent. They were doing so because the burgeoning movement of rank-and-file farmers, working-class consumers, and their allies in the federal government was mounting a real challenge to the most dearly held prerogatives of the capitalist class—indeed, to the very prerogatives that made them capitalists: the rights to invest, to price, and to profit without restraint.

The AAA Consumers' Counsel then became one of the first victims of the red-baiting that would undermine so much of the New Deal Left in the immediate postwar years. In mid-1939, the Hearst Magazines executive Richard E. Berlin began accusing Montgomery of enabling "subversive elements, pretending to serve the consuming public but actually motivated by communistic theories" and demanded that "this subversive movement [be] publicly exposed."[36] Some months later, J. B. Matthews, an assistant to Martin Dies, charged that the *Consumers Guide* provided favorable coverage to organizations in which "Communists had played the leading role."[37] The top leadership of the USDA responded by instructing Montgomery to stop pursuing "activity with regard to things of consumer interest" and to instead limit its purview to "the programs provided for in the act."[38] In particular, they demanded that the *Consumers Guide* narrow its editorial scope, presenting only "information relating directly to the programs administered by the Department."[39] That year the Consumers' Counsel budget was cut by 25 percent, and it would only shrink from there.[40]

In the wake of this offensive, the Institutional Keynesians in the USDA began to emphasize what might be considered their conventionally *Keynesian* beliefs. If campaigns targeting specific industries were too politically risky, a similar agenda might be achieved by couching their proposals in the new language of economic aggregates. Achieving a "greater abundance" of milk, the *Consumers Guide* reported in March 1940, had become the principal goal of consumer organizers.[41] Whereas in the early years the *Guide* consistently featured the tagline, "consumption is the end and purpose of production," the Consumers' Counsel staff was now contending that only through maximum production could consumers get the things they needed at prices they could afford. The great scourge, in other words, was underconsumption. As Milo Perkins, the head of the AAA's food stamp plan, put it, the only way to end this "black plague of the twentieth century" was complete utilization of resources and "full employment."[42] Perkins's statement came on the heels of Mordecai Ezekiel's 1939 publication of *Jobs for All*— together these Institutional Keynesians in the Department of Agriculture were some of the first proponents of the idea of full employment, an idea that would become central to postwar liberalism. But this new rhetorical approach did not imply an abandonment of their concern with economic structure and corporate power. Full employment and maximum production geared toward achieving balanced and equitable growth, the Institutional Keynesians understood, was only possible through a planning regime that included intervention in corporate decision making. In other words, their adoption of a different language was not so much a concession as a calculation made in the heat of political struggle.[43]

The Politics of Inflation and the Attack on Institutional Keynesianism

World War II turned the economic conditions of the Depression on their head. Maximum production for the war effort along with high levels of federal spending provided more of a jolt to investment and employment than the New Deal ever could. But strong economic performance only made the politics of the cost of living more acute. And if Institutional Keynesians in the USDA had offered one of the most powerful explanations for the rising price level in the 1930s, conservative forces joined them in offering their own theories of price inflation during the 1940s. Two causes in particular drew their ire, and both were integral to the Institutional Keynesian program: federal deficits and growth in labor costs.

Confronted by these conditions, and by a corporate class emboldened and valorized by its centrality to the war effort, the Institutional Keynesians suffered significant defeats in the immediate postwar years. The first was over the labor question. The experience of war had convinced rank-and-file workers and consumers, along with their allies in government, that the vision of full employment with price control, which Institutional Keynesians in the USDA had called for, was indeed possible. Next came agriculture. The myopic focus on commodity prices, Institutional Keynesians had argued through the 1930s, benefited commercial agriculture at the expense of both the rural working class and urban consumers. An agricultural policy that instead directed support to ordinary farm workers and encouraged maximum production could serve the dual purpose of providing industrial workers and their families with affordable food and incorporating that rural working class into the New Deal coalition. Their failure on both of these fronts would have lasting consequences.

Full employment sounded nice, but it had a lot of enemies. Indeed, as Michal Kalecki had predicted in 1943, even under the best of circumstances the obstacles capitalist society placed in the way of full employment might just be too great to overcome. His prescient words are worth quoting at length:

> Under a regime of permanent full employment, "the sack" would cease to play its role as a disciplinary measure. The social position of the boss would be undermined and the self-assurance and class consciousness of the working class would grow. Strikes for wage increases and improvements in conditions of work would create political tension. It is true that profits would be higher under a regime of full employment than they are on the average under *laissez-faire*.... But "discipline in the factories" is more appreciated by the business leaders than profits. Their class instinct tells them that lasting full employment is unsound from their point of view and that unemployment is an integral part of the "normal" capitalist system.[44]

That is what proponents of full employment could expect to confront if successful. But their struggle did not get that far.

By all accounts, a full employment policy without attendant economic controls would prove inflationary. When times were good, high levels of investment and employment would drive up demand and take prices with it.

And when times were bad, the federal government would have to prime the pump with heavy doses of deficit spending that would in turn fan the flames of inflation. The defeat of the Office of Price Administration (OPA) and the great inflation of 1946, then, gave business conservatives just the issue they needed to kill the full employment campaign.

That the original version of the bill itself had been drafted by none other than Mordecai Ezekiel and Louis Bean of the BAE along with the NFU legislative director Russell Smith highlights both the centrality of the Institutional Keynesian tradition to this struggle and the significance of the drafters' failure.[45] In its final form, sponsored by the Montana senator James Murray, the Full Employment Act of 1945 called for the president to submit to Congress an annual National Production and Employment Budget that forecast the number of jobs and the amount of investment that would be required to provide work for everyone in the national labor force. If private investment was expected to fall short of the necessary amount, the federal government would step in to make up the difference. The idea was to break capital's monopoly on the investment function, and the corporate class understood the threat. Through 1945 and 1946, until the midterm elections bought them some breathing room, they waged a relentless two-pronged war against the OPA and the full employment bill, finally using the demise of the first to justify their opposition to the second.[46]

But popular demand for full employment was high—not least because the war had proved it possible—so the business community responded with a measure of its own. The Employment Act of 1946, differed from the Institutional Keynesians' measure in fundamental ways. First, it had two goals, not one: maximum employment, which it defined as an unemployment rate of 3 percent; and price stability. Whether those goals might run at cross-purposes its sponsors failed to mention. Second, it dispensed with the National Production and Employment Budget, the substantive core of the law. The Employment Act did create the Council of Economic Advisers, charged with publishing an annual *Economic Report of the President*, and a congressional Joint Committee on the Economic Report (later changed to the Joint Economic Committee), both of which have remained mainstays of the federal economic policymaking top brass.[47] But the dream of full employment, for which Institutional Keynesians in the USDA had been some of the first advocates, was dead.

The labor question in the immediate postwar years was rivaled in significance only by the question of what to do about agriculture. War had transformed the issues facing the U.S. countryside, as two decades of downward pressure on commodity prices, which the New Deal met with production restraint, gave way to a booming demand and the threat of inflation. The political economy of war, that is, called for a different approach than seemed appropriate in a time of depression. But old habits die hard. As Donald Montgomery and others had learned in the 1930s, commercial agricultural producers and processors fixated on price movements alone would resist any obstacle in the way subsidies and support. Complicating matters was the changing character of the USDA. In 1940, Roosevelt put Henry Wallace on his ticket, and as a result of the personnel shakeups and the exigencies of war, the Institutional Keynesians lost much of the ground they had held since 1933. When Montgomery departed for the UAW in 1943, for instance, the Consumers' Counsel shut down.

Throughout the war, tensions flared between big agricultural interests, along with their representatives in the USDA and the planners in the OPA. And during reconversion these tensions erupted to catastrophic effect. Indeed, agribusiness and corporate processors bore as much responsibility for the death of the OPA, the inflationary spike that followed it, and the political consequences that resulted, as any other element of the body politic. Freed from price control, the cost of food surged through 1946—and as one of the largest items in working-class household budgets, this took a more immediate toll than did climbing industrial prices, which crept into consumer goods more gradually. Arriving at a national agricultural policy that ensured both stable incomes for farm workers and affordable food for urban consumers—a challenge that had bedeviled Institutional Keynesians in the New Deal— therefore took on renewed urgency.[48]

Donald Montgomery continued to voice concern about it from his position with the UAW. Commercial agriculture, he noted to a New York State committee on nutrition in late 1943, "always has been concerned primarily with price." Judging by recent federal policy, Montgomery continued, borrowing a formulation coined by Mary Taylor, an observer could reasonably "think that the purpose of agriculture was to produce prices" rather than "food as something to eat." Why? Because "the big farmers who control government policy" and who, through depression and war, had accumulated a larger and larger "proportion of the total agricultural productive capacity of this country," profited from the continuation of the status quo. Not unlike their industrial cousins GM and U.S. Steel, the owners of the means of agricultural production would always charge as much as they could get away with.

The difference was that they did so with government sanction. As a result, Montgomery soberly concluded, while there "will certainly be enough food for our country as a whole" after the war, "mismanagement" would lead to unfair distribution and waste. Poor "families will continue to starve on their feet, as they always have," and, he feared, many middle-class "families are going to have to join their low-income colleagues because of the rise in the cost of food."[49]

The Institutional Keynesians got their shot in the late 1940s, when Truman, in a nod to the CIO and NFU, named as secretary of agriculture the well-known Colorado progressive Charles Brannan. His Brannan Plan, unveiled soon after the inauguration in 1949, represented the culmination of more than fifteen years of Institutional Keynesianism inside and outside the federal government. The proposal was complicated in its technical details, but straightforward in principle: the purpose of agricultural policy should be to guarantee farmers stable incomes, not high prices. This the government could achieve by providing producers with subsidies and encouraging high production to bring down consumer prices. To protect natural resources and to direct production toward low supply but nutritionally valuable crops, receipt of the subsidies would be conditional on following USDA guidelines about conservation and diversification. And, most controversially, to promote family farming over large-scale commercial agriculture, a cap would be placed on the number of acres for which a producer could collect the subsidy.[50] No more handouts to the southern planter class.

The Brannan Plan, it should be noted, was premised on the understanding that U.S. agriculture was undergoing a wholesale transformation through which mechanization on farms and employment opportunities off them would substantially reduce the number and proportion of farm workers.[51] This process had been under way since early in the century, and it accelerated during World War II. Brannan felt it should not be resisted. Greater support for resettlement and a full employment economy, he felt, would offer security for the landless, and the institutionalization of a mosaic of independent, midsized farms, could serve as a New Dealized version of the old republican dream for those who remained. A healthy urban economy, that is, was a precondition for rural prosperity. As Donald Montgomery put it a few weeks before the plan was announced, in an NBC broadcast debate with representatives of the American Farm Bureau Federation (AFBF) and the Chamber of Commerce, whatever "the details of the farm program are, it is not actually going to get prosperity and security for the farmers unless we make up our minds that we are going to maintain full employment and a full productive economy year after year."[52] To the NFU president James Patton, the synthesis Brannan had achieved represented "a milestone in the history of American agriculture."[53] As Truman had hoped, the proposal had the potential to formally incorporate an urban–rural alliance under the auspices of the Democratic Party, one that would have tilted the balance away from both Republicans and the reactionary South once and for all.

Conservatives were aware of that threat, and the campaign they waged against the Brannan Plan was accordingly determined. Republicans, southern Democrats, and every farm organization excepting the NFU opposed it, with more than a few labeling it "socialistic," "Communist bunk," "un-American," and other watchwords of the paranoid style then gaining currency in U.S. political rhetoric.[54] The most powerful criticism of the Brannan Plan, however, was that it would be inflationary—just as was the case with the Full Employment Act. Although the secretary insisted that its cost would be comparable to that of the existing agricultural program, critics charged that it would encourage dangerous amounts of deficit spending and thereby serve to depreciate the value of the dollar. This was an argument Institutional Keynesians had heard since early in the New Deal, and it was one from which they could not escape. Led by the freshman senator and former secretary of agriculture Clinton Anderson, backed by the AFBF and its processor allies, the anti-Brannan forces prevented the bill from coming to a vote. Brannan tried again in 1950, but his proposal did not even make it out of committee. With the onset of the Korean War the Truman administration abandoned its pursuit of the Fair Deal, of which a new agricultural policy had been a central part.[55] Never again would there be a sincere effort to incorporate the ordinary people of the rural United States into the New Deal order. The political consequences of that failure continue to be felt to this day.

From Corporate Power to Productivity and Beyond

With the 1952 election of Dwight D. Eisenhower to the presidency, Institutional Keynesians lost their last opportunity to transform either U.S. industrial or agricultural policy. Moreover, the defeats that they had suffered immediately after the war had been compounded in 1951 by the Treasury-Federal Reserve Accord. This little remembered but significant policy shift granted the central bank the independence—for the first time since early in the New Deal—to use monetary policy however it saw fit. The accord, which was ratified by a handshake and not a statute, introduced an eminently powerful and hawkish adversary to the Institutional Keynesian agenda.[56] This post-accord Federal Reserve could use its control over the monetary leash, through which it sets the terms of federal borrowing and affects overall rates of economic growth, to make it difficult if not impossible to implement any kind of sustained deficit spending program. Even if McCarthyism had not gutted the New Deal Left, the structural obstacles they would have encountered in the 1950s were formidable indeed.

But the forces arrayed against Institutional Keynesianism did not just come from conservatives. A new cohort of liberals did their part too. During the Kennedy administration, economists who had come of intellectual age during the late New Deal grappled not with the chronic stagnation of the 1930s but with the challenges of affluence, including, importantly, creeping inflation. They therefore understood the problems of industrial policy far differently from their New Deal predecessors. To Paul Samuelson, Walter Heller, and others, the object of liberal statecraft was to ensure that the dividends derived from economic growth were distributed with a measure of equity. The power to make investment decisions, to set prices, and to reap profits was not something over which they felt they had much control. But if a rising tide could lift all boats, an economic downturn would sink them. When the crisis of stagflation—recession together with inflation—arrived in the 1970s, it was this new liberalism that had few answers.[57]

Still, the road to what has since been called neoliberalism, which began with the Federal Reserve Chair Paul Volcker's program of monetary austerity at the end of the 1970s and continued through the Reagan administration, was not foreordained. In 1971, confronting the first tremors of what would become stagflation, the Nixon administration responded with nothing less than wage and price controls. Though these paled in comparison to the interventionist machinery built by the OPA, it was unlikely that a Republican president—in particular one who launched his political career in opposition to that wartime body—would have taken such a turn without the work done by Institutional Keynesians in decades past. Nor would the Humphrey–Hawkins Act of 1978, which established the Federal Reserve's dual mandate of inflation control and employment maximization, have been achieved.[58]

Indeed, even a few decades of market ideology and bipartisan aversion to statist intervention did not fully extinguish the Institutional Keynesian impulse. To this day, economists at left-liberal think tanks like the Economic Policy Institute, the Center for Economic and Policy Research, and the Washington Center for Equitable Growth continue to elaborate policy prescriptions that draw on the Institutional Keynesian tradition.[59] And many of the ideas advanced since the Great Recession by leading progressives in the Democratic Party have their origins in proposals developed by those in that orbit. The challenges their predecessors confronted and the opposition they faced have much to teach those who hope to build a new New Deal more robust and durable than that which came before. The complete inability of the existing system to address the deepening crises of economic inequality and environmental degradation—indeed, the way it intensifies those problems and erodes democratic processes—makes the Institutional Keynesians' radical vision as relevant as ever.

PART II

New Deal Headwinds

Contestation and Resistance

CHAPTER 5

The Unanticipated Consequences of
New Deal Poor Relief

Welfare Rights, Empowered States,
and the Revival of Localism

Karen M. Tani

As historians of the twenty-first century look with fresh eyes on the New Deal, most still agree that it was a transformative event—not entirely "new," but a significant break from the past. New Deal *welfare* programs, by contrast, have remained part of a different story, one that we might call "the more things change, the more they stay the same." Alert to the continued subordination of poor women, children, and racial minorities in their own times, historians have tended to emphasize how New Deal–era welfare programs perpetuated, rather than broke from, dark traditions. Yes, these programs came with a new name—"public assistance"—but much like their colonial-era and nineteenth-century predecessors, these purported reforms regulated the low-wage labor market, policed women's sexuality, and reinforced racial and gender hierarchies, all while offering only the stingiest financial support. So goes the dominant narrative.[1]

Such critiques of the U.S. poor relief tradition are well founded and deserve their prominence. But in placing so much emphasis on continuity, these critiques have also tended to obscure important, large-scale changes—changes that are foundational to our current legal and political order. Phrased differently, scholars have devoted so much energy to showing what New

Deal poor relief did not do for its ostensible beneficiaries that we have neglected what these programs *did* do, not just for people in need but also for the nation at large.[2]

This chapter emphasizes three changes, none of which feature prominently in New Deal historiography, but all of which help explain the fate of the New Deal order by the 1960s. First, New Deal public assistance programs laid crucial groundwork for a new, rights-oriented way of thinking about poverty and the poor.[3] The federal administrators of these programs, along with some of their state and local counterparts, encouraged Americans to see public assistance benefits as a type of entitlement and to treat the programs' intended beneficiaries as rights-holding citizens of state and country. In the short-term, these efforts did not always succeed, but they helped create the conditions for subsequent organizing, both by those who embraced rights language and those who opposed it. Second, New Deal public assistance programs helped create more robust and empowered state governments. The enabling legislation (the Social Security Act of 1935) demanded that federal funds go through professional, centralized, state bureaucracies—many of which had to be created from scratch. With these enhanced capacities, states were better partners to federal reformers, but they also became more formidable opponents. Third, New Deal public assistance programs contributed to the endurance and reinvigoration of localism in political discourse: those who attacked these programs so fiercely in the 1940s, 1950s, and 1960s often invoked a golden age of local control. Conservative politicians used that romanticized image to craft, and sell, the next generation of policy solutions. Ironically, these solutions continued to involve central-state supervision. But they appealed to proponents of localism by imposing on the poor harsher and more restrictive rules, all of which tended to undercut the rights claims that New Dealers had invited.

Together, these three changes bring into view a specific pattern of governance: centralized, interventionist, and bureaucratic, but never truly dominated by the federal government or its administrators; "socialized" in many respects, but insistent on disaggregating subjects into rights-bearing (and obligation-owing) individuals; and capable of redistributing resources and recognizing citizens' common humanity, but equally capable of perpetuating inequality and punishing difference. This pattern of governance—*this* New Deal order—remains with us today.

Welfare as a Right, the Poor as Rights-Holders

The notion that rights concepts existed, much less flourished, in New Deal poor relief goes against the grain of much historical writing on U.S. social welfare law and policy. Most scholars associate the pairing of rights and welfare with a brief period in the late 1960s and early 1970s, when Americans witnessed the broadening of the modern civil rights movement, the establishment of the War on Poverty's Legal Services Program, the emergence of grassroots welfare rights organizations, and a series of bold pronouncements from the Supreme Court about the Constitution's protections for poor citizens. Most scholars also continue to accept the "two-track" model of the U.S. welfare state, and with it, a particular assumption about rights. According to the two-track account, Americans have tended to frame the benefits of insurance-type programs (e.g., Social Security, unemployment insurance) as earned rights or entitlements; they have characterized the benefits of means-tested programs as charity, the quintessential nonright.[4]

There are good reasons for conceiving of the U.S. welfare state in terms of separate "tracks," but the notion of a transhistorical rights/nonrights binary is dubious. My research shows that rights concepts were part of the world of welfare well before the 1960s, and further, that some New Deal welfare administrators were devoted purveyors of rights language, especially after President Franklin D. Roosevelt made such language a staple of his public communications.[5]

For example, starting almost as soon as the Social Security Act took effect, administrators working for the federal Social Security Board (SSB) used rights language to talk about how to interpret the law—and not just the act's much celebrated Old Age Insurance title but also the titles dealing with what we would call *welfare* (and New Dealers called *public assistance*).[6] In 1936 the SSB's Office of the General Counsel circulated a memo to the agency's leadership insisting that public assistance recipients had "vested rights" in their assistance payments, not unlike the beneficiaries of Old Age Insurance ("Social Security"). These poor individuals therefore also had a right to due process of law before their benefits could be taken away.[7] By the same logic, a lawyer warned in 1937, the board's public relations department should not be telling the American people that only Social Security was a legal right.[8]

As states around the country began administering federally subsidized public assistance, rights language also appeared in communications between federal administrators and the people administering these programs at the ground level. For example, in 1939, a high-ranking member of the General Counsel's office urged social work educators to be aware that in administering public assistance, social workers dealt "with rights and privileges of citizenship."[9] It was up to public welfare experts, the same agency lawyer emphasized two years later to the National Conference of Social Work, to vindicate the rights that modern social legislation created—to make these rights operate with "certainty and regularity."[10] And it was not just the lawyers using this language. At that same social work conference, Jane Hoey, the director of the Social Security Board's Bureau of Public Assistance (BPA), offered very similar guidance. She characterized rights as "inherent" in the Social Security Act's commitments to its beneficiaries.[11]

Along similar lines, rights language appeared in the guidance that federal administrators issued to state administrators, for their own education and for distribution to their local counterparts.[12] One widely circulated example is the BPA's 1944 directive on "Money Payments." This was an effort to clarify an often-neglected piece of the Social Security Act: the provision requiring payments in cash—to be spent as the recipient pleased—rather than in the form of food, clothing, or some other "in kind" benefit. The "Money Payments" directive reduced this apparently confusing requirement to a "basic principle": "that assistance comes to needy persons as a right."[13]

A second example is Public Assistance Report No. 8 (1945), titled *Common Human Needs: An Interpretation for Staff in Public Assistance Agencies*. The BPA's Division of Technical Training commissioned it in 1944 to assist supervisors in state and local welfare agencies interpret "the basic philosophy of the program" and thereby facilitate "constructive attitudes" toward their poor clients.[14] Here again, rights language is prominent. The author Charlotte Towle opened the report by emphasizing the notion of "sound individualization" (that is, tailored social casework) "in a program based on right." The administrator must approach all cases, she continued, with "genuine conviction as to the applicant's rightful claim on society in time of need."[15] By the mid-1940s, rights language was a staple of federal agency communications and an emerging feature of state agency documents.[16]

This rights language had consequences. Whether it resulted in better treatment of the poor or greater generosity is a question that historians must continue to explore,[17] but it almost certainly contributed to a broad shift in

U.S. governance—to the weakening of an old pattern of governance, in which local communities had the strongest claim on citizens, and to the emergence of a new pattern, characterized by direct, individualized links between citizens and the state.

Two bodies of evidence support this conclusion. The first is the records of administrative "fair hearings" before state welfare boards and the appeals of these administrative decisions to state courts. Scholars of U.S. social welfare law generally assume that, until the 1960s, welfare recipients were relatively quiescent: they did not take to the streets or the courts to claim public benefits or demand fair treatment from public authorities. Looking at federal court records, that assumption seems well founded. State and local agency records tell a different story. They suggest that between 1935 and 1960, tens of thousands of Americans contested the decisions of local welfare officers. In other words, tens of thousands of poor individuals stood up in front of state officials and said, in effect, "My local agency got it wrong; I deserve something more."[18] Dozens—likely hundreds—of these individuals took their cases a step further, to state court, where their posture was, "*State* administrators got it wrong; I deserve something more." To these individuals, at least, poor relief was no longer a matter of local whim, but a matter of right, established in state and federal law.[19]

A second source of evidence is the reactions of critics—those who noted the appearance of rights language in the poor relief context and registered their discontent. As just one example, consider the following quote, from the controversial city manager of Newburgh, New York, Joseph McDowell Mitchell. After gaining national fame in 1961 for proposing an extremely punitive set of local welfare reforms (I discuss these later in the chapter), he attributed his success to his willingness to question the era's new rights. In his words, he challenged "the right of social parasites to breed illegitimate children at the taxpayers' expense, the right of moral chiselers and loafers to squat on the relief rolls forever, the right of freeloaders to make more on relief than when working, the right of those on relief to loaf by State and Federal edict, the right of people to quit jobs at will and go on relief like spoiled children, [and] the right of citizens to migrate for the purpose of becoming or continuing as public charges. . . ."[20] That such sentiments resonated with even a fraction of the public (which they did)[21] shows that rights language was circulating in and around local welfare operations, and that it was a matter of deep concern.

The source of this concern is worth pondering. One reason that critics disliked rights language, it seems, is for the same reason that federal administrators liked it. This language suggested a direct relationship between the federal government and impoverished individuals. It cast the federal welfare state, rather than local notables, as the friend and protector of these citizens. It augured a new type of governance, in which centrally determined individual needs trumped locally determined understandings of the good of the community. These seeds of conflict would erupt into pitched battles by century's end.

Empowered States, Capable State Bureaucracies

The second way in which New Deal public assistance programs contributed to deep and lasting change pertains to state administrative power. Elsewhere I have emphasized the way that New Deal public assistance programs empowered the *federal* government, especially the federal administrative state.[22] But New Deal public assistance programs also empowered state governments. These programs were a crucial factor in what Jon Teaford calls "the rise of the states"—from "spare" governmental units "with little administrative muscle" in the nineteenth century to "dynamic molders of domestic policy and vital providers of government services" by the end of the twentieth.[23] As with the use of rights language, this story is largely missing from the historiography.[24]

  Consider the precise mechanism by which New Deal reformers attempted to remake the landscape of American poor relief. Rather than attempting a complete federal takeover, the Social Security Act incentivized states to become the federal government's partners in reform. The act did so by offering states generous grants-in-aid for particular categories of poor relief and attaching conditions to those grants.[25] (Subsequent amendments to the act expanded those categories and imposed additional requirements on states.)[26] Today, the word *conditions* invokes images of the federal government twisting states' proverbial arms—coercing them into uncomfortable postures, forcing them to yield power. To accept that image is to forget what states used to look like. In terms of collecting revenue, building and maintaining infrastructure, regulating public health, and so on, many states were primitive by today's standards.[27] In almost all cases, the Social Security Act's conditions, once implemented, actually *increased* states' strength.

The central-state-agency requirement is the best example: states that wanted federal money could not simply funnel those dollars to the cities, counties, and towns that had traditionally cared for the poor. Via a central state agency—the likes of which many states did not have before the New Deal—states had to assume responsibility for the administration of federal funds,[28] either through supervision of local welfare authorities or through their own state machinery. Other federal grant conditions included uniform, state-wide rules and procedures; systems for reviewing local benefit decisions; and, after 1939, personnel standards for state and local welfare workers (i.e., the use of a merit system). These were the hallmarks of "good government," according to a generation of progressive reformers and academics. Thanks to the Social Security Act (and the Great Depression), these ideas finally made headway in at least one significant pocket of state government. State officials even had a convenient response to critics: "We need money, and this is the price." Phrased differently, "The feds made us do it."

The federally subsidized empowerment of states did not happen overnight, of course. As New Deal public assistance programs got off the ground in the mid- and late 1930s, many states did not fully comply with federal requirements. In some instances, they couldn't: state bureaucracies simply lacked the capacity to oversee local welfare operations in any meaningful way. In other instances, they wouldn't: some state officials were concerned about upsetting the status quo and essentially abdicated their power to local officials. Contemporary accounts of New Deal public assistance are filled with stories of state government intransigence, incompetence, and inefficacy.[29] Establishing state supervision over local operations was "a slow and tedious process," summarized a 1941 report from the BPA's Field Division.[30]

Taking a longer view, however—into the 1940s and 1950s—reveals that federal administrators persisted, and that state welfare agencies did become the capable, modern governmental units that the Social Security Act demanded. Though often headed by political appointees, they were staffed with professionals, including social workers, public administration experts, and lawyers. They had structures that mirrored those of the federal Social Security Board. They maintained manuals of state-wide rules, and they had mechanisms for distributing and interpreting those rules to their local counterparts. In this they epitomized New Deal reform, even if their policies have caused scholars to see mainly conservatism or reaction.[31]

Another way of charting the growth of state power is by observing the decline of local autonomy, as political scientist Martha Derthick did in her classic study of public assistance administration in Massachusetts. By the mid-1960s, she observes, "there was almost nothing of importance" that the state's historically powerful local boards of public welfare "were free to decide for themselves." Where local discretion existed, it was exercised by civil servants, whose employment was governed by state-prescribed rules.[32] In other words, to the extent that traditional relief structures survived, they had become embedded in state government machinery. This was a direct result of the Social Security Act and its conditional grants-in-aid.

This intergovernmental shifting of powers matters because it increased state officials' ability to contest the authority of the federal government and to thereby undermine some of the New Deal's more egalitarian commitments. As Margaret Weir has noted, the "issue-oriented liberal Democrats" who were the New Deal's strongest supporters enjoyed prominence at the state level for only a brief window in the 1930s. In most states, Republicans and "traditional organization Democrats" were much more powerful, especially after 1938; together they made states "inhospitable terrain for advancing the liberal goals o[f] activist government."[33] My research extends this argument beyond hospitability (or lack thereof) to *hostility* and its weapons: critics of the New Deal benefited from the sophisticated state-level administrative machinery that the New Deal bequeathed them. The very tools that New Dealers used to incentivize state cooperation in national reform projects became tools of resistance in the longer term.

Consider, as an example, the classic story of "suitable homes"—retold here with the benefit of different sources.

Among those working for the federal Social Security Board, there was a widely shared distaste for moralism in public welfare administration. Conditioning relief on such factors as religion, drinking habits, and sexual behavior was characteristic of the archaic "old poor law" tradition, federal administrators argued, and not a trait of modern relief practice. In the words of one federal agency lawyer, discussing worrisome tendencies in the Aid to Dependent Children (ADC) program, "the sins of [the] parents" should never enter the equation. Federal administrators used their power over state grants to signal as much to their state counterparts. Recipients of New Deal public assistance—unlike recipients of old-fashioned local poor relief—must be free to spend their money as they pleased; they should not be told how to live their lives, or whom to spend their time with. In fact, federal administrators insisted, no one outside of the public welfare bureaucracy should even know the identities of public assistance clients.[34]

These views came under siege in the late 1940s and 1950s, for reasons that are now well documented in the literature. First, the Aid to Dependent Children program had continued to grow, and the deserving white widow was no longer its most common face. Instead—and in an age of deep anxiety about gender roles, white privilege, and the nuclear family—the public saw benefits going to unmarried African American women and their children. Second, Americans were developing a sense of themselves as "taxpayers," and of welfare recipients as "taxeaters." "Relief Chiselers Are Stealing Us Blind," warned an article in the popular *Saturday Evening Post* in 1951.[35] More than ever, the practices of public welfare administrators seemed like everyone's business. Third, public welfare programs seemed to epitomize everything that a growing coalition of anti–New Dealers detested, including unchecked federal and state spending, pushy and idealistic bureaucrats, and the implicit desire to "level" society.[36] One way that states responded in the late 1950s and early 1960s was through "suitable home" policies: policies that allowed for (or required) an administrator to turn away an applicant for Aid to Dependent Children if, based on the mother's sexual history or other behavior, the home appeared "unsuitable" for the child in need.

Previous scholars have written about "suitable home" policies as if they had existed from time immemorial—a problematic oversimplification. It is true that among Progressive Era mothers' pension programs, suitability of the home (which, at the time, meant respectability of the mother) was often an eligibility consideration. It is also true that these mothers' pension programs were the predecessors to the New Deal's Aid to Dependent Children program. With greater federal involvement, however, came the strong suggestion that states eliminate or reimagine such policies. By 1950, fifteen states had repealed their "suitable home" provisions and others maintained theirs only to identify genuinely neglected and abused children.[37] Thus, there was something distinct about the nine state-level suitable home policies that cropped up in the later 1950s.

What was novel about these emergent suitable home policies was state officials' willingness to challenge federal administrators and offer up their own interpretations of federal law. Back in the late 1930s, if federal welfare administrators did not like something happening in a state, they communicated as much to state administrators and the problem generally improved. States badly needed their federal grants and resistance seemed futile.

This was so even when federal administrators had a weak legal basis for their demands. By the late 1950s, by contrast, state administrators had accumulated years of experience with federal rules and procedures. They also had a better sense of federal administrators' motivations and constraints and used that knowledge to their advantage. Consider the actions of the Mississippi Department of Public Welfare, after the 1954 state legislature prohibited assistance payments to a child whose mother subsequently had a child outside of marriage. In short order, federal administrators raised concerns about this law: Didn't such a prohibition violate citizens' right to equal treatment, not to mention contradicting federal guidance? Through legal-administrative wrangling, state officials kept a debate going for four years and eventually won federal administrative approval for an only slightly liberalized interpretation of the blatantly discriminatory state law. State politicians now knew that federal officials did not want to cut off the state's funds, and state bureaucrats knew enough law to make plausible arguments. Officials in Alabama and Florida achieved the same result, simply by watching their neighbor and demanding similar treatment from the federal agency. (That networking, in and of itself, was evidence of enhanced state capacities.)[38]

Meanwhile, at the ground level, states' now-robust administrative machinery ensured that the new suitable home policies had a real effect on poor women and children. Before the New Deal, most states had no way of enforcing policy across the myriad local welfare departments within their jurisdictions. The New Deal brought with it the idea of statewide uniformity—and uniformity did not necessarily mean liberality or generosity. Florida's short-lived suitable home policy, for example, affected 17,999 ADC cases between July 1, 1959, and June 30, 1961, resulting in a statewide caseload drop of 13.7 percent and a significant decrease in the proportion of nonwhite families on the rolls.[39] To the extent that state legislators wanted to undermine, rather than vindicate, poor citizens' sense of themselves as rights holders, they now had the means to do it.

To sum up: Scholars like James Patterson and, more recently, Margaret Weir, are right when they conclude that the New Deal had a limited effect at the state level. But this truth coexists with another truth. States generally welcomed New Deal funds, and with those funds came conditions; those conditions, in turn, brought structural changes. Public assistance grants brought centralization, professionalization, and bureaucratization, in varying degrees, to every state in the union. When we fail to notice this, we also fail to notice an important set of tools that states had for rolling back the New Deal in later decades.

The Reinvigoration of Localism

A third change that I attribute, at least in part, to New Deal public assistance is the resurgence of an ideology of localism. This modern ideology of localism often wore the garb of nostalgia: somewhere in the not-too-distant past, its proponents implied, governance was simpler, more personal, and more effective. On closer inspection, this modern ideology of localism was also often laden with coded references to women and racial minorities, with the implication that a more locally oriented mode of governance kept people in their proper place. Poor relief seemed to offer a perfect example. "Unhampered by the rules Washington imposes as a price for [its] 'aid,'" explained one critic in 1952, localities could "take care of [their] own at a fraction of the present cost"; "we would make sure that no one was cold or went hungry, as we have always done." Rather than alleviating poverty, such critics contended, the federal government had simply made the problem worse, by creating dependency, rewarding indolent behavior, and encouraging people to migrate willy-nilly into communities where they had no roots.[40] If such arguments sound familiar, they should: by the end of the twentieth century, they animated the policymaking solutions of both the major political parties.

This argument draws inspiration from scattered work in urban history and the history of modern consumerism,[41] but is in tension with important interpretations of the New Deal. For example, in his enduring account of the twin populisms of Huey Long and Father Coughlin, Alan Brinkley ties the ultimate failure of these two figures to the limits of their localist ideology. Long and Coughlin railed against centralization and concentration, but could not imagine viable solutions, and at times even urged the expansion of federal government power; they celebrated local institutions, but did not offer concrete plans to revive those institutions. It was not long before other leaders—most notably Franklin D. Roosevelt—seized the imagination of the public.[42] Much writing in U.S. history continues to present localism in this way: as a sort of throwback to premodern times, capable of appealing to Americans' baser instincts, but inconsistent with prevailing values.

And yet, localism was far from dead. If some New Deal programs helped Americans become comfortable with a more interventionist and centralized government,[43] others—such as public assistance—helped preserve Americans' faith in local government. This was especially so as journalists documented the rising number of women receiving Aid to Dependent Children in the late 1940s and 1950s, and the rising proportion of those women who were nonwhite and never-married. In the days before federal involvement, critics implied—the days of true local control—such women knew better than to expect public support. They turned to marriage and the labor market, and everyone was better off. The same suggestion was made regarding African American migrants from the rural South: when poor relief was a local function, available only to settled residents, African Americans knew their place and stayed there. Locally controlled poor relief, in other words, represented a tried and true alternative to the emerging order.[44]

Attacks on local welfare operations are actually the best evidence of a reinvigorated localism. Such attacks were so common by the early 1950s that public welfare workers referred to them as an "occupational disease."[45] Particularly noteworthy, for purposes of this chapter, is that although these attacks often highlighted the incompetence of local public officials and the unfair strain placed on local resources, they ultimately blamed the federal government, for tying the hands of local administrators and imposing on them a foreign, socialistic ideology (including, as I mentioned earlier, the notion of welfare as a "right").

An early example comes from Baltimore. In 1947, in the course of investigating the city's seemingly spendthrift public welfare department, conservative civic leaders stumbled upon *Common Human Needs*, the federal agency's widely circulated statement on the right to public assistance. Federal officials quickly became the scapegoats for all the city's ills. If the federal government would simply stay out of the local department's way, critics explained, practicality would once again reign and Baltimore's relief problem would disappear.[46]

A better-known example comes from Newburgh, New York, in 1961, City Manager Joseph McDowell Mitchell proudly unveiled a thirteen-point welfare reform plan targeting the hundreds of "chiselers and loafers," "freeload[ing]" migrants, "social parasites," and "illegitimate children" whom he perceived to be dragging down the once-glorious city. The specific proposals were nothing new—relief "in kind" rather than in cash, limited assistance for outsiders, no assistance for "able-bodied" men and sexually deviant women—but the plan nonetheless attracted national headlines and many admirers (as well as many critics).[47] Fans of the plan particularly liked Mitchell's reassertion of local control—his determination to stand up to federal and state officials and to replace their edicts with locally grounded commonsense. A Gallup poll conducted in the wake of the controversy found that a majority of respondents favored greater local control over public relief programs.[48]

It is tempting to treat the Newburgh incident and other local welfare "scandals" as curious artifacts—relevant, perhaps, for the insights they offer into modern conservatism, but otherwise a small footnote. After all, these episodes did not result in the restoration of autonomous local poor relief operations, much less the dismantling of the large-scale bureaucracies that Mitchell and others so detested. That aspect of New Deal reform remained untouched. Newburgh-style localism matters because when tethered to the powerful notion of "states' rights"—a notion that, unlike localism, had constitutional standing—it produced policy changes that were antithetical to the spirit of the New Deal and at cross-purposes with the idea of poor people as rights-holders. (It is no coincidence that among Newburgh's fans was the presidential hopeful Barry Goldwater, a staunch advocate of states' rights and sharp critic of the New Deal.)

Consider the public assistance reforms that emerged over the next forty years: not only did states retain authority over benefit levels, but states must also be allowed to tailor their public assistance program to local conditions and capitalize on local innovation, federal legislators came to agree; states should not be simply enforcers of federal law. This thinking emerged as early as 1962, in the Kennedy administration's offer to "waive" certain federal program requirements and thereby facilitate experimentation in the states. It was also apparent in the gradual transition from highly restricted matching grants to much-less-restricted block grants. In practice, state officials tended not to devolve policymaking power to the local level, but they often wielded their new power in ways that accorded with conservative, localist critiques of the New Deal welfare state. Recipients of Aid to Dependent Children were the most frequent target. Using waivers, states imposed work requirements and time limits on recipients, discouraged childbearing out of wedlock, and adopted new, more invasive technologies of information-gathering and surveillance. In short, states used waivers to undermine those aspects of the New Deal that had once appeared to liberate individuals from the oppressive features of the locally administered "old poor law."[49]

By the late 1990s, these more restrictive policy preferences had come full circle, to become actual federal requirements rather than case-by-case exceptions to the more generous federal rule. The Personal Responsibility and Work Opportunity Reconciliation Act of 1996 (PRWORA) is often associated with devolution of authority—a restoration to smaller governmental units of the flexibility and autonomy that New Deal reformers wrong-headedly took away. But as Joe Soss, Richard Fording, and Sanford Schram have shown, PRWORA was equally about nationalizing some of the states' most paternalist and exclusionary innovations.[50] Under the cover of decentralization, Uncle Sam is an energetic and largely unsympathetic overseer of the poor.[51]

*   *   *

Historians have often characterized New Deal public assistance programs as minimally reformist—little more than federal subsidies for old-fashioned, locally controlled poor relief, and nowhere near as significant as the new programs of Old Age and Unemployment Insurance. To the extent that this critique helps us see the inadequacies and inequities of our current welfare system, it remains vitally important. We must also recognize, however, how New Deal public assistance altered the logic and workings of American poor relief, with notable ripple effects. In the decades after 1935, programs of Aid to Dependent Children, Old Age Assistance, and Aid to the Blind allowed both the federal government and the states to claim a permanent stake in this policy area, and to develop bureaucracies to match. Autonomous local poor relief operations became largely a relic of the past. Statutes and regulations replaced local mores as the governing source of authority. Relief givers became subject to civil service rules. Professionalism, uniform treatment, and adherence to law became the yardsticks of acceptable practice.

The changes described above matched the intentions of at least some New Deal reformers. Other changes appear to have been unintended, or at least beyond reformers' predictive powers. This chapter has emphasized three, all of which directly affected the broader landscape of politics and policymaking in the second half of the twentieth century. First, the emergence of a language of welfare rights: important New Deal administrators used rights language in their dealings with state and local administrators, as a way to contrast "modern" public assistance with old-fashioned, locally controlled "poor law." Such language may well have helped inspire the welfare rights claims of the 1960s and 1970s, by enabling poor people to reimagine their relationships to the polities around them. In the meantime, it most certainly created enemies for the New Deal. Second, the empowerment of the states: the success of New Deal public assistance programs depended on capable state bureaucracies—many of which had to be created from scratch. After federal administrators helped build up these bureaucracies, they saw their tools turned against them, to fight off federal "dictation" and add new restrictions to New Deal programs. Third, the revival of localism: even as the New Deal permanently deprived localities of their exclusive jurisdiction over the poor, the tactics and attitudes of its federal administrators gave new strength to the ideology of localism. This ideology infused politics by the 1960s and informed the shape of the conservative and neoliberal welfare reforms of the late twentieth century.

This volume asks: How should we think about the political economy of the New Deal era? How did the "New Deal order" take shape and how do we explain its trajectory? This chapter, like others in this volume, invites us to see vulnerabilities built into the New Deal's architecture—vulnerabilities that, to reformers, may have seemed like victories, or necessary compromises, or that perhaps went unnoticed at the time.[52] In the case of New Deal poor relief programs, real reform occurred—poor relief will never go back to being an exclusively local responsibility—but the most enduring reforms proved capable of advancing various ideologies. Most notably, the institutional pattern that New Dealers created to execute their vision lives on, but is now infused with a decidedly antiwelfarist sensibility.

CHAPTER 6

Financing Security and Opportunity

The New Deal and the Origins of the Millennial Student Debt Crisis

Elizabeth Tandy Shermer

Many consider mass higher education to be a part of the New Deal order. The country had 1.1 million college students in 1931; sixty years later, 14 million were enrolled. By 2015, 59 percent of the population had some postsecondary schooling and a third held at least a bachelor's degree.[1] That jump expanded upward mobility after World War II and has buoyed the U.S. economy since the 1960s, when knowledge-based service industries became more lucrative than manufacturing sectors. Yet this celebrated expansion did not reflect New Dealers' eagerness to educate the majority of Americans. The Roosevelt administration never offered a comprehensive higher education program because few policymakers initially considered such an undertaking possible or desirable. Those interested also hesitated to confront hidebound educators and lawmakers openly hostile to 1930s experiments. As such, New Dealers' delayed, limited efforts to help schools and enrollees through a federal student assistance program did less to reform higher education and more to serve the administration's larger goals of stabilizing the labor market and keeping people off the dole.

Those choices ended up exacerbating inequality in the long run. Even though New Dealers did not fundamentally overhaul the federal government's relationship to the academy, their work-study program created important precedents that complemented the intents and practices behind more iconic legislation, including the Banking, Social Security, Wagner, and Fair

Labor Standards Acts. Postwar policymakers, for example, preferred to finance student assistance, not directly fund higher education. That approach helped navigate political quagmires over federalism, school autonomy, government spending, equal opportunity, integration, and the separation between church and state in the 1940s, 1950s, and 1960s. Fees steadily grew in those years but really spiked after the erstwhile New Dealer Lyndon Baines Johnson signed the 1965 Higher Education Act (HEA), which contained an important provision for federally guaranteed student loans modeled on the New Deal's mortgage program.

Since then, lawmakers have arguably done less for students, parents, and schools and far more for financiers. HEA's periodic reauthorizations and indirect modifications provided the financial infrastructure for the student-loan industry, to which more than 44 million Americans owed almost $1.4 trillion by 2018. By then, the majority of families and students had to borrow, which ensured that they ended up paying more, over time, than the wealthy do. The expense of having to pay some expenses upfront, work at least part-time, and borrow to cover the rest has led to an actual decrease in the proportion of young people completing college and their likelihood of finding the kind of work capable of enabling them to ever pay back debts, buy homes, or start families.[2]

Today's student-loan crisis underscores how many of the Roosevelt administration's policy choices, political compromises, and signature achievements nurtured inequality and established a penchant for indirectly financing, not directly funding, social welfare. That tendency supports and contradicts scholarship highlighting how much economic security the New Dealers provided for white, male, industrial workers, which historians have noted exacerbated long-standing racial and gender inequalities. Providing blue-collar workers with white-collar living standards also benefited big businesses, whose chief executive officers (CEOs) profited enormously from providing the financial products, like mortgages and health insurance, that were critical parts of the public–private welfare state bolstering manufacturing workers and, by extension, their families who no longer had to or could send aging parents and young children to work.[3]

But recent scholarship has suggested that the Roosevelt administration may have given the largely white-ethnic industrial workforce new rights on the job but they did not really fund their improved living standards at home. New Dealers actually granted them access to the kind of debt arrangements, financial products, and insurance policies that had buoyed the generally white, Protestant families in the Gilded Age and Progressive Era's growing middle- and professional classes. Many Depression Era experiments mitigated the risk of extending credit to blue-collar Americans by making the national government the payer of last resort in financial arrangements that required consumers, workers, and employers to buy into pension, unemployment, savings, and mortgage programs. Such innovations inspired new financial products after World War II, when 1930s regulations had made banking safe. Private options slowly supplemented and sometimes took the place of public pensions, federally guaranteed home loans, and unemployment or disability compensation policies. In the case of student assistance, New Dealers' preference for financing security and indirectly underwriting higher education eventually made federal postsecondary aid programs a pathway into, not out of, poverty for many Americans. Most now have no choice but to try to finance a degree in order to have the chance to compete for harder-to-find well-paying jobs with benefits.[4]

Working and Studying for Individual Wants and National Needs

Few Americans wrote to the president asking for a loan to help them or their children afford college, which (at the time) was not considered "financial aid." Only in the late twentieth century did educators, policymakers, and citizens start using that phrase to describe help for students. The term previously described direct business, philanthropic, or state support for private colleges, small state schools, or great public and private research universities. Donors and legislators were capricious. Many colleges depended on student fees to stay open. Rates nevertheless remained relatively low because enrollees' real financial sacrifice was time not spent working for money or on the family farm.[5]

Students started to need cash more than time in the 1920s, when enrollment doubled nationwide. More Americans graduated from high school, could afford to send their children to college, and willingly risked the expense because matriculation offered the chance of joining the growing managerial and professional classes. Those jobs required at least some college coursework to train for and acculturate into that white-collar world. Blue-collar applicants found enrollment opportunities in junior colleges, teachers colleges, and urban universities, which offered useful, part-time programs in engineer-

ing, home economics, and business. By 1930, the largest postsecondary institutions were municipal schools, like the College of the City of New York.
Yet the academy still remained a largely privileged and rarified world. The
majority of enrollees, particularly at long-standing schools and elite institutions, were white, Protestant men from the middle and upper classes. Increased demand allowed top private schools' admissions personnel to limit
enrollment and start a quota system that excluded Jews, Catholics, immigrants, and racial minorities in order to cultivate an air of lily-white exclu-
sivity. That character could even be found in state schools since the children
of urban professionals greatly outnumbered farmers' kids.[6]

Loans were one way to ensure both enrollment and tuition revenue.
Schools had a long tradition of rarely lending to students. Dartmouth, for example, stood out in 1806 for graduating thirty-three students (out of a class
of thirty-nine) who together owed their alma mater $1,222.18. A century later,
most Association of American Universities members extended credit to only
1 percent of their student bodies. Few institutions could afford to let students
borrow but college administrators nevertheless toyed with charging students
the full cost of instruction and letting them pay over time in the speculative
1920s, when clubs, business associations, churches, individuals, and philanthropies also started offering student loans. As a result, roughly $8 million
to $10 million in credit was available to undergraduates in 1930. Two years
later, half of the U.S. student body financed their studies by working part-time
and borrowing between $25 and $200. Credit had become so commonplace
that the *New York Times* reporter Dorothy Woolf celebrated the "changed
attitude of borrowers and lenders. No longer can the loan be considered an
act of charity," she enthused, "today it is held an honorable and praisewor-
thy means of financing higher education."[7]

But those advances epitomized risk. Admission was a student's collateral.
Neither degrees nor college credits could be repossessed. School loan officers
generally asked that undergraduates repay them when and if they could.
Twenty-five percent of debts made under such agreements proved uncollect-
able. Schools with stricter agreements also struggled to recoup funds. Staff
had to dun 15 percent of borrowers, turning over 1 percent of such cases over
to lawyers. Philanthropists were equally lax. Whitney Benefits lent the foundation's income to students but never charged interest. The Felid Co-operative
Loan Fund, in contrast, required borrowers to take out a term life insurance
policy to guarantee repayment. Only a handful of bankers and philanthropists sought stricter standards but even the American Banking Association's

Foundation for Education only offered suggestions since, as top financiers admitted in 1934, "even with the best of judgment it has not always been possible to estimate correctly either the desire or the ability of the student to repay his obligation."[8]

Such unsound loans hardly helped U.S. higher education's rickety finances during the Great Depression, when hundreds of schools faced bankruptcy. College loan officers, private lenders, and philanthropic organizations started receiving far more inquiries in 1930, including from Americans who would have been able to afford college or find part-time work before the stock market crashed. Such continued interest reflected a faith in education to provide economic opportunity but enrollments still fell after 1932, when budgets set before the crash had expired and tuition rates had to be raised as endowments, private donations, and state allocations shrank. Between 1932 and 1934, attendance dropped by 8 percent, which accounted for a 61 percent reduction in tuition revenue nationwide. Two years later, 31 of the country's 1,700 postsecondary institutions had closed and 22 others had merged. Elite schools fared better since they feverishly competed for the wealthiest applicants even if they were, as Wesleyan's president lamented, "white dullards."[9]

Desperation forced less prestigious colleges to try anything to stay open. More than 10 percent of private colleges and universities accepted IOUs. Some schools bartered for admission. Some college officials promised students the chance to split their time between work and study but many students complained that college officials reneged on promises of decent hours and pay. Some schools gave needy students grants and loans. The amount and availability of money was still small (just a 38–44 percent increase between the 1928–1929 and the 1936–1937 school years).[10]

Leading academics still did not want a New Deal. Harvard's James Conant and Columbia's Nicholas Baker continually warned against federal interference in schooling matters, which had historically been left to local and state governments as well as individual schools and churches. Even the heads of land grants shied from federal support. Science and engineering faculty tended to share the political proclivities of these administrators as well as manufacturers, who had given them far more support than the federal government had.[11]

Educators' fears had little to do with the way in which Roosevelt conceived of the New Deal or actually presided. Right-wing critics lambasted him as a dictator demanding unconstitutional, if not downright un-American, expansions of federal power and executive authority. But FDR was a moderate who favored keeping Americans off the dole, making work a condition of relief, managing the labor market, balancing the budget, preserving federalism, and saving capitalism by working with amenable CEOs. He also trusted his staff to experiment with new ideas as well as existing state, local, and private initiatives to aid and empower the citizenry, help the country recover from the Great Depression, and also complete the country's reconstruction. These appointees ran the federal agencies that both congressional legislation and executive orders had placed under presidential purview. Higher-ups also gave a lot of power to the men and women whom they hired to run initiatives out of federal offices at the local and state level. Together, these New Dealers fashioned the 1930s programs that defined the Roosevelt administration.[12]

Many of these iconic New Deal experiments sought to manage the labor market in ways that historians now recognize reified inequality. Policymakers, for example, insisted that work be a condition of relief even though many economists doubted there would be enough jobs for every American in the Roosevelt administration's early years. A range of initiatives subsequently strove to reduce the number of Americans competing for jobs and depending on government support, which even Roosevelt insiders maligned as the dole. The 1935 Social Security Act, for example, created a public pensions system for the elderly as well as a welfare program for single mothers so they would not need to work. That legislation complemented the 1935 Wagner Act, which guaranteed the rights of employees not toiling in homes, fields, or government offices. This iconic labor law, in effect, enabled men (generally white) to join unions that bargained for the kind of wages and benefits that could support an entire household without any additional income from wives, kids, or elderly relatives. Families could trust banks with their savings by 1936 because a series of banking acts offered deposit insurance and regulated the speculative financing that epitomized the Roaring Twenties. Blue-collar Americans could still get lines of credit, which were much more restrictive than the early student loans. Savings helped working men buy their brood a home through the 1934 National Housing Act's mortgage program, whose low-interest, fixed-rate, long-term loans and the government-sponsored enterprise that traded them (the Federal National Mortgage Association, aka FNMA or Fannie Mae) became the template for the lawmakers who designed the student-loan program thirty years later. There would be many more Americans eligible for college then because the 1938 Fair Labor Standards Act included a prohibition outlawing child labor among the many other sections devoted to improving life on the job.[13]

The spirit behind and even the nuts and bolts of these celebrated policies shaped the way New Dealers aided the academy, which had historically been the purview of states, schools, donors, and philanthropies. Long-standing decentralization had created a postsecondary system best described as fragmented, which made a broad federal bailout unthinkable. Only public grammar, secondary, and postsecondary schools were eligible for direct federal support, which did little to expand advanced learning options in the 1930s when most colleges were private. Policymakers also never dictated that schools participate. The Works Progress Administration (WPA) generally supplied workers for projects, leaving institutions to cover material expenses. The Public Works Administration only fronted half the costs for public colleges and universities that applied to build $200 million worth of dorms, classrooms, labs, and libraries.[14]

Such limited support also reflected the president and his advisers' initial personal and political disinterest in a New Deal for higher education. FDR's storied Brains Trust hailed from the country's top schools, where their politics certainly made them outsiders but had not divorced them from the country's gentry.[15] The executive branch staff eager to experiment, whether from the country's prosperous white Protestant middle and upper classes or from striving white-ethnic or minority working-class communities, had often been educated in the Midwest or Northeast, like Roosevelt. The president did not have fond memories of his years in the country's most elite schools. He disliked the Harvard faculty's politics, did not think he had learned all that much as a student, and initially doubted the country needed more public postsecondary schools. That conviction came from governing New York, whose higher-education institutions (as in much of the Northeast) had largely trained teachers and left the liberal arts, sciences, and engineering to private colleges and universities. Therefore, the president initially insisted that high unemployment rates, particularly for educators, made bailing out public colleges and universities wasteful.[16]

Only citizen demand from around the country led the president and his advisers to start interweaving educational opportunities throughout many New Deal programs. For example, Civilian Conservation Corps higher-ups presumed their all-male recruits just needed vocational training since enlistees had been hired to help conserve and harness the country's natural resources. Recruits worked but eight hours a day planting trees, improving parks, and building roadways. They had spare time and asked for courses in basic literacy, civics, and even advanced classes in the fine arts and humanities. Requests shocked well-educated administrators, like the Grinnell graduate Harry Hopkins. He and other officials soon deemed courses in literature, history, and current events vital for relief, recovery, and long-term reform. Classes offered a chance to explain policies crafted in Washington to a citizenry who, appointees had discovered, often did not understand the Constitution or know the country's history. Hopkins subsequently recruited the famed labor-college educator Hilda Smith in 1933 to oversee a Workers Education Program, a popular initiative that sent teachers into hamlets, city neighborhoods, and unused college classrooms in order to offer the vocational, law, liberal arts, and other types of classes, for which communities applied.[17]

Those experiments coincided with the demands of East Coast journalists, politicians, and social reformers that the administration do something for unemployed youth. By fall 1934, suggestions circulated in and outside the White House for some kind of coordinated effort to help young people. Roosevelt insiders, the businessman Brains Truster Hans Taussig and the southern Democrat Aubrey Williams considered many of those ideas in the winter and spring of 1935. Taussig feared that the high unemployment rate for sixteen- to twenty-five-year-olds might make them converts to the kind of radicalism stirring in the United States and roiling Europe at the time. Williams, in contrast, considered educational opportunities critical to individual aid and national recovery. Both suggested Roosevelt create a new agency dedicated to young people's specific needs. They envisioned the National Youth Administration (NYA) offering a range of programs to keep young people off welfare rolls and out of competition for jobs. But the NYA did more than complement the Wagner and Social Security Acts' efforts to manage the labor market. Both men predicted that young people who stayed in school would be able to compete for skilled or professional positions that the country needed to be filled.[18]

But Taussig and Williams still wanted FDR to use an executive order to create the NYA. Both feared that the president would be asking Congress to undertake too much in one calendar year. By June 1935, lawmakers had already secured passage of bills in the House or Senate (in some cases both) for some of the New Deal's major legislative achievements, including the 1935 National Labor Relations, Social Security, and Banking Acts. Those laws, and many others already passed, had required lawmakers to approve of a substantial increase in the executive branch's size and authority. No one could be sure that Congress would acquiesce to more, especially over schooling. A few senators and representatives had indicated support for improving colleges and aiding young people but an outspoken contingent also fought the president's reform agenda, a growing coalition that historians have noted included Republicans and Democrats from across the country.[19]

Even if Congress created an agency to help young people, Roosevelt appointees could hardly expect such far-reaching guarantees to have gone unchallenged from the president's many critics. Both he and his advisers recognized that a federal program for young people smacked of the kind of state efforts to indoctrinate children and draw them into the European fascist and communist movements that Taussig and many other Americans disdained. New Dealers also had no guarantee that they would be able to ensure all young people, including women and minorities, could benefit from this agency since southern Democrats represented a powerful contingent in the congressional coalition forming against the New Deal. Their sizable numbers had already forced liberals to compromise their reform agenda by excluding from New Deal legislation those Americans working in the domestic, agricultural, and public sectors, which effectively prevented many women and people of color from receiving a New Deal.[20]

Executive Order 7086 subsequently strove to shield the administration from criticism while endeavoring to meet growing demands that New Dealers do something for young people. FDR cited the 1935 Emergency Relief Appropriation Act in order to allocate $50 million for a new WPA agency. The 1935 directive also placed Williams in charge of "a program of approved projects which shall provide relief, work relief, and employment for persons between the ages of sixteen and twenty-five years who are no longer in regular attendance at a school . . . and who are not regularly engaged in remunerative employment." Williams had permission "to accept and utilize . . . voluntary and uncompensated services" but could only expect help from state and local officials with their consent. He also had to answer to the head of WPA, an executive committee of six representatives from other federal agencies, and a National Advisory Committee whose delegates the president appointed. Taussig headed this panel, a motley crew (like many New Deal advisory committees) of educators, manufacturers, labor leaders, and celebrities, including the flying ace Amelia Earhart and the Olympic runner Glenn Cunningham.[21]

Williams represented a good but unlikely pick to head the NYA. Education had lifted this Alabaman out of poverty before he and his wife flocked to Washington, like so many other young professionals, in order have the chance to experiment. He took on a number of roles, leaving him hard-pressed to give any one task, including overseeing the NYA, his full attention. He also could not muzzle his disdain for the Jim Crow South and eagerness for a truly expansive federal welfare state. Top New Dealers rarely shared his distrust of corporations and monopolies or his desire for the government to do far more to ensure opportunity for all Americans, regardless of race or sex. He still, like other New Dealers, feared high unemployment, hated the dole, and never deviated from the basic principle that "relief shall be in the form of wages for work done."[22]

Those principles structured many New Deal programs, including work-study. Recipients received neither a handout to go to college nor a student loan, the kind of speculative financing anathema to this era's banking legislation. They instead received another kind of help that colleges had already started to offer in order to keep students enrolled and paying tuition: part-time work that would give them both money and the time to go to class. Both public and private schools could participate in work-study since New Dealers designed it not to be a direct bailout but indirect aid through relief for individuals, which also preserved the academy's long-standing reliance on fee-paying students. The NYA officials never imposed this program on students or schools. Young men and women had the choice to apply to college, not a presidential directive to do so. Colleges could and did decline to participate in work-study, over which they had enormous discretion. Any nonprofit, tax-exempt postsecondary school received enough money to pay $15 a month for 8 percent of undergraduate and graduate students in residence under age twenty-five. Federal officials insisted that undergraduates could only receive $20 a month, half what graduate students could receive by 1938 (an easily enforced rule since the government still paid recipients' wages). Applicants had to give schools educational and financial records as well as reputable witnesses who could vouch for an enrollee's inability to afford fees, books, and basic living expenses, including clothing, food, housing, and transportation. Those stringent requirements hardly stopped young people from applying. Most schools received double, sometimes triple, the number of applicants that their quotas permitted. Administrators did not just have their pick of recipients. Faculty and staff assigned jobs, decided hours, set wages within the general federal guidelines, and oversaw student workers. Even though state directors, including the Texas office's Lyndon Baines Johnson, reviewed schools' work-study plans, NYA staff let schools use only a portion of the funds allotted, limit hours to assist more pupils, and offer work-study students additional help to make ends meet.[23]

Work-study quickly became popular and vital. Schools that cooperated reaped much from the $93 million Williams spent educating over 600,000 Americans. Most schools (1,466 of the 1,700 eligible) immediately accepted work-study and many holdouts, like Harvard, eventually participated. A few educators actively campaigned against the NYA but many soon praised the program since, as a University of Colorado president enthused in 1937, "students have been so eager, so earnest, and so hard-working."[24]

The vast majority came from families, who could hardly help with expenses (75 percent had annual family incomes less than $2,000). A few, generally those who lived at home, made enough to pay all their fees and expenses, but most recipients only earned 50 percent to 10 percent of what they needed. Paychecks, averaging $6 to $10, still meant a lot to the many students who faced extraordinary hardships. Groucher College, for example, admitted two sisters, whose father (a minister) had lost his savings. Scholarships, loans, summer babysitting jobs, and work-study positions kept them enrolled and active in their Baltimore church. An MIT student, from a midwestern family of eight surviving on just $1,620 a year, used NYA money to make up the difference between the loans and scholarships the school provided. Investigators found that seemingly paltry sums helped destitute students excel. A twenty-three-year-old orphan had started the semester alternatively living in a park and a University of Illinois building before staff gave him a work-study job and found him a room. He undoubtedly would have had to drop out but finished the term with top marks. A University of North Dakota undergraduate actually won a Rhodes Scholarship after work-study enabled him to pay for the tuition, room, and board that his widowed mother could not afford while trying to support his two younger siblings.[25]

Recipients considered the work for which the NYA paid them to be as worthwhile as studying. Almost 90 percent of students in an Ohio State University survey considered the tasks that they did educationally valuable. A lot of their work also kept campuses running in an era of extremely tight budgets. More than 20 percent of all work-study students helped with research, tasks that included compiling statistics and making surveys. On-campus maintenance and community service in public libraries and government agencies rounded out the top three job categories. Recipients could subsequently be found in academic departments, libraries, and laboratories where they worked as clerics, construction workers, janitors, printers, photographers, graders, and tutors. Their tasks included mounting art exhibits, building machine tools, repairing library books, remodeling buildings, repairing windows, transcribing legal debates, editing manuscripts, preparing atlases, improving teaching materials, and reshaping agricultural practices.[26]

Success and popularity failed to shield Williams, the NYA, and the entire New Deal. Complaints and accusations turned into investigations after the disastrous 1938 midterm elections, when liberal Democrats' losses turned the once fledgling coalition of anti–New Deal Republicans and southern Democrats into a force to be reckoned with once Congress reconvened in early 1939. Many in that coalition disdained Williams who publicly decried Jim Crow. The White House tried to protect the NYA by moving the agency under the Federal Security Administration (FSA), the sprawling bureaucracy safeguarding the country's long-term economic health and stability. That 1939 reorganization put the agency's budget at the mercy of an increasingly uncooperative Congress. Even though military leaders had considered harnessing the NYA's training programs to be vital to arming European allies and preparing Americans to fight since 1938, liberal lawmakers (including then-representative LBJ) struggled to preserve earmarks in the early 1940s. Williams subsequently found himself compromising the scope and spirit of his agency in order to save it. The fight escalated as private college presidents colluded to besmirch work-study as wasteful and lawmakers launched investigations into what the NYA did to aid the war effort as well as quietly undermine Jim Crow. Those inquiries were a part of a larger assault on the Roosevelt administration, which included abrupt congressional defunding of the NYA and many other New Deal agencies in 1943.[27]

Rewarding Schools and Servicemen

Senators and representatives nevertheless passed the storied G.I. Bill of Rights the very next year, which dramatized how both the spirit of and opposition to the New Deal continued during and after World War II, particularly over concerns (like higher education) that New Dealers had not squarely addressed. The 1944 Servicemen's Readjustment Act, more commonly called the G.I. Bill or G.I. Bill of Rights, has most often been remembered for the schooling programs in Title II. Most Americans only cite those provisions when lauding this legislation for helping the so-called Greatest Generation and starting the expansion of U.S. higher education that would be needed to admit their children, the baby boomers.[28]

But the Roosevelt administration crafted this legislation, as the historian Keith Olson surmised, on the principle that "the economy and not the veteran needed adjusting."[29] Roosevelt and his aides had no interest in just giving soldiers a reward for services rendered. Fears of another Bonus March made that idea unpalatable. Mustering-out pay went against the very vision of improved, sustained, permanent social welfare and economic security for everyone, not just special classes of citizens (like veterans).[30] By the mid-1940s, many erstwhile New Dealers recognized mass higher education was not only possible but also useful and desirable. Student assistance was thus a part of intense discussions in and outside of Washington about how the country might transition to a peacetime economy since colleges might once again ease pressure on a labor market that desperately needed more skilled workers.[31]

Many doubted most veterans would be interested in education and leading educators opposed schooling guarantees. Ivy League faculty, including James Conant, had eventually accepted work-study and certainly had embraced federal support for science departments during the war. They had no interest in welcoming working-class veterans, regardless of race or ethnicity, onto campus. Conant feared "sentimental pressures and financial temptation" might enable "the least capable among the war generation, instead of the most capable," to flood "the facilities for advanced education in the United States." The University of Chicago president Robert Hutchins shared many of Conant's concerns even though he had a reputation as a liberal Democrat. The famed legal scholar considered the G.I. Bill likely to become "a substitute for the dole or for a national program of public works," meaning schools would be "converted into educational hobo jungles." Cost also concerned the conservative coalition of congressmen who had used 1943 budget negotiations to destroy New Deal agencies like the NYA. These senators and representatives questioned generous educational entitlements, which would come in the form of actual tuition payments and subsistence allowances, not loans. Roosevelt aides and allies nevertheless fought for Title II but still assumed most GIs would prefer home, small-business, and farm loans.[32]

The administration also faced opposition from long-standing critics who wanted substantial educational opportunities but insisted that only veterans be eligible. The conservative American Legion and other veteran organizations envisioned robust programs to help GIs readjust but worried Congress would never pass such guarantees, particularly for schooling. So legionnaires went to the aging William Randolph Hearst, whose papers stood out at the time for their open, strident criticism of the Roosevelt administration. The publisher spared no expense or editorial-page space on promoting the legion's preferred bills. Reporters insisted that returnees had earned these benefits but spent far less time explaining the particular difference between the legion's preferred legislation and the Roosevelt administration's proposals, which differed in the amounts allocated as well as which agency would oversee the program. The legion, the Hearst papers, and their congressional allies wanted the Veterans Administration (VA) to oversee it, whereas Roosevelt officials sought to give the FSA oversight. Liberals feared that the VA's authority would permanently wall off these social guarantees from the rest of the citizenry, whereas FSA control might eventually enable veterans' entitlements to be offered to all Americans, a possibility that fueled the objections of the legion, the Hearst publishing empire, and their congressional allies.[33]

The Roosevelt administration and its allies in Congress lost that fight but the omnibus legislation preserved liberal Democrats' preference for creatively financing higher education. Like work-study, this federal aid directed support through students, not schools that remained fiercely protective of their institutional autonomy and academic freedom. This tuition assistance plan continued to enable liberals to indirectly fund the expansion of schools willing to accept ordinary Americans. The Roosevelt administration and its congressional allies considered such institutional growth necessary for advanced learning, of which many Americans had already proved themselves capable and desirous. Unlike work-study, veteran students received their stipends directly from the VA but did not pay tuition out of that allowance. Schools decided whom to admit and billed the VA for veterans' fees. The maximum tuition reimbursement was far higher than most schools charged, which enabled administrators to raise rates and encouraged them to admit the ordinary Americans, whom Conant, Hutchins, and other elite academics insisted did not belong on college campuses. That extra tuition revenue seemed capable of indirectly underwriting the expansions needed to accommodate the small number of applicants that lawmakers, military leaders, veterans groups, and educators predicted. That growth seemed likely to ready schools to accept subsequent generations of Americans, whom Roosevelt insiders rightly predicted would need and demand more learning.[34]

Soldiers shocked everyone with their eagerness to enroll as well as their general disinterest in loans to start farms or small businesses. Access to such financial products had greatly increased since the 1930s but broad, direct support, especially for schooling, remained rare. Soldiers subsequently clamored to continue their education. Many wanted the opportunity to study and recognized that schooling guaranteed upward mobility far more than farming or entrepreneurship did. Congress subsequently had to revise this legislation within a year, increase the money earmarked for Title II, and even provide some limited, temporary support to help colleges and universities expand to meet this unexpected demand.[35]

Former soldiers still had to fight for these educational benefits. Underfunded schools needed this help and tended to readily accept veterans, less so the elite institutions, such as Harvard, the University of Chicago, and Columbia. Top universities generally admitted those GIs, who would have been able to get in and afford fees (such as the already wealthy future Rhode Island senator Claiborne Pell). Those institutions still operated under a quota system but Roosevelt and Truman administration officials did not intervene even after front-page stories about these restrictive admission policies outraged the public, who put pressure on these institutions to end restrictions that went against the spirit of what the administration had called the all-American war effort and the dream that many African Americans had of a double victory against fascism abroad and racism at home. Former soldiers openly discussed Title II's limitations with reporters, who published numerous accounts of cramped classrooms and unsanitary dorms. GIs also demand that VA officials give them their entitlements. Many returnees waited months for their subsistence checks, even though schools tended to receive tuition reimbursements on time. Delays receiving even these meager allowances forced former service personnel to dip into their savings, ask parents for help, cash in war bonds, take part-time jobs, procure loans, or just drop out of schools.[36]

Journalists noted that veterans excelled despite these terrible conditions. Within two years of the bill's passage, faculty continually and publicly praised GIs for being eager, capable students. Even Conant admitted in 1946 that soldiers had already proved "the most mature and promising students Harvard has ever had." The University of Wisconsin president E. B. Fred also deemed troops a "stabilizing influence on Wisconsin student life." They studied intensely, famously outperforming their younger peers who had never served. Soldiers' success sometimes annoyed their civilian classmates, including the Stanford students who labeled GIs "Damn Average Raisers," or "D.A.R.'s."[37]

Veterans' successes epitomized how many Roosevelt-era policies often exacerbated, not lessened, inequality over time. Almost 8 million made use of Title II, with over 2.2 million using it for college. The $14.5 billion spent on education still only helped 37 percent of eligible veterans, 80 percent of whom had expected to continue or start additional studies. White males once again benefited the most, much as they had during the New Deal. Graduates enjoyed better educational opportunities, had better living standards, and saved more over the course of their lifetimes than the civilians who did not have access to these specific learning entitlements or the veterans who could not take advantage of them. Title II also reified the federal government's indirect approach to aiding education to avoid political fights, which had disastrous consequences. Using tuition as a means to underwrite schooling hid the way student assistance placed higher education increasingly out of reach of poor and working-class Americans even as the number of seats available increased. Colleges' physical growth in the early postwar years required admitting more Americans. Schools would not be able to stay open, much less expand, after veterans' benefits expired. That $500 tuition maximum had also encouraged schools to raise rates for everyone, not just the GIs whom the law had singled out as uniquely deserving of this support. College subsequently became more expensive for every American after GI benefits expired. Even though those guarantees fell short of many soldiers' needs, subsequent generations of soldiers received far less under the later G.I. Bills over which Congress doggedly fought.[38]

A Pathway into, Not out of, Poverty

Civilians did not receive substantial assistance until almost twenty years later. More Americans had wanted to go to college after World War II but costs put that dream out of reach. Neither work-study nor the G.I. Bill had provided the kind of direct support needed to underwrite schools and free them of their reliance on tuition. After World War II, few legislatures allocated money for the much-needed expansions, much less to keep fees down. Some states, most notably New York and Massachusetts, did experiment with student assistance programs, including helping students and parents secure loans from banks. That method did little to contain education costs, a key concern of the businesses and philanthropies that desperately tried to secure donations for private schools in order to sustain them without additional revenue from students. The relatively little funding available through government defense contracts and grants for health or scientific research hardly helped. That money went to specific projects, labs, and departments at well-established state and private universities able to compete for support, but that money could never have paid for an entire university's expansion.[39]

Laggard, conditional support worried the lawmakers who introduced various bills for federally underwriting colleges and universities. Senators and representatives found educators, including Conant, increasingly amenable, especially since national funding had not compromised their authority. That aging administrator's political weight had started to fade as a new generation of academics started demanding national support. At the forefront of this vanguard stood the University of California president Clark Kerr, a former New Deal–era labor economist who foresaw a postindustrial America needing "multiversities" that would serve everyone in an increasingly metropolitan America. Yet congressional efforts to directly underwrite those ambitions generally died over the issue of supporting private, religious, or segregated schools in the 1950s and early 1960s.[40]

Those concerns almost scuttled the 1958 National Defense Education Act (NDEA). That much-celebrated law only ended up promising limited, temporary assistance to universities and college students after a year of fighting between and within Congress, the White House, and the Department of Health, Education, and Welfare. Money only went to science, engineering, math, and foreign-language programs with obvious importance for defense, which could not cover the collegiate growth needed. Student assistance also went to applicants promising to study something related to defense. Only graduate students received a grant because, at the last minute, lawmakers balked at offering undergraduates such support and instead created a complicated loan program that gave schools' discretion over who received aid and how this supposedly self-perpetuating loan program was administered. Financial aid officers had tremendous difficulty managing these ten-year, low-interest loans since federal deferments delayed how quickly an individual school's loan fund was replenished to meet steadily increasing needs and demands, a problem that had plagued 1920s and 1930s campus loan programs.[41]

The NDEA also did not resolve the fights over federalism, segregation, and welfare that had roiled Washington since the New Deal's heyday. Those same conflicts hamstrung the Kennedy administration's efforts to offer genuine assistance to colleges and universities just as the baby boomers began to apply in record numbers. He died before he could sign the 1963 Higher Education Facilities Act, a long-forgotten but important law that provided five years of money to build higher-education facilities. This limited legislation represented a breakthrough of sorts because parochial and denominational institutions could apply for and receive funds as long as that money did not pay for buildings dedicated to religious purposes.[42]

That law, the G.I. Bill, and work-study nevertheless provided the precedent for the 1965 Higher Education Act. The former Texas National Youth Administration director LBJ promised the HEA would ensure "deeper personal fulfillment, greater personal productivity, and increased personal reward" because any "high school senior . . . can apply to any college or any university . . . and not be turned away because his family is poor." The president could offer that guarantee after the 1964 Civil Rights Act's passage, which ended concerns about public money going to segregated institutions. The HEA's eight titles seemed to offer substantial, general, direct support for colleges, universities, and their libraries to keep fees down, something a handful of Democrats had been seeking since the late 1940s. Higher-education spending did jump from $1.4 billion to $3.7 billion between 1963 and 1966. Yet lawmakers and White House staffers did not advocate fully funding the HEA since they had a larger War on Poverty to wage, Great Society to build, and Vietnam War to fight, costly endeavors at a moment when neither the White House nor Congress wanted to repeal the business tax cuts passed under Kennedy. Many experts still deem those mid-1960s educational outlays an unprecedented achievement, whereas others consider that increase as well as much of the rest of Johnson's domestic record "a mixed story of initial failure and frustration, of political brilliance and luck, of partial success, of unintended consequences, and ultimately of being overwhelmed, even in triumph, by stronger forces."[43]

That analysis captured the long-term consequences of the Johnson administration's and Congress's enthusiasm for Title IV's grants, work-study opportunities, and loans. As in the 1930s and 1940s, those 1960s offerings arose out of earlier experiments, state innovations, and long-standing ideas.

For example, the Guaranteed Student Loan Program's (GSLP) low-interest, ten-year loans mimicked what some states had started brokering for undergraduates in the 1950s (not what a handful of lenders and colleges had offered students in the 1920s). Federal officials secured GSLP offerings from private lenders but gave these credit lines to school financial aid officers, who could include them in individually tailored financial aid packages. Students could over the course of their college career receive a mix of grants, NDEA loans, work-study opportunities, and GSLP advances. The latter echoed New Deal innovations that used regulated financial products to both save capitalism and finance social welfare since lawmakers and White House staffers had designed the GSLP, like the New Deal mortgage program, to nurture a new financial sector, which lawmakers presumed would enable the government to cheaply help a lot of schools and undergraduates.[44]

The HEA's indirect loans differed substantially from the Federal Housing Act's mortgage program, which had recrafted an industry around that safe low-interest, long-term financial product. The GSLP epitomized the kind of risky, speculative financing that had made a federal student-lending program unthinkable among Roosevelt insiders in the 1930s. Credit, as in earlier campus loan programs, only required admission. A borrower did not have to go through a credit check or prove their likelihood of being able to make future payments. Loans were small enough to ensure that everyone had to put some money down for the chance to pursue a college degree that could not be repossessed.[45]

The GSLP also differed in important ways from the NDEA's small loan program, which lawmakers started calling *direct loans* to differentiate them from the GSLP's even more indirect offerings. The federal government had offered 90 percent of the money for an NDEA loan fund that campus personnel had to set up and administer. Financial aid officers lent a prescribed amount directly from this slush fund, which borrowers should have helped replenish with interest within ten years of graduation. Unlike the NDEA, the GSLP (like the federal mortgage program) offered a real guarantee to lenders. School financial-aid staff had to ensure repayment and wait to see whether Congress would appropriate additional NDEA funding. In contrast, the government promised financiers repayment for loans that the government brokered in order to provide schools in the pool of money for all federal financial aid resources. Neither the NDEA nor the HEA guaranteed students a loan since college financial aid staff decided what mix of aid, if any, applicants received.[46]

Reauthorizing Guarantees for Lenders

Lawmakers, not campus personnel, nurtured and protected the student-lending industry through the HEA's periodic reauthorizations. Mandatory legislative reconsideration did not feature in some of the New Deal's major legislative achievements, including the National Housing, Social Security, Banking, and Wagner Acts. Such compulsory reviews could be found throughout a lot of postwar legislation, including many Great Society laws. Mandatory periodic revisions theoretically gave lawmakers the chance to expand, change, and reduce social entitlements. In the HEA's case, lawmakers altered titles, added new programs, ordered studies, added repayment options, renamed assistance offerings after their colleagues, tinkered with loan rates, and included initiatives with little connection to higher education in the 1968, 1972, 1976, 1980, 1986, 1992, 1998, and 2008 reauthorizations.[47]

The 1972 changes did the most to nurture a powerful student-loan industry. That reauthorization, like much of the Great Society, has usually been heralded for expanding opportunities for the many Americans left out of the New Deal. Title IX, for which Oregon Democratic Congresswoman Edith Green and Hawaii Democratic Senator Patsy Mink fought, decreed that sex discrimination would come at the expense of federal financial assistance for all colleges and universities. That boon for women's educational advancement accompanied another form of student aid intended to help the poor: the Basic Educational Opportunity Grants (BEOGs). Lawmakers have since renamed that offering after Pell, the Rhode Island senator who promised this scholarship would give every American the right to an education. At the time, many presumed this entitlement would disproportionately help minorities, who had the most need. Yet this program did not prescribe affirmative action for any one set of undergraduates but merely promised to help any aspiring poor students who needed a scholarship, which federal officials, not college financial aid personnel, gave out.[48]

Neither Title IX nor Pell Grants ensured college would remain affordable or accessible. Title IX barred discrimination but did nothing to ensure that women or their families could pay for school. Similarly, the small Pell grants purposefully did not cover the full projected costs of going to college. Low-income students, like their better-off peers, still needed whatever mix of assistance college administrators offered them. That program also alienated some lawmakers, including Green, who disliked the idea of a guaranteed federal handout to students. This former teacher wanted only colleges to determine who was worthy. She subsequently left the education subcommittee that she had served on for years in order to join the budget committee, where she could ensure that Pell Grants never received the full amount earmarked in the 1972 reauthorization.[49]

In retrospect, the most important, costly, and deleterious 1972 addition was the Student Loan Marketing Association (SLMA or Sallie Mae), a clearinghouse for student-loan debt modeled on the New Deal's Fannie Mae but privatized between 1997 and 2004. President Richard Nixon's advisers had urged Congress to create this government-sponsored enterprise (GSE) in order to encourage lenders to participate in the laggard student-loan industry just as Fannie Mae had coaxed more banks into the mortgage sector. Few lawmakers raised objections to this idea. They instead spent their time fighting over Title IX, the BEOG proposal, and busing, a K–12 issue roiling the country and Congress at the time. The conference committee barely discussed the SLMA during the lengthy sessions to reconcile the final House and Senate bills on this legislation, which reflected how commonplace GSEs had become since the New Deal had borrowed the idea from Progressive Era reformers.[50]

The SLMA, like the FNMA, did much to make student lending profitable. The promised rate of return may have been relatively low, but federal officials guaranteed both the principal and interest on these incredibly risky financial products, which could then be more easily and profitably sold like federal-backed mortgages had been for decades. Insuring that part of a financiers' portfolio enabled them to offer private student loans, a vital ingredient in this financial sector's explosive growth. These liens came with no assurance of government repayment and could have interest rates double those brokered and guaranteed by the government. Undergraduates and their parents often found themselves taking out such advances since the cost of going to college greatly outpaced the maximum allowances for federal loans and grants. Pell Grants, for example, had covered 46 percent of college costs in the mid-1970s. A decade later, that small award paid only about 30 percent. That drop reflected that tuition was rising far faster than consumer prices. The total cost of going to school rose roughly 45 percent in the 1980s, triple the increase in the median amount of disposable income. The debt incurred through private loans could also be bought and sold through the SLMA as well as other private clearinghouses. The GSE remained the largest assurer, whose 1983 debut on the stock market raised $357 million in private capital.[51]

The Third Rail of U.S. Politics, Education, and Finance

Lawmakers created Sallie Mae just as the costs to attend college began to outpace families' ability to afford these increases. That historic shift reflected working- and middle-class wage stagnation since the 1970s as well as the simultaneous, rapid decline in state support for schools. Neither federal research grants nor state expenditures has ever really come back to previous levels. Voters have instead proved far more supportive of tax cuts than of funding for critical parts of social welfare, such as health care, basic infrastructure, and education. By the 1990s, twenty years of steadily rising tuition rates left most students and families expecting to pay a substantial out-of-pocket amount, work at least part-time, and borrow in order to afford all college expenses. They really did not have a choice since postsecondary schooling had already become necessary for entry into or just staying in the middle class. These trends continued into the new millennium, when certain experts noted that some young people, particularly women and minorities, found that they could not afford to go to or to skip college.[52]

Students' and parents' growing reliance on loans expanded the financial aid industry. Financiers added additional costs and spent time lobbying for both the periodic direct congressional reauthorizations of the HEA and indirect modifications, which by 1999 were laid out in an estimated seven thousand sections of federal regulations just pertaining to loans. By 2007, this industry included a complicated web of campus financial aid officers, lawmakers, legislators, federal policymakers, state officials, and student-loan industry insiders, whose ranks then included three thousand lenders, thirty guarantee agencies, seventy loan-servicing companies, several clearinghouses, and countless consultants who gave advice on how to navigate the application process.[53]

Size made reform, let alone abolishment, difficult. For example, Bill Clinton had hoped to get rid of the guaranteed loan program. Yet a hostile, Republican-controlled Congress only enabled him to slightly expand the small experimental direct loan program first introduced in the 1992 reauthorizations that his Republican predecessor had begrudgingly signed into law. Clinton had a far bigger influence on higher education when he signed off on the 1997 Taxpayer Relief Act, which finally put into law the kind of higher-education tax credits and deductions that conservative Republicans and a handful of Democrats had been publicly championing since the 1950s. Such credits had already been passed in a handful of southern states but the federal breaks soon became one of the third rails in U.S. politics, arguably as untouchable as Social Security.[54]

That supposed relief represented an affront to the New Deal. The Roosevelt administration had intended taxes to provide the revenue for social-welfare initiatives that benefited individual citizens and the country as a whole. But experts estimated that the 1994 write-offs would result in a $9 billion reduction in revenue, little of which colleges and universities could easily expect to recoup. Specialists also warned that these deductions would not ease alumni's financial burdens, since (as with the deduction for mortgage interest) they disproportionately gave the biggest breaks to the wealthiest Americans who could already afford to send their children to pricey exclusive schools.[55]

Those deductions survived the GSLP's sudden, dramatic 2010 end. During the early months of the Obama administration, financial aid lobbyists struggled to marshal their formidable resources and defend indirect lending as they had when Clinton had fought for the direct loan program in the early 1990s. Toward the end of congressional fights over the passing and enacting of the Affordable Care Act (Obamacare), lawmakers included a provision in a hotly contested budget agreement that cut out the banking middlemen who stood between the Department of Education and the millions of students enrolled in American colleges and universities. President Barack Obama, who had only recently paid off his student loans, subsequently proclaimed "two major victories in one week" when he signed off on the Health Care and Education Reconciliation Act. The first was, of course, health care. The second was the end of the once revered Guaranteed Loan Program that LBJ had signed into law, which Obama called "a sweetheart deal in federal law that essentially gave billions of dollars to banks." That victory was still pyrrhic. Enrollees and their families still needed direct federal loans and possibly private loans to afford college. Debtors would also have to repay what they owed on indirect liens.[56]

Americans could not expect much more during the Great Recession. Social welfare assurances had long come in the form of insurance products, financial schemes, and tax breaks that overwhelmingly benefited financiers. Residents needed far more since that catastrophe outscaled all other downturns in U.S. history, save for the Great Depression. The more recent calamity also occurred at a moment when the wealth gap matched Gilded Age inequality, the era when middle-class and some working-class Americans could really only find assistance in complicated fiscal offerings to mitigate risk. A century later, the real legacy of the New Deal hence seems to be offering more Americans access to complicated provisions to finance basic social needs like housing, health, and education. In the long run, the Roosevelt administration subsequently seems to have ensured that these public necessities remained largely private luxuries.

CHAPTER 7

The Shackles of the Past

Constitutional Property Tax Limitations and the Fall of the New Deal Order

Isaac William Martin

On April 26, 1979, George Hardy, the president of the Service Employees International Union, wrote a letter to his fellow union presidents to warn them of a new threat. "The right wing is spending millions of dollars this year to organize American workers—including our members—to support their political aims. For the first time in our history, they are succeeding," he wrote. "Conservative organizations supporting Proposition 13 initiatives have captured the attention of the nation by presenting a unified national voice calling for tax relief for the everyday taxpayer."[1]

Hardy was right to sound the alarm. The 1978 ballot initiative called Proposition 13 had amended the California state constitution and imposed a new, and permanent, condition of austerity. Local governments could no longer levy property tax rates in excess of 1 percent. Revenues from real estate taxes could no longer grow with the California real estate market. State legislators could no longer approve new taxes by a simple majority. In one blow, the amendment ended the era of easy finance that had enabled decades of progressive innovation in California's public sector in the postwar decades.

Worst of all, from the perspective of Hardy and other labor leaders, was that Proposition 13 appeared to symbolize the fracturing of the New Deal coalition. Proposition 13 was approved by 65 percent of the state's voters. Even before the polls were closed, legislators in other states had begun to copy the language of Proposition 13, in hopes of claiming credit for a populist tax cut of their own. National polls showed that a majority of Americans favored "a measure similar to Proposition 13." Within weeks, talk of Proposition 13, and the new mood of austerity that it was thought to symbolize, came to dominate congressional debates over taxing and spending on programs from transportation to welfare.[2]

Previous scholarship has explained the success of Proposition 13 by pointing out how it exploited long-standing weaknesses of the New Deal order. As characterized by Steve Fraser and Gary Gerstle, this "order" was more than an electoral alignment; it was also a set of policies and institutional arrangements that supported that alignment. The fundamental political and institutional settlement of the New Deal order combined rising wages, modest public social provision, the promise of home ownership, and macroeconomic stabilization through government-subsidized housing finance. This combination had provided many working-class Americans with economic security—but it had also made them acutely sensitive to property taxes, and had encouraged them to develop loyalties to a particular suburb rather than to a class or a workplace. The two-tiered structure of the New Deal welfare state had locked in support for federal old-age pensions while ensuring that state and local public finance was linked to welfare programs that were comparatively stigmatized and unpopular. It was these deep structural flaws in the New Deal order that made a state and local property tax crisis into a political crisis for organized labor and its liberal Democratic allies.[3]

But why was the crisis resolved by a constitutional amendment that limited the taxation of property? There was nothing about the tensions in the New Deal order that made this outcome inevitable or even particularly likely. Until the California primary election of 1978, homeowners' grievances about property taxes could be, and often were, yoked to campaigns for progressive tax reform. Working class resentment of rising property taxes helped propel the populist Dennis Kucinich into the mayoralty of Cleveland in 1977. It provided fuel for new populist community organizing projects from the Association of Community Organizations for Reform Now (ACORN) in Little Rock to Massachusetts Fair Share in Boston. For most of the 1970s, a loose coalition of progressive labor unions and former civil rights and welfare rights organizers competed successfully for leadership of the property tax revolt. They demanded tax relief for low-income homeowners and increased taxation of business and the rich.[4]

To explain how this populist rebellion became a force for permanent austerity, we need to understand the intellectual roots of Proposition 13 itself. It was not until this policy was ratified by California voters in 1978 that the promise of economic security for working-class homeowners came to be bound up with a policy regime that imposed austerity on the public sector. We have learned a great deal in recent years about the intellectual foundations of the broad assault on the public sector. Intellectual historians such as Nancy MacLean and Angus Burgin have illuminated the conservative traditions that survived alongside the New Deal order and informed the political visions of its opponents. But the intellectual genealogy of Proposition 13 had less to do with the airy visions of neoliberals, and the think tanks and academic centers that supported them, than with the history of practical strategies by which a changing constellation of interest groups sought to limit the property tax. At the time that California voters cast their ballots for Proposition 13, the tradition of property tax limitation already stretched back a century, and the links in this chain were forged in a series of improved responses to property tax crises.[5]

The First Constitutional Property Tax Limitation

The roots of Proposition 13 can be traced to an antidemocratic counterrevolution. The first people to draft a constitutional limitation on the local property tax were delegates to the Alabama constitutional convention of 1875. They sought to protect white supremacy by depriving the fledgling multiracial democracy of its power to tax.

Reconstruction had precipitated a property tax crisis throughout the former Confederacy. Financing economic reconstruction was expensive. The defeated states issued bonds for railroad development backed by property taxes, and they assumed new responsibilities for the education of the formerly enslaved labor force. The war, however, had left them with a diminished tax base from which to raise the revenues to meet these expenditures. Not only had the war destroyed the value of some taxable lands and luxury goods, but much of the taxable wealth of the antebellum South had consisted of enslaved people. Emancipation shifted the tax burden from owners of slaves to owners of land. Some white smallholders who had never owned slaves faced steep tax increases. Some of them, particularly in the hill country of North Alabama, had little cash income with which to pay their taxes.[6]

The crisis came to a head in the election of 1874. The financial crisis of September 1873, and the ensuing depression, discredited radical Republican rule in the eyes of many voters and exacerbated intraparty conflicts between freed black voters and upcountry whites. Democrats swept the elections in 1874 after a campaign of intimidation and violence in which organized terrorists suppressed black turnout by burning crops, homes, and ballots, leaving at least nine people dead. Many black leaders in and outside of the Alabama legislature appealed to Congress for federal military intervention, but Congress adjourned in March 1875 without action; the Alabama Democratic Party then moved to consolidate its rule by calling a constitutional convention with delegates apportioned in a manner that favored sparsely populated, majority white counties. In the words of the Democratic state representative Thomas H. Price, the purpose of a convention was to "put a reasonable limit on taxation, make it impossible to increase the public debt, [and] put it out of reach of counties to tax the people out of house and home."[7]

Putting a limit on taxation was the first order of business when the convention met in September 1875. The president of the convention, Leroy Pope Walker, urged tax limitation as a substitute for suffrage restriction. Walker had voted for secession, and he had served as secretary of war in the Confederacy. But in 1875, with the Fifteenth Amendment newly ratified, federal troops still stationed in Louisiana, and the restoration of military rule a live possibility, he urged his fellow delegates to accept universal manhood suffrage as a fait accompli, even if they did not embrace it as a principle. "Let us recognize this fact with broad significance," he told the assembled delegates, "and incorporate into the Constitution the National spirit and the National law of the perfect political and civil equality of all men, of whatever race, color, or previous condition." Political and civil equality, but not economic or social equality: the task for the convention, as he saw it, was to limit the damage that freedmen could do with the franchise—by limiting the power of their elected governments to tax. "An eminent statesman has said, 'The power to tax is the power to destroy,'" Walker advised the delegates, paraphrasing Chief Justice John Marshall's opinion in *McCulloch v. Maryland*. "Governments should provide against possibilities, as possibilities often become facts. Limit, therefore, the legislative power of taxation; and yet so impose this limitation as to shield from suspicion the honor and credit of the state."[8]

Walker's dual charge to the delegates—limit the power to tax, but don't hurt the state's credit—corresponded to the delicate political situation of the Alabama Democratic Party. Some agrarian delegates from the northern part of the state argued for repudiation of the state's railroad debts. Walker, along with Governor George Houston and other "Bourbon" party leaders, agreed that the total debt was unpayable, but thought that repudiation would hurt the state's industrial development. They argued for adjustment rather than repudiation. The governor hoped to persuade bondholders to accept a haircut in exchange for a credible repayment plan, and thereby to preserve the state's credit so that it could borrow again. Writing a low tax rate into the constitution could strengthen the state's bargaining position, by demonstrating its determination to keep taxes low—but only if the rate was not so low as to foreclose *all* possibility of repayment. The optimal tax rate to solve this bargaining problem was anyone's guess.[9]

It was this peculiar political situation that accounted for the unprecedented and essentially quantitative nature of the constitutional exercise. Existing models for constitutional limits on the power to tax were useless. The federal Constitution limited the qualitative choice of tax instruments—"no capitation, or other direct, tax shall be laid, unless in proportion to the census or enumeration herein before directed to be taken"—but its only quantitative limitation was a dead letter that was irrelevant to the problem at hand, namely a cap on slave import duties expressed in dollars per capita ("not exceeding ten dollars for each person"). The Confederate Constitution of 1861 had merely copied the relevant sections of the federal Constitution. No state constitution had ever imposed a maximum percentage tax rate; indeed, Louisiana voters had only the previous year amended their constitution to establish a *minimum* state property tax rate in order to secure a favorable interest rate on state bonds. Alabama delegates had the unprecedented task of solving an imponderable political equation to yield a definite number.[10]

They ultimately solved the problem by a simple application of the availability heuristic. After some debate, the delegates agreed that the maximum rate of tax should be three-fourths of 1 percent, the statutory tax rate already in effect. The specific numerical parameter did not derive from any high principle or draw on any careful analysis of the debt problem. It merely responded to a temporary crisis by freezing the current tax rate in amber so that future legislative majorities could not increase it.[11]

The constitution of 1875 also imposed limitations on local property tax rates, and those limitations, too, simply codified existing legislative practice. The Alabama legislature regularly authorized property tax rates for particular cities and counties. The delegates merely generalized this principle, adopting the rules that "no county in this State shall be authorized to levy a larger rate of taxation, in any one year, on the value of the taxable property therein, than one-half of one per centum" and that "no city, town, or other municipal corporation . . . shall levy or collect a larger rate of taxation, in any one year on the property thereof, than one-half of one percentum of the value of such property, as assessed for State taxation during the preceeding year," with allowances for additional millage to pay off existing debts of county and municipal governments. These rules were not designed to limit local decision-making bodies. If delegates had sought to limit the behavior of city council members or county commissioners they might have accomplished that purpose by statute. A constitutional provision was only necessary to constrain the actions of future *state* legislative majorities.[12]

In short, constitutional property tax limitation was invented as way to lock in the policies of a fragile legislative majority, itself of questionable democratic legitimacy, whose members feared that future majorities might attempt to overturn those policies. The Democratic Party campaigned for ratification of the new document with explicit appeals to protect white supremacy against the "Jacobin Republicans" who wrote the previous constitution of 1868. "Who made the present constitution?" the Montgomery *Advertiser* asked rhetorically, and answered: "Corn field Negroes, corrupt carpetbaggers and United States soldiers. Vote for the new one, made by your own representatives." The Republicans, for their part, denounced the new constitution as fiscally unsustainable, and accused it of choking off resources to public schools. The partisan and racial basis of the conflict was clear to everyone involved. Four Black Belt counties voted against ratification. The rest of the state voted for it. In 1901, when the state was convulsed by the debate over another constitutional convention, the *Advertiser* explained to its readers that the main purpose of the 1875 constitution had been to "fix things so the Republicans could do little harm if they should return to power."[13]

The new constitution fixed things perhaps too firmly. Before long even many Bourbon Democrats began to chafe at the state's constitutional property tax limitations. Businessmen complained that the state's constitutional tax limitations held back infrastructural improvements and forced municipal governments to borrow at unfavorable rates. The state's schools complained that the limitations impaired the availability and quality of public education. Cities regularly petitioned the legislature for constitutional amendments to relieve localities from the strictures of the property tax limitation. When a convention was finally called for 1901, a coalition of Alabama cities petitioned the delegates to repeal the property tax limitation altogether. The delegates declined. Property tax limitation was too popular with the state's white farmers, and the threat of repeal was alarming to landowners who thought they might thereby lose an important guarantee of their economic security. Alabama "incorporated no new ideas on taxation in the Constitution of 1901"—which would remain the state's constitution for the rest of the twentieth century and into the twenty-first. The property tax limitations of 1875, in short, have remained stuck in the Constitution of Alabama. But they have not remained *only* there.[14]

How Property Tax Limitation Became a Thing

Leroy Pope Walker, in his address to the Alabama constitutional convention of 1875, described the ideal constitution as an organic whole, which he contrasted to the "unseemly mosaic, composed of shreds and patches gathered here and there, incongruous in design, inharmonious in action" that was the Alabama Constitution of 1868. In his romantic constitutional theory, the property tax limitation was part of this organic unity and inseparable from the whole. But constitutions abstract. Their power to bind the future conduct of government comes from their articulation of general principles purified of the particulars that belong to the immediate context of their drafting. Constitutions thereby become machines for standardization of political action. Once translated into the abstract language of constitutionalism, an expedient decision undertaken to solve an idiosyncratic problem becomes an abstract policy device that can be copied and applied in circumstances far removed from its immediate origins. So it was with constitutional property tax limitation. The Alabama delegates of 1875, by writing maximum property tax rates into their constitution, not only bound future Alabama legislators but also invented a device that could be taken out of its originating context and used to bind state and local legislators in other times and places: constitutional property tax limitation.[15]

It did not take long for others to adopt it. The first were Redeemers in other southern states. Texas Democrats wrote limitations on local property tax rates into their constitution in 1876. Arkansas, Georgia, and Louisiana followed suit, as did the border states of Missouri, Kentucky, and West Virginia. Property tax limitation spread through these states as part of a wave of reactionary constitution writing that, in the words of Eric Foner, aimed to "dismantl[e] the Reconstruction state, reduc[e] the political power of blacks, and reshap[e] the South's legal system in the interests of labor control and racial subordination." From there, property tax limitation spread to the West, for no better reason than that several new western states held their first con-stitutional conventions in the 1880s and 1890s, and the delegates copied parts of other constitutions that sounded good. Constitutional conventions in states such as Utah, Wyoming, and North and South Dakota copied southern states' property tax limitations into their founding documents. By the end of the century, eighteen states, almost all of them in the South or the mountain West, had adoped constitutions that imposed at least some quantitative lim-itation on the rate of state or local property taxes.[16]

Constitutional property tax limitation proved to be a multipurpose tool. In the early twentieth century, some Progressives in the northeast and mid-west discovered new uses for constitutional tax limitation as part of a gen-eral package of property tax reforms intended to rationalize state and local taxation. In practice, the assessment of property values for tax purposes of-ten permitted local officials enormous discretion, and favorable assessments could be a valuable political currency. Some civic reformers hoped that leg-islation to limit property tax rates would curb corruption and disempower the political machines. If revenue-seeking local governments could not in-crease property tax rates, then they might have to increase their property *assessments* up to the legal standard—and thereby give up on favoritism. Other civic reformers saw property tax limitation as an indirect way to ensure economy in government.[17]

But it was not until another property tax crisis that constitutional prop-erty tax limitations began to spread rapidly. The Great Depression provoked a revenue crisis for state and local governments: while property values plunged, the expense of state and local government did not. State and local officials struggled to collect property taxes from income-constrained prop-erty owners who were being taxed at historically high rates on assessed val-ues that had not been adjusted adequately for worsening market conditions. Homeowners and apartment owners in several big cities threatened property tax strikes in 1932 and 1933. City managers described "hysterical attacks on government" by "local chambers of commerce, real estate board[s], taxpay-ers organizations, city club[s], and other organizations" that demanded prop-erty tax limitations and reduced spending. Farmers and bankers joined in. So did mortgage lenders, who discovered a sudden new interest in property tax limitation when they took possession of foreclosed properties and became liable for paying the taxes on them. The National Association of Real Estate Boards (NAREB) actively encouraged the campaign for property tax limi-tations by disseminating arguments and model legislation. "It must not be supposed that the proponents of tax limitation put forward such a measure as something ultimate, to be retained always," explained NAREB's secretary, Herbert Nelson. "We advance it only as a method which meets, ultimately, an urgent present need."[18]

Property tax limitation spread because it met *many* urgent needs. Interest groups campaigned successfully for new constitutional limitations on local property taxation in Ohio, Michigan, West Virginia, and Oklahoma. In California, after a grassroots initiative campaign for property tax relief failed at the ballot box, voters approved a compromise amendment to the state constitution that limited annual growth of city, county, and school district expenditures to grow no faster than 5 percent per year—an expedient designed to limit the growth of property taxes.[19] Tax experts who studied the "property tax limitation movement" of the 1930s were struck, often unfavorably, by the sheer variety of problems that constitutional property tax limitation was purported to solve. Advocates argued for property tax limitations to improve property values, restrain public expenditures, force state and local governments to broaden the tax base, and combat creeping socialism. The advocates of tax limitation reminded the economist Jens Jensen of the parable of the blind men and the elephant: they mistook it for a whip, an awl, a crowbar, a cloth, or a wall, depending on which part of the animal they touched; everyone agreed it was a tool, but a tool for what? The Princeton economist Harley Lutz dismissed the movement as an incoherent jumble of "diverse, illogical motives." An expert committee convened by the National Tax Association to evaluate property tax limitations titled the opening section of its report "A Movement of Mixed Purposes," and concluded wryly at the end of three years' study that the committee members were not in a position judge whether property tax limitations accomplished their intended purpose, because they could not tell what that purpose was: "Advocates of property tax limitation are apparently not agreed on the choice of emphasis as to the most important end to be achieved by the movement."[20]

These economists, despite their unanimous condemnation of constitutional property tax limitation, may have contributed to its spread by reifying it as a discrete policy tool. The progressive critics of constitutional tax limitation did not think of constitutions as organic wholes. Jensen ridiculed constitutional tax limitation as "an elephant of a new species . . . escaped from some menagerie of Untried Taxation Devices, into the green pastures of Ohio"; but ridiculous or not, it was an animal that stood on its own, and might wander from one pasture to another. Harley Lutz called it a "crude, unscientific device," but thereby conceded that it *was* a device, severable from the constitutions in which it was embedded. The proliferation of commentaries by experts like Lutz and Jensen—classifying types of constitutional property tax limitation, evaluating them, arraying them in tables, and debating their merits—all contributed to codifying the idea that constitutional property tax limitation was in fact a discrete and transposable object. It was a provision that could be cut from one constitution and pasted into the next, like a standardized part that could be lifted out of one machine and fit into another, there to accomplish a different purpose.[21]

Species of Property Tax Limitation

The property tax limitation movement of the Depression years left the legal landscape littered with constitutional tax limitations that would be rediscovered when the next property tax crisis came. It was decades in coming. World War II further increased the fiscal reach of the federal government, and for a time the combination of rising living standards and a new influx of federal funds relieved the pressure on the local property tax. But the New Deal had already laid the groundwork for the next crisis. The bargain that brought prosperity to working class Americans also made millions of workers into first-time homeowners who were newly sensitive to property taxes. The New Deal also popularized a language of rights that would come to be wielded against local government. The rising cost of schooling and other local government services in the postwar era exacerbated conflict over property taxation in the courts. By the mid-1960s, the combination of a rights revolution in the judiciary and a technological revolution in public administration were forcing local governments to rationalize the assessment of property. Computer-assisted mass appraisals replaced the whim of the assessor and its attendant potential for abuse; but they also increased the speed and accuracy with which real estate price increases turned into tax increases. Housing inflation drove up residential taxes, and long-term residents in many urban and suburban markets began to fear that rising tax bills could drive them out of their homes.[22]

The crisis came early to California, and policymakers and activists in that state turned to many different sources for policy ideas that might address the crisis. Liberals allied with organized labor generally argued for progressive tax reforms that would shift the burden from working-class homeowners onto business property and high-income individuals. Conservatives picked up and repurposed property tax limitations that had been devised in crises past, and drew on a century of experience to propose new constitutional limits on the taxation of wealth.

One strategy, devised by the Los Angeles county assessor Philip Watson, was modeled directly on the property tax limitations of the Depression era. Watson was an avid student of fiscal history who read deeply in the economics and law of the property tax. Watson collected boxes of material on the Depression-era campaign against the property tax in California, and consulted this history in drafting his first proposal for a new property tax rate limitation. His first attempt was a constitutional amendment to ensure that "the total ad valorem tax burden imposed in any tax year on all property in the State . . . shall not exceed one percent of market value to provide for the total cost of property related services," with an additional allowance for debt service. Following his Depression-era forebears, he recruited the backing of the California Real Estate Association. His proposal was opposed by the state's education lobby (schools objected to the exclusion of education from the definition of "property related services"), and voters rejected it roundly in 1968. His second effort, drafted after consulting with schools and a wider range of business interests, allowed for a more generous limitation: "The property tax shall be limited to 1.75% of market value for all purposes." It then added a long list of detailed instructions on how this total percentage was to be apportioned to cities, counties, and other local agencies. The resulting complexity may have hurt it at the ballot box. The provision applying to most school districts, for example, read as follows: "The tax levied by or on behalf of all intra-county taxing agencies, the boundaries of which are wholly within one county, or one city and county, shall not exceed in the aggregate FIFTY CENTS ($0.50) per ONE HUNDRED DOLLARS ($100) of assessed valuation of taxable property within each such county, or city and county." There were similar sections describing limits for *inter*-county taxing agencies, alongside detailed instructions for the number of "DOLLARS per ONE HUNDRED DOLLARS" that could be levied by a city, a county, or a consolidated city and county. Voters rejected it by a two to one margin.[23]

Another strategy, pursued by California's governor Ronald Reagan, had intellectual roots in neoliberal economics, and in particular in the Virginia School of political economy championed by James Buchanan. In the spring of 1972, Reagan convened a small group of advisers to draft a new proposal for a constitutional amendment that would restrain the growth of state and local government. The chair, Lewis Uhler, was a former John Birch Society activist who shared Reagan's mistrust of the welfare state. He managed to recruit a veritable *Who's Who* of neoliberal economists to the campaign advisory board, including Buchanan alongside the other future Nobel Memorial Prize winners Milton Friedman and Armen Alchian. The committee assumed a theory of government as a revenue-hungry Leviathan staffed by crafty, revenue-maximizing bureaucrats.[24] After months of deliberation, it produced a comprehensive plan that was designed to leave those bureaucrats no wiggle room at all. There were pages of dense definitions and equations ("the State Tax Revenue Limit," for example, to be derived from the "State Tax Revenue Limit Income Quotient" and the "State Tax Revenue Limit Population-Inflation Quotient," each of which had a formula of its own). They included a section with instructions for the proper computation of inflation rates—and then authorized an independent state commission to do the computation, presumably because existing state agencies could not be trusted even to do arithmetic when their budgets were on the line. The drafters plainly sought to minimize flexibility in interpretation and implementation. In the process they produced a constitutional amendment that read like exactly what it was, a document produced by a committee of economists.[25]

This was a losing strategy. These men were ideologues, not campaigners, and they lacked a feel for the politics of the property tax. Their amendment included property tax limitation almost as an afterthought, and with much less attention to detail than they devoted even to the computation of inflation rates. The property tax rate for each local government was to be limited to the rate levied in fiscal 1972 or 1973, whichever was higher, with a subsequent adjustment of some kind "to reflect cost variations due to cost-of-living or population changes not offset by assessed valuation changes or to allow for other special circumstances creating hardship for individual Local Entities." The precise adjustment formula and the precise definition of special circumstances and hardship were left to the state legislature—perhaps even, incredibly enough, to the Local Entities themselves. Democrats argued quite plausibly that it would not actually limit property taxes at all. Voters rejected this measure, called Proposition 1, by a vote of 54 to 46.[26]

Howard Jarvis devised a winning strategy for property tax limitation by taking yet a third approach: he stuck with the idea of a constitutional limit on the property tax, but radicalized the Depression-era precedent into a limitation on the growth not only of the *aggregate* local tax levy, but also of the tax bill of *every individual* property owner. Discovering the proximate intellectual sources of this strategy is not easy. Jarvis left few records and told many fables. He was not very knowledgeable about—or, apparently, very interested in—the details of state and local tax policy. Watson, who often debated him, complained that Jarvis sometimes misremembered, or simply misrepresented, the tax policies of other states, in order to invent precedents for his own ideas. Jarvis later claimed to have been involved in Depression-era state tax reform efforts in Utah, but he seems to have been lying. It is, indeed, easiest to say what his sources were *not*. They were not the neoliberal economists in the orbit around Ronald Reagan: Jarvis dismissed Reagan's Proposition 1 as an unintelligible policy—"you had to be a genius to figure out whether a yes vote or a no vote was a vote to reduce taxes," he said. Nor were they the historical researches of Philip Watson: although Jarvis copied the general idea of tax limitation from Watson, he deliberately ignored Watson's advice on just about every matter of detail. In early 1977, the two men met with an activist named Paul Gann to work out the legislative language of a new property tax limitation proposal. But when Watson, his health failing and his office under investigation, backed out of the campaign, Jarvis and Gann threw out his draft and penciled a new one that became Proposition 13.[27]

It was short but effective. In contrast to previous property tax limitation measures, which had presented the voters with pages of dense prose filled with fine conceptual distinctions and detailed schedules of tax rates and adjustment factors, Jarvis and Gann were brief, vague, and ungrammatical: "The maximum amount of any ad valorem tax on real property shall not exceed One percent (1%) of the full cash value of such property. The one percent (1%) tax to be collected by the counties and apportioned according to law to the districts within the counties." They allowed an exception to the 1 percent cap for servicing previously incurred debts, permitted the state legislature to increase other tax revenues upon two-thirds majority of each legislative house, and permitted local governments to impose "special taxes" if and only if two-thirds of their voters approved. The whole proposal was contained in ten short sentences.[28]

There was one additional, wholly original provision: a freeze on assessed values. The Jarvis–Gann proposal defined "full cash value" as the value that had been assessed for tax purposes in 1975, henceforth to be updated only upon change of ownership, and otherwise adjusted upward by not more than 2 percent per year. This assessment limitation effectively froze the distribution of property taxes in place. All of the other parts of Proposition 13, from

the rate limitation, the exception for debt service, to the use of legislative su-
permajorities to constrain tax increases, had precedent in the tradition of
constitutional property tax limitation. But the assessment freeze had no
precedent.[29]

The assessment limitation may have been a wholly improvised response
to a temporary emergency. At the time that Jarvis and Gann drafted their
amendment, assessed values in Los Angeles County were increasing rapidly,
in some cases doubling or tripling within a single year. Watson was of the
opinion that limiting the growth of assessments was terrible policy, but he
was not surprised when voters approved Proposition 13. Under the circumstances, he later said, "anything that got on the ballot would have won."[30]

The Shackles of the Past

Something else *was* on the ballot—a labor-backed alternative to Proposition
13 that might indeed have won but for a stroke of bad timing. In the spring
of 1978, while Jarvis and Gann were campaigning for their constitutional
property tax limitation, the California Federation of Labor and a broad coalition of its Democratic allies were campaigning for a more progressive alternative. Proposition 8 would have expanded property tax relief for
low-income senior citizens, lowered the tax rate on residential property,
limited the revenues of local government, and reduced homeowners' property taxes by 30 percent. In April, it was polling neck and neck with Proposition 13. On May 16, Watson's successor in the Los Angeles County assessor's
office released new assessments that showed the average home had doubled
in value—and the average homeowner would face double the taxes. The
nightly news filled with stories of Los Angeles homeowners who said they
would have to take second jobs or sell their homes to pay their property taxes.
By the end of May, polls showed a decisive lead for Proposition 13.[31]

The victory of Proposition 13 was not the inevitable result of deep frac-
tures in the New Deal order. This constitutional amendment was one among
many competing solutions to the property tax crisis, and its eventual triumph
over the alternatives was accidental. Once it was written into the state constitution, however, this policy became difficult to dislodge. Constitutional
property tax limitation created a new coalition where none had existed before. Homeowners now reckoned with fixed tax rates and low property assessments in perpetuity. As California real estate continued to increase in

value in the decades after 1978, the gap between the property taxes that Californians paid and the property taxes that they *would* have owed if they were
taxed on the market values of their homes grew wider and wider. The implied tax break was especially valuable to low-income homeowners. Polls
taken on the thirtieth anniversary of Proposition 13 showed it was more
popular even than when it had passed, and most popular of all among elderly
homeowners who were being taxed on market values that were decades out
of date. In a perverse parody of the New Deal bargain, a vested interest in
retirement security now bound working-class homeowners to a policy regime
that imposed permanent austerity on the public sector.[32]

Understanding how this bargain was made requires us to understand the
genealogy of the policy that made it. The drafters of Proposition 13 did not
deduce property tax limitation from an economic or political theory. They
improvised it to meet an urgent political crisis. But in doing so, they borrowed
elements of other public policies, themselves abstracted from other urgent
crises and archived for future use by earlier practitioners of the practical arts
of constitution writing and constitutional interpretation. Their political
imaginations were bound by, and often bounded within, the tradition of constitutional property tax limitation.

Some of the most celebrated theorists of neoliberalism offered theoretical justifications of Proposition 13 after the fact that characterized it as a blow
for liberty. Milton Friedman welcomed it as a sign of growing popular distaste for government and a preference for the freedoms of the market. James
Buchanan and his coauthor Geoffrey Brennan proposed a new theory that
justified constitutional limitations on the power to tax as devices for precom-
mitment. "Constitutional commitments or constraints become means by
which members of a polity can incorporate long-term considerations into
current-period decisions," they explained in their 1985 text, *The Reason of
Rules*. We should agree to constitutional limitations on taxation, in other
words, because we would rationally prefer fiscal restraint, but we know that
we cannot resist immediate gratification at the public expense. "Ulysses has
himself bound to the mast of his ship as it approaches the sirens' shore," they
wrote. "He recognizes his weakness of will; he does not trust his ability to
resist temptation, and he knows that if he succumbs, the larger purpose of
the voyage will be undermined."[33]

The allegory was inapt. In Homer's telling, Ulysses bound only himself,
and left his oarmen free, trusting that they would guide him past the sirens and
untie him when the danger was past. But the authors of constitutional prop-

erty tax limitations were, from the beginning, interested in shackling *other* people. They ruled certain tax decisions outside the bounds of the ordinary political process, turned fine quantitative distinctions into absolute prohibitions, and replaced majority rule with a minority veto, all because, unlike Ulysses, they trusted themselves and mistrusted the majority. Voters approved permanent constitutional limitations on the property tax when these were presented to them as the way to address temporary emergencies. But when the sirens were past, there was no one left free to unbind them from the mast.

CHAPTER 8

The Koch Network

Property Supremacist Ideology and Politics in the Twenty-First Century

Nancy MacLean

President Barack Obama's team had barely begun to settle in to their new offices when the ground began to heave beneath them. After an exhilarating inauguration that inspired viewers worldwide, Obama and his staff got to work on plans to save an economy hit by the worst financial crisis since the Great Depression. Just four weeks in, though, on February 19, 2009, the CNBC financial analyst Rick Santelli railed on camera against the president's plan to assist struggling homeowners who had been sold subprime mortgages by the banks. "Government is rewarding bad behavior!" he fumed. There should be no subsidies for "the losers' mortgages." Santelli summoned "capitalists" to his home city for a "Chicago Tea Party" protest. Right-wing media pounced on the call, spreading it far and wide with their hosts' embellishments. The dazed new denizens of the White House watched as their stimulus plan, the American Recovery and Reinvestment Act, criticized as far too modest by the leading economist and columnist Paul Krugman, among others, was re-branded as a "porkulus" fest by fast-multiplying local groups that claimed the Tea Party mantle. By April 15, Tax Day, some 850 communities had seen lo-cal Tea Party gatherings, given outsized coverage from Fox News and other right-wing media outlets.[1]

Seizing their name from the tax revolt in Boston Harbor that had helped launch the American Revolution, the Tea Party groups branded the president a "socialist." The label seemed kooky to Obama and most of the electorate, but it accorded with the Mont Pelerin Society founders' definition that any-one who relied on government to achieve social justice was a socialist (in time, the Americans came to include public education, the post office, national parks and just about anything beyond armies, courts, and police). "Libertar-ians led the way for the tea party," boasted a Cato Institute publication. They were "more than twice as 'angry' with the Republican Party" as other con-servatives going into the election, and that rage fed the challenge to Obama. "The tea party is united on economic issues," Cato's polling data showed, if "split on the social issues"—gingerly gesturing to the libertarians' willing-ness to exploit the religious Right and the racist reaction to the first black president. Through that unity on the economy, Cato kvelled, Tea Party ac-tivism was pushing the GOP to become "functionally libertarian."[2]

How is it possible that at the very moment the cause of capital suprem-acy should have been completely discredited by the conduct of Wall Street firms, it instead gained ground? Many smart political observers have tried to solve this puzzle. The explanations they have produced are not wrong so much as partial—but partial to the point of distortion because they were un-familiar with the core ideas driving the mobilization to block the new presi-dent from achieving what a resounding majority of voters wanted from him. Not knowing the deep history behind the sudden barrage from the radical Right in 2009 and thereafter, the analysts could not see how the actors who obstructed Obama were acting on an approach to government developed by James McGill Buchanan, the Nobel Prize–winning founder of public choice economics (more narrowly, the Virginia School of political economy), and other scholar activists with whom he worked from the late 1950s forward. Nor did they understand how Charles Koch and the network of organizations he cultivated from the 1970s forward had determined that Buchanan's ap-proach could get them what they wanted: a property supremacist transfor-mation of U.S. government and law that could advance by stealth, precisely because it was—and is—so unpopular it could not be achieved in the usual manner.[3]

The short answer, then, to the mystery of why market fundamentalism gained ground instead of enduring a historic rout is that the Koch network applied "a technology" that worked: an integrated long-game strategy to ap-ply Buchanan's insights and recommendations to change the very ground-ing of U.S. public life. Working from a base at George Mason University (GMU), now the very prototype of the corporate university, Koch and the cadre he had subsidized for decades as they built up a vast institutional apparatus were able to divert the course of history when a crisis created a vacuum. The strategy devised by applying public-choice thought is thus the essential missing piece needed to explain the events that followed the historic 2008 election. Without awareness of the ideas informing the various moves, it was difficult for even the most talented and determined observers to see how all the key players were playing their parts in an intricate composition whose choreography was as audacious as its endgame.

This chapter is its story. It could not be told without the revelatory investigations by some of the country's best journalists. But it also could not be told without attention to history: to how the ideas coming from Virginia School political economy as it developed after the 1950s linked battlefronts hitherto not seen as connected in a stealth plan to enchain democracy, which they deemed too troublesome to capitalists' liberty. Because the Koch team knew that voters would never willingly support this endgame, they concluded that it must be imposed upon the people, piece by piece. The mechanisms of imposition, this chapter shows, were many, and integrated for maximum effect. They included securing donor control of the Republican Party; defunding of the Democratic Left, by deception where needed; gaining control over easily manipulated statehouses (thirty as of this writing) both to rig the rules of the political process in favor of corporations and the political Right and to undermine both hard-won national standards and local progressive victories, and capture of the courts, the ultimate arbiters of the ground rules of U.S. public life.

*   *   *

The libertarian economist Tyler Cowen began laying the conceptual groundwork for all that would unfold after 2008 with a paper in 2000 called "Why Does Freedom Wax and Wane?" The heir to James Buchanan's realm, now spread over three Virginia zip codes, Professor Cowen has served as the general director of the Mercatus Center at George Mason University, working together with Charles Koch to make it into a libertarian citadel—and prime case of corporate donor capture of a public university—since 1998. The Mercatus Center enlists the authority that comes from association with a large public university, yet enjoys autonomy to advance the private political agenda its faculty members share with their top donor and the nonacademic operatives who staff the center. In fact, Charles Koch was initially Cowen's codirector of the enterprise; he remains on the nine-member Mercatus

board of directors. Koch was joined in that role by his top political strategist, the former GMU economics professor Richard Fink, and by Edwin
Meese, a leading figure on the Right all the way back to Ronald Reagan's first
governorship. Conveniently, Meese was presiding over GMU as rector, the
top oversight position, when Koch launched the bid to reroute history in
1997. The team was nothing if not well-funded, well-staffed, and determined.
In the new century, with Buchanan effectively retired to his country home,
Cowen stepped up as the top academic architect of Koch's daring project: to
transform America by stealth.[4]

"The strategy of Mercatus is to integrate theory and practice," Cowen's
paper informs readers from its downloadable spot on the center's public website. Indeed, Cowen produced the piece as a guide for Mercatus's Social
Change Project, reviewing research that could inform plans to achieve economic liberty. The project supplies what in today's parlance are called "de-
liverables" to policymakers, think tanks, foundations, media, and others with
kindred aims. (With its location on the Arlington campus of GMU next to a
Metro stop, Mercatus is but a twenty-minute ride from Capitol Hill, making
such contact easy.) Cowen was particularly interested in findings that could
help to eradicate the "restrictions on liberty" characteristic of twentieth-
century democracies.[5]

One key finding was that by the 1920s, in both Europe and the United
States, "the expansion of the voter franchise" beyond "wealthy male landowners" had produced the unfortunate result of enlarged public sectors. It
seemed that when other citizens, notably women in this timetable, could influence government policy, taxes went up. Cowen further explained that
"the elimination of poll taxes and literacy tests leads to higher turnout and
higher welfare spending." Mobilized voters pushing governments to act resulted in exactly the kinds of policies that Koch-style libertarians despise and
the Mercatus team works to combat, so Cowen next turned attention to the
few countries that "have reformed."[6]

Cowen offered Chile under General Pinochet as "the most successful"
such case. Through structural "reforms" locked in by constitutional revision,
Chile starkly reduced "rent-seeking through government favors" (translation: organized citizens making claims on government for what they cannot get as individuals from the market). As a case in point, the military
junta converted social security to a system of self-funded individual accounts
invested with private financial corporations. The results were so good,
Cowen joked, that others began to clamor that they "need a Pinochet." Chile

was the shining example of root-and-branch transformation, though there were others.

"The freest countries have not generally been democratic," Cowen observed of what the islands of economic liberty had in common. He pointed to Hong Kong and Singapore as free as well as to other cases: Peru under Alberto Fujimori and New Zealand from the mid-1980s to the early 1990s, which deregulated financial markets, privatized extensively, slashed taxes on the wealthy to create "a (nearly) flat tax," and undermined labor unions' bargaining power.

Cowen observed another interesting commonality, related to the lack of democracy, in the success stories: "In no case were reforms brought on by popular demand for market-oriented ideas." Again and again, he observed of the previous experiences, the pro-liberty cause had run up against a persistent problem: it wanted a radical transformation that "find[s] little or no support" in the electorate. Professor Cowen delivered the domestic action implication of his survey without mincing words: "If American political institutions render market-oriented reforms too difficult to achieve, then perhaps those institutions should be changed."

To inform the bid to change U.S. political institutions, Cowen offered tactical "generalizations" from the previous trials. In every case, "a precondition" was to make sure that "a small number of critical decision makers were conversant with market-oriented ideas on a highly intellectual level." A second precondition was that although most citizens would not want what those insiders sought, they would need to feel that "some form of radical change was necessary." This might just prove sufficient, because "public toleration is more important than deep public involvement." But an additional condition would likely help in securing such acceptance: "In each case traditional democratic constraints were to some extent attenuated." Although the economist was not specific about how traditional small-*d* democratic constraints might be attenuated, clearly, finding ways to keep voters from the polls would help. (In hindsight, it would be easy to build a list of other intentional efforts from the Koch-funded Right to offset long-standing guardrails.)[7]

The U.S. nut would be a tough one to crack, it seemed. Cowen counseled that "the weakening of the checks and balances" in the U.S. system "would increase the chance of a very good outcome" for the cause. Yet, given the pervasive regard for the U.S. Constitution, a direct bid to manipulate the system, if it set off alarms, could also prove "disastrous." Cowen's best advice was sudden percussive bombing. When the right opportunity arose, apply "big-bang style clustered bursts" to dispense with multiple restraints on economic liberty in the same surge.[8]

In the meantime, shaping public opinion was crucial, so as to prepare for success when the opportunity to inflict such a surge arose. Efforts should probably focus on men, because they "are more likely to think like economists" (women tend to anticipate the downside of economic liberty and therefore support government intervention, leading the Mont Pelerin Society's Fiftieth Anniversary conference planners to complain that feminism was "heavily socialistic"—and Charles Koch to fund the antifeminist Independent Women's Forum).[9] Research being done at George Mason suggested a good deal of irrationality in the electorate, which might be turned to advantage. "It might be possible for 'irrationally held' views to in fact support good policies," particularly if the cause were to enlist insights from "cognitive science and perhaps evolutionary biology." Knowledge of just how vulnerable humans are to hardwired drives that resist reasoned evidence, it seemed, might prove helpful in winning voters to an "unpopular" agenda.[10]

Changes under way in the media offered still more promise for the cause. Television's new fixation with private peccadilloes, as seen in the Clinton era, could leave viewers jaded and suspicious, thus sowing helpful mistrust of government (although some caution was in order, as the "cynicism may undercut some of the values needed to sustain a free society"). Moreover, Cowen pointed out, the emerging Internet, "appears especially well suited for rumor, gossip, and talk of conspiracy." Seeing the Internet's potential "to encourage minority political groups and radicals," Cowen had launched his own blog; more than a dozen Koch-linked GMU faculty members followed suit. The department chair, for his part (Walter E. Williams, the John M. Olin Distinguished Professor of Economics), began serving as a regular guest host for Rush Limbaugh's right-wing talk radio, the first out of the gate in the weaponizing of white conservative identity for unprecedented personal and political profit after the end of the fairness doctrine in broadcasting.[11]

Media visibility, though, would be the least of the team's influence on the country. Hillary Clinton had famously used the phrase "vast, right-wing conspiracy" in 1998, to characterize the coordinated forces that seemed determined to destroy her husband's presidency. She was widely mocked for this, because most educated citizens understandably discount explanations that smack of "conspiracy theory." But Clinton was sensing something very real then emerging, if not exactly capturing it. What the Koch-funded cadre and its allies were undertaking was not a conspiracy by a dictionary definition, for that involves agreement to commit an illegal act or a combination for an unlawful purpose, whereas the available sources suggest that the team exercised scrupulous care in staying within the law (with the possible exception of tax law for nonprofit entities). But it is also obvious from all that followed that theirs was an extraordinarily shrewd and well-coordinated effort. And it is one that from the outset concealed relevant information from the public and spread disinformation while actively exploiting false and "'irrationally held' views," to use Cowen's phrase. The truth is, social theory does not yet have an apt concept or term for such a venture because it is so utterly new in human history, unimaginable without the emergence of a multibillionaire determined to enchain democracy, advised by the best legal talent and strategic wizardry a vast fortune can buy, and enlisting state-of-the-art technology to achieve his ambitious endgame. A case in point: by the time of this writing, the Koch network had leveraged the vast reams of purchasable data on individual citizens to build a database (i360) with "detailed personality profiles on 89 percent of the U.S. population" for use in its political persuasion targeting. As the reporter says, drily, this "is a dangerous development, with potentially dramatic consequences for our democracy."[12]

The audacity of this quietly coordinated power grab is the more notable because the Koch-funded GMU team bore no little responsibility for the economic devastation that helped put Obama in office. Actors guided by public-choice thought had contributed to Wall Street's meltdown. The Law and Economics movement entrepreneur Henry Manne, recommended by James Buchanan to the university president to transform the George Mason School of Law, had first made his name by pushing for financial deregulation. The national lobbying operation conceived and led by GMU's Richie Fink as Citizens for a Sound Economy (CSE) had, since its founding in the 1980s, pushed Congress to free Wall Street from previous restraints. Senator Phil Gramm, a former Texas economics professor and the most devoted Capitol Hill convert to public-choice economics, had achieved the liberation of the financial sector in sponsoring and winning passage of the 1999 Gramm–Leach–Bliley Financial Services Modernization Act. As head of the Senate Banking Committee from 1995 to 2000, Gramm also deserved, according to a leading study of the crisis, "much of the credit—or blame—for [the] meteoric rise" of the credit default swap derivatives that encouraged Wall Street speculation on the people's homes, creating perverse financial incentives for the wildly irresponsible corporate risk taking that helped cause the collapse. Gramm's wife, Dr. Wendy Gramm, for her part, as head of the Commodity Futures Trading Commission from 1988 to 1993, assiduously advocated deregulation. While on the staff of the Koch project at GMU thereafter, she served as an inattentive audit committee member of the board of Enron Corporation, whose 2001 collapse through fraudulent accounting was an unheeded early warning of the catastrophe ahead.[13]

A season of shame and reflection might have seemed in order, then, for the Koch cause's thinkers and operatives alike. After all, the resulting near collapse of the financial system wiped out $14 trillion worth of household wealth, caused nearly eight million families to lose their homes, and rendered millions more jobless—and that was just in the United States.[14] The simple truth is that the cause of capital supremacy, built up since the founding of the Mont Pelerin Society in 1947, had been horribly wrong; its panaceas proved reckless beyond any of its members' imaginations.

As chilling as the economic outcome was, the political project continued, also despite empirical refutation. James Buchanan's prime argument for en-chaining the demos had already been decisively disproved by the opening of the new century. The policy decisions of the 1990s refuted what had be-come the core thesis of his later career: that government spending could only be contained with locks and bolts on democracy. By eliminating the deficit while shoring up Social Security and Medicare, President Bill Clinton and Congress, in testy countermoves, had shown that democracy could both balance its books and maintain highly popular programs to ensure citizens' economic security: in 1998 the federal budget went into the black for the first time since 1960. It was "the fiscal equivalent of the fall of the Berlin Wall," said the *New York Times*. As the new century opened, the federal surplus hit an unprecedented $236 billion. This surplus showed, it bears underscoring, that elected officials could solve a problem Buchanan had portrayed as en-demic and inescapable in a situation of unshackled majority rule. The Democratic Party under Bill Clinton had embraced markets to a degree that understandably alarmed many in the party's base.[15]

But the new bipartisan solicitude for corporate well-being and concern for disciplining government (to say nothing of labor unions, welfare recipi-ents, and those accused of crime) was not enough to satisfy the Koch-funded cadre. It was too late for facts to make a difference to them. The donors had invested big chunks of their immense disposable income in the plan to achieve the dream. True believers were at the switches. Operating the kind of "gravy train" that Buchanan had recommended back in the 1970s, they now had thousands of loyal "cadre" on retainer and at the ready.[16] No one, according to the extant documentary record, suggested even a pause.

*   *   *

Together, the Koch-allied cadre enlisted the joint shocks of 2008 to advance their world-historic mission. Its components were multiple. The crucial first task was to capture the Republican Party so it could be made into a battering ram for their ends. This would be achieved through a kind of pincers movement: it combined suasion of, as Cowen had recommended, "a small number of critical decision makers" with power plays to coerce the recalcitrant. The operatives of Americans for Prosperity (AfP), successor to Citizens for a Sound Economy, launched to avoid its public relations problems and legal liabilities after the Justice Department's vast and successful RICO suit against the tobacco corporations CSE served, would help organize bottom-up pressure on any GOP officials who failed to march in line, backed by top-down donor-funded primary challenges against those who balked. The team could then use this new party discipline to pass laws to break up or at least defame groups that pushed for government action, from the Association of Community Organizations for Reform Now (ACORN) to labor unions and Planned Parenthood. Those attacks did double duty, disempowering potential opponents while also being popular with the Tea Party base of older white Americans long suspicious of such groups (indeed, a notable number had been Barry Goldwater supporters in 1964).[17] Also in keeping with Buchanan's counsel, the team's members used U.S. federalism to advantage, gaining control of a growing number of state governments that could be used to hem in Washington. And following Tyler Cowen's outline, their allies in office acted with breakneck speed once they gained control to push through multiple radical changes in a percussive manner before stunned opponents could obstruct them.

Established groups linked to George Mason and the Koch funding network rushed to use both the Tea Party groups and the Republican Party to achieve economic liberty. Starting in 2009, their operatives pressed party officials to radically change the rules of U.S. governance at the national and state levels and through the courts and government agencies. The combined measures they rolled out over the next several years would end, wherever possible, long-standing rules that facilitated popular mobilization and claims on tax revenues and institute new rules that undercut inclusive democracy by impairing government's ability to respond to majority desires. With the double shock of the financial crisis and the hugely costly and unpopular Wall Street bailout dovetailing with the election of the country's first black president, the cause at last had its chance to reboot governance. The "science of liberty" Charles Koch had found at GMU and envisioned applying with "the kind of force that propelled Columbus to his discoveries," could now prove its value. It was time for America's "clustered big bang," with far-flung blows that would, Koch said, "mak[e] it in the nature of things for liberty to gain ground rather than yield."[18]

A slew of seasoned operatives steeped in Buchanan's variant of public-choice thought helped the Tea Party activists to compel Republican office-holders to do the cause's bidding. As two leading scholars of the unusual new movement note, the "unelected leaders of ultra-free-market advocacy groups based in Washington," despite their lack of ongoing contact, "were all too happy to speak in the name of grassroots Tea Partiers."[19]

The most powerful such force was the Koch project's grassroots arm, Americans for Prosperity. The GMU alumna Nancy Pfotenhauer led it, applying the insider political knowledge she had gleaned from work at Koch Industries, as chief economist on the Republican National Committee, and as a member of president-elect George W. Bush's transition team and then chief economist of his Council on Competitiveness. Showing how the cause affixed itself to those Cowen called "critical decision makers," Pfotenhauer went on to serve as a top economic adviser to the GOP presidential nominee John McCain in 2008, as did the longtime public-choice enthusiast Phil Gramm. That was quite a résumé for an MA economist but Koch Industries and GMU provided excellent grooming.[20]

But Pfotenhauer was outdone by her successor, Tim Phillips, appointed president of Americans for Prosperity in 2005. Phillips had trained in political science in the early 1980s at Buchanan's then home, Virginia Tech; he went on to found a political strategy firm with the Christian Coalition's Ralph Reed. There he helped clients from Dick Armey to George W. Bush win election, while also "servic[ing] Fortune 500 corporate clients" with "successful issue advocacy campaigns in a number of states."[21] Phillips had a keen grasp of how to get the atheist pursuers of economic liberty to link arms with the faithful enthusiasts of the religious Right, whose millions of votes would be needed to push the dream to victory.[22] By 2011, Americans for Prosperity claimed 1.5 million members in thirty-two states. Being so well-endowed by donors, Theda Skocpol and Vanessa Williamson report, the group "regularly pays to transport protestors across the country and even to international events."[23]

Two other public-choice devotees ran a kindred outgrowth of CSE called FreedomWorks: the former House majority leader Dick Armey and the much younger Matt Kibbe, who trained in economics at George Mason University and had earlier edited the journal published by Mercatus. One day after Santelli's outburst on CNBC, FreedomWorks rushed to connect with the sudden and still small protests. Armey was ready to make the most of them, having worked to cultivate just such a popular movement with Koch support since leaving Congress, without much luck. But now, right-wing outrage over the bailout and the first black president, a former community organizer (aka "rent seeker" in public-choice terms) no less, was enabling a breakthrough. The team at the helm of FreedomWorks rushed to turn the new groups into vehicles to carry out their political strategy.[24] Positioning themselves as spokesmen of the unrest with a *Tea Party Manifesto* and outreach to news outlets, Armey and Kibbe and their staff also provided guidance to local and state Tea Party groups in how to act as "watchdogs" to ensure that the kinds of Republicans who had defied Armey's pressure for discipline in Congress in the 1990s would now capitulate—or find themselves driven from office.[25] Indeed, the coauthors devoted a chapter of their manifesto to "Why We Must Take Over the Republican Party."[26]

Allied journalists assisted as they could. "This era brings yet another PC: 'public choice' theory," Amity Shlaes exulted in *Forbes* in August 2009. The Yale-trained libertarian journalist was well-known to followers of the financial press, from Bloomberg to the *Wall Street Journal*; at least half a million others knew her from her best-selling 2007 revisionist history of the New Deal based on Buchanan's thought. Now she wanted her followers to understand how his thinking spoke to contemporary affairs.[27]

What neither Shlaes nor the many other media figures who trumpeted the new energy on the Right explained to the public, however, was that fundamental to the interlocked public-choice-influenced strategy was an aggressive offense to break down the kind of group power that had opened up U.S. democracy over the twentieth century to working-class voters—those whose growing enfranchisement, in Cowen's accounting, limited economic liberty. The irony was sharp, because that attack relied on determined grassroots members who imbibed just enough public-choice analysis to believe that government had become a systemically corrupt enterprise to allow tax eaters to exploit taxpayers (a "swamp" to be drained), yet not enough to know that the ultimate goal was to take away programs they, too, valued, such as Social Security and Medicare and federal protection of their air and water quality.

The first big target was the Association of Community Organizations for Reform Now. Since its founding by veterans of the welfare rights movement in 1970, ACORN had become the most effective national federation of groups devoted to organizing residents of low-income communities to play a larger role in the political process. In campaigns for affordable housing, better schools, urban gun control, an end to predatory lending, the blocking of privatization, and more, its members' actions had won tangible improvements in the lives of hundreds of thousands of Americans—using the political process in precisely the way that so outraged libertarians. ACORN chapters had helped put living wages on the ballot (and won) in scores of cities and states. In 2008, it registered more than a million voters, many of them first-time voters, to promote a progressive political agenda. For all this, ACORN attracted bilious rage from the Right—and became the target of a 2009 sting operation out to destroy it with duplicity. They succeeded.[28] Wielded without scruples, the revolution in communications Cowen had heralded as potentially helpful had, indeed, provided a mighty weapon.

"Defunding the Left is going to be so easy," exulted the newly elected Tea Party leader Michele Bachmann after Congress rushed through the Defund ACORN Act, "and it's going to solve so many of our problems." Indeed, defunding the Left was an approach the public-choice enthusiast Dick Armey had urged since he was House majority leader in the 1990s. The Capital Research Center, on whose board the GMU team member Ed Meese had served, had been promoting the approach for years, lately with Tea Party groups as partners and ACORN as a particular target.[29]

The scheme worked so well that two years later, another alumna of the Koch-funded Leadership Institute would, as one report put it, "give Planned Parenthood the ACORN treatment" (that is, use doctored-video entrapment and disinformation in an effort to destroy it). Planned Parenthood's effectiveness in lobbying for federal and state public health funding (aka rentseeking, in Buchanan-style public-choice terms) was its real offense to the corporate libertarian cause. But its provision of abortion services made it an ideal foil to engage—and please—religious Right voters, just as attacking ACORN's registration of poor voters of color had outraged erstwhile grassroots white conservatives.[30] A colleague of Buchanan's had earlier warned of both ACORN and Planned Parenthood in a 2004 manifesto. "Uncle Sam: Sugar Daddy to the Feminists" proclaimed the chapter that included Planned

Parenthood. The book closed with a call to "get [the] lobbyist leeches off the taxpayer's tit." (Its author has since been promoted to Eminent Scholar and a chaired professorship in political economy at George Mason.)[31]

Meanwhile, the big-bang strategy moved forward on a crucial strategic front for which groundwork had been laid over the preceding years: action at the state level. If the cause and its allies in legislatures could successfully transform the public agendas and governing rules of enough states, on matters ranging from redistricting and the conduct of elections to labor policy, taxation, public education, and the environment, then those states could act as a kind of tourniquet on national policy, slowly but radically reducing federal actors' room for maneuver.

The principal coordinating agency was the State Policy Network (SPN), ostensibly independent but linked to the Koch apparatus in personnel and donors as well as mission. The SPN illustrates the way in which the apparatus throws sand in the eyes of citizens to conceal how centralized it is. "They appear to be advocating purely local interests," explained the astute researcher Lisa Graves, then executive director of the Center for Media and Democracy, "but what they are promoting is part of a larger national template to radically remake our government in a way that undermines public institutions and the rights of workers."[32] Building on Buchanan's ideas about how competitive federalism could advance economic liberty (as one of several "actions on the spectrum of secession" that used the threat of exit to countermand democratic governance), the SPN by 2009 had fifty-two think tanks operating in forty-five states. "We're all comrades in arms," announced the chair of the network, and indeed they were, working together much more closely than ordinary nonprofits. That is because the donor-imposed rules require network members to share their publications and best practices. Such forced collaboration leverages to maximum effect their research, publicity, and lobbying to privatize public education, push antiunion measures, curtail progressivity in tax codes, oppose increases in minimum wages, advocate restrictions on voting, and more. A team of GMU-affiliated fund-raisers including Stephen Moore, founder of the Club for Growth, implored wealthy donors to invest generously in the SPN. Seeing its great value to them, many did.[33]

One of the most gifted such network rainmakers was the SPN board member Whitney Ball; her career illustrates the interpenetration of the Koch network's ostensibly separate wings and the billionaire backing on which the entire enterprise depended. Ball had been a top fund-raiser at the Cato

Institute and the Philanthropy Roundtable before creating DonorsTrust. There to help her run it with the broadest possible influence was the GMU-based and Koch-backed Atlas Network, which organized ideological cross-pollination between groups and across nations (claiming over 450 partners in ninety-six countries by 2019). Over its first sixteen years, DonorsTrust raised and contributed almost $750 million to right-wing causes, and provided practical coordination of the far-flung apparatus. A case in point: DonorsTrust paid the fees for the purportedly independent State Policy Network groups to join the American Legislative Exchange Council (ALEC), for which Charles Koch had long ago contributed seed money.[34]

Winning power at the state level was crucial for another front of the battlefield that the GMU team had been studying and preparing for some years: redistricting for statehouse and congressional races. Specifically, they explored how drawing district lines in particular ways could reduce the influence of some voters and expand the influence of others in such a way as to reduce support for taxation and public spending.[35]

The North Carolina–based libertarian James Arthur ("Art") Pope had suggested at the time of Koch's first big gift to George Mason in 1997 that the project should consider "implementation at the state level." A longtime ally of Charles Koch's, Pope was a founding director of Americans for Prosperity.[36] Over the ensuing dozen years, Pope enlisted his family fortune to build up a model state apparatus to drive the effort to enchain democracy in North Carolina. On the eve of the 2008 election, the website of one of his SPN affiliates, the Civitas Institute, tutored readers in Buchanan's ideas about how and why government grows: "competition between political agents for constituency support through the use of promises of discriminatory transfers of wealth." Translation: elected officials who could spend other people's money would be approached by grasping hands and would fill them to get votes. The only way to stop it was to deny them that ability. This, a Civitas analyst argued, was "a lesson we must tattoo on our brains."[37]

Pope was a key player in an ingenious project to amass state-level power to transform the country by using redistricting to boost the power of Republican minorities over Democratic majorities and to pull the Republican Party to the right of its own voters in the process. The official name was the Redistricting Majority Project, or REDMAP. It demonstrates how minute attention to the rules enables the cadre to capitalize on the inattention of the electorate, and the opposition for that matter, to the particulars of the political game that make all the difference to the outcomes. Run by the Republican

State Leadership Committee for a trivial investment relative to a presidential election year (which enhanced the pitch to corporate donors), the investment helped produce massive Republican successes in the 2010 midterm elections, winning enough power in statehouses to enable the GOP to then control the all-important 2011 redistricting process using the results of the decennial census to shape the political map for the next decade or more. The project yielded vast overrepresentation of the Right in Congress, owing to a technologically sophisticated and aggressive application of that power to redraw district lines with an eye to their probable partisan—and policy—consequences, and in a manner kept secret to a degree never before seen.[38]

Nationwide, the plan worked with brutal effectiveness. As many Obama voters sat out the midterms, well-funded insurgents won historic Republican majorities in many state legislatures, gaining veto-proof control of twenty-one states, more than twice the number the Democrats controlled. Given the way Democratic voters were corralled by REDMAP, notes the investigative journalist Jane Mayer, who first revealed both the Koch attack on Obama and REDMAP, the U.S. "map looked red, with small islands of blue."[39] The toll is conveyed well by *Salon*'s editor in chief, David Daley, who wrote a revelatory book on REDMAP: "Without the protection of a fairly drawn district, the citizen is a pawn of billionaires who use the map of the country as a checkerboard to play politics on." And the game was a long one, all but invisible to those it was locking out. Daley explains that the GOP was, in effect, seeking "an unimaginable goal in a country that sees itself as a beacon of democracy: a veto-proof supermajority operating without majority support." Shrewd, amoral gerrymandering, guided by public-choice thought and state-of-the-art map-drawing programs informed by reams of purchasable data on voters and their communities, put that conquest within the funders' grasp.[40]

The bid gained invaluable help in mid-2010 from success in court on another measure that the Virginia School team had urged: opening the spigots to corporate money in politics. In *Citizens United v. Federal Election Commission*, a 5–4 majority on the Supreme Court ruled against any limit on election spending by individuals, corporations, and other entities, applying a grotesque interpretation of the First Amendment to dub campaign finance laws "censorship" of corporations. The victory came from the judges closest to the cause's affiliated Federalist Society, for which Koch had provided "seed money" and continuing support.[41] It was a startling instance of judicial activism from justices who had promised judicial restraint. "Through artful questioning," notes the veteran court reporter Jeffrey Toobin, Chief Justice John Roberts and Justices Samuel Alito and Anthony Kennedy raised the stakes of a relatively inconsequential case "into a vehicle for rewriting decades of constitutional law."[42] "The Roberts Court, it appears," Toobin concluded, "will guarantee moneyed interests the freedom to raise and spend any amount, from any source, at any time, in order to win elections."[43]

Between REDMAP and the influx of money after *Citizens United* on a scale that state races had never before seen, the result was a remarkable sweep of new Tea Party gubernatorial, congressional, and legislative candidates—goaded by the donors' team to deliver a big bang.

In a midwestern state once known for the absence of sharp elbows in politics, a governor newly elected with Koch-team backing showed how much control over state governments could advance the stealth cause—and how that control could introduce a new nastiness into public life. The Wisconsin governor Scott Walker proposed a "Budget Repair Bill" that took away collective bargaining rights that public employees had enjoyed for half a century—and that a vast majority of voters in his state and the country supported. The state's unions had already agreed to cuts to help fix the state deficit, and most taxpayers were willing to pay higher taxes to preserve benefits and services, so the alleged reason the governor offered was disingenuous. Rather than openly stating that he sought to lastingly debilitate the labor movement, he used the state's budget troubles as an alibi for a historic power play. Other changes in the bill showed, in their elaborate precision, the clear stamp of the public-choice emphasis on changing rules and altering incentives to get outcomes that democracy would not yield. Public employees could no longer be allowed to negotiate working conditions and benefits but only wages (with those held to the rate of inflation). Each contract would be only a year in duration, thus draining staff time and energy from addressing membership grievances or organizing new employees. Unions would lose the right to have dues deducted from members' paychecks and instead have to chase down individuals in a manner that encourages what public-choice economists call free riding, when those who benefit from goods or services do not pay for them. And, in a final slap, with the unions no longer able to do anything of substance for their members, they would face recertification elections each year. Walker's revolution in labor relations left most state residents and national observers gobsmacked—and set off an epic battle.[44]

Speaking privately, Governor Walker made clear that his bill was the culmination of a carefully considered strategy. "This is our chance to change
the course of history," he regaled his team. He gleefully reported to a caller
he believed to be David Koch, "We dropped the bomb." What Walker was
gesturing at in these comments was not, as so many commentators imagined,
simply a hyperpartisan bid to shrink a constituency that tended to vote Democratic. It was the essential first step of the multipronged plan informed by
Virginia School thought: to debilitate the labor movement before seeking a
thoroughgoing transformation of public life.[45]

Understanding the inner logic of the battle plan, the *National Review*,
the Right's premier conservative journal of opinion and a beneficiary of
Koch largesse, heralded "'public choice' theorists" as the inspiration behind
Governor Walker's abrogation of collective-bargaining rights for public-
sector workers. The magazine explained to readers not in the know that in
public-choice parlance, the concept of "special interests" meant something
distinct: it referred to people who turn to the government for advantages
they cannot get as individuals from the market. Public employees were its
case in point.[46] Further, Walker assured a donor that ending public-sector
collective bargaining "opens the door" to other radical changes, among
them turning over public resources and services to corporations through
privatization.[47]

The strategic plan to come at public-sector unions first and hard also
answered the question posed by one headline: "Teachers Wonder, Why the
Heapings of Scorn?"[48] The Right had been targeting public-sector educators
as enemies as far back as the New Deal era. And teachers' unions had lately
proved the most significant barrier to the Right's decades-long quest to
privatize schooling. "It would be difficult to find in the United States any
profession so dedicated to socialism as that of educators, and difficult to find
any argument for socialism as popular as the cause of public education,"
complained the *National Review*'s Kevin Williamson.[49] In other words,
public school teachers must be defamed precisely because they lead people
to believe in the kind of government libertarians hate. The demonizing of
teachers and their organizations is thus a necessary part of the overall political strategy.[50] Again, the subterfuge of the Koch quest for power: do not
admit openly that you despise the very idea of public education (what you
derisively call "government schools"), because most voters like it. Instead,
advance obliquely, by blaming "educrats"—language from the massive-

resistance-era attack that has reappeared among libertarians—for an alleged crisis that can be solved only by privatizing.[51]

* * *

Just as breaking down the potential for less-wealthy citizens to exercise group power was an essential part of the plan for slow-motion revolution, so, too, was transformation of the courts and constitutional understanding. Here, the first need was defense: to enlist the judiciary to prevent the acceptance of any new program that might come to have the popularity of Social Security—in particular, President Obama's signature achievement: the Affordable Care Act (ACA), which provided access to health insurance for millions of Americans who lacked it. At the helm of this effort was Michael S. Greve, who announced of the ACA: "This bastard has to be killed as a matter of political hygiene. I do not care how it is done," he said, "whether it's dismembered, whether we drive a stake through its heart, whether we tar and feather it and drive it out of town, [or] whether we strangle it."[52]

Greve, needless to say, was a devoted operative of the cause. As the chairman of the Competitive Enterprise Institute, a Koch-funded "do tank," by its own depiction, he helped devise the surprise litigation plan against the ACA that one court watcher predicted could send it into "a death spiral" when it reached the Supreme Court. Although he had a PhD in government from Cornell, law became his main focus. Influenced by James Buchanan, he became an advocate of "constitutional revolution" and a litigation strategist to control "the *demos*" they deemed too profligate. To shackle the power of the people, Greve cofounded and for a decade directed the Center for Individual Rights (CIR). Famed first for its landmark legal successes against affirmative action, it went on to file the *Friedrichs v. California Teachers Association* case that aimed to permanently hobble public-sector unionism in America by changing the rules on dues collection in the state with the highest number of public-sector union members in the country. The CIR-backed plaintiffs looked likely to win by the usual 5–4 right-wing majority in the Supreme Court, until its strongest ally on the court, Justice Antonin Scalia, died suddenly in 2016, leaving his colleagues deadlocked and the case moot.[53]

Greve left no doubt about what the courts could do for the cause: "We want to withdraw judicial support for the entire modern welfare state."[54] His work was deemed so valuable that the George Mason University School of

Law hired him in 2012. If Greve did not sound like a normal law professor, what with his calls for dismembering and tarring and feathering, nor was George Mason a normal law school. From the time the Law and Economics entrepreneur Henry Manne took it over in 1986 to its apt 2016 renaming after the newly deceased Scalia with Koch funding and laundered monies from the Federalist Society, the institution's inner circle had a distinctive mission. It was and remains a prime base of the cause.[55]

The long-term bid to transform both the law and the political process scored another 5–4 massive victory in the Supreme Court with the *Shelby County v. Holder* decision of June 2013. Republicans in Congress did not want to openly oppose the supreme victory of the civil rights movement, the Voting Rights Act (VRA), near the fiftieth anniversary of the 1965 Selma beatings that had made the country's majority see the need for federal action. Voting against renewal of the VRA's section 5, which required preclearance with the Justice Department of proposed voting restrictions in states that had historically discriminated at the polls, would cost incumbents votes, which is why the cause needed litigation and judicial activism for the big bang to succeed. In a case funded by DonorsTrust, Chief Justice John Roberts wrote for the court's majority. He portrayed the former Confederacy as a picked-upon region for no good reason anymore, saying that it was unfair that efforts to protect voters applied "only to some disfavored states." Those protections, Roberts insisted, now violated the "equal sovereignty" of the states.[56]

A surge of state-level measures to reduce turnout quickly followed, pushed by affiliates of the Koch donors' network, above all the American Legislative Exchange Council, and passed by allied GOP legislators. Once again, commentators portrayed the laws as a push for partisan advantage and racially motivated exclusion. There was plenty of evidence for both. Yet once again, there was something more far-reaching going on than they saw. Restrictive measures were aimed at those least likely to share libertarian views on political economy: not only African Americans and Latinos, but also young adults and lower-income elderly people. Because allegations of racial bias were the only ones that would have legal standing, critics could lose sight of how the measures aimed to keep voters away to insulate libertarian policies from likely opposition. Legal strategy, that is to say, skewed understanding of what was going on and why. This was not coming from atavistic white supremacy but from twenty-first century capital supremacy, even as the strategy relied on popular racism to prevail.[57]

Moreover, although the Koch-affiliated think tanks, advocacy organizations, and elected officials focused public attention on the new requirement for photo IDs, which polled favorably, they failed to explain why they pushed so hard also to eliminate or cut back practices popular among all voters. These included early voting, same-day registration, Sunday voting, programs for high school students to become automatically registered voters, the option of straight-ticket balloting, and more. As the new century opened, the irony was palpable: the modern world's first experiment in collective self-government was now nearly alone among peer nations in trying to make voting harder. The racial anxieties used to rally support for the legislation, pushed through with deceitful allegations of fraud, could be seen in one GOP governor's rationale: "Just because you haven't been robbed doesn't mean you shouldn't lock your doors."[58] It was a good dog whistle to activate the irrationally held views of conservative white voters, the kind of views Tyler Cowen had suggested might advance economic liberty, in this case among lower-income white voters who failed to understand that they themselves were also targets for the funders who believed that their fellow citizens were voting themselves a living.[59]

Pleased with the progress on so many fronts, the cadre created a new arm in late 2011 to fund the still more ambitious work of effectively taking over the Republican Party to use it to their ends: Freedom Partners Chamber of Commerce, soon dubbed "the Koch ATM" by the investigative journalist Kenneth Vogel. Freedom Partners supplied the dark money that network donors contributed in the millions to wings of the effort, such as Americans for Prosperity, the Club for Growth, and Heritage Action for America. All worked together, mobilizing varied constituencies, to force the Republican Party to do the donor's bidding in Washington and the states.[60]

As the 2012 elections approached, the team was heady with expectation. Mitt Romney was something of an empty suit, eager to please the cause yet also so opportunistic in lurching from earlier moderation to the far right of the GOP's presidential lineup that few trusted him. Romney's biggest gift to the Koch project was his choice of a running mate: Representative Paul Ryan of Wisconsin, an old friend of Governor Scott Walker. Grover Norquist spoke for the whole operation when he told an interviewer "he did not expect Mr. Romney to lead as president. He just wants him to sign the bills that put Mr. Ryan's vision into practice."[61]

Ryan had outlined a revolutionary vision in his detailed budget proposals, "A Roadmap for America's Future." Ryan was a devoted lieutenant on whom the team could rely. He credited the libertarian novels of Ayn Rand for his worldview (and made his staff read them), but the intellectual and strategic content of his road map owed more to his mentor Jack Kemp and the Virginia School of political economy orbit around him. Indeed, after leaving Congress, Kemp had gone on to found a policy "action tank" called Empower America that merged with the Kochs' Citizens for a Sound Economy in 2004 to form FreedomWorks. Ryan had served as Kemp's assistant in that effort before running for the House himself, so it is not surprising that the Ryan plan, as one critic jabbed, was a blueprint to "repeal the 20th century." Substituting "self-provision" for social insurance was its long-gestating purpose, one translated by an editorialist as "a sweeping attempt to dismantle the social compact."[62]

Here again, smooth operating belied the calculated exploitation of what Cowen had called "irrationally held views" to advance ends not wanted even by those upon whose votes the cause counted. The rank-and-file Tea Party activists who backed Ryan saw him as the House leader of their quest to slash federal spending and stop "moochers" from laying claim to their taxes. Their tendency to assume the abhorred "freeloaders" said to be undermining America were racial minorities and immigrants—even as whites like themselves actually received the lion's share of government benefits—was a perfect illustration of the kind of wrongheaded beliefs that Cowen had suggested could be useful. As the political scientist Theda Skocpol notes, "U.S. federal spending is overwhelmingly channeled to national defense, military veterans' benefits, Medicare, and Social Security," and virtually no grassroots Tea Party members wanted to see Social Security or Medicare privatized, which was a core part of the Koch team's plan. To put it in blunt terms, the libertarians exploited the GOP base's animus against President Obama and lack of understanding of who the actual beneficiaries of most federal spending were to advance the Koch network's program against the Tea Party members' own commitments to the social welfare programs that accounted for most federal spending.[63]

Guided by public-choice thought and professional pollsters and message crafters, Ryan and his insider allies became adapt at disinformation: framing measures to ultimately destroy programs as "reforms" to improve them. His "Roadmap" assured such voters that it "rescues and strengthens Medicare, Medicaid, and Social Security—allowing them to fulfill their missions and making them *permanently* solvent." If making the programs permanently solvent and trimming the deficit were really the main concerns as stated, though, Ryan would have acceded to increasing tax revenues, which many leading economists urged. But he was mapping a route to a different goal, one long desired by the strategists backing him: to privatize Medicare and Social Security and, as some editors observed, to "liberate business and the rich from the inconveniences of oversight and taxes."[64] It was "an enormous, destructive con job," warned the Nobel laureate and columnist Paul Krugman, to move in "a policy direction the public would not support if it were clearly explained."[65]

The states have a particular advantage for advancing this project: the vast majority of citizens do not follow state politics closely. The minority that does skews older, whiter, and wealthier than the electorate that tracks national politics. Moreover, with geographically based representation, state-minded voters carry power far beyond their numbers. The Virginia-guided strategy exploits this vulnerability of the U.S. federal system. After all, Tyler Cowen had advised them that only "toleration" was really needed, not active public support.

The state strategy had yet another virtue for the long game: it could accustom growing numbers of citizens to changes that most would see as too radical to consider at the national level by first normalizing them where they would face less resistance. A case in point: flat taxes. Ending progressivity in the tax system would undo a principle that by the Eisenhower era was bipartisan and widely viewed as an application of Judeo-Christian ethics and the New Testament maxim "For unto whomsoever much is given, of him shall be much required." But the libertarian Right had never gotten over its outrage at the income tax, which had spawned the first modern "rich people's movements," as the historical sociologist Isaac Martin aptly dubbed them.[66] Today, when members of the Koch cadre choose a specific date for when democracy went awry in the twentieth century, they often point to 1913, when a majority of Americans, through their representatives in Washington and the states, gave the government license to levy taxes on income, assigned in proportion to ability to pay, in ratifying the Sixteenth Amendment. The most vocal individual advocates of flat taxes to replace graduated income taxes are enthusiasts of public-choice economics. They include the FreedomWorks founder Dick Armey, the former Texas senator Phil Gramm, the Americans for Tax Reform president Grover Norquist, and the billionaire investor Steve Forbes.[67]

The team had a chance for a state trial of flat taxes when the 2012 elections supplied the GOP with complete control of North Carolina, including the governorship and both houses of the General Assembly. Guided by the donor-funded institutions built over the previous decade, North Carolina's new Republican majority instituted the most far-reaching version of the overall strategy. "They scrapped North Carolina's progressive income tax and replaced it with a flat rate," explains the budget and tax expert Alexandra Forter Sirota, thus "shift[ing] the tax load further onto working- and middle-class taxpayers while giving millionaires a significant tax cut."[68]

One additional tax measure they pushed illustrates well how radical change of rules of the kind Buchanan long advocated could lock in the libertarian agenda: the Taxpayer Bill of Rights (TABOR) proposed a constitutional amendment that limits state spending to population growth plus inflation. The idea is to prevent the people's representatives from adjusting spending without inflicting massive cuts to compensate for any increases.[69] No one caught its purpose better than the veteran state politics reporter Rob Christensen, who wrote of the ALEC-affiliated legislators promoting it: they "fear that their libertarian brand of conservatism is not politically sustainable in a democracy, and they are trying to constrain future legislatures."[70]

Another key base of oppositional power that had obstructed the cause of economic liberty for decades was higher education. Buchanan had set up his own first outpost at the University of Virginia in 1957 with a mission to undermine the prevailing scholarly support for twentieth-century interventionist government. In 1969, to combat the student movements sweeping campuses, he had produced a blueprint for how to undercut dissent by radically changing rules and incentives in public universities with measures such as full-cost tuition, an end to shared faculty governance, and administrators who would behave more like chief executive officers (CEOs). After 2010, as the Koch-funded project moved forward in the states, its representatives pushed to enact proposals along these lines. They sought to cut spending, raise tuition, end need-based scholarships, reduce faculty governance, and undermine support for the liberal arts curriculum (particularly those parts of it most known for dissent). In North Carolina, Louisiana, Mississippi, Iowa, and Wisconsin they pushed out chancellors who would not do their bidding.[71] "There is a difference between a conservative and a vandal," wrote a Milwaukee corporate attorney and alumnus of the University of Wisconsin. "What Scott Walker and the Republican legislature are doing to the University of Wisconsin is not conservative. It's an act of destruction."[72] Creative destruction, one might add, to advance the libertarian cause by further clearing the field of obstacles.

*   *   *

When the *New York Times* reported in 2013 that "open warfare is breaking out among rival Republican groups," it grossly exaggerated, because by then the so-called Republican establishment was subordinated by the once-outsider cause's cash and deeply enmeshed with its various wings.[73] The GOP was ever more visibly cowering under the pressure of occupation by the Koch-backed Right, startlingly so in Congress. On issue after issue, a minority of determined advocates of economic liberty was running the show from the wings and upstaging the official leadership, secure in the knowledge that their cothinkers and benefactors would reward them and punish GOP office-holders who failed to comply. Together, they and the operatives who backed them had made the party, in the words of one bipartisan analysis, "ideologically extreme; contemptuous of the inherited social and economic policy regime; scornful of compromise; unpersuaded by conventional understanding of facts, evidence, and science; and dismissive of the legitimacy of its political opposition."[74]

And that was four years before the victory of Donald Trump.

The decades-long struggle charted here illustrates just how serious the Koch plan to transform the country is. Its bottomless reserves of cash, weaponization of Buchanan-style public-choice thought to reverse engineer the policies of the twentieth century, and vast network of interconnected organizations working toward the endgame have advanced the project so far that it is, boasted the leading operative Mark Holden in 2015, "close to winning"— not least because the critics "don't have the real path."[75] Perhaps they do now.

PART III

Capital and Labor in the Twilight
of the New Deal

CHAPTER 9

Economic Royalists and Their Kingdom in the New Deal Era and Beyond

Nelson Lichtenstein

In his June 1936 speech accepting the Democratic National Convention's re-nomination, President Franklin Delano Roosevelt famously denounced the "economic royalists" who had "carved new dynasties" and "created a new despotism." Decrying the pervasive influence of the corporations and banks, which had flourished since the late nineteenth-century merger movement, FDR saw concentrated industrial and financial power as a threat to democracy itself. "The hours men and women worked, the wages they received, the conditions of their labor—these had passed beyond the control of the people, and were imposed by this new industrial dictatorship."[1] The New Deal solution, of course, called upon the "organized power of Government" to counter "economic tyranny" and reanimate democratic norms in both civil society and within the world of work and market exchange.

The metaphorical language deployed by FDR—citing royalists and despots—made clear to all his auditors that the object of presidential scorn was not an economic abstraction, like inequality, financial speculation, or an unpredictable market, but concrete institutions often led by men—Ford, Du-Pont, Morgan, Sloan, and Whitney—whose names were familiar to many a household. They presided over a set of giant, highly integrated institutions whose regulation and democratization was essential if the New Deal were to truly transform the country and uplift plebian America. In truth much New Deal statecraft regulating agriculture, the service sector, local banking, and the coal and garment industries faced no set of powerful executives at the command of giant corporations. But the ideological and policy heart of the reform impulse from the Progressives onward saw the taming of the oligopolistic, highly integrated corporation as essential to the fate of U.S. democracy. "Combinations of industry are the result of an imperative economic law which cannot be repealed by political legislation," asserted Theodore Roosevelt in his "New Nationalism" speech of 1910. "The way out lies, not in attempting to prevent such combinations, but in completely controlling them in the interest of the public welfare."[2]

Although U.S. corporations have been chartered and structured in a remarkably wide variety of ways over the past two centuries, the corporation form that Progressives and New Dealers saw as the object of the reform impulse was one in which managerial authority coincided with virtually the entire process that produced and/or distributed a tangible good or service.[3] Most U.S. companies have not been as vertically integrated as Ford, U.S. Steel, or IBM in their heyday, but that unified organizational structure served as a template whose imaginative reach was enormously influential, certainly in terms of regulatory law, labor relations, and public perception. To the extent that these entities could be held responsible and accountable, they could be regulated and reformed. Laws governing the health, safety, and environmental conditions under which production took place or services were rendered covered all operations of a corporation that lay within the legal and administrative reach of management. Wagner-era labor law sought the internal democratization of the corporation by postulating a pluralistic division of economic power in which "management" committed a large slice of the entire production organization—today we would call this the supply chain— to abide by a contract negotiated between itself and a union or unions representing a majority of the workforce.[4]

That vertically integrated structure is today largely in eclipse because of the disaggregation and fragmentation of the firm. We live in a world, domestic and international, of supply chains, contract production, temp work, franchising, and self-employment. Regardless of the actual content of regulatory law, such atomization has subverted the capacity of the polity to subject the corporation to regulatory control, thereby marginalizing a core New Deal impulse. But it would be a mistake to assert that the global market has simply become more potent and pervasive, depriving even the management of modern firms like Amazon, Walmart, and Nike of the administrative power held by those once at the command of General Motors and General Electric. Nothing could be farther from the truth because, as this chapter demonstrates, contemporary supply chains, whatever the legal, corporate, or global form, are highly integrated production and service entities in which top management uses new forms of technology to exercise a level of comprehensive and intrusive control that would have been the envy of even the most energetic executives of the early twentieth century.

This essay explains some of the reasons, often labor-related, for the erosion of the vertically integrated corporation, not just in terms of their global sourcing strategy but also from a domestic perspective. From the 1950s onward, the attempt to elude the burden of the New Deal–era regulatory regime, including the encouragement it offered to trade unions, proved a powerful incentive for management in many heretofore highly integrated firms to outsource labor, disaggregate production, and franchise their products and services. This has created a regime of "fissured employment," to use the phrase coined by management theorist David Weil, in which executives and the firms over which they preside have sought to absolve themselves of the legal and economic responsibilities that were once thought intrinsic to the managerial function.[5]

During the first half of the twentieth century the large, vertically integrated corporation seemed the template for business organization and an engine of economic growth. The radical decrease of transport and communication costs in the nineteenth century created conditions for a collapse of geographical barriers and the increasing integration of the domestic market. Larger markets allowed a shift to higher-fixed-cost methods of production and distribution, which in turn lowered unit costs at higher and higher levels of output. Not all firms and markets underwent this transformation, but many of the most iconic firms, employing large and growing workforces, underwent a transformation in which wholesalers, vendors, merchants, and other market makers were marginalized in favor of a visible managerial hand. With its own rubber plantations, glass plants, and steel mills, and a dealer network that was formally independent but under Dearborn's thumb, Ford took vertical integration to an organizational extreme; likewise United Fruit with its own Central American banana plantations, came to define the imperial corporation; and U.S. Steel, with its captive coal and iron mines seemed an industrial autocracy. AT&T advanced corporate research and development (Bell Labs) even as women manufacturing operatives at Western Electric served as research subjects for innovations in what we would today call human resource management. For these companies and all those that sought to emulate their vertical structure, supply chains and labor markets gravitated toward an internalization and bureaucratization during these decades. Even midcentury retailers like Sears and A&P took ownership control of some heretofore independent manufacturing firms whose appliances, hand tools, and baked goods now became store brands.[6]

In the early 1930s, when Ronald Coase, then a young British socialist, first spent time in the United States, he visited Detroit and came up with a puzzle: How could economists say that Lenin was wrong in thinking that the Russian economy could be run like one big factory, when Ford, General Motors (GM), and other vertically integrated firms seemed to be doing very well indeed? They were privately owned planning bureaucracies, a point Peter Drucker would later make in his own far more extensive study of GM management. But not all corporations were gigantic. Some were small, highly competitive, and limited to but one part of the value production chain. In his seminal essay of 1937, "The Nature of the Firm," Coase answered his own query with an insight about why firms exist in the first place. They were "islands of conscious power" like lumps of butter coagulating in a pail of free-market buttermilk. Outside the firm, price movements direct production, but within a firm, market transactions are eliminated and in their place is substituted the entrepreneur-coordinator, who directs production.[7]

So firms are organizations that self-consciously plan, but unlike in the Soviet Union, where coercive methods were the norm, in a capitalist economy differential market or transaction costs determine the degree of vertical integration of any given firm in any given market. If markets were costless, reliable, and transparent, firms would not exist. Instead, executives would build products or sell services through a plethora of arm's-length transactions. But because markets, both for goods and labor, are costly to use, which is a function of transport and communication expenses on the one hand, and custom, expectations, and regulation on the other, the most efficient production processes often take place in a firm, which requires a managerial strata necessary for nonmarket coordination. Alfred Chandler would later historicize this insight in his masterwork, *The Visible Hand: The Managerial Revolution in American Business*, published in 1977.[8]

The accommodation of the vertically integrated corporation to a more democratic and republican ethos has therefore been a central hallmark of political and economic reform. What is not so obvious, however, is that the very subordination of the market to the bureaucratic management of these corporations greatly strengthened the hand of the early twentieth-century reformers. If managers rather than markets guided the fate of these large

institutions, then their legitimacy, or at least that of their governance structure, might well be called into question.[9]

The key text for this effort, the book that a contemporary described as
"the law, the logic and the philosophy of the New Deal," was *The Modern Corporation and Private Property*, published in August 1932 by Adolf Berle and
Gardiner Means. Berle was a lawyer and Means an economist. Both were the
offspring of Congregational ministers, and both were familiar with the practical operation of the U.S. corporation. Their collaboration began before the
financial crash; indeed, when the book appeared three years later, they hardly
took note of the Great Depression, because their argument hardly depended
on the existence of an immediate economic crisis.

But the book, which instantly became a controversial classic, provided an
ideological rationale for New Deal planning, consumer activism, labor organizing, and financial regulation of the large corporation and, by extension, of
all U.S. capitalism. Berle and Means argued that America's two hundred largest corporations, which then controlled one-third of the national wealth,
had themselves abridged the fundamentals of a liberal capitalist order. Berle
and Means were not Brandeisian "small is beautiful" trustbusters. The giant
corporation was "the flower of our industrial organization." Concentration
was a problem, but not for its own sake. Something more fundamental was
wrong in that the immense power of those who ran America's largest corporations was essentially unfettered, not only by the state but also by those who
were their ostensible masters: the shareholders themselves.[10]

Not only had oligarchy replaced competition, but also, and of even more
consequence, management had usurped the prerogatives of traditional
ownership. If the shareholders had therefore lost control of the corporation
to a set of unelected, self-perpetuating managers, then the modern corporation could best be understood not in terms of "the traditional logic of property and profits . . . not in terms of business enterprise but in terms of social
organization." And like the church, the military, and the state, such power
had to be either regulated or democratized if a republican government were to
exist. The rise of these illegitimate controlling elements, with their potential
for abuse, has now "placed the community in a position to demand that the
modern corporation serve not alone the owners or the control but all society."
Over and over again they wrote, the U.S. corporation has "ceased to be a
private business device" and has become "a major social institution."[11]

Although historians have subsequently demonstrated that in the early
twentieth century there were relatively few firms in which a dispersed range

of stockholders were effectively disenfranchised by professional managers, this critique of the corporation nevertheless exemplified a turn toward the "socioeconomic" mode of reformist thought identified by Howard Brick in his *Transcending Capitalism: Visions of a New Society in Modern American Thought.* With Thorstein Veblen, who denounced the "make-believe" property rights of modern shareholders, and Rudolf Hilferding, who postulated a new era of "organized capitalism," many reformers in the middle decades of the twentieth century rejected the vocabulary of Smithian competitiveness.[12] Private property, private enterprise, individual initiative, the profit motive, wealth, and competition have simply "ceased to be accurate" ways of naming the most important features of modern business.[13] The Tennessee Valley Authority (TVA) head David Lilienthal thought he presided over the kind of technocratic organization that would prove a template for other big combinations of management and modern science. In the 1950s he became a business consultant, but as Richard Hofstadter has pointed out, this shift in roles represented no change of heart; rather it "underscored his ability to find in private organization many of the same virtues that as TVA administrator he found in public enterprise."[14] As Roland Marchand has noted, large corporations themselves adopted some of this perspective, if only to accommodate reform impulses, by describing themselves not so much as a competitive business entities but as "institution[s]" infused with all the connotations of civic beneficence characteristic of other nonmarket entities, including hospitals, universities, foundations, and even government agencies. Colby Chester of General Foods admonished fellow industrialists that the U.S. businessman could no longer "consider his work done when he views the income balance in black at the end of an accounting period." Now it was "necessary for him to demonstrate the social virtue of these accomplishments to the public." Likewise, Owen D. Young of General Electric remarked in 1936 that as "a great public institution," General Electric had to accept "more and more obligations for public discourse and public activities."[15]

If big, vertically integrated corporations were not market mechanisms themselves, and if shareholders were thought to exercise neither proprietary nor popular control, then the door was open to outside regulation and internal reform. As a Roosevelt Brains Truster, Adolf Berle and other like-minded reformers played a large role in writing some of the key regulatory laws of the early New Deal, laws designed to correct the specific abuses illuminated by *The Modern Corporation and Private Property* and the many books, investigations, and congressional hearings that followed.

Even more important, and important for the thesis of this chapter, was the rise of labor. Corporate reformers of the New Deal era wanted a labor movement, first to serve as a Keynesian mechanism whereby aggregate demand might be enhanced without an even greater dependence on government spending and public employment projects. Without a broad income tax, a welfare state, or a large military, the state capacity for such countercyclical Keynesianism simply did not exist.[16] But even more important and at the time far more popular, was the effort to get inside the black box of the corporation to constitutionalize its internal operations, equalize wages, and make top management responsible and responsive to other stakeholders, of which organized labor seemed the most significant. Such a labor movement would police the new wage and hour laws, rationalize and make more equitable wages throughout every stage in the corporate value chain, and make corporate executives accountable for decisions once thought the exclusive prerogative of management.

During World War II and the generation that followed, experiments in tripartite governance—labor, management, and public/government—were frequently proposed and sometimes instituted. Corporatist arrangements of this sort almost always faced bitter opposition from the private sector, but a sizable slice of top executives did, reluctantly, accommodate themselves to collective bargaining over wages and the quaintly named "fringe benefits" that would loom so large on corporate account books from the 1950s onward. These New Deal/laborite reforms had a large effect on the internal structure of the working class and of the corporation itself: real wages more than doubled in the years 1939 to 1973; wage inequalities between working-class occupations declined, internal labor markets, often with formal systems of seniority promotion, became highly validated, and during a midcentury era that economists have called the great compression, income inequality declined. The pay gap between executives and line workers shrank, but of equal import, so too did the distance between the incomes of janitors and office workers, between garment workers and auto workers, and between retail clerks and truck drivers.[17]

The mid-twentieth-century heyday of the vertically integrated firm coincided with the rise of a social democratic reformism in the United States that promised to marginalize the market and subordinate the profit motive to institutional growth and stability. This may have been wishful thinking in the long run, but for several decades it offered Progressives and New Dealers a powerful sense that history was on their side.[18] Berle and Means thought that if capitalism were to survive, "the control of the great corporations should develop into a purely neutral technocracy, balancing a variety of claims by various groups in the community and assigning to each a portion of the income stream on the basis of public policy rather than private cupidity."[19] Indeed, many students of postwar management now saluted the separation of share ownership from management control. It would not lead to the hegemony of an overweening and self-interested executive strata, but instead to a more rational business technocracy. "We now know that management is a generic function of all organizations, whatever their specific mission," wrote Peter Drucker in *Post-Capitalist Society*, "it is the generic organ of the knowledge society."[20] Since the vertically integrated corporation had, in effect socialized production, corporate managers could pursue goals other than profits, including sales, growth, and the prestige that came from producing high-quality products of advanced technology. "Progress Is Our Most Important Product," asserted General Electric in one of its midcentury advertising campaigns. And as Ralph Dahrendorf put it, "Never has the imputation of a profit motive been further from the real motives of men than it is for modern bureaucratic managers."[21]

All of this seemed antiquated by the end of the 1970s, a decade characterized by a chronic profit squeeze, a stock market slump, and the dramatic rise to policy prominence of conservative intellectuals, politicians, and economists who sought to return to a world antedating that of Berle, Means, Drucker, and Keynes. Milton Friedman's 1970 manifesto, "The Social Responsibility of Business Is to Increase Its Profits," published in the *New York Times Magazine*, proved a clarion call. Asserting that the corporation was an "artificial person," in which the shareholders should reign supreme, Friedman declared those executives who concerned themselves with the "social responsibilities of business" little more than thieves, who abrogated unto themselves or their favored interests the corporate earnings that rightfully belonged either to shareholders, consumers, or even workers, whose wages were depressed when companies failed to maximize profits.[22] Corporations had to obey the law, of course, but Friedman's repudiation of the idea that corporations did have or should have a social and political character devalued the idea that these institutions were bureaucratic entities whose growth and perpetuation necessarily marginalized the profit motive.[23]

The ideas of intellectuals like Milton Friedman might have had little traction had not corporate America already been faced with two highly consequential challenges. The first was the demise of the corporate conglomerate, itself a product of the hubris that infected top management during the prosperous postwar era. Conglomerates like the now forgotten Textron, Ling-Temco-Vought, and Litton Industries were aggregations of once distinct companies in wildly disparate industries, linked together by sophisticated management and the sort of clever finance and stock manipulation designed to avoid taxes and boost share prices. They were all the rage during the "go-go" sixties, but their Icarus-like flight came crashing down at the end of the decade when stock prices dropped and the Securities and Exchange Commission finally became more skeptical and aggressive. In the fire sale that followed, a new generation of management consultants convinced executives and investors that all firms, conglomerate or otherwise, should be thought of as composed of a portfolio of investment opportunities in which the "dogs" must be eliminated, the "cash cows" milked, and the "stars" nurtured with new money and executive attention. Once this mental revolution was assimilated and propagated, the successful chief executive officer (CEO) would understand his function not as that of a bureaucratic manager but rather as an investor continuously evaluating the value and prospects of each unit within the enterprise over which he or she presided. All this was advanced by the digital revolution that greatly reduced those transaction costs whose existence Ronald Coase had thought such an important key to the construction of big, bureaucratic business enterprises; but now savvy managers could efficiently buy rather than build component parts and services on the open market. Not unexpectedly, the pace of business divestments, mergers, and reorganizations accelerated mightily in the 1970s and afterward.[24]

The rise of foreign economic competition in the 1970s—it was not yet called globalization—also contributed to the potency of Friedman-like ideas about the structure and purpose of the corporation. The idea that the top two hundred U.S. firms monopolized a continental market, thereby administering prices and devaluing wage competition, vanished as oil prices surged and East Asian manufacturers shipped cars, consumer electronics, and clothing to U.S. consumers. There were no longer three car companies with an oligopolistic grip on the North American market, but nearly a dozen global competitors in this key industry, for the first time in decades subjecting the once-insular managers at Ford and General Motors to real competitive pressures and an insecure hold on power. When the GM board, frustrated by the Japanese competitors who had stolen market share, actually fired the CEO Robert Stempel in 1992, the shock waves spread far and wide.[25]

Indeed, many firms now seemed ripe for a takeover by another set of managers who could, in the parlance of the time, boost "shareholder value," now increasingly seen as the essential raison d'être of the firm. By the end of the 1980s, nearly one-third of all companies on the *Fortune* 500 had received takeover bids during the previous decade.[26] Since the 1980s, a new economic theory of the firm has shifted the focus of corporate law and analysis from questions of social and economic power to the maximization of value for investors—from collective concepts to individualist ones, thus sharply devaluing the message Berle and Means offered almost a century ago. Asserting that "market forces and the information age" had beaten the Soviets, the *Forbes* columnist Peter Huber argued that such impulses would soon dissolve America's largest economic organizations. "If you have grown accustomed to a sheltered life inside a really large corporation," he advised, take care: "The next Kremlin to fall may be your own."[27] And to the increasingly influential "Law and Economics" school of business scholarship and advocacy, the corporation had become less a social or even economic organization than a bundle of contractual arrangements, "a tool of making profits for investors."[28]

By the end of the twentieth century the vertically integrated firm was well into the process of disaggregation. Apple makes no computer products, but purchases them from Foxconn and other Asian vendors. Nike operates in similar fashion when it comes to the hundreds of millions of shoes it sells each year. FedEx uses independent contractors to drive its fleet of red-and-blue trucks. Likewise, virtually every container that reaches one of America's great port complexes is driven away by an owner-operator, tens of thousands of whom have replaced the corporate trucking companies that once serviced U.S. ports and distribution centers.[29] Amazon too hires labor contractors, including Schneider Logistics, Roadlink Workforce Solutions, and Skyward Employment Services to staff and supervise scores of new fulfillment centers.[30] The franchising of hotels, motels, and restaurants is now a pervasive way to off-load risks and generate virtually capital-free growth. In 1999, Wyndham Corporation, which owns Ramada, Howard Johnson's, Super 8, and Days Inn brands, franchised all of its 6,383 properties.[31] Cash-strapped municipalities outsource a remarkable range of services once thought core functions of government, while even the most secretive and sensitive federal agencies contract with a vast array of outside vendors for the most important work. General Motors spun off dozens of its auto parts plants to create Delphi and Ford did the same to create Visteon. In both instances, these newly independent companies faced intense low-wage competition

from nonunion parts suppliers, thus forcing them to slash wages and benefits. Delphi went bankrupt in 2005, thereafter moving much production to
East Asia.[32] In an essay titled "The Vanishing Hand," the economist Richard
Langlois wrote, "Vertical disintegration and specialization is perhaps the
most significant organizational development of the 1990s."[33] And there is
little evidence to say that the process has ceased in subsequent years.[34]

The economic and sociological effect has been significant. Employment
in the temporary help services industry—which includes firms like Kelly
Services for office workers, and various suppliers of blue-collar warehouse
labor—more than doubled to 2.3 million between 1990 and 2008.[35] And if
one adds to this number all those workers who are ostensibly self-employed
or contract workers, the total number of contingent workers rises to over 11
million. Meanwhile more than 8 million workers are employed by companies that are franchisees, beholden to much larger firms, like McDonalds.[36]
Indeed, the Census Bureau reports that of the 4.3 million business establish-
ments it has surveyed, more than 10 percent were franchisees, accounting for
$1.3 trillion in sales.[37] And finally there are the contract manufacturers, at
home but mainly abroad, who are integral and subordinate links in the global
supply chains that put athletic shoes, consumer electronics, and so many
other products on big box shelves. Walmart alone is estimated to have more
than 30,000 vendors in East Asia, employing a workforce that numbers in
the millions.[38]

It would be a large mistake to think that the transformations outlined
above mean that the hand of management has become any less potent or that
the market now governs decisions once made on a command-and-control basis within the firm. Coase's buttermilk remains highly coagulated because
even when supply chains exist in a formally free market economy, firms at
the apex of those chains retain enormous power amounting to de facto op-
erational control. What has changed are the power relations within the supply chain and the legal, political, and moral imperatives that once governed
and constrained the administration of the vertically integrated corporation.

Two consequential examples of the process are offered here. The first explores the rise of temporary employment firms whose enormous success in
transforming employment relations within many heretofore vertically integrated corporations required a minor revolution in New Deal–era employment law. The second traces the way in which giant retailers came to create
a series of supply chains—first domestic and then global—that, while composed of a disparate set of legally and organizationally autonomous "vendors,"

have in fact been as well-controlled and as hierarchical as the most vertically integrated corporation of the old economy.

In the Progressive Era and for many years afterward, reformers thought private employment agencies hardly a step above the exploitative padrones who herded immigrant laborers to construction projects and truck farms in order to skim wages, win kickbacks, and sell jobs. As a consequence, most states strictly regulated employment agencies while making the job-search function an integral part of the services provided by state unemployment-compensation agencies. Many state laws required employment agents to register, obtain a state license, and post bond. They capped fees charged to workers and banned the practice of sending scabs to replace union workers on strike. For example, in 1955 the Supreme Court of Nebraska ruled that Manpower, Inc. was not an employer itself, but "obviously" an employment agency that must comply with state licensing laws.[39]

Manpower and other early temp agencies resisted such a classification, arguing that they were themselves employers of labor who performed a service, like a painting firm whose employees worked at the direction of the homeowner. In the late 1950s and throughout the 1960s temp agencies advanced this organizational theory in all the key state legislatures, their case materially advanced by the Kelly Girl imagery they propounded, a cultural trope designed to convince the public that glamorous female office workers, whose relationship to the paid employment was advertised as episodic and voluntary, in no way sought to undermine existing wage standards, employment ladders, or union power.

Temp agencies waged a two-pronged fight: avoiding the classification of employment agency would satisfy the industry's own desire to be free from unwanted state regulation, whereas gaining designation as the actual employer of temporary workers would give their clients access to labor without the obligations or expectations that had been politically or culturally embedded in core industry and office jobs. Although the former goal was important, the latter was absolutely essential. Unless the temporary-help firms were accepted in practice as legal employers, their raison d'être would disappear.[40] They won a sweeping victory, both judicial and political. By the 1980s the U.S. Employment Service began to refer job seekers at its free public offices to private employment agencies; and indeed, the federal government itself greatly expanded its own use of part-time and temporary workers in the 1980s.[41]

The impulse powering their vast expansion in the 1970s and 1980s arose out of a corporate determination to subvert or displace the New Deal–era labor regime by severing the employer-employee relationship between workers and those user firms on whose premises they worked. As Louis Hyman has pointed out in *Temp: How American Work, American Business, and the American Dream Became Temporary*, this managerial ideology had its origins well before the onset of hard times in the 1970s. Consulting firms like McKinsey and temp agencies like Manpower spread the gospel of corporate outsourcing and employment flexibility both as a profit maximizing strategy in boom times and as a necessity for survival when U.S. firms came under competitive pressure from abroad.[42] Labor costs had to become more flexible and not a fixed item on the account books. As the recession of the mid-1970s exacerbated corporate anxieties, *Management Review* cataloged the advantages of hiring what were now often called permatemps: "The employees do not affect the unemployment insurance rate if they have to be terminated, they do not add to the cost of fringe benefits or payroll maintenance, and they are outside the company's normal policy requirements for personnel."[43] This arrangement allowed the clients of temporary employment firms to deploy a labor force while avoiding many of the specific social, legal, and contractual obligations that have increasingly been attached to employer status since the New Deal. By giving user firms almost absolute control over the duration of a worker's stay and over what tasks workers could be directed to do while on the job, the "temporary" solution enabled large firms to "downsize" their labor force and deprive it of "voice" without actually reducing labor input or limiting control and direction of that workforce.[44] New Deal employment relations—of the sort expected at vertically integrated firms—have therefore been utterly fissured and then rhetorically scrambled. In this new frame, all the terms in the resultant triangular employment relationship are given new meanings. The employment agent becomes an "employer": the client employer becomes a "customer"; the work performed becomes a "service"; and the worker becomes a "consumer" of the services of the temporary employment firm.[45]

Thus, when in a recent lawsuit Walmart and its labor contractor, Schneider Logistics, were charged with depriving some 568 workers at a California distribution center of nearly $5 million in wages, the big retailer declared itself disinterested and innocent. Although the warehouse was partially owned by Walmart and all the goods therein were destined for Walmart stores, a retail company executive declared that Walmart was merely Schneider's customer. "We have a set of business needs that we pay them to meet just like any company might hire an accounting firm to do taxes or an advertising firm to help launch a new product."[46]

Franchising and independent contracting function in the same spirit, although in this case the workers, or the petty managers who employ so many fast-food or other service workers, are defined as entrepreneurs themselves, even though their product is uniform across the country, their work routine is hyperstandardized, and their profit margins are small—thus leading to high levels of franchisee bankruptcy. As the Taco Bell franchise agreement states:

> You must operate your facilities according to the methods, standards, and procedures (the "System") that Taco Bell provides in minute detail. . . . [The franchisee] shall faithfully, completely, and continuously perform, fulfill, observe and follow all instructions, requirements, standards, specifications, systems and procedures contained therein; including those dealing with the selection, purchase, storage, preparation, packaging, service and sale (including menu content and presentation) of all food and beverage products, and the maintenance and report of Restaurant buildings, grounds, furnishings, fixtures, and equipment, as well as those relating to employee uniforms and dress, accounting, bookkeeping, record retention and other business systems, procedures and operations.[47]

Given such a contractual imbalance of power—some have likened it to sharecropping—it was only reasonable for a *Washington Post* reporter to ask, "Here's a problem for the protesters demonstrating at fast-food restaurants across the country to demand $15 an hour: Whom are they talking to, exactly? A global megacorporation or a locally-owned small business?"[48] In Chapter 12 of this volume, Kate Andrias is also cognizant of this problem, noting how inadequately contemporary labor law deals with such fissured employment issues and how the labor movement and its liberal allies might nevertheless seek to achieve better wages and working conditions. Likewise, Annette Bernhardt, the noted scholar of low-wage work, argues that the real problem lies not with the rise of Uber and TaskRabbit, icons of the high-tech "gig" economy, but rather with endemic wage stagnation in regular employment, which has forced so many workers to look for a "flexible" second job, one readily supplied by the new employers of contingent, fissured, and contracted-out work.[49]

As in fast-food and other franchising operations, many of these same patterns have become apparent and pervasive with the rise of the big-box retailers who command a set of global supply chains, made possible by the telecommunications revolution, innovations in container shipping, and the growth of low-cost East Asian manufacturing. These supply chains are functionally well integrated and utterly dominated by big-box retailers like Walmart, Amazon, and Home Depot. Managers running those companies in Bentonville, Seattle, Atlanta, and elsewhere exercise the kind of organizational control, sans legal or financial responsibility, that has become apparent in the temporary employment industry and once so offended critics of corporate governance in the first half of the twentieth century. Ironically, the retail-industry universe demonstrates how a renewed commitment to vertical integration at one end of the supply chain can coexist in simultaneous fashion with a disaggregation elsewhere.

The brands and retailers that stand at the apex of these supply chains have generated a highly integrated production and distribution entity that has subordinated both manufacturing and logistics to a powerful set of merchant capitalists. Walmart pioneered many of these innovations in the 1970s and 1980s as cargo containerization, high-speed communications, interstate highways, and distribution-center efficiencies transformed logistics and greatly reduced the transaction costs that once incentivized vertical integration. Meanwhile, the now ubiquitous bar code enabled Walmart and other retailers to leverage their enormous buying power against that of manufacturing "vendors" and others down the supply chain. The information created by all those swipes over the checkout scanner generated trillions of bits of information that poured into Walmart's data warehouse. This meant that Walmart was sitting on an information trove so vast and detailed that it far exceeded what many manufacturers know about their own products. Soon followed by other brands and retailers, Walmart was in a position to virtually dictate the terms of its contact on price, volume, delivery, schedule, packaging, and quality. Indeed, each year the company hands its suppliers detailed "strategic business planning packets," thereby cementing Walmart's power over its vendors.[50] "Wal-Mart lives in a world of supply and command," observed a *New York Times* retail analyst in 2004.[51]

Many manufacturers established offices in northwest Arkansas with teams fully dedicated to furthering their partnership with Walmart. One of the first was Procter & Gamble (P&G). But so intimate was the relationship between P&G and Walmart that soap company executives feared that the autonomy and creativity of their company had been compromised. "The people were paid by P&G and sat in P&G's office, but it was like they were working for Wal-Mart and P&G equally," admitted one Cincinnati-based executive. "The payroll just happened to come from P&G."[52]

It did not take long for Walmart and other retailers to put this system into operation on a worldwide basis. These merchants control the supply chain, they squeeze their commodity-producing vendors, and they shift production from one venue to another with ease and economy. Just as nineteenth-century cotton houses could switch their source of supply from Mississippi to India or Egypt, so too can cell phones, sweat shirts, and tennis shoes find their manufacturing home in Honduras, the Pearl River Delta, Ho Chi Minh City, or Bangladesh.[53]

The phrase "supply chain" is of recent derivation. The historical sociologist Emmanuel Wallerstein had first developed the idea of a "commodity chain" in the 1970s as part of his world systems schema.[54] A decade later, consulting firms like Bain and Company coined the phrase "value chain management" or "supplier rationalization" to describe how large companies, often retailers and branded manufacturers, purchased components and materials from foreign vendors and transformed them into salable goods. The industrial relations scholars Frederick Abernathy and John Dunlop used a similar phrase, "commodity channels," in 1999 to describe the way apparel moved from Asian and Central American suppliers to North American retailers. In the twenty-first century, however, the artful "supply chain," with its sense of hard linkages and buyer- not producer-driven dominance, has become the pervasive terminology, both among executives in the field and scholars in the academy.[55]

However, this tight coordination takes place not by formally integrating the supply chain into one legal, corporate entity, but by creating a pseudo-market whereby management exercises its will and power. Therefore, the great retailers of Europe and the United States have no legal or even much moral responsibility for those who labor along many of the links in their supply chain. In China, Bangladesh and elsewhere millions of workers supply the products that end up on the shelves of all the big-box retailers. But none of these people work directly for Walmart, Apple, or the other big retailers and powerful brands that require the production of such a continuous stream of consumer durables. Most firms have established "corporate social responsibility" staffs, but such initiatives are but a pale substitute for the absolute legal and administrative responsibility that reformers once thought a core function of management.[56]

No one knows how many companies or how many workers supply these brands and retailers because no one really knows or can know the extent of the vast subcontracting system that stands at the heart of the sweatshops universe filling the production end of these buyer driven supply chains. They all consist of a series of subordinate entities whose prices, production schedules, and labor costs are put under relentless pressure by the firm or institution that is the ultimate buyer of the product.[57] They are hard to tax, regulate, unionize, or even measure. Indeed, this is the essence of "sweatshop" production, which derives its historic, derogatory meaning from the "sweater," the Victorian-era middleman, who took advantage of the poverty and unemployment endemic in London's East End to subcontract garment cutting and sewing to scores of desperate families, many of whom were migrants to the British metropolis from a countryside where tenants and farmhands had been dispossessed by the new international trade in wheat and wool.[58]

New Dealers faced many of these same problems nearly a century ago, and their solution may well offer instructive guidance to twenty-first-century reformers. In the early twentieth century there were some vertically integrated clothing firms, such as Hart, Schaffner & Marx, that were also pioneers in the sort of welfare and collective-bargaining arrangements that prefigured the New Deal. But most of the rest of the garment industry—as well as many other low capitalization sectors including laundries, food processing, local cartage, and other urban services—was fragmented and disorganized. This is the world explored by the historians of capital and labor in early twentieth-century America: Andrew Wender Cohen, Shane Hamilton, Philip Scranton, and others.[59] In the "rag trade" well-established designers, apparel firms, and retailers were the "jobbers" who contracted out all or part of their work to "a protean sea of tiny enterprises," described by the historian Steve Fraser as inhabiting "an economic underworld where chiseling, subterfuge, and tainted goods were the common currency." As in East and South Asia today, where manufacturers scramble for contracts from Nike, Zara, Target, and H&M, the "outside" manufacturer of early twentieth-century New York "defended his razor-thin margin of profit by means both legitimate and shady, but especially by exerting a constant downward pressure on wages and working conditions."[60]

The International Ladies Garment Workers Union (ILGWU) argued that jobbers and contractors were actually "joint employers" in an "integrated process of production," if only because the small, labor-intensive firms that actually did the sewing and assembling of the garments did not own, design, invest in, or purchase any of the materials needed for production. Their sole task was to supervise the productive process in the same way that a foreman or plant supervisor got out production and controlled labor costs in an "inside shop."[61] The union insisted that ultimate responsibility for labor conditions in sewing factories resided with the companies that provided the orders, not with the contractors who were the official employers of garment workers in the outside shops.

For two midcentury generations, the ILGWU prevailed. The New Deal's National Recovery Administration (NRA) created codes of fair competition that did in fact mandate joint liability for jobbers and contractors, eliminating the capacity of the jobber to evade industrial responsibility and thereby greatly ameliorate "the jobber-contractor evil."[62] Although the NRA itself imploded in 1935, the garment unions created a stable system of triangular bargaining in which the union first negotiated a collective-bargaining agreement with the jobber, then negotiated an agreement with the contractors, and then finally the jobber and the contractors negotiated an agreement with each other. As a retired union official told the sociologist Jennifer Bair decades later, "The ILGWU recognized that the jobber was the lynchpin of the industry. Contractors couldn't pay anything unless the jobber paid it to him or for him. The trick was to get as much as you could in the contract to protect the workers and the union."[63]

In the immediate postwar era the garment industry had its brief moment of domestic stability. Sweatshops were eliminated, apparel firms brought much production "inside," and garment industry wages stood at nearly 85 percent of those in the rest of manufacturing. Price competition and wage arbitrage moderated.[64] When the labor law was revised in 1959, Barry Goldwater, the conservative senator from Arizona linked arms with liberal New York politicians to shield the garment industry from a prohibition against union-organized secondary boycotts, sometimes necessary to enforce collective-bargaining contracts that required jobbers to contract only with registered contractors. Having been the manager of a Phoenix department store in the 1930s and 1940s Goldwater knew the industry, and he had "seen order come out of chaos," which made profitable and stable retailers and apparel firms. From the Senate floor Goldwater declared, "None of us wants to disturb for one second the status that the garment trade now occupies under the present law"[65]

Of course, this system soon fell apart as jobbers shifted production to nonunion contractors in the United States and abroad. The garment unions tried to follow the work to Pennsylvania, North Carolina, California, and even Puerto Rico, but once the work moved to the Caribbean, Mexico, and East Asia, unions in the garment and textile industries could only seek some form of trade protectionism to defend industry standards. But the 1993 enactment of the North American Free Trade Agreement and the 2004 phaseout of the Multifiber Arrangement (which limited apparel imports) accelerated the decline of the domestic garment industry. As jobbers were liberated to subcontract production across the globe, the market proved the most potent arbitrator of wages and working conditions. Brands like Adidas or Levi Strauss and retailers sourcing their own apparel have circumvented the labor standards that the union had once imposed on the domestic clothing industry. And with the return of the sweatshop came spectacular disasters like the collapse of the Rana Plaza manufacturing complex in Bangladesh, in which 1,132 workers lost their lives.[66]

The vertical integration or disaggregation of corporate supply chains, both domestic and international, are indeed products of a technical-organizational calculus that measures transaction costs in such a way as to make a distended value chain possible and profitable. Ronald Coase was right about that, but so too are all those analysts of corporate management, from Adolph Berle and Gardiner Means on down to our own time, who understand that managerial capacity to command and control is also created and sustained by a set of legal structures and political/reputational pressures that create incentives for the distended sourcing strategies and fissured employment regimes that have diminished the vertically integrated corporation. This kind of enterprise reconfiguration has proved just as damaging to efforts to regulate and democratize the corporation as is the new latitude these entities have won when it comes to their capacity to spend large amounts of money in U.S. politics.

The reintegration of the corporation, both global and domestic, is therefore a decisive frontier in the century-long battle to once again impose on these large economic entities a measure of social responsibly and legal accountability. It seems unlikely that global supply chains will anytime in the foreseeable future actually transform themselves into a vertically integrated institution, à la General Motors or IBM in the 1950s, or that McDonalds will simply purchase from its franchisees 10,000 brick-and-mortar restaurants. But a measure of de facto integration especially in terms of environmental and labor-related issues, seems entirely possible.[67] If changes in the law and social mores force corporations to recognize that they are, in effect, "joint employers" when they contract with a much weaker link in the supply chain, then a large step forward will have been taken, once again creating a legal and organizational environment in which the real holders of economic and administrative power can be held responsible for their activities or lack thereof.

CHAPTER 10

The High-Tech Revolution and the Disruption of American Capitalism

Margaret O'Mara

During the last months of 1980, three extraordinary things happened in quick succession. On October 14, the California-based gene-splicing firm Genentech went public. Although Genentech had only made a profit in one year of its four-year history, Wall Street dealmakers salivated at the prospect of getting in on the ground floor of a new and hugely lucrative field. *New Issues*, a stock-industry newsletter, called the company "the Cadillac, Mercedes and Rolls-Royce of the industry rolled into one." Genentech opened trading at $35 a share and shot upward to a peak of $86 within three hours. It was the biggest initial public offering (IPO) run-up in Wall Street history.[1]

Exactly three weeks later on November 4, Ronald Reagan defeated Jimmy Carter in a landslide, winning more electoral votes than any nonincumbent presidential candidate in history. It happened swiftly, with networks calling the election even before polls closed in California. Washington's chattering class was quick to observe that Reagan's victory meant a big win for business interests, notably the new-breed entrepreneurial capitalists who had made fortunes in sectors like financial services and real estate development. In the Class Reunion, a DC bar crowded with political insiders, the mood started to turn "around 8 o'clock when the lobbyists moved their drinks closer to the Republican end of the bar," observed one reporter. "By 10 o'clock they were buying the drinks."[2]

On December 14, as Jimmy and Rosalynn Carter prepared to light their last White House Christmas tree, Apple Computer made its stock market debut. Based in Cupertino, California, the firm was even a hotter offering than Genentech, partly because of its charismatic chief executive officer (CEO), twenty-five-year-old Steve Jobs. "It's like bears attracted to very sweet honey," remarked one analyst.[3] Within weeks of its debut, four-year-old Apple had a valuation of nearly $2 billion: larger than the valuations of Ford Motor Company, Colgate-Palmolive, and Bethlehem Steel. Two years later, its annual sales neared $600 million and the company had minted about three hundred millionaires, most in their twenties. The euphoria baffled even seasoned tech-industry veterans. "We are living in a goofy time," one venture capitalist mused to a reporter.[4]

"When Ronald Reagan assumed office in January of 1981, an epoch in the nation's political history came to an end."[5] Steve Fraser and Gary Gerstle's opening words in their now-classic *The Rise and Fall of the New Deal Order* (1989) rightfully framed Reagan's landslide as a critical turning point in U.S. political history. November 1980 marked the culmination of a conservative groundswell that had been brewing for decades, a turn away from questions of labor and race that had defined liberal politics for two generations, and the beginning of a neoliberal era of tax-cutting, deregulation, and privatization.

However, the Reagan years also marked the beginning of another reinvention of the United States: the consumer high-tech revolution. In the span of a few short years, powered by ever-faster and cheaper semiconductor technology, the desktop "microcomputer" went from an oddball hobbyist's toy to a standard piece of office equipment and an increasingly popular home appliance. At exactly the same moment, consumers discovered the video game, another silicon-chip-powered phenomenon that made the world of tech an increasingly inescapable and addictive force in popular culture. *Time* magazine named Ronald Reagan "Man of the Year" for 1980. It named the personal computer "Machine of the Year" two years later.

The high-tech moment and the Reagan revolution seemed perfectly matched. Throughout his presidency, Reagan invoked industrious high-tech entrepreneurs as paradigms of U.S. free enterprise—and as a validation of his embrace of deregulated markets and rejection of the labor-business compact set in place by the New Deal. They were "the explorers of the modern era . . . men with vision, with the courage to take risks and faith enough to brave the unknown," Reagan proclaimed toward the end of his second term. "They are responsible for almost all the economic growth in the United States."[6]

The high-tech community, particularly in the antiestablishment confines of Northern California's Silicon Valley, sang a similar tune of fearless individualism, personal empowerment, and free markets. "The personal computer operator is the Electronic Man on Horseback riding into the (sinking) Western sun," wrote the tech journalist William Schenker in the Valley insider newsletter *InfoWorld* in early 1980. "He is the last of the rugged individualists, and the personal computer is his only effective weapon."[7]

However, it was a crop of younger Democratic lawmakers who became most closely associated with technology during this period, laying the groundwork for a deeper political affiliation between national Democrats and Silicon Valley in the 1990s and beyond. They included senators like Colorado's Gary Hart, congressmen like Massachusetts's Paul Tsongas and Colorado's Tim Wirth, and governors like Arizona's Bruce Babbitt and Massachusetts's Michael Dukakis. By early 1982, the Beltway columnist Elizabeth Drew had given the group a cheeky nickname: "the Atari Democrats."[8] They called themselves liberals—but ones with little fealty to the manufacturing industries and labor unions of the New Deal Order. "The clearest feature of the emerging world economy," wrote Wirth in 1982, "is that the future will be won with brainpower."[9]

*   *   *

The people and companies of the modern U.S. technology industry, and its command-and-control center of Silicon Valley, like to characterize themselves as "disrupters" of traditional industries, markets, and state institutions. This chapter argues that they have indeed been "disrupters" of the capitalist order since the 1970s, but not in the way that techies assume. Rather than being actors outside of or in opposition to mainline U.S. political and economic institutions, peripheral to the larger dramas of state transformation and partisan realignment after 1970, high-technology industries are precisely at the heart of them.

First, tech disrupted the business-government relationship. While contemporary conventional wisdom may hold that the tech revolution occurred independently of (and despite) the liberal state, the reality is that generous, privatized, and federalized state investment—set in place by the New Deal and vastly enlarged during the early Cold War—enabled the U.S. technology industry to fly as high as it did. The indirect and parastatal nature of much of this spending (in contrast to other industrialized countries) was critical in enabling a competitive and highly innovative tech marketplace to emerge. Simply put, the government shoveled a massive amount of money in Silicon

Valley's general direction, and then it got out of the way. The nature of this funding relationship and the emergence of multiple small firms—venture-backed startups—and different varieties of industry (computer hardware, software, games, biotech, telecom) and near-total absence of labor unionism meant that a set of industries seeded by government contracts had remarkably weak ties with national policymakers.

Tech leaders forged a very different sort of public–private relationship than the three-legged stool of manufacturing industries, labor unions, and government leaders that had characterized the peak decades of the New Deal Order. Instead, this was a relationship built on the (often top-secret) foundations of the national security state, in which technology companies received a great deal of support from government—in the form of contracts, tax breaks, and general political goodwill—along with a great deal of leeway to do as they pleased. This was a two-way street between tech tycoons and policymakers, forged in the heyday of supply-side economics and strengthened in the age of the New Democrats. Rank-and-file tech workers, who supposedly were intent on building entrepreneurial fortunes of their own, were not part of the negotiation.

Second, tech disrupted the prevailing economic trends of the 1970s (and their contemporaneous interpretations). What Judith Stein characterizes as "trad[ing] factories for finance" destabilized the business and labor constituencies of the New Deal but also opened up avenues for small, agile new businesses that could quickly globalize supply chains and had fewer fixed labor costs. Although tech industries were not immune to the economic woes of the "pivotal decade" of the 1970s, their upward growth trajectory presented a stark contrast to old-line manufacturing industries like autos and steel. In turn, high-tech companies presented themselves as a highly attractive new model for U.S. capitalism: culturally liberal, meritocratic, and unencumbered by old constituencies and traditions. The ability of tech to succeed during a period of malaise gave heft to the political argument that the struggles of old-line industries resulted in part from their internal weaknesses and strategic failures, rather than macroeconomic and political shifts beyond manufacturers' control.[10]

Third, high technology disrupted partisan politics. Tech became a golden ticket, rhetorically and materially, for national politicians on both sides of the aisle seeking the votes of an increasingly independent-minded electorate after 1980. For Republicans like Reagan and his inheritors, the scrappy high-tech entrepreneur was the perfect poster child for the U.S. free enterprise system and the tax cuts, regulatory relief, and privatization at the heart of Reaganomics. The "think different" self-presentation of tech companies held particular appeal for a rising generation of "Atari Democrats" seeking to reinvent their party along more centrist lines. Ultimately, Democratic liberals aided and abetted the mythos of the iconoclastic, self-sufficient technology entrepreneur and helped reaffirm a free-enterprise ideology of capitalism unfettered by the regulatory state and organized labor.

The people and companies in Silicon Valley and the U.S. technology industry soared while so many other things—from big cities to large manufacturing industries to Americans' faith in political leadership—were falling apart. But Silicon Valley did not just fill a vacuum. The entrepreneurs and financiers of the technology industry evangelized a new model of U.S. capitalism with immense traction and influence on both state and markets in the subsequent four decades. Rather than existing apart from and indifferently to politics, Silicon Valley—as place, idea, and millionaire-saturated reality—had a profound influence on legislative, regulatory, and partisan realignments of the late twentieth and early twenty-first centuries.

Recent literature on the 1970s has made important interventions explicating the relationship between political and economic realignments. Much of the emphasis has, deservedly, focused on the transformation of manufacturing and unionized labor.[11] Relatively few historians of labor, business, and politics have reckoned with the high-tech phoenix rising from this much broader landscape of industrial decline and retrenchment.[12] Yet when we place the two revolutions—Reagan and personal computers—in conversation with one another, we can see how high-tech becomes another powerful lens through which to understand the partisan realignments that signaled the end of the New Deal order, and to further contribute to a historiography of rightward-bound America that includes both Democrats and Republicans as contributors to the conservative swing.[13]

The First Venture Capitalist: The Indirect Nature of Federal Spending

The federal government built the computer industry, but it did so in a way that made leaders of that industry believe they did it all on their own. This structure was long in the making: Washington, DC, was a critical investor and customer for computer hardware and software well before the massive public expenditures during the Cold War on defense research and development (R&D).[14] The New Deal itself created overwhelming information-technology demands and rich new contracting opportunities for business-machine companies. Giant new federal programs for wage and price controls, agricultural subsidies, and public works generated masses of data in desperate need of rapid, sophisticated processing. The demand only intensified with World War II and the Cold War.[15]

By the end of the Eisenhower administration, as the economist Fritz Machlup observed in his seminal 1962 study of the "knowledge economy," 524 mainframes hummed and blinked away in government offices, representing "almost 20 per cent of the sales value of all computers produced and delivered in the United States up to the end of 1959." More fundamentally, "a large portion of the nation's expenditures on knowledge has been financed by government."[16] This included huge investments in university-based basic research and education in science and mathematics, as well as development of blue-sky innovations in computer hardware, software, and networking. This spending was geographically skewed toward particular states, regions, and congressional districts, almost all of which were in the South and the West. Many political and economic factors played into this high-tech geography, not the least of which was the abundance of cheap electricity in these regions as a result of the hydroelectric dams and electrification projects built during the New Deal itself.[17]

The political gut-punch of the Soviet Union's successful launch of Sputnik in 1957 spurred Congress and Eisenhower to create the National Aeronautics and Space Administration one year later. The space race drove demand (and provided another deep-pocketed government customer) for small, light, fast, and sophisticated electronic equipment—just the sorts of things produced by the audacious little companies beginning to cluster in the suburbs south of San Francisco, near aerospace giants like Lockheed and the blooming technical powerhouse of Stanford University. It was also good news for other regions on the forefront of transistor-powered electronic technology, Boston, Massachusetts, and Dallas, Texas, chief among them.[18]

Hewlett-Packard (HP) and Fairchild Semiconductor, the two most influential first-generation Bay Area tech companies, got big chunks of early business from military and space-related projects. As the Stanford provost Fred Terman recalled, "it just turned out that these expensive things that Hewlett-Packard had developed just were right in where the line of great progress was." At Fairchild, government contracts made up 80 percent of its book of business in 1959. As late as 1969, HP got 35 percent of its revenue from government projects.[19]

The *structure* of these funding flows is critically important to understanding why the mid-twentieth-century U.S. state was so remarkably effective at spurring technological innovation. At a moment when commercial customers for small electronics could be few and fickle, the Cold War state effectively acted as a very large, forward-thinking seed capital fund. It forced private enterprises to compete fiercely with one another to build more and more sophisticated products, and it spurred a larger ecosystem of subcontractors (and sub-subcontractors) who supplied the hundreds of different, specialized components needed for a missile or rocket.

Both military and domestic activities (soon to include the large bureaucracies created by Great Society programs like Medicare and Medicaid) provided a large, stable set of clients and customers. In such a novel, geographically concentrated industry, contracts flowed relatively unhampered by congressional earmarks and political favoritism. The model was particularly fruitful for small enterprises without mass production capacities, and the subcontracting structure allowed most of the operators of these companies to escape the bureaucratic burdens of being a defense contractor.[20]

Ironically, this big-government funding helped lay the foundation for Silicon Valley's small-firm startup culture. In the late 1950s and early 1960s, starting a company on your own was an odd and risky choice, even in relatively open-minded Northern California. Federal money mitigated this risk, provided economic security, and created a market of wide-open opportunities. The existence of this market in turn incentivized the creation of a new kind of private financing, venture capital, which generated astounding rates of return. There was so much work on offer, and so few firms able to do it. "There was no competition," recalled one early venture capitalist.[21]

The decentralized and parastatal nature of government R&D funding, like much of the New Deal state, hid the extent of its influence. Being two or three degrees removed from the contracting process, and engaged in a lively tussle with other small companies to win new business, it was easy for tech startups to imagine themselves as purely private-sector enterprises.

This ethos endured even as the political economy of high-tech changed significantly at the end of the 1960s. Vietnam-era spending cuts ate into defense budgets, throwing thousands out of work in Northern California, Seattle, and other hubs of the military-industrial complex. By 1971, the United

States had entered a recession that shook the foundations of a society accustomed to individual economic security and national economic supremacy.

As malaise and stagflation settled in, however, a different story emerged in the computer and electronics industries. Tech was not immune to the economic woes of the decade; inflation, a sagging stock market, and risk-averse investors made it tough for new startups to raise money and attract talent. Yet in a period of relentlessly bad economic news for U.S. manufacturing, the small-electronics and computer industries seemed to buck prevailing trends.

Nationally, between 1950 and 1980, jobs in manufacturing shrunk from 30 percent to 20 percent of gross domestic product (GDP). Within this category, however, computer and electronics manufacturing grew, ultimately employing about two million people and capturing 1.6 percent of GDP by 1980. True, even after adding the white-collar managerial and engineering workforce to the total, the sector accounted for a tiny fraction of the overall national economy. But both the industry's intense geographic concentration and its remarkable capacity to create personal and regional wealth gave it a hefty economic and social impact.[22]

In the San Jose, California, metropolitan area, where defense cuts contributed to the disappearance of more than 10,000 manufacturing jobs between 1969 and 1971, employment in manufacturing turned around quickly, growing by nearly 8 percent in 1971 and another 17 percent in 1972. From 1969 to 1980, manufacturing employment nearly doubled, to over 245,000 jobs.[23] Instead of defense-related aerospace jobs coming back, the resurgence in manufacturing came from a burgeoning cluster of computer chip makers. The same story played out along Boston's Route 128, where minicomputer makers like Digital Equipment and Data General became some of the region's most visible, dynamic, and fast-growing companies. By 1974, Digital employed 20,000 people, had sales of $422 million, and joined the ranks of the Fortune 500.[24] By the mid-1970s, observers estimated that the Northern California technology community had somewhere between 100 and 500 high-tech millionaires, most of whom were under age thirty-five.[25]

It was partly because of defense cutbacks that this high-tech surge became possible. At the same moment that thousands of engineers and scientists were thrown out of work because of a shrinking military-industrial complex, computing was reaching a technological inflection point that made mass commercialization viable. It also benefited from Vietnam being a relatively high-tech war, as the waves of returning veterans also included a cadre of college-educated officers possessing deep familiarity with sophisticated military electronics.[26]

With every year, semiconductor firms managed to cram even more memory onto a computer chip, making machines faster, smaller, and more powerful. Gordon Moore of Fairchild Semiconductor had predicted in 1965 that the number of components per chip would double every year. Within a decade, Moore's law proved true, and Intel, the chip company he cofounded, had become one of the dominant firms in the industry.[27]

Defense money did not disappear; one great market success of the 1970s, the computer and telecommunications equipment maker ROLM, earned 99 percent of its $10 million revenue in 1975 from "mil spec" sales of rugged, impact-resistant equipment designed for soldiers' use in the field.[28] The decade saw new government investments in medical research as well, spurred in part by President Richard Nixon's declaration of "war on cancer," expanding university research labs and the ranks of research scientists. The biotechnology boom would not come until the early 1980s, however, after a series of court decisions permitting the patenting and commercialization of medical discoveries, as well as the passage of the Bayh–Dole Act of 1980, which allowed universities and their researchers to patent and profit from federally financed inventions. In the meantime, tech remained chiefly a computer-and-chip, business-to-business game.

By the end of the 1970s, government contracts made up less than 10 percent of semiconductor-industry revenue.[29] As the industry shifted in a more private direction, its entrepreneurial, free-market mythos strengthened. Much of this talk came out of the Bay Area electronics community, which a local business journalist had dubbed "Silicon Valley" in early 1971.[30] "If you are a capitalist—and I am—you graduate to the Olympics of capitalism by starting new businesses," remarked Steve Brandt, one Silicon Valley businessman, to a reporter in 1974.[31] Entrepreneurial thinking drew a young college graduate named Ellen Lapham to Stanford's business school in the fall of 1975. For this East Coast native, Silicon Valley was "young, open-minded, entrepreneurial. It had a missionary spirit. The micro revolution was also a cultural revolution."[32]

The Cold War apparatus had given way to a new set of startup companies, headed by leaders who wore their hair long and embraced the sexual and social mores of the new generation. Along with it came a fresh conception of technology as a tool of personal empowerment, of computers as enablers of authentic human connection, of software as the means to create more meaningful social networks. One pioneering software developer of the period, Lee Felsenstein, summed up the new capitalist philosophy on display in Silicon Valley: "You don't have to leave industrial society, but you don't have to accept it the way it is."[33]

Bit by bit, the message started to percolate outward from the Valley to the rest of the country, including politicians in Washington. There was no such thing as a "technology reporter" in national newspapers and magazines in the 1970s; most reporting on the industry occurred in the pages of trade and more specialist publications like *Datamation* and *Scientific American*. Yet a smattering of articles by high-profile journalists in magazines ranging from *Rolling Stone* to *Fortune* began to sketch a portrait of a new kind of business enterprise. Iconoclastic, brilliant, risk-taking, wealthy, and male, Silicon Valley techies were the apotheoses of the Schumpeterian entrepreneurial idea, the antitheses of William Whyte's faceless organization men.[34]

Weeding out the hype, Silicon Valley high-tech companies clearly practiced a new strain of U.S. capitalism. It was not a complete upending of the old regime: the organization charts of these growing companies looked a lot like those of typical "old economy" corporations, with all the requisite support functions (sales, marketing, human resources) that had become critical to doing business in the modern era. But many companies, particularly those in Northern California, departed from the rest of corporate America in their management style, workplace culture, and labor relations.

Founders of firms often stayed at the helm as their CEOs or chairmen, and their priorities could have a large influence on company culture.[35] The original models were Bill Hewlett and David Packard, who founded their eponymous company in 1939, when both were in their early twenties. The two engineers made a hands-on, build-as-you-go management approach central to their corporate ethos from the start, something Hewlett liked to call "management by wandering."[36] Employees and shirt-sleeved executives ate lunch together on a sun-drenched patio at the center of HP's Palo Alto headquarters. They played volleyball and horseshoes on the lawn out back, and spent off-work hours socializing together with their wives. To build loyalty and camaraderie, HP gave all employees (not just executives) stock in the company, and their fortunes rose and fell along with its share price. "I think many people assume, wrongly, that a company exists simply to make money," David Packard once told HP executives. "While this is an important result of a company's existence, we have to go deeper to find the real reasons for our being."[37]

When company founders were sober-minded engineers like Hewlett and Packard, this highly personalized approach worked well. When they were more mercurial and freewheeling, it could generate chaos. The video-game maker Atari, creator of the arcade phenomenon Pong, was cofounded in 1972 by a group whose leader was a charismatic and mercurial twenty-nine-year-old named Nolan Bushnell. The company's early years were characterized by management squabbles among its young executives, drug use on the manufacturing line, and goofy product ideas that never would have made it past ordinary corporate marketing structures. It was 1970s California, recalled one early Atari employee, and the company was "a bunch of free thinking, dope smoking, fun loving people. We sailed boats, flew airplanes, smoked pot and played video games."[38]

Perhaps because of this loose and casual organizational structure, Atari stumbled repeatedly in trying to convert Pong's success into a lasting business. In 1976, after deciding against a Wall Street IPO, Bushnell sold Atari to Warner Communications for $28 million, netting $15 million personally. It would take several more years—and the eventual ouster of Bushnell from the company he helped found—for Atari to find its footing, but by the early 1980s it had become the dominant player in the booming home video-game industry, and shorthand for the technology industry itself.[39]

The change-the-world vibe of the technology industry was a stark contrast to business-page stories about besieged automakers, unemployed machinists, long gas lines, and spiraling inflation. In an era when "big business" was deeply unpopular, here was a type of business that seemed kinder, better, and even rather fun. Yet the feel-good overlay veiled a fundamentally altered model of employer-worker relations, one that hinged worker economic security on stock price, and substituted company swimming pools and cafeterias for more substantial benefits and protections that were some of the New Deal era's most important legacies.[40] Employees benefited greatly from this bargain when a company was successful. When a company failed—and many did—its workers could be left with nothing.

The economic unpredictability of high-tech life was both a cause and a consequence of something else being absent from the sun-dappled suburban landscape: labor unions. It was perhaps not surprising that the engineers and programmers at work in these companies would be immune to the persuasions of labor organizers. U.S. unions had been trying to organize private-sector office workers since the 1950s, with little to show for it. Arguments for worker solidarity had particularly little appeal amid the entrepreneurial, individualistic, and nonhierarchical ethos of an industry in which even the most junior employees were well-paid, well-educated, and expected to get quite rich. "In good times," remarked one electronics-industry spokesman to a reporter in 1984, "employees know that if they are not happy where they are working or want more money, they can just go across the street."[41]

Yet as labor organizers understood well, the shirt-sleeved engineer and hippie hacker only made up one part of the high-tech workforce. Far outnumbering them were the blue-collar workers on the computer-hardware assembly lines and in the clean rooms of chip fabrication plants. In Silicon Valley, the contrast was particularly stark, as unlike the overwhelmingly male managerial ranks of the tech industry, the manufacturing workforce was mostly female, and disproportionately Asian or Latino/Latina. This was in part a legacy of the Valley's agricultural past, filled with orchards and canneries that employed a large immigrant and female workforce in the 1930s and 1940s. It also reflected the nature of small-electronics manufacturing, where manufacturing of miniature components and postage-stamp-sized microchips required less physical brawn and more precise manual dexterity.[42] Unlike their colleagues in the research parks up the road, workers in the fabrication plants rarely got stock options. Instead of perks, there were hazards. The making of a microchip involved many toxic ingredients, and repeated exposure had potentially disastrous long-term health consequences.[43]

Unions attempted to organize both white- and blue-collar workers in the technology industry for decades, with dismal results. In 1962 the International Brotherhood of Electrical Workers (IBEW) tried to organize workers at the Georgia-based research firm Scientific Atlanta. Eighteen years and five more failed IBEW drives later, Scientific Atlanta still did not have a union. As semiconductor manufacturing began to take off in the Valley in the early 1970s, the United Electrical Workers (UE) set their sights on the industry leaders National Semiconductor, Fairchild, and others. They found fiercely resistant managers and dispirited and disempowered blue-collar workers. As the UE general secretary-treasurer Amy Newell recalled, "it was very hard organizing a union in those plants, because the feeling of powerlessness among the workers was so difficult to overcome."[44]

When the computer industry exploded in size and wealth in the early 1980s, national unions renewed their efforts to organize the tech industry. On his first day in office as head of the Communications Workers of America (CWA), Mort Bahr announced a campaign to organize what he called the "virulently antiunion" IBM, calling it "the J. P. Stevens of the international

telecommunications industry."[45] Company executives scoffed at union organizers' accusations that they were running "high-tech sweatshops." High-
tech was a different breed of workplace from the smoke-belching factories of
old, they argued. Unions were no longer necessary. As Jeff Bartman, spokesman for the Boston-based tech giant Data General, noted rather primly: "I
think the general impression is that the high-tech industry has working conditions and sensibilities that are sophisticated enough so that unionization
is not an issue."[46]

By the time the PC revolution was in full swing, only a handful of the
two thousand-plus companies that belonged to the American Electronics
Association had unionized workforces. This was not just a result of the industry's Sunbelt geography; none of the 162 member companies of the
Massachusetts High-Technology Council had a union. In the Valley and elsewhere, many labor activists threw up their hands, declaring the industry
"unorganizable."[47]

Why did technology entrepreneurs reject, and sometimes strenuously
resist, unionization campaigns? Although part of their resistance was
philosophical—many techies truly believed they were building different sorts
of companies—it also reflected the cutthroat competition and precarious
market position of a very new industry. Tech entrepreneurs had to convince
their venture-capital backers that they were running lean, efficient operations.
Companies that had only recently gone public had to maintain shareholder
value—not only for Wall Street investors but also for the employees whose
own financial security rose and fell with the price of the stock. In the semiconductor industry, where demand fluctuated wildly and where overseas
competition regularly undercut U.S. chipmakers on price, having a unionized
workforce reduced flexibility in hiring and firing. Technology firms had
weathered recession years in the 1970s and early 1980s partly because of their
agility and low fixed costs; union drives challenged that.

Tech was not the only entrepreneurial sector operating along these lines.
Yet its breathtaking financial successes brought it outsized attention and ac-
claim, and tended to inoculate it from criticism. In contrast to union-busting
corporations of an earlier era (General Electric comes to mind), the high-tech
industry did not take a public relations hit for its resistance to union organizing. Stories about working conditions in the fabrication plants got little traction in the mainstream national media. There, they were far outnumbered
by breathless accounts of the computers, video games, and other high-tech
marvels being pumped out by Silicon Valley companies.[48]

As labor unions and other manufacturing industries lost public support and political clout, the new-economy boys of high tech retained their golden sheen. The decline of the manufacturing and labor constituencies of the New Deal created an opening for tech to become a model for the next generation of capitalist enterprise. The political challenge to the old order—reflected in Jimmy Carter's one-term struggles and Ronald Reagan's 1980 victory—created the right policymaking environment to accomplish this.

Cutting Taxes and Picking Winners: The High-Tech Industry and Party Politics

All this talk of entrepreneurial techies bubbled up right at a time when Washington politicians on both sides of the aisle were casting around for remedies for the ailing U.S. economy, and amid a mood of political reform. Starting in the late 1970s, tech-industry interests became part of the "network of elites" described by Thomas Byrne Edsall in the final chapter of *The Rise and Fall of the New Deal Order*, benefiting particularly from "the vacuum of power in the Democratic Party" that allowed "the Party to be taken over, in part, by its most articulate and procedurally sophisticated wing: affluent, liberal reformers."[49]

Two sometimes competing, sometimes overlapping policy approaches emerged out of this conversation between 1978 and 1984. The first argued for more supply-side incentives (lower taxes, less regulation) to spur innovation and investment, and engaged Republican lawmakers and interest groups as key advocates and allies. The second argued for a more interventionist, demand-side approach (research investment, education and training, trade protections, and a "national industrial policy" akin to that of Japan) to protect the tech industry from foreign competition and to turn away from bailouts to old-economy manufacturing and toward strategies promoting "sunrise industries" like tech. This was the place where the "Atari Democrats" took center stage, but also gained support from GOP-leaning interests. Both policy streams served as venues for a new generation of politicians to find a national spotlight. In the process, they transformed an informal assortment of tech entrepreneurs into a set of organized political interest groups.

The high-tech community had had a less visible role in Washington politics while other business interests mobilized through organizations like the Business Roundtable at the start of the 1970s. The main trade association representing small California-based electronics ventures was the Western

Electronics Manufacturers Association, which at that time did not have a Washington office, and in which policy operations consisted chiefly of informing companies of any tweaks to army procurement regulations or patent law.[50] Small electronics firms and young venture capitalists did not find that these mainstream associations spoke much for their interests. Tech's political problem did not have to do with labor or outmoded production techniques, and it did not—at least not yet—have to do with foreign competition. Its biggest problem was a shortage of cash.

After a stock-market boom in the late 1960s, initial public offerings of venture-backed companies had gone from a flood to a trickle. In 1969 about one thousand went public; between 1973 and 1977 the number dropped to as few as twenty per year. While established manufacturing operations (like semiconductors or minicomputer makers) were growing during this period, the smaller firms that needed to raise money from public or private markets struggled mightily. Venture capital commitments had reached $171 million in 1969. By 1975 they were at $10 million.[51] It was, in the words of one investor, "the Death Valley days" of high-tech venture capital.[52]

A sour stock market could not be entirely responsible for the drop, the venture capitalists and tech executives reasoned. There had to be another culprit. Looking into the U.S. tax code, they found one: the capital gains tax, which had crept upward from a rate of 25 percent in 1969, and topped out at 49 percent by 1976. The tax hikes had come about without much notice or opposition. Historically, the main beneficiaries of low capital gains rates had been the extremely rich, members of clans like the Rockefellers and Whitneys, who for decades had been about the only people doing this sort of seed-stage investment.

The capital gains cash crunch brought high tech to Washington. First, in 1974 and 1975, came emissaries from the newly formed National Venture Capital Association (NVCA): a courtly, fifty-something Clevelander named David Morgenthaler, and a preppy Californian dealmaker named Reid Dennis.[53] By 1977 the venture capitalists were joined by a higher-octane, more Washington-savvy organization, the American Electronics Association (AEA) and its DC ambassador: an exuberant, kinetically energetic Silicon Valley CEO named Ed Zschau.

For all their business savvy, the three were neophytes when it came to the workings of Washington. "We were so green back then," Morgenthaler recalled later. "We sort of mentally associated ourselves with the big boys from New York, until we got there and we found the congressmen were seeing us as these nice little guys from the country."[54] In a down economy, when there was little political upside to seeming as rich as Rockefeller, the team quickly realized that outsider status was an advantage. The NVCA and AEA commissioned studies showing the job-creating power of high-tech industries. They testified at hearing after hearing that high taxes on tech were "killing the goose that lays those golden eggs." Zschau in particular displayed uninhibited zeal in his pursuit of a tax cut, going so far as to compose and sing an original ditty titled "Those Old Venture Capital Blues" and pressing cassette tapes of the recording into the hands of every congressman and senator on the Hill. Those that listened reported back that Zschau sang in "a plaintive moan that sounds somewhere between Leadbelly and Frank Sinatra with a cold."[55]

It was Jimmy Carter, however, who turned the capital gains tax from a boutique issue into a mainstream political debate. In early 1978, the president unveiled an unabashedly populist tax reform plan that promised the end of corporate tax loopholes and a fairer shake for regular taxpayers. "The privileged few are being subsidized by the rest of the taxpaying public," declared Carter, "when they routinely deduct the cost of country club dues, hunting lodges, elegant meals, theater and sports tickets, and night club shows."[56] Nestled within the red-meat proclamations was a proposal for capital gains: not to cut the rate, but to raise it even higher. The high-tech lobbyists were outraged, and so were other Republican-leaning interest groups who saw low corporate taxes as the key to U.S. economic recovery.

As often happens in politics, a personal connection helped channel Morgenthaler and Dennis's dealmaking and Zschau's exuberance into actual legislation. It came via Silicon Valley's congressman, Paul "Pete" McCloskey, a moderate Republican, ardent environmentalist, antiwar activist, and—reflective of the intimate little world that was the Valley in the 1970s—a law school classmate and neighbor of Reid Dennis.

McCloskey was sympathetic to the cause, but he had very little clout. He was a member of the minority party with little patience for playing the political gamesmanship needed to succeed on Capitol Hill. Moreover, he had managed to royally tick off most of his partisan comrades by running a primary challenge against President Nixon in 1972 to protest the continuation of the Vietnam War. However, this self-described "bad boy of the Republican Party" had an influential friend: an up-and-coming young Republican legislator from Wisconsin named William Steiger, who held a seat on the tax-writing Appropriations Committee.[57]

Then in his late thirties, Steiger's boyish looks often had him mistaken for a congressional page. Although hailing from America's Dairyland, the congressman was sold on the entrepreneurial pitch of the Silicon Valley executives. He agreed to introduce legislation to return the capital gains tax back to 1969 levels.

Business interests had already come out swinging in response to Carter's tax plan—more than three hundred people testified before the House Ways and Means Committee in the spring of 1978 about the package—and the Steiger Bill intensified the political firestorm. By late June, the little bill sponsored by an obscure GOP legislator had garnered a great deal of support, from Democrats as well as Republicans. Other, more established business interests joined the chorus, lending their lobbying muscle to the cause.[58]

The tech interests and their allies had helped reframe the tax as something that benefited scrappy entrepreneurs, small-business people, and plucky inventors. Although there was scant evidence that the general public actually cared about capital gains tax cuts—polling in fact found that Carter's tax plan had good support among voters—official Washington bought into the new definition with enthusiasm.[59]

One *Washington Post* op-ed in support of the bill did a clever retake on New Deal rhetoric by calling the U.S. investor "today's 'forgotten man.'" Making matters worse was the passage of the property-tax-cutting Proposition 13 in California. Worried legislators looked westward at a brewing tax revolt and did not want to be on the wrong side of history. "It's the old Horatio Alger vision" said one analyst. "People want to keep taxes on investments low in case they strike it rich themselves someday." "It's obvious," observed the *Post*'s editorial board that June, "that there has been a profound change in basic opinions about the tax structure—particularly among Democrats."[60]

The Carter administration initially struck back quite forcefully—Treasury Secretary Michael Blumenthal scoffed that the bill should be called the "Millionaire's Relief Act"—but as the summer session neared its end, it was clear that the measure had a veto-proof majority. The White House had to back down.[61] The tax reform package that Carter eventually signed in fall 1978 cut the capital gains tax to 28 percent. The NVCA and AEA had won, and their emissaries had become seasoned political operators in the process.[62]

The tax bill taught the Carter team a potent political lesson. High-tech business was now a virtuous, even populist, political actor. They would score no points by appearing to stand in the way of giving entrepreneurs access to cash. The following year, venture investment got an even bigger boost when the Department of Labor (also a target of tech-industry lobbying) expanded its interpretation of the Employment Retirement Income Security Act's "prudent man" rule and allowed pension funds to make riskier, venture-backed investments, opening up another huge source of capital to the world of tech startups. Between 1978 and 1980, a staggering $1.5 billion in additional venture investment flowed into the tech world, allowing companies to scale up into corporate behemoths just as the PC and the home video game reached the technological and price point that made a large consumer market possible.[63]

In the wake of the summer of 1978, high-tech investors and executives became wise to the ways of Washington, and national politicians on both sides of the aisle increasingly gained an appreciation of how support for tech issues might win the votes of an increasingly independent-minded electorate. As a result, bipartisan support emerged for critical tax and regulatory changes that accelerated the growth of technology and telecommunications industries.

By the fall of 1980, more than seventy-five pieces of legislation had been introduced in Congress that had to do with industrial innovation. The House and Senate passed several new measures aimed at further helping startup companies raise capital and cut red tape. "Small business in general and the high-technology companies in particular have suddenly become the darlings of Washington," noted *Business Week* on the eve of the November election. Even before Ronald Reagan won the White House, politicians of both parties clamored to help the high-tech entrepreneur.[64]

The capital gains tax fight was one of many blows to the liberal agenda during the Carter years, and a sign that the interests and priorities of the New Deal order were on precarious footing. Another sign was the rising power of a new generation of Democrats on Capitol Hill and in the country's statehouses, many of them "Watergate Babies" elected in the wake of Nixon's disgrace in 1974 as part of a sweep that picked up forty-nine seats for Democrats in the House and five seats in the Senate.[65]

All male and all white, these politicians were socially liberal but had little engagement in the activist social policy agenda of the groups that had remade the face of the post–civil rights Democratic Party since the 1960s. Many represented places that had been epicenters of Cold War defense spending and now were emergent high-tech hubs (see Table 10.1). They were roughly the same age, race, and gender as many of the beanbag-inhabiting hackers and engineers-turned-entrepreneurs of Route 128 and Silicon Valley. Yet the two communities might have inhabited different planets. One had decided to change the world through policymaking; the other through business. One ardently believed in the power of political ideas and of government action;

Table 10.1. From Watergate Babies to Atari Democrats: Lawmakers Described as "Atari Democrats" and/or "High-Tech" Advocates in National Publications, 1980–1986

Name	First elected	Positions held	Policy priorities, 1975–1980*	Policy priorities, 1980–1984*
Gary Hart	1974	Senator, CO	Energy; tax reform	Education; trade; energy
Timothy Wirth	1974	Congressman, CO (1st) Senator, CO	Government reform; energy	Research; tax reform; energy
Paul Tsongas	1974	Senator, MA	Research; energy and environment	Education; research; tax reform; energy
Jerry Brown	1974	Governor, CA	Government reform; energy and environment	Technology; education; environment
Michael Dukakis	1974	Governor, MA	Government reform	Technology; education; transportation
Richard Gephardt	1976	Congressman, MO (3rd)	Government reform; energy	Tax reform
Al Gore Jr.	1976	Congressman, TN (4th, 6th) Senator, TN	Trade	Technology; education
Bill Bradley	1978	Senator, NJ	Education; energy	Tax reform
Bruce Babbitt	1978	Governor, AZ	Energy; government reform	Government reform; tax reform

*Policy emphases of legislation sponsored or cosponsored; major state initiatives and national leadership roles.
Source: Database searches of the New York Times, Wall Street Journal, Washington Post, Newsweek, Time, and Businessweek using individual names and the terms Atari Democrats or high-tech, or technology.

the other had a political temperament that ranged from nonpartisan to avowedly libertarian.[66]

High tech was not on the minds of these lawmakers as they arrived in Congress, but New Deal liberalism held little allure. "The Democratic Party, under penalty of irrelevance and extinction, must bring forward a new generation of thinkers who are in touch with the real world," Gary Hart wrote in 1973, months after the defeat of the McGovern campaign of which he had been the manager.[67] As the new generation's ranks swelled with the 1976 and 1978 elections, they started to display a hybrid sort of politics that blended fiscal conservatism with social liberalism in ways unseen since the era of the "Modern Republicans" of the 1950s.[68] On top of that, however, was a layer of decidedly post-1960s cultural influences and ideas. Building on the tax reforms enacted in 1978, Democrats in the Ninety-Sixth Congress swung toward using tax expenditures to accomplish policy goals. Bill Bradley introduced a bill to provide tax credits for electric cars. Dick Gephardt proposed tax incentives for alternative energy development. Gary Hart proposed tax credits for homeowners who used solar panels.[69]

As Jimmy Carter and Ted Kennedy battled it out for the 1980 nomination, the new-breed Democrats on the Hill began to articulate a broader economic vision. Current trade policies, tax rates, and subsidies were not enough. It was time for an industrial policy on par with Japan and Singapore. Furthermore, such a microeconomic strategy should not focus on the old manufacturers who were struggling, but on the new high-tech industries that were skyrocketing. Because these were knowledge-driven industries, the government needed to invest in the raw materials—people and research knowledge—that fueled productive capacity. At its essence, the industrial policy idea was about *reforming* the system to make it work better. The vision had intellectual kinship with the Silicon Valley hacker culture: take over the system, and retrofit it for the modern age. The ideas were progressive and hopeful and promised liberals they could have new economy without leaving the New Deal coalition behind.

The vision had plenty of critics, on the Left and Right. The liberal economist Robert Kuttner observed, "If you switch from steel to semiconductors, you go from union to nonunion and I don't see how you can get [AFL-CIO President] Lane Kirkland to sign onto that bargain." From the Right, Bruce Bartlett, the Republican staff head of the congressional Joint Economic Committee, scoffed, "It's just new rhetoric to disguise economic planning."[70] And despite their relish for wading into the policy details, the group now known as the Atari Democrats could not shake the accusations that they were more style than substance. "These new-breed guys were born in the TV studio, and the old breed were born in the political clubhouse," scoffed Chris Matthews, then an aide to House Speaker Tip O'Neill. "The old guys worked their way up through the chairs. . . . They dance with the girl they came with. The new-breed guys are one-night stands."[71]

Yet as the 1982 midterm elections neared, the House Democratic Caucus decided to sponsor a report on long-term economic policy and asked Tim Wirth to write it. The result, titled *Rebuilding the Road to Economic Opportunity*, demonstrated how far the new-breed ideas had percolated into the political consciousness. Some of Wirth's passages channeled the spirit of the venture capitalist: "It is up to our party to rekindle the entrepreneurial spirit in America, to encourage the investment and the risk taking—in private industry and in the public sector—that is essential if we are to maintain leadership in the world economy." Others echoed bedrock New Deal liberalism: "Free-market capitalism is the basis of our economy, and remains the first and best hope for long-term growth and jobs. But just as it has done throughout our history . . . government must be a vital partner." The report also showed how the entrepreneurial rhetoric of business interests like the AEA and NVCA in the late 1970s had changed the conversation about business and taxes. "It is particularly important," Wirth observed evenly, "that revised business tax laws take into account the special needs of small entrepreneurs who have produced so much innovation in our economy."[72]

Despite the Democratic embrace of tech, the industry and its Washington representatives maintained close ties to the GOP side of the aisle. One reason was Ed Zschau, who had moved from the Silicon Valley boardroom to Republican politics, and was elected to the House in 1982 as "Silicon Valley's Congressman." Another was the continued focus of the AEA and NVCA on the supply-side realm of capital gains and other tax cuts.[73]

It was also personal; like other businesspeople of their age, region, and tax bracket, the venture capitalists and industry executives active in the two trade associations often voted Republican. Furthermore, the hawkishness and escalated military spending of the Reagan administration had revved defense contracts back up for Silicon Valley and other regions with defense ties. The elevation of the Bay Area power broker (and tech advocate) George Shultz further strengthened the ties between high-tech defense contractors and the Reagan administration.[74]

Despite this, many in the high-tech industry were little impressed by early Reaganomics, chiefly because it did little to stem what was now the biggest threat to the industry's growth: Japan. Partly as a result of the Japanese government's extraordinary government investments in research and strict market regulations (the same policies that had inspired the Democrats' industrial policy proposals), Japan's semiconductor manufacturers had been ahead of Silicon Valley in bringing higher-speed chips to market and had been able to significantly undercut the Americans on price. By 1982 Japan had captured 40 percent of the market for 16K RAM chips, and had gotten ahead of Valley firms in developing and manufacturing the next-generation 64K and 256K RAM devices. Although the overall market had doubled since 1978, the U.S. merchant producers no longer had the near-monopoly they once enjoyed. Vertically integrated Japanese manufacturers could build a chip and put it in a finished consumer product in less time and at less cost.[75]

California semiconductor manufacturers had long felt that the distinct challenges facing their industry made their concerns different from the rest, and had organized themselves separately from the AEA as the Semiconductor Industry Association (SIA), which emerged as the result of a 1977 dinner of top chip-making executives in Palo Alto. But Washington lobbying efforts made up only a tiny fraction of the SIA budget.[76] One year into the Regan era, Japan's share of the semiconductor market continued to climb, and the Reagan tax reforms of 1981 left high-tech industries paying higher taxes than smokestack industries. "We're really taxing winners and subsidizing losers," said John Albertine, the president of the American Business Conference, a Wall Street–based lobbying group for small- to medium-sized companies.[77]

Worried Silicon Valley CEOs decided to come to Washington in person to press their case. At the helm of this effort was the Intel cofounder Robert Noyce, who had decided to step back his involvement from the day-to-day workings of his company and was casting about for a next act. Noyce, along with fellow chipmakers like Charlie Sporck of National Semiconductor and Jerry Sanders of AMD (Advanced Micro Devices), descended on the White House and Capitol Hill starting in 1981 and made repeated visits over the course of Reagan's first term. Their message was dire and sounded eerily familiar to the laments of the Rust Belt. Noyce warned that Silicon Valley might become another Detroit. Even more despondent, the National Semiconductor executive John Nesheim declared, "It is just a matter of time before we fall and are crushed."[78] The SIA's request, somewhat surprising given the political mood and its own politics: *more* government intervention, via trade sanctions, market quotas, and investments in next-generation research.[79]

Not all U.S. chipmakers agreed. Texas Instruments, which had successfully entered Japanese markets, scoffed at the Californians' lobbying, saying that this was a crisis of their own making. "Those fellows on the West Coast sort of have schizophrenia," said TI's president, Fred Bucy. "They had the same leverage as we did in dealing with the Japanese."[80] But by the summer of 1982, Sanders was proudly reporting back to a group of fellow technology executives, "We are gaining champions in Washington; we're no longer considered Cowboy Capitalists, Boutique Manufacturers or California Crybabies."[81]

In 1983, in an effort to respond to all the anxieties swirling around Washington about foreign competition, Ronald Reagan established a Committee on Industrial Competitiveness, headed by the Hewlett-Packard chief John Young and including Bob Noyce among its several other Silicon Valley members. The makeup of Reagan's committee demonstrated that Republicans had plenty of powerful high-tech allies, but it indicated the persistence of the generational divide that had marked new economy politics for a decade. When it came to thinking about high technology in the future tense—beyond manufacturing, beyond big companies, beyond trade wars—the business-minded Republicans lagged behind the high-tech Democrats.

En Route to the Google Economy:
Post–New Deal Liberalism

In *Rebuilding the Road to Opportunity*, the congressional Democrats made the case that the New Deal coalition could have its high-tech cake and eat it, too. Shifting government resources and political attention away from the lumbering "sunset" industries of heavy manufacturing and toward the "sunrise" industries of high technology would not only give the U.S. economy the jolt it so desperately needed, but it could be done in a way that would not leave the union rank and file behind. Just as retooling could save the Rust Belt factory, they argued, so could education and training retool the blue-collar manufacturing workforce, giving them the skills that high technology needed.

In March 1983, however, the Atari Democrats' namesake company demonstrated quite forcefully that what the high-tech industry actually needed was a cheaper workforce, not necessarily a more highly skilled one. Feeling the lingering effects of the recession that had hit Silicon Valley with nearly equal force as it had the rest of the country, and still never having quite gotten a sound business footing in the first place, Atari announced that it was moving its 1,700 manufacturing jobs to Asia. "What people have tended to forget," noted one industry analyst, "is that eventually high-technology industries become competitive, like any other industry. And keeping labor costs down is a crucial part of being competitive."[82] Atari was not alone. By the time it made its move, more than 90 percent of the semiconductor manufacturing industry's assembly work was happening overseas, chiefly in Singapore, Taiwan, and South Korea.

After that, the Atari Democrat label started to fade. Paul Tsongas had been the only member of the group who had actually embraced the nickname in the first place, and by the time Gary Hart made his first run for president he, Tsongas, and the rest were more often referred to as "neoliberals" or "postliberals." Neoliberalism was also a moniker that the lawmakers bore with reluctance; ultimately, the most enthusiastic, self-identified neoliberals during the era were pundits and academics, not elected officials.[83] Instead, many of these new-breed Democrats insisted, they were *liberals*—but liberals who were in touch with the realities of the new economy.

Even so, many of them could not shake the slick, made-for-TV label that Democratic rivals had pinned on them. As Walter Mondale famously quipped during his 1984 primary debate with Gary Hart: "Where's the beef?" The headline-making barb—which the Mondale team had included at the suggestion of the AFL-CIO chief Lane Kirkland—reinforced the narrative that Hart lacked the gravitas for the job, and his once-ascendant candidacy never quite recovered from it.[84] The territory of Reagan's landslide included the rolling hills and low-slung tech parks of Silicon Valley, where the combination of the PC boom and Reagan defense and space contracts had made the place into what one observer called "a satisfied society."[85]

Yet only eight years later, the Democrat Bill Clinton (and his vice president, the former Atari Democrat Al Gore) took back the White House after a campaign whose platform echoed so many of the policy ideas put forth during this earlier moment of high-tech politics. A key moment on Clinton's road to victory came in September 1992, when a bipartisan group of high-tech executives publicly declared their support. "I am still a Republican," the Apple chief John Sculley told the *New York Times*, "but I am voting for Bill Clinton because I don't believe America's industries can survive four more years of President Bush."[86]

At the start of the 2020s, the PC is middle aged, the consumer internet nearly three decades old, and the twelve largest technology companies in the world have catapulted beyond multimillion-dollar valuations to a combined market capitalization of over $2.8 *trillion*.[87] Some tech companies—Google, Apple, Microsoft, Amazon, Facebook—have achieved such ubiquity that it is nearly impossible for a middle-class American to move through daily routines without encountering or using one or more of their products.

Despite this saturation, the iconoclastic, freewheeling, and free-market mythos of the tech world persists. Many in the technology industry have gravitated toward what Shane Hamilton has characterized as "a radically antistatist capitalist ideology" that emerged in the wake of 1970s realignments, even as they have moved away from the political disengagement that characterized tech's early years and have become political power brokers, particularly on the Democratic side of the aisle.[88]

Yet when we step back from "the new economy" nomenclature and historicize this politics, we can recognize that much about these companies is not all that new, and that their success has old-economy roots. Tech giants like Google and Amazon may style themselves as firms of the future, but their success stems in part from managerial hierarchies that blend the organizational chart of the twentieth-century corporation with the personal sensibilities of the nineteenth-century sole proprietorship. They are creatures of the state in ways both seen and unseen, originating in the military-industrial complex but extending far beyond it.

Looking at high technology through a political lens debunks the myth of high tech as a free-market meritocracy. Similarly, looking at politics through a high-tech filter complicates our understanding of what happened in Washington after 1970. National lawmakers on both the right and the left ends of the political spectrum have aided and abetted the pervasive mythology of the iconoclastic, self-sufficient technology entrepreneur. With technology companies having become as much a political story as a business one, it is high time to write the state back into this iconic post–New Deal story.

Silicon Valley's products have disrupted markets, to be sure, but the companies themselves have been important disruptors of the political order as well. By stepping away from and disavowing the foundational role that government spending played in the industry's growth—public policy had "absolutely nothing to do with" the success of the Valley, one thirty-year Apple veteran told me not too long ago—and by giving austerity-minded lawmakers a compelling example of corporate success without unionization and with tax cuts and free trade policies, the computer hardware and software industries of Silicon Valley created a new and politically alluring model of U.S. capitalism that has had ripple effects far beyond the realm of tech.

CHAPTER 11

The Other Operation Dixie

Public Employees and the Resilience of Urban Liberalism

William P. Jones

In April 1946, the *New York Times* reported that leaders of the Congress of Industrial Organizations (CIO) were launching "two major organizing drives" at neighboring hotels in Atlantic City. At the Breakers, the United Textile Workers of America devoted a million dollars to Operation Dixie, a "holy crusade" aimed at organizing textiles, lumber, and other major industries in the southern United States. Meanwhile, down the boardwalk at the Chelsea, the United Public Workers of America (UPWA) set out to unionize the nearly five million workers employed by local, state, and federal governments across the country and its territories. Noting that the American Federation of Labor (AFL) was planning similar campaigns in both fields, the *Times* estimated the rival federations would invest more than $4 million to expand their ranks by the end of the year. *Businessweek* noted that southern industrial workers and public employees represented the largest remaining nonunion workforces following organized labor's unprecedented expansion in the previous decade, making the "Dual Campaign" a major test of the labor movement's power and relevance in the United States following World War II.[1]

Although Operation Dixie is now widely recognized as a "decisive juncture" in the rise and fall of the New Deal order, scholars have largely forgotten the postwar campaigns to organize the public sector. A large body of literature shows that the southern industrial campaign was undermined by staunch resistance from southern employers, elected officials and clergy; and union leaders who prioritized white textile workers who proved ambivalent toward organized labor and failed to confront racial segregation and discrimination in the region. In addition to halting the expansion of industrial unionism nationally, this left the South as a bastion of conservative opposition to both the social liberalism of the New Deal and the racially egalitarian liberalism of the civil rights movement. In stark contrast, however, public-sector unions faced less hostility from employers, focused on low-wage, mostly female and nonwhite service workers who proved enthusiastic supporters of organized labor and went out of their way to confront racial discrimination and segregation. That approach allowed public-sector unions to grow steadily despite a backlash against organized labor in the late 1940s and early 1950s, and to emerge as the fastest growing affiliates of the newly merged AFL–CIO after 1955.[2]

Unions did not grow rapidly enough in government to offset their losses in manufacturing, but the postwar campaign established an important foothold for organized labor in the late twentieth century. The biggest barriers to public-sector unionism in the 1930s and 1940s were high turnover rates in government employment, particularly in low-wage service jobs where wages and benefits lagged far behind unionized manufacturing, and the lack of legal protections that aided industrial unionism on those decades. Unions stabilized labor markets by pushing for better wages, benefits, and informal work rules that provided a degree of security and protection to workers who were often excluded from both federal labor laws and state civil service protections. The increased size and militancy of public-sector unions also pushed cities and states to develop local laws governing unionization and collective bargaining by public employees. Those laws were weaker and more restrictive than the National Labor Relations Act, which regulated collective bargaining in the private sector. Nevertheless, the share of public employees who belonged to unions jumped from 13 percent to more than 35 percent between 1962 and 1984, while private sector unions shrunk by a similar proportion.[3]

Just as the defeat of Operation Dixie marked a turning point for New Deal liberalism in the South, success in the public sector allowed unions to remain key players in the economic and political history of the late twentieth-century United States. By improving wages and benefits for the most exploited public servants, unions transformed the public sector from a low-wage employment ghetto into "the principle source of black mobility, especially for women, and one of the most important mechanisms for reducing black poverty." Beyond their economic impact, public-sector unions also emerged as important political forces in U.S. cities. Allying with civil rights and feminist organizations, they attacked discrimination in employment and access to public services, worked to expand opportunities for leadership by African Americans and women in organized labor, and wielded significant influence in electoral politics. In these respects, public-sector unions forged an early model of the "social bargaining" that Kate Andrias highlights as a path forward for organized labor in her contribution to this volume (Chapter 12).[4]

Thus, in addition to extending the social democracy of New Deal liberalism into the late twentieth century, public-sector unions expanded and transformed that legacy by linking it to the egalitarianism of the civil rights and feminist movements. Nelson Lichtenstein points out that this shifted the debate over collective bargaining in the public sector from fear that unions would undermine the sovereignty of the state to the charge that they used their power to push for the state's expansion. In the context of a conservative campaign to dismantle the welfare state, such criticism often rested on misleading claims about the rising cost of government and the lavish pay and benefits of public employees. Yet, as Lichtenstein indicates, conservatives were correct in their observation that public-sector unions had emerged as powerful defenders of both the jobs of public employees and the public services they provided. By the end of the twentieth century, in fact, the collapse of industrial unions meant that public-sector unions were often the only institutions left to oppose the dismantling of public education, health care, and other public services.[5]

That shifting context gains additional relevance in light of recent attacks on the collective-bargaining rights of public employees. Starting in Wisconsin, the state that first extended collective-bargaining rights to public employees in 1959, elected officials scaled back protections that had been critical to government workers' ability to sustain unions and improve their wages and working conditions in the past half century. Retrenchment gained steam from the U.S. Supreme Court ruling, in the 2017 case *Janus v. AFSCME*, which prohibited public-sector unions from charging fees to nonunion workers that unions were required to represent. Wisconsin saw a sharp drop in union membership among public employees and, although union membership held steady and even increased in some states, the Supreme Court ruling devastated union treasuries and inspired further attacks on the legal rights and political influence of unionized public employees.[6]

With this rising effort to reverse the legal protections that public employees gained in the 1960s and 1970s, it is important to understand how and why they were won and the influence they had on both public employees and the broader society in the following decades. The sociologist Jake Rosen-field has cautioned correctly against the hope that the success of public employee unionism could counteract the collapse of industrial unionism in the late twentieth century. He points out that government employs far fewer workers than the private sector, that collective bargaining rights vary significantly from state to state, and that the relatively high wages of public employees limit the economic and political benefits of unionization for both union members and the broader society. This does not consider, however, the degree to which unions have already improved wages and working conditions in government, particularly for the lowest-paid, mostly marginalized workers, while also defending public services in the face of a broader backlash against the social democratic legacies of the New Deal. At a time of increased criticism of public-sector unionism, we should ask how different the postwar era would have looked without it.[7]

The contrasts between the CIO's two postwar organizing drives were obvious from their beginnings in Atlantic City. Leaders of Operation Dixie went out of their way to distance themselves from demands for racial equality, which they believed would make it impossible to win support from white workers in the South. "They believe that the question, 'You want your pay raised, don't you?' is a more effective gambit than a long talk about human equality and human rights," reported the Saturday Evening Post. In stark contrast, several newly elected officers of the United Public Workers were arrested for protesting racial discrimination at Hackneys, an iconic seafood restaurant on the boardwalk. Turned away by a manager who explained, "I have no waitress who will wait on colored people," the interracial group walked out and started picketing. Police warned that the picket was illegal because they had "no labor dispute" with the establishment and, despite their insistence that New Jersey's civil rights law prohibited racial discrimination, several were arrested and two spent the night in jail. The following morning the executive committee of the United Public Workers pledged its "fullest backing" to defending those arrested and to suing Hackneys under the civil rights law, established a special committee to investigate racial discrimination in public employment, and urged locals of their union and the CIO more broadly to publicize the incident. "This is a fight for all that is decent in American life," the union newspaper declared, "and we are proud that the first official action" of the new leadership came "in fighting for these basic principles."[8]

Although industrial unionists characterized the fight against racism as a distraction from economic issues such as wages and benefits, organizers found it more difficult to separate them in the public sector. Ewart Guinier, one of the black UPWA leaders refused service at Hackneys, was in the midst of a campaign to organize maids, janitors, and other low-wage workers at municipal hospitals in New York City. At a time when New Deal labor policies empowered industrial workers to demand health-care benefits from their employers, many of the workers who provided those services worked forty-eight-hour weeks and still depended on public relief to support their families. "Large numbers of these workers are women and Negroes," Guinier said at a city budget hearing the week before the Atlantic City convention, indicating that city officials practiced the policy common in the private sector "of paying Negroes the lowest wages for the hardest jobs." Municipal hospitals remained central to the public-sector campaign, Guinier explained, because they employed the "largest group of Negro workers in public service in New York State and one of the largest concentrations of Negro workers in any industry in New York City." In addition to improving wages and working conditions for the lowest-paid and hardest-worked city employees, union organizers contended, a successful campaign would improve health care for all people in New York City, facilitate unionization of other public employees, and "serve as a major base for the election of progressive candidates."[9]

The United Public Workers grew most rapidly in liberal northern cities, but the union also made significant headway in the conservative South. In addition to pledging support for Guinier and others arrested on the boardwalk, delegates to the Atlantic City convention denounced an "act of intimidation" against Ruby Jackson, an African American teacher who led a UPWA local in Birmingham, Alabama. The previous year, Jackson's union had secured a federal court order requiring "equal pay for equal work, regardless of race or color," for all teachers in the state. She and another teacher were fired after suing their districts for noncompliance with the order, but the UPWA launched a nationwide campaign that gained support from unions, churches, and black newspapers and civil rights groups and eventually secured their reinstatement along with statewide compliance with the equalization order. The victory inspired unionization by black and white teachers in Alabama, as well as maids and janitors at public schools and universities, cafeteria and laundry workers at state and federal hospitals, and municipal street and sanitation workers in Alabama, Georgia, Tennessee, North and South Carolina, Virginia, and Maryland. The UPWA grew most rapidly among low-wage service workers but, in addition to teachers, the union gained support from professors at black colleges in Tuskegee, Alabama, and Hampton, Virginia.[10]

Wherever they organized, UPWA leaders insisted that workplace issues such as wages and benefits could not be isolated from broader questions of equality and human rights. Four months after the Atlantic City convention, in August 1946, the CIO announced that seventeen thousand federal employees in the Panama Canal Zone had formed a UPWA local and won wage and benefits increases, a grievance procedure and collective bargaining rights. Their next step, according to the *New York Times*, was the "elimination of racial discrimination in employment." AFL unions had represented U.S. citizens on the canal since its construction in the early twentieth century and persuaded canal authorities to provide their members with wages and living standards comparable to those in the United States. They denied union membership to West Indians, however; and demanded that they be paid far lower wages and excluded from the housing, health clinics, schools, and other public services provided for U.S. citizens and their families. Over time, that arrangement evolved into a pattern of racial segregation, known as the "Silver/Gold" system, in which nonwhite workers—including West Indians, Asians, and even black citizens of the United States—were barred from public services reserved for white workers and their families. Ewart Guinier had grown up in the Canal Zone, and he enlisted the black activists W. E. B Du Bois and Paul Robeson to cochair the union's Committee to End Silver-Gold Jim Crow. After a yearlong campaign, they convinced authorities to desegregate public services in the Canal Zone and raise wages and benefits for West Indian workers to the standards of the U.S. civil service.[11]

The United Public Workers' approach was so effective that it pushed more conservative AFL unions to pay closer attention to low-wage workers in the public sector. The American Federation of State, County and Municipal Employees (AFSCME) had been founded in the 1930s by state bureaucrats in Madison, Wisconsin, and expanded by organizing mostly white professionals, law enforcement, and skilled workers in county and state governments across the Midwest and Northeast. Convinced that public servants could improve their conditions most effectively through quiet lobbying and negotiation, the union prohibited locals from going on strike and rejected calls for collective bargaining rights similar to those used by unions in the private sector. That caution led AFSCME organizers to avoid African American workers as they moved into the South, arguing that they were "disgruntled" and likely to strike, "which would hurt our organization rather than benefit it."

They reconsidered during World War II however, after black garbage collectors won a strike in Atlanta and white truck drivers complained that union policies prohibited them from following suit. After the war, the AFSCME hired former CIO activists to organize low-wage hospital and janitorial workers in Detroit, New York, and Los Angeles, and started pushing local officials to recognize unions and to bargain for better wages and contracts.[12]

The UPWA's militancy proved effective but, as leaders of Operation Dixie predicted, it also provoked a backlash. In June 1946, three months after the Atlantic City convention, five members of the new union were fired from their jobs at Aberdeen Proving Ground, where the U.S. army tested rockets and missiles. Although the War Department stated that the action had "no connection whatever with their union activities," it seemed to have been related to a resolution, adopted after considerable debate at the convention, that "was widely interpreted as" authorizing strikes by federal employees. Congress responded to news of the resolution by prohibiting federal funds from being paid to members of unions that asserted the right to strike. A War Department spokesman explained that "only a few dozen" workers were dismissed "in the interest of national defense," and that they were physicists and chemists engaged in sensitive areas. "This ought to show," he stated, "that the War Department hasn't gone off half-cocked to 'witch-hunt, red bait, or to bust' unions." Nevertheless, UPWA president Abraham Flaxer called the move "an obvious union-busting device."[13]

Tensions increased after the UPWA established its local in the Panama Canal Zone. In October 1946, the U.S. House Un-American Activities Committee (HUAC) opened an investigation into reports that the union was "bent on spreading subversion among the 17,000 non American colored employees in the Canal Zone." UPWA leaders insisted they were "not threatening nor will we ever threaten the security of the United States; we are merely trying to alleviate low pay and viscous discrimination." When Canal authorities sought, however, to alleviate tensions by raising wages and promising equal treatment for "silver" and "gold" workers, anticommunists complained that they were allowing union organizers to "plant the Communist seed of 'racial discrimination.'" A report circulated to HUAC and then printed in the anticommunist magazine, *Plain Talk*, explained that UPWA members worked in schools, hospitals, hotels, and restaurants that served the U.S. citizens who operated the canal, and were represented by AFL craft unions. Nevertheless, the author insisted that the mostly Panamanian and West Indian service workers were "as vital to our defenses as the civilian employees of our War Department."[14]

Union leaders responded to these attacks by affirming their loyalty to the United States and their independence from the Communist Party, but that grew more difficult as anxieties rose over Soviet subversion during the Cold War. A committee of CIO leaders, which included UPWA president Abram Flaxer, issued a resolution condemning communist interference with the CIO and pledging to "resist with all our might" any attempt "to undermine or destroy our free institutions." After meeting with Flaxer and other union leaders, the attorney general decided not to include the UPWA on a list of subversive organizations that federal employees were forbidden from joining. CIO leaders also cooperated with AFL unions and the American Civil Liberties Union to protest proposals to require public employees to sign "loyalty oaths" in federal agencies and New York, Los Angeles, and other cities. That unity broke down, however, when UPWA locals disrupted public signing ceremonies and refused to answer questions about their own party affiliation. In June 1947, Congress passed the Taft–Hartley Act, which required union officials to sign an affidavit stating they were not communists. The law did not apply to the public sector, but many public officials stopped negotiating with unions that did not meet that standard. At least one UPWA local president was fired on charges of leading "a Communist-dominated" union, a decision that an appeals court found to have "run counter to every known precept of fairness" but justified in response to subversion.[15]

By undermining negotiations with employers, the fight over anticommunism also bolstered opposition from union members who believed their leaders were placing political commitments ahead of the economic interests of public employees. That complaint emerged initially at the Atlantic City convention, when delegates adopted a resolution calling on the United States to withdraw from China and India and stop trying to "isolate" the Soviet Union but rejected a similar statement condemning the Soviet occupation of Poland. Soon afterward, members in Washington, DC, formed a "Build the Union" caucus to challenge leaders who "abuse their position in the union to advance their views." A meeting of dissidents from Washington, New York, Chicago, Detroit, Atlanta, and other cities condemned restrictions on political expression but charged the current leadership with allowing the union to be "branded in the press as a 'left-wing,' pro-Communist union," which made it "virtually impossible" to recruit new members. By the spring of 1948, locals representing thousands of workers were leaving the UPWA and seeking affiliation with other unions. Abram Flaxer deepened the rift by suspending leaders of a Detroit local for holding a "secret meeting" to draft a resolution demanding he sign an affidavit stating he was not a communist.[16]

CIO leaders responded to the crisis by expelling unions whose leaders refused to sign the affidavits but, although this weakened those unions considerably, it did not end the campaign to organize the public sector. The CIO president Philip Murray gave the unions a year to bring their leadership in order, but authorized the "Build the Union" caucus to begin organizing the thousands of public employees who had already left the UPWA. "We believe it would be a great tragedy if the CIO were to lose those loyal adherents by its failure to act," stated representatives from more than fifty public-sector locals who gathered in Washington, DC, to reorganize "the country's largest single industry." In 1950 CIO leaders finalized the expulsion of nine unions, including the UPWA, and created the Government and Civic Employees Organizing Committee (GCEOC) to resume the job of organizing the public sector. Leaders of both rival factions traveled across the country vying for the loyalty of existing locals. Under increased attack from anticommunists, and stonewalled by public officials and other unions, the UPAW collapsed quickly. The expulsion also deprived the CIO of finances, which were already depleted by the 1946 campaigns, but the GCEOC managed to regain over half the UPWA's membership by 1954.[17]

The expulsion aimed to depoliticize the issue of anticommunism, but CIO leaders took pains to demonstrate that it would not diminish their commitment to racial equality. When Chicago organizers complained that the lack of black leadership in the GCEOC reinforced the UPWA's claim that it was expelled "because they stood up for the Negroes and other minorities," the GCEOC director Milton Murray hired John Yancey, of the black led CIO Transport Services union, as his assistant director. Yancey led a team of black and Mexican American organizers who helped revive the CIO local in Panama, and then directed efforts to revive former UPWA locals in Chicago and Milwaukee. In 1951, the GCEOC secured a U.S. State Department scholarship for Edward Gaskin, the president of the Canal Zone local, to meet with leaders of both the CIO and AFL unions in Los Angeles, Chicago, Birmingham, Alabama, and other cities. "Brother Gaskin has long been a leader in the fight to oppose Communist control of workers in the Canal Zone," wrote the CIO leader Milton Murray, adding that "as a Negro, he has endured the discrimination both social and economic practiced in the Canal Zone." The CIO also redoubled its use of strikes to improve wages and working conditions for the lowest-paid public servants, particularly in the South. After supporting two strikes in Birmingham, Alabama, the organizer Carey Haigler boasted that the union secured grievance, seniority, vacation, and sick leave policies for African American sanitation and janitorial workers who had previously been employed as day laborers.[18]

Ironically, the legacy of the UPWA was sustained most effectively by the AFSCME and other AFL unions that had previously rejected both its militancy and its commitment to racial equality. Having struggled to organize white-collar workers in New York City, the AFSCME took advantage of the CIO's crisis by hiring anticommunist radicals to organize "blue collar" laborers in the parks and streets departments and in municipal hospitals. Jerry Wurf, who rose quickly to leadership of the AFSCME's New York District Council 37, hired civil rights activists to organize mostly African American hospital workers and dispatched union staffers to picket discriminatory stores and restaurants. The AFL Building Services Employees International Union (BSEIU), which had previously focused on mostly white janitors and elevator operators in the private sector, absorbed a UPWA local with nearly ten thousand mostly black and Latino/Latina maids and janitors in Los Angeles. The AFL Teamsters union also expanded by recruiting locals from the UPWA and hiring former UPWA organizers who, according to the labor reporter Daniel Bell, "long followed and have never publicly broken from the Communist line."[19]

The convergence of CIO and AFL approaches solidified with the merger of the two federations in 1955, and set the stage for the dramatic expansion of public-sector unions in the following two decades. Daniel Bell remarked in *Fortune* magazine that only 10 percent of the nearly five million Americans employed by state and local governments belonged to unions. Because increasing demand for education, health care, transportation, and other public services made the public sector "one of the major 'growth areas' of the workforce," he warned, the "failure of unions to win a following among them presents a serious problem for labor." Yet, two developments gave him hope. The first was that, despite their low levels of unionization, public employees are "remarkable joiners" and various civil service associations and mutual benefit groups representing millions of workers were moving increasingly toward affiliation or merger with formal unions. Second, Bell observed that public officials were starting to rethink the long-standing assumption that unions did not belong in government, which stood in stark contrast to Europe where the public servant was seen "as the intellectual leader of the working-class." He pointed to an executive order issued the previous year by New York's mayor, Robert Wagner, whose father had written the National Labor Relations Act to promote private-sector unions in the 1930s. In addition to encouraging department heads to meet with union representatives, it created a City Labor Department to develop a collective-bargaining policy for city agencies. "If this system is successful," Bell predicted, "and if the city's final code grants full collective bargaining rights, then unions will press for the adoption of similar codes throughout the country."[20]

Collective-bargaining rights have been described as "harmless" gestures designed to "mobilize the public-sector workforce behind" Wagner and other liberal politicians, but they were adopted because public employees had already mobilized. Wagner promised to issue the order during his campaign for Mayor in 1953, after the AFSCME organized a "mass demonstration that pointed up the union's growing strength," and after his election, the union "constantly had to threaten and plead to win any concessions on labor-management relations." The mayor of Philadelphia granted "sole and exclusive bargaining rights" to the AFSCME in 1957, but explained it was to prevent "wasteful union competition" rather than to empower the workers. He also may have hoped to help union leaders constrain the militancy of mostly African American sanitation workers who paralyzed the city with a wildcat strike in 1953. Even in the AFSCME's home state of Wisconsin, the Socialist mayor of Milwaukee rejected requests for a collective-bargaining system on the grounds that "dealing with public employees is a legislative function that cannot be delegated to a bargaining committee." In New York City, Wagner waited until 1958 to finally adopt a policy that was so vague that unions "were obliged to resort periodically to demonstrations, mass meetings, full-page newspaper ads, radio announcements, and even job actions, at almost every important point of negotiations."[21]

By 1959, when Wisconsin adopted the first statewide collective-bargaining law for the public sector, 1.5 million government workers had already joined a union. That represented a 60 percent increase over the previous decade, slightly higher than the 51 percent increase in state and local government employment. The most impressive growth came from the AFSCME, which had doubled its membership since 1956 to reach 200,000 by the end of the decade. AFSCME president Arnold Zander was particularly proud of the "voluntary character" of his membership, which was necessary because most states and cities had no formal policies for determining representation. Without collective bargaining rights, and often legally barred from striking, workers relied on "the tactic of the calculated squeeze," such as "an embarrassing picket line" or a well-timed demonstration at City Hall, to pressure politicians into doing the right thing. That was costly and inefficient, however, and relied on the goodwill of elected officials facing pressure to control costs while expanding public services. "We believe in collective bargaining instead of collective begging," explained Jerry Wurf, who led the union's rapidly expanding District 37 in New York City. Based on its "growth, potential, and ability to outlast others," *Businessweek* magazine predicted that the AFSCME could become the largest and most influential union in the AFL–CIO.[22]

Even as other cities and states followed the examples of Philadelphia, New York, and Wisconsin, the weakness and inconsistency of collective-bargaining policies forced the AFSCME and other unions to maintain the militancy that had sustained public-sector unionism in previous decades. In 1962 President John F. Kennedy directed federal agencies to negotiate with unions over working conditions and policies for grievances, transfers, and promotion. He set unusually high standards for unions to meet before representing all workers, and forbade bargaining over wages or benefits, but the order lent legitimacy to state and local collective-bargaining laws. By 1968 nine states had adopted collective bargaining laws similar to Wisconsin's and three others allowed public officials to "meet and confer" with union representatives. The others varied widely, from permitting unions but not collective bargaining to prohibiting them completely. Most states that allowed collective bargaining prohibited public employees from striking, which proved unenforceable and, when coupled with vague and confusing collective-bargaining rules, was blamed for provoking strikes and other forms of militancy. Ohio faced thirty public-sector strikes in 1967 alone, despite a state law allowing the strikers to be fired. "Public employees will strike unless there are acceptable alternatives," said one of the many industrial-relations professors tasked with developing a statewide policy. "I don't have any answers, and nobody else has any answers."[23]

The struggle for collective bargaining rights also deepened the alliance between economic and racial liberalism that had distinguished the CIO's public-sector campaign in the 1940s. Jerry Wurf allied District 36 with the civil rights movement in New York City, building on the roots that Ewart Guinier established a decade earlier. In 1956 he helped black labor leader A. Philip Randolph form In Friendship to support civil rights activists in the South and he helped the Congress of Racial Equality, which was headed by the AFSCME hospital organizer James Farmer, organize a boycott of Woolworth Stores in New York City to protest the company's discriminatory policies in the South. "The establishment of a closer relationship between labor and the civil rights movement is, in my view, one of the most important contributions to be made in the struggle of our Negro citizens for full equality in our society," Wurf stated in 1963. Cooperation paid off when Randolph and Farmer supported the AFSCME in an election to represent 35,000 workers in the municipal hospitals that Guinier had started organizing in 1946. Building on that victory, District 65 organized a broad range of service workers at city schools, libraries, jails, and laboratories. By 1966 the AFSCME represented over 80,000 workers in New York City.[24]

The AFSCME also built on the CIO's legacy in Chicago. With the AFL–CIO merger, the AFSCME inherited a local of six hundred mostly African American nurses' aides, janitors, cafeteria and laundry workers, and other non-professional employees of hospitals operated by the University of Illinois and the University of Chicago. The union was initiated by the UPWA in the 1940s, and John Yancey had doubled its size after the GCEOC took it over in 1950, but it faced staunch resistance from administrators and Mayor Richard Daley. The AFSCME revived the organization in 1957 and, after building considerable support among workers, launched a strike at two hospitals on the city's South Side. The action enraged Arnold Zander and the AFL leaders in Chicago, who feared it was "doomed to failure," but gained support from black-led CIO unions, student groups, and the National Association for the Advancement of Colored People. Administrators refused to recognize the union, which conceded defeat after five months of picketing, but a wage increase, grievance procedure, and a reduced workweek with no cut in pay. Led by Lillian Roberts, a charismatic nurse's aide who emerged as an influential leader of the AFSCME, the strike also became "a symbol for many of the fight against black exploitation by the Daley machine and by business leaders who viewed themselves as liberals."[25]

As with the UPWA, the AFSCME made its most dramatic impact in the South. Having focused its southern organizing on mostly white professionals, police, and prison guards, the AFL union struggled to incorporate African American sanitation, laundry, and janitorial workers who had joined the CIO. Initially, AFSCME leaders maintained segregated locals but, starting in 1956, encouraged local leaders to confront "the issue of integration." They also supported strikes, which increased as southern state legislatures resisted the trend toward collective-bargaining laws. When four hundred sanitation workers walked off their jobs in Miami, in violation of the AFSCME's policy of preauthorization from national leadership, local leaders still recruited support from the Central Labor Council and the Negro Ministerial Alliance, and arranged a meeting during which the mayor agreed to grant paid vacation, holiday and sick leave, and to rehire strikers with no penalty. A one-day "sit-down" strike secured a similar arrangement for white truck drivers and black sanitation workers in Charlotte, North Carolina, despite a pledge by the segregationist United Southern Employees Association to run the integrated AFSCME local out of town. Birmingham, Alabama, which had been the center of UPWA strength in the South, saw strikes by African American laundry and sanitation workers, resulting in recognition of the AFSCME, despite a city ordinance requiring the dismissal of any city worker who went on strike.[26]

One major city where the AFSCME did not build on the CIO's legacy was Los Angeles, and that was because the AFL Building Service Employees International Union was more proactive. Following the UPWA's expulsion from the CIO, the BSEIU saw an opportunity to establish itself in Southern California by merging the union's massive janitorial, health-care, and sanitation locale without any changes to leadership or staff. Led by Sidney Moore and Elinor Glenn, former UPWA activists with close ties to the communist Left, the BSEIU sustained alliances with civil rights activists, black churches, and other local groups. As Glenn recalled, the older union "really taught other unions how they needed to have this connection with neighborhood organizations and the unions." In 1955 the union set out to win higher wages, benefits, and collective-bargaining rights for twenty thousand streets, sanitation, parks, hospital, and airport workers employed by the city and county of Los Angeles. The BSEIU's first major victory was a three-year contract to represent seven hundred nurses' aides, janitors, and cafeteria workers at two hospitals and sixteen clinics owned by the nonprofit Kaiser health care. Won after a threatened strike in 1963, the agreement set a basis for bargaining with the city and county in the next decade. Reflecting its expanding membership in health care, sanitation, and food service, the union dropped "Building" from its name in 1968.[27]

The SEIU and AFSCME represented a broad spectrum of government workers across income, skill, race, and gender, but the rise of large urban locals shifted their emphasis decidedly toward the low-wage, mostly nonwhite and female, service workers who had been the focus of the CIO's postwar campaign. Jerry Wurf, Lillian Roberts, and other urban militants built on that shift when they challenged Arnold Zander and other white-collar bureaucrats for control of the AFSCME's national office in 1962. Zander narrowly defeated Wurf in the presidential election, but reformers passed constitutional reforms that allowed their slate to sweep the elections two years later. By the end of the decade, roughly a third of the AFSCME's half a million members were African American and Latinos and Asians made up a substantial portion of the remainder. A similar portion of the SEIU's membership was nonwhite, concentrated primarily in public-sector locals. "In California, where the SEIU is the dominant public employee union, minority membership—mostly black but also Mexican-American and occasionally Indian—approached 90 percent in some locals and was very substantial in others," the economist Jack Stieber wrote in 1973.[28]

The transformation of public-sector unionism received international attention in 1968, when Martin Luther King Jr. traveled to Memphis, Tennessee, to support an AFSCME sanitation local that was on strike for better wages and working conditions and the right to bargain collectively with the city. The strike was resolved only after King was assassinated, but it awakened many Americans to the fact that their public services were provided by workers who worked for poverty wages with few benefits and enjoyed few of the rights and protections that most private-sector workers had enjoyed since the 1930s. "So often we overlook the work and the significance of those who are not in professional jobs, of those who are not in the so-called big jobs," King declared in one of his last speeches, "but let me say to you tonight that whenever you are engaged in work that serves humanity and is for the building of humanity, it has dignity and it has worth." Building on what the AFSCME organizer William Lucy called "the Spirit of Memphis," the AFSCME and SEIU played key roles in electing black mayors in Atlanta, Los Angeles, and Chicago and helped to establish the Coalition of Black Trade Unionists and the Coalition of Labor Union Women to further egalitarian politics within the AFL–CIO.[29]

Although the failure of Operation Dixie dealt a devastating blow to industrial unionism in the United States, the CIO's other postwar campaign was an important, if delayed, success. By 1973 nearly 40 percent of public employees belonged to unions, while the unionization rate for industrial workers had fallen to 25 percent from a postwar high of 33 percent. Nearly half a million public employees belonged to the AFSCME and another 124,000 made up nearly a third of the SEIU's membership. The long-term success of the CIO's campaign to organize public employees did not reverse the effects of its failure to organize southern industry, but it did forge a model for social democratic and egalitarian unionism that would prove essential to the survival of organized labor in the postindustrial United States. By demanding legal rights that were comparable to, although never as robust as, those enjoyed by industrial workers since the 1930s, public employees succeeded in bringing their wages and benefits in line with the private sector. Those victories were most beneficial to low-wage public-service workers, particularly African Americans and nonwhites who used unions not only to improve their economic situation but also to challenge their exclusion from the political system. By the end of the twentieth century, public employee unions had emerged as some of the most consistent voices for economic and racial liberalism in the United States.

CHAPTER 12

Constructing a New Labor Law
for the Post–New Deal Era

Kate Andrias

Since the 1970s, U.S. union membership has declined precipitously, with dire consequences for working people. In the aftermath of the New Deal, more than a third of U.S. workers belonged to unions. Today, the rate is about 6 percent of workers in the private sector and only about 10 percent of workers overall.[1] As unions have declined, the New Deal Order has eroded: the United States has lost a critical equalizing institution in politics and the economy.[2] Economic inequality is at its highest point since the Gilded Age, when unionization rates were similarly low.[3] Workers have minimal influence not only in their workplaces but also in policymaking at the state and federal levels.[4]

Though the causes of labor's decline are multiple, law is chief among them. Labor law enacted in the New Deal promised to protect workers' rights to organize and bargain, to exercise voice in the economy and the democracy. But in the decades after the New Deal, labor law's protections were attacked by employers, narrowed by Congress, disfigured by courts, and ultimately rendered inapt by a global and fissured economy. Employment law, which protects employees on an individual basis irrespective of unionization, was unable to fill the void.

This essay argues, however, that the story is not all bleak. From the remnants of the New Deal collective-bargaining regime, the outline of an aspirational new legal regime is emerging, one more attuned to the needs of workers and better matched to the characteristics of workplaces in today's economy.

Wagner, Taft–Hartley, and Voluntary
Enterprise Bargaining

The story of labor's rise—and then its steady and relentless decline—is, in large part, a story about law. When Congress enacted the original National Labor Relations Act (NLRA), also known as the Wagner Act,[5] it recognized the right "to self-organization, to form, join, or assist labor organizations, to bargain collectively through representatives of their own choosing, and to engage in other concerted activities, for the purpose of collective bargaining or other mutual aid or protection."[6] A sweepingly broad statute, the act established the types of organizations workers could form, the procedures for doing so, and the subjects over which employers were required to negotiate, as well as an independent regulatory agency—the National Labor Relations Board (NLRB)—to enforce the regime.

At its inception, the act was "perhaps the most radical piece of legislation ever enacted by the United States Congress."[7] It announced an affirmative national policy in favor of collective bargaining and economic redistribution; worked a fundamental change in the common-law employment relationship; and promised a system of nationwide industrial democracy.[8] Section 7 was particularly revolutionary. It protected not only the right of unionized workers to bargain but also the right of all workers to engage in concerted action for mutual aid or protection. Senator Wagner went so far as to assert that the act was "the next step in the logical unfolding of man's eternal quest for freedom."[9]

But the act simultaneously embodied the values of the more conservative elements of the U.S. labor movement, particularly the early twentieth-century American Federation of Labor's (AFL) commitment to private, voluntaristic bargaining at the firm level. Instead of the industrial or social bargaining that was advocated by other strands of the U.S. labor movement, and that subsequently developed in most European countries, the NLRA was premised on a principle of exclusive representation at particular worksites.[10] Bargaining was to occur between an employer and its employees sharing a "community of interest," but only if the majority of those employees selected a union representative.[11] The NLRA also represented a compromise with southern democrats and industry, while reflecting the AFL's own gendered and racialized conception of the "able-bodied worker." The statute excluded millions of the most vulnerable workers—namely, domestic and agricultural workers, largely African American—from its coverage.[12]

In the years following the Wagner Act's passage, unions experienced a period of rapid growth. But they were also met with significant resistance from the business community, including in the form of legal challenges.[13] At the urging of employers, Supreme Court interpretations of the statute soon began to curtail utopian aspirations for a radical restructuring of the workplace and the political economy.[14] Wartime mobilization temporarily strengthened labor's position. But in 1947, at the behest of business, and buoyed by popular concerns about rising labor militancy and union abuses, Congress passed the Taft–Hartley Act over President Truman's veto.[15]

Taft–Hartley amended the NLRA to make it far less favorable to unions.[16] No longer did the act favor concerted action and collective bargaining: instead, it embraced employees' "full freedom" to engage in or refrain from such activity.[17] In addition, Taft–Hartley cemented the act's commitment to enterprise-level bargaining. In particular, it limited the ability of unions to exert economic pressure across employers by prohibiting secondary boycotts, wherein workers target an employer other than their own.[18] It also restricted mass picketing, enabled state-level right-to-work laws, and augmented the ability of employers to oppose unionization.

The passage of Taft–Hartley was widely viewed by the labor movement as a resounding defeat.[19] Yet the extent to which the law would ultimately harm workers would not become clear for some time. Rather, the postwar years were marked by relative prosperity among organized workers—and a good deal of industry-wide bargaining. Because unions in industries like auto and steel had already achieved significant density among the few major employers, they were able to force those employers to engage in pattern bargaining, despite the absence of any legal obligation to do so and despite the various restrictions placed on union activity.[20] Ultimately, unions won substantial wage increases, pensions, and generous health benefits, in exchange for assurances of industrial discipline and stability. The result was that workers in these highly organized, oligopolistic industries—albeit largely white men—made significant gains, helping produce one of the most economically egalitarian periods in U.S. history.[21]

Globalization, Fissuring, and Deunionization

Over the course of the 1970s, 1980s, and 1990s, however, the picture transformed. By that time, many unions had become more inclusive of minority and women workers and had organized large numbers of public-sector employees as well as some key parts of the growing service sector.[22] But, in manufacturing, unions were on the verge of losing much of their economic power—and the law would prove to be of little help. U.S. corporations, many already unreceptive to unions, faced increased domestic and international competition, as well as restive capital markets and a push for higher profits. They responded by reshaping themselves, moving capital away from union workers to the nonunion south and overseas. And they "fissured." They shed activities deemed peripheral to their core business models and contracted out work to low-wage domestic and foreign subcontractors—again, almost always nonunion. They also shrank the portion of their labor force that enjoyed full-time work, vastly increasing their use of "contingent" workers, including part-time and temporary workers and independent contractors.[23]

Hostility to unionization became routine and overt. Following the lead of President Reagan in his fight against the air traffic controllers, employers began to aggressively retaliate against employees who exercised their right to strike.[24] They also closed union plants and opened up low-wage nonunion plants in other locations; double-breasting and subcontracting allowed employers to bypass existing collective-bargaining arrangements. And they developed sophisticated campaigns to try to stop workers from organizing new unions.[25]

The courts largely permitted these tactics, privileging employers' managerial and property rights over employees' rights to organize, bargain, and strike. In a series of cases, for example, courts ruled that employers were not required to bargain over entrepreneurial decisions, including where to operate.[26] They also permitted the use of permanent replacements, the National Guard, and state police against striking workers who sought to resist concessionary contracts.[27] Even where the law prohibited employers' antiunion activity, remedies were delayed and penalties were slight, making evasion of the law an economically rational decision on the part of employers.[28] Meanwhile, deregulation reduced barriers to entry by nonunion, lower-wage firms, particularly in industries like transportation and telecommunication, resulting in more competitive markets, but further contributing to unions' declining power.[29] Many unions, complacent with their negotiated benefits and recognizing the obstacles, failed to organize in the newly developing industries.

The Limits of Labor Law in the New Economy

The trends of deindustrialization, outsourcing, and antiunion campaigning continued during subsequent decades, resulting in a contemporary U.S. economy almost unrecognizable from the one that defined the New Deal.[30] Business gained more flexibility and higher profits, although disintegration of the production process meant that firms often had less control over their labor forces and decreased ability to achieve brand consistency and market power. Corrupt and excessive union practices were curtailed. But so too was the ability of unionized workers to negotiate for better terms and conditions of employment. The effect on workers overall was substantial. New jobs were created, and prices on many consumer goods decreased. But wages stagnated.[31] Workers increasingly came to fill contingent, nontraditional positions. And as a proportion of the entire workforce, union membership declined from 29 percent in 1973 to about 15 percent in the early 1990s, even though more than 60 percent of workers continued to report a desire for collective representation.[32]

In the face of this economic transformation, the NLRB no longer could effectuate employees' statutory rights to form and join labor organizations.[33] Indeed, by 1984 the House Subcommittee on Labor-Management Relations released a report announcing "The Failure of Labor Law." The NLRA, the House committee concluded, "has ceased to accomplish its purpose."[34] Countless scholars and commissions subsequently echoed the assessment.[35] Indeed, even those academics, judges, and politicians who celebrated the NLRA as a continued success did so for its ability to further industrial peace— not for its ability to protect the right to organize or to facilitate workers' collective economic or political power.[36]

One problem, upon which most scholars and commentators focused, was that the NLRA did not provide significant tools to combat employer resistance to unionization. Its weak enforcement mechanisms, slight penalties, and lengthy delays allowed employers to evade the law with near impunity.[37] But another, more significant problem existed: Even when the law was enforced, the NLRA's mechanisms—geared toward voluntary worksite bargaining between single employers and their employees—no longer matched the economy.[38]

Consider, for example, an auto manufacturer that once produced primary parts, assembled those parts into vehicles, and stored, transported, and distributed the vehicles to market.[39] By the 1990s, the manufacturer was more likely to own only the assembly stage of production, relying on separate corporations, some foreign, some domestic, linked by exclusive or nonexclusive supplier–purchaser contracts, to perform the remaining functions.[40] Or consider the modern retailer, which obtains goods from a host of factories and warehouses. Those factories are staffed by workers who are employed by entities other than the retailer itself. Several contractors likely stand between any given factory or warehouse worker and the retailer. And the workers themselves are as likely to be classified as temporary employees or independent contractors as full-fledged employees. Within the retail store, some of those who labor may be employees—many temporary or part-time. But those who clean, repair, and secure the building are more likely to be subcontracted.[41] Or consider Uber, part of the new "platform" economy,[42] which has a team of lawyers, engineers, and high-tech workers at headquarters, but, it contends, only independent contractors providing the rides that make up the company's core business.[43]

For several reasons, the NLRA is of diminished relevance throughout these and other ecosystems of disintegrated or fissured employers. First, the statute does not cover nontraditional work relationships. It expressly exempts independent contractors and excludes many temporary workers as well.[44] Thus, if an entity like Uber or FedEx is correct that its workers are independent contractors—an issue now hotly contested—federal labor law would not protect them.

Second, because the NLRA is designed to channel organizing drives between groups of employees and *single* employers, it does not facilitate collective action across the multiple interrelated employers that structure most contemporary workplaces. Only "employers" can be held liable for retaliating against workers for exercising their right to organize.[45] The law does allow for "joint employers," but from the 1980s until 2015, employers had been successful in advancing a narrow interpretation of the term—and they continue to press for a reinstatement of the narrow definition.[46] Moreover, even the more expansive legal standard from the Obama era is still limited by the NLRA's enterprise focus. The rules do not reach companies that participate in a supply chain or economic network, without sharing control over terms and conditions of employment, nor do they reach separate employers in a single industry.

Third, even if a worker organization were to succeed in organizing several units across multiple employers, the NLRA does not require the merger of different units for purposes of bargaining.[47] Multiunit bargaining is permitted and has been used in various industries where employers have agreed to it.[48] But it is not required. Indeed, from the 1980s until the recent Obama-era joint-employment decision, only direct employers, not employers sharing control over terms and conditions of employment, would have been under an obligation to bargain with downstream employees.

Finally, the law significantly limits the ability of workers to engage in cross-employer economic action. When seeking to win improvements in wages, benefits, or working conditions, the worker organization is not permitted to exercise economic pressure over a "secondary" employer to put pressure on another, even when their businesses are intertwined, as long as they are not formally joint employers.[49] A picket at corporate headquarters designed to coerce franchisees to negotiate a contract (assuming no joint-employment status) is thus illegal.[50] Nor may a worker organization sign an agreement that commits an employer to contract exclusively with unionized suppliers or buyers.[51]

Unions and Politics

All the above features of labor law make it exceedingly difficult for unions to exercise economic power on behalf of workers in the contemporary, fissured economy. The law is structured around an ideal—or imagined—labor-management relationship that, for the most part, no longer exists. The legislative decisions to cover only traditional employees, to mandate bargaining only with individual employers, and to penalize cross-employer economic strategies leave workers with little private, economic power in the modern economy.

Making problems worse, workers also lack significant political power. As union membership has plummeted, unions have fewer workers to mobilize in politics and fewer resources to deploy on behalf of workers' goals in electoral politics.[52] But the problem is more fundamental than the decline in union membership and resources. The local, firm-based structure of labor law and restrictions on cross-employer concerted action leave unions weakened in their ability to mount a powerful political defense of workers on a national or regional level. Unions must develop extensive bureaucracies to provide representational services, diminishing resources available for broader organizing and political work; the structure also provides an incentive to engage in political work that benefits existing members, as opposed to workers generally. Although many unions have been powerful advocates for legislation that benefits all workers—including health care, workplace safety, antidiscrimination, and wage and hour law—others have focused almost entirely on contract administration, or on legislation that serves their own members, sometimes at the expense of more vulnerable and nonunionized workers.[53]

Finally, the law gives unions no formal role in negotiating generally applicable wages or workplace standards—or other social benefits. This sharply differs from many European systems. For example, in Germany, the union federations participate in basic decisions concerning national wage policy and policies relating to employment, economic growth, and social insurance.[54] Meanwhile, collective bargaining occurs on a regional basis, with unions and employers responsible for negotiating wage scales that cover all workers, at least in manufacturing sectors; those agreements then provide a floor above which local bargaining may occur.[55] In Denmark, unions have played an even more active role in negotiating social policy. Unions and employers have, for example, collectively negotiated national policies on worker training and parental leave.[56] Throughout many other industrial democracies, the law provides for various forms of "contract extension," which extend collective-bargaining agreements to apply to workers throughout a region or sector, effectively forming the basis for employment policy in those sectors.[57]

To be sure, the NLRA does protect, to some extent, workers' political activity. Section 7 has been interpreted to extend to workers' concerted activity that occurs through political channels—as long as such activity relates to employment issues.[58] In addition, unions, like other organizations, may engage in electoral politics and lobby government officials.[59] In some circumstances, they may also use political pressure to bring about concessions from employers regarding organization and collective bargaining.[60] In practice, many unions spend a great deal of energy and money on political activity, with significant effect.[61] But although the law permits political action, it fails to empower unions at the political level, and it incentivizes a bureaucratic focus.

These features of U.S. labor law matter not only for the way unions spend their time and resources but also for society more generally. When unions were large and strong, they helped engage workers in the political process and helped ensure that the government was responsive to the actual preferences of working people. When particular unions moved beyond a focus on workplace representation of existing members and pursued a broader social justice mission at the sectoral, national, and political level, they helped bring about significant improvements in the lives of all working Americans.[62] Conversely, the decline in unionization rates and the failure of U.S. law to structure unions in ways that facilitate workers' collective political power have contributed to a politics in which government is particularly responsive to the wealthy.[63]

Employment Law: Distinct and Insufficient

Of course, labor law, which aims to protect collective action among workers, represents only one facet of U.S. workplace law. Another is employment law, which offers "rights and protections to employees on an individual—and individually enforceable—basis."[64] As labor law became ossified and decreased in relevance, employment law grew increasingly important.[65] In particular, the antidiscrimination statutes—the Civil Rights Act of 1964, the Equal Pay Act, the Age Discrimination in Employment Act, and the Americans with Disabilities Act—worked an important transformation in the U.S. workplace. Together they opened up employment opportunities for millions of Americans.[66] More recently, the Family and Medical Leave Act and the Affordable Care Act have provided important new guarantees of economic benefits—unpaid family leave and the right to purchase medical insurance.

To a great extent, the expansion of employment law was compatible with labor law. Like labor law, much employment law aims to improve workers' economic and social position to create greater societal equality.[67] Rather than displacing collective bargaining, most employment law statutes set a floor in the workplace above which unions can negotiate. Employment law thus functions to fulfill the substantive goals of unions and to extend the benefits won by unionized employees to a broader set of workers. Certain employment law statutes also include provisions that facilitate and protect collective action among workers.[68]

At the same time, scholars have documented tensions between the two regimes. Employment law and labor law, some argue, embrace fundamentally different approaches to protecting workers: bestowing individual rights in the case of employment law; facilitating collective power in the case of labor law. Though these two approaches can be—and have been—mutually reinforcing, they can also conflict. Historians have documented how the rise of rights-conscious liberalism undermined trade unionism in particular ways.[69]

In any event, employment law was unable to fill the void left by a weakened labor movement and a labor law that failed to protect workers' ability to organize and bargain. Enforcement of employment law is lax and violations are rampant, particularly in the fissured workplace.[70] Moreover, as with labor law, when employment is contracted out, fewer rights attach. And court remedies are often unavailable because of mandatory arbitration clauses.[71] Finally, the substantive rights provided by employment law, even when enforceable, are paltry compared to those in other industrialized countries and to those guaranteed by most collective-bargaining agreements. Most nonunion workers are employed "at will" with few protections against termination;[72] federal law and most state laws lack guarantees of paid family leave, vacation, or sick time; and statutory minimums do not provide the wages or benefits necessary to keep workers out of poverty.[73] Despite the existence of a wide range of employment law statutes, in practice, many workers enjoy few rights at work, and workers' real income has barely increased since the 1970s, even though total working hours are longer and educational attainment greater.[74]

Efforts at Resuscitation—and Abandonment

Against this background, the labor movement has been trying to rejuvenate itself, in part by developing new organizing strategies and in part by trying to reform the governing law. In particular, unions have pushed for amendments to the NLRA that would make organizing and bargaining easier. They have sought to reduce employer interference in organizing drives and to strengthen the bargaining obligation. The most recent bill that gained traction, the Employee Free Choice Act (EFCA), would have required that the NLRB certify unions based on a showing that a majority of workers in a unit had signed cards indicating their desire for representation; the goal was to allow unions to avoid the NLRB's dilatory election process. EFCA also would have mandated that parties unable to reach agreement on a first contract within four months submit to binding arbitration.[75] But EFCA and other prior law reform proposals all failed, garnering insufficient support from Democrats as well as staunch opposition from Republicans.

While seeking law reform, unions also worked around the existing law by developing alternative mechanisms to obtain traditional recognition and collective bargaining arrangements.[76] One approach was to engage in private ordering by seeking private agreements with employers in order to alter the ground rules for union organizing and first contract bargaining. In such agreements, employers typically pledge to remain neutral with respect to whether their employees organize; they also may allow unions access to employer property, recognize the union when a majority of workers sign cards requesting representation, or agree to some form of expedited election or first contract arbitration.[77]

Another approach was to create pathways to organization for workers excluded from federal law. For example, unions used innovative lawyering and legislative strategies to transform state-funded home-care workers into state employees, or quasi-state employees, in numerous jurisdictions. After doing so, they won the right to hold representational election for these workers.[78] The organization of home-care and childcare workers thus added to labor's ranks in the public sector, using a model that tracked the NLRA.

Finally, while unions sought to bring new workers under the NLRA's basic framework, other worker advocates attempted different forms of collective action. One important innovation to that end was the emergence of organizations known as worker centers. Worker centers, which became increasingly prevalent in the 1990s and 2000s, are community-based, nonprofit organizations that provide legal and social services to low-wage, often immigrant workers. They also engage in advocacy work, leadership development, and collective action in order to improve working conditions in the lowest-wage industries.[79]

The worker center campaigns filled an important void in vulnerable communities, and the innovative union campaigns brought tens of thousands of new workers—largely women, immigrants, and people of color—into the labor movement. Yet, for the most part, neither produced any fundamental change in labor law or the structure of labor relations. With a few notable exceptions, most worker centers expressly rejected the goal of collective bargaining and remained local in structure, without substantial power to affect the national economy or politics.[80] Meanwhile, the union campaigns did not aim to transform the basic system of labor law established by the NLRA. As Cynthia Estlund remarked in 2006, unions engaged in trying to revitalize labor law were "largely committed to a more or less recognizable regime of union organization and collective bargaining." Their innovations did not so much "transform the nature of labor relations—of unionization, majority rule, and collective bargaining—as they [sought] to smooth the path that leads there."[81]

For several decades, most scholars urging labor law reform operated in this vein as well. For example, they argued in favor of amending the NLRA's election machinery to remove the obstacles to unionization;[82] for more frequent elections to facilitate workers' exit from unions, as well as their entrance;[83] and for a private cause of action to enforce NLRA rights.[84] They also explained why judicial and agency opinions that narrowly interpret the NLRA ought to be reversed.[85] Other scholars sought to rewrite First Amendment doctrine to better protect ongoing collective action among workers.[86]

Whereas unions and many academic supporters sought to invent new ways to bring workers under the NLRA's basic framework, others abandoned the project of labor law, asserting the need for a postunion approach. Indeed, some abandoned the idea of traditional law. Most notably, since the 1970s, a movement has emerged in support of corporate self-governance. That is, multinational corporations, on their own, or when pushed by human rights groups, unions, and nongovernmental organizations (NGOs), have adopted corporate codes of conduct and agreed to let outside groups monitor their compliance with these codes. For businesses, these voluntary codes of conduct are a tool to enhance brand reputation and to achieve regulatory forbearance. For NGOs and worker advocates, they are a way to improve labor standards when domestic and international law fail.[87]

Some scholars, including some labor and employment law experts, have celebrated the turn toward self-regulation as a way to create more flexible and modern governance systems.[88] In their view, self-regulation can help fill the void left by the decline of unions and the weakness of employment law. Indeed, where strong worker organizations are present, as in the case of the Coalition of Immokolee Workers in Florida, corporate codes of conduct have been remarkably successful.[89] But for the most part, corporate social responsibility efforts are characterized by profound weaknesses. The programs suffer from low levels of transparency; effective sanctions are rare; and, without strong regulatory systems or unions, workers are typically unwilling to report problems to private monitors, even when the monitors operate in good faith. Even the most aggressive self-monitoring programs have had mixed success at best, with studies documenting pervasive code violations.[90]

*　*　*

In short, by the metrics of protecting workers' associational rights and facilitating greater economic and political equality, the innovations of the past decades have all failed. Since the early 2000s, when scholars began exploring a revitalized labor law and reporting the rise of both worker centers and self-regulation, economic inequality has increased;[91] union density has declined;[92] most workers still lack a meaningful voice in their place of employment; and working people's influence in politics remains feeble.[93]

No doubt, there are numerous explanations for the failure of labor law's revitalization and the continued weakness of employment law. The extraordinary opposition to reform mounted by conservative groups and business interests cannot be overstated, nor can the efforts to weaken the existing regimes. Limitations within the labor movement itself also played a role. But even if the reforms identified thus far had been achieved and the innovative strategies more fully realized, they would have done little to ameliorate the failure of labor law to provide workers significant power in the contemporary political economy. In short, although the failure to pass the EFCA and its predecessor reform bills represented significant losses for the labor movement,[94] the import of the defeats may be overstated. The proposed reforms all centered on altering the existing mechanisms of organizing and bargaining to make them more amenable to unions, without addressing the fundamental mismatch between the law and the structure of the contemporary political economy.

The Contours of a New Legal Framework

An incipient labor law is, however, being forged by today's social movements. The emerging labor law is nascent and contested; chances of success are uncertain at best; and the specifics of what success would look like are far from clear. But compared to the rutted road of the existing labor law, this new path offers a more promising way forward.

Since 2012, more than two dozen states and many more localities have raised their minimum wages.[95] Several of these, including California, Massachusetts, New Jersey, and New York, have enacted increases to $15 an hour—nearly $8 an hour more than the federal minimum—to be phased in over time.[96] The wage laws have been accompanied by new regulations providing scheduling protection, sick time, and other benefits.[97] Just a few years ago, increases of this scope and magnitude would have been unthinkable.

At first glance, these seem to be ordinary state and local employment statutes, separate and apart from the law that governs collective activity by workers.[98] But the sea change comes in response to the efforts by unions, especially the "Fight for $15," a campaign of low-wage workers organized by the Service Employees International Union (SEIU).[99] The express goal of these campaigns is not just higher wages but also union rights for all.[100] And many of the new laws they have won are a product of tripartite *bargaining*, either formal or informal, among unions, employers, and the state.[101]

The wage increase achieved in New York is the most prominent example. In 2015, after growing protests and strikes organized by the Fight for $15, and at the request of Governor Andrew Cuomo, the New York labor commissioner exercised his authority to impanel a wage board to recommend higher wages in the fast-food industry.[102] The board members—representatives from labor, business, and the general public—held hearings over the next forty-five days, across the state.[103] Workers organized by the Fight for $15 participated in great numbers at these hearings.[104] On July 21, the board announced its decision: $15 per hour for fast-food restaurants that are part of chains with at least thirty outlets, to be phased in over the course of six years, with a faster phase-in for New York City.[105] The wage board order was a significant victory, followed by another victory: a bill to raise the statewide minimum wage to $15.[106] But New York is by no means the only example—in cities and states across the country the movement has achieved similar victories.

Critics point out that despite the new wage and benefit laws, the unionization goal remains elusive for many of the workers involved in the movement. This is true. But from the social movements' efforts one can glimpse the outlines of an alternative legal regime that, if achieved, would have the capacity to vastly expand workers' power in the political economy— the outlines of an aspirational new labor law.

The new labor law would break from the legal regime that has governed since the New Deal in several ways. First, it would reject the old regime's commitment to the employer/employee dyad.[107] It would locate decisions about basic standards of employment at the sectoral, industrial, and regional levels, rather than at the level of the individual worksite or employer. That is, the Fight for $15, the teachers, and other contemporary worker movements are refusing labor law's orientation around the narrow employer/employee relationship. They are demanding $15 an hour and the right to *a union for all workers*, whether employed by the franchise or the franchisee, whether classified as an employee or an independent contractor. They are striking on a regional or statewide basis rather than on a shop-by-shop basis, and they are seeking to bargain at the sectoral and regional level, rather than at the local, enterprise level.

Second, the new labor law would reject the principle of private ordering that was cemented in the years following the New Deal, under which labor negotiations are a private affair and the state plays a neutral and minimal role.[108] Instead, the new labor law would position unions as political actors representing workers generally and would involve the state as an active participant in supporting collective bargaining—in a system one might call "social bargaining," but it is also sometimes known as "labor tripartism" or "labor corporatism."[109] Specifically, the Fight for $15 and other contemporary worker movements are rejecting the notion that unions' primary role is to negotiate traditional private collective-bargaining agreements, with the state playing a neutral mediating and enforcing role. Instead, they are seeking to bargain in the public arena: They are engaging in bargaining with the state on behalf of all workers.

Third, and related to the first two moves, the contemporary worker movements are offering a vision of labor law that would reject the bifurcation between employment law and labor law that has governed since the end of the 1940s. Instead of one system of employment law that protects individual rights and a separate system of labor law that protects collective rights, the new movements are forging a regime in which the basic terms of employment for all workers are subject to social bargaining.[110]

At the same time, the new labor law would not abandon worksite organization. To the contrary, the movements pressing reforms are using sectoral and political bargaining to strengthen and supplement traditional collective bargaining. Union leaders report that the political demands for $15 and a union have made it easier to obtain successful contracts; the broader campaign has shifted employer expectations and softened opposition.[111] In addition, worker movements are beginning to experiment with new forms of workplace organization. For example, at the urging of various worker groups, New York City recently enacted a law that enables employees to contribute, via paycheck deduction, to qualified nonprofit organizations that will advocate on their behalf but without engaging in traditional collective bargaining with employers.[112] Seattle recently passed a Domestic Workers Ordinance that not only gives domestic workers rights to minimum wages, rest breaks, and meal breaks but also creates a Domestic Workers Standards Board through which domestic worker organizations, the public, and hiring entities can engage in negotiations about conditions of employment.[113]

Meanwhile, the recent teacher strikes across the country represent another example of the emerging new labor law. Teachers are organizing not just at one school, or in one neighborhood, but across their cities and states, on a sectoral basis, and they are winning not only fair wages and good benefits for themselves but also improved education funding for their students. In the coming months and years, more reforms are possible at the state and local level in labor-friendly jurisdictions, albeit within the confines of federal preemption doctrine.[114] Long term, with new social mobilization, more substantial reform might become possible at the federal level as well.

*   *   *

Of course, in an important sense, the new labor law emerging from the remnants of the New Deal labor law regime is not, in fact, new. It is a reinterpretation of principles advanced by earlier incarnations of the U.S. labor movement[115] and embraced by systems abroad.[116] But support for a system of labor law that empowers unions to bargain on behalf of all or most workers, with active support from the state, has long been considered to exist only in the "political ozone."[117] The goal of state-supported sectoral bargaining, the conventional wisdom long held, is unmoored from reality, and with no hope of passage.[118]

This sentiment is beginning to change, as the nascent form of inclusive, sectoral bargaining develops in the United States.[119] To be sure, in a political environment hostile to reform, the new labor law is by no means certain. Moreover, the nascent regime has limitations, including the inherent shortcomings of a domestic labor regime in an increasingly global economy, and the challenge of maintaining worker voice and union funding in a system not based primarily on traditional exclusive bargaining agreements.

But the nascent sectoral labor law is increasingly recognized as one component of a broader solution to the problems of economic and political inequality facing the country, as well as a way to protect workers' fundamental associational rights. Sectoral bargaining has significant advantages when compared to enterprise-based bargaining: It is more effective at reducing economic equality; it provides workers a stronger voice in the policymaking process; it avoids the issues that arise when workers attempt to bargain with fissured employers; and it takes many economic disputes out of the workplace, potentially facilitating more harmonious and collaborative relationships between workers and employers.[120]

Ultimately, the path out of the ashes of the New Deal labor law is only beginning to emerge. But the contours of a new legal regime are discernible from action in workplaces, on the streets, in legislatures, and before agencies. While the temptation to patch up the old model remains, to do so without confronting its core weaknesses would be a mistake. Likewise, to abandon collective bargaining altogether in favor of governance and regulation would offer little hope of addressing the deep structural inequities in our politics and economy. The revitalization of U.S. democracy and a return to shared prosperity depend on the development of a new, more inclusive, and more political form of unionism.

NOTES

Introduction

1. See, inter alia, Steve Fraser, *The Age of Acquiescence: The Life and Death of American Resistance to Organized Wealth and Power* (Boston: Little Brown, 2015); Nelson Lichtenstein, *The Retail Revolution: How Wal-Mart Created a Brave New World of Business* (New York: Picador, 2010); Leon Fink, *The Long Gilded Age: American Capitalism and the Lessons of a New World Order* (Philadelphia: University of Pennsylvania Press, 2014); and Jefferson Cowie, *The Great Exception* (Princeton, NJ: Princeton University Press, 2015).

2. Thomas Piketty, *Capital in the Twenty-First Century* (Cambridge, MA: Harvard University Press, 2014).

3. Simon Kuznets (1901–1985), who was born in Pinsk, Russia, researched labor statistics in the Soviet Union before emigrating to the United States in 1922. He worked at the NBER from 1927 to 1960 and was awarded the Nobel Prize in Economics in 1971.

4. On Kuznets, see also François Nielsen and Arthur S. Alderson, "The Kuznets Curve and the Great U-Turn: Income Inequality in U.S. Counties, 1970 to 1990," *American Sociological Review* 62, no. 1 (February 1997): 12–33; Piketty, *Capital*; and Romain Huret, *The Experts' War on Poverty: Social Research and the Welfare Agenda in Postwar America* (Ithaca, NY: Cornell University Press, 2018).

5. Notably, Kuznets was no reformist, and he remained aloof from the political world, leaving his perch at the NBER only to take academic appointments. Even at the time, however, there were dissenters among economists and intellectuals.

6. Indeed, Piketty calls it a "fairy tale." See *Capital*, 11; and for Piketty's own analysis of Kuznets, 11–15.

7. Nelson Lichtenstein, *State of the Union: A Century of American Labor* (Princeton, NJ: Princeton University Press, 2003); Jake Rosenfeld, *What Unions No Longer Do* (Cambridge, MA: Harvard University Press, 2014); Michael Yates, *Why Unions Matter* (New York: New York University Press, 1998); and Robert Gordon, *The Rise and Fall of American Growth: The U.S. Standard of Living Since the Civil War* (Princeton, NJ: Princeton University Press, 2017).

8. Lisa McGirr, *Suburban Warriors: The Origins of the New American Right* (Princeton, NJ: Princeton University Press, 2001); Michelle Nickerson, *Mothers of Conservatism: Women and the Postwar Right* (Princeton, NJ: Princeton University Press, 2012); and Theda Skocpol and Lawrence Jacobs, eds., *Reaching for a New New Deal: Ambitious Governance, Economic*

Meltdown, and Polarized Politics in Obama's First Two Years (New York: Russell Sage, 2011). As Skocpol and Jacobs explain, "'The *New* New Deal—What Barack Obama Can Learn from F.D.R.—and What Democrats Need to Do' was the feature story in the *Time* magazine of November 24, 2008" (1).

9. American Political Science Association, "Task Report on Inequality and American Democracy," 2004, http://www.apsanet.org; Lawrence Jacobs and Desmond King, eds., *The Unsustainable American State* (New York: Oxford University Press, 2009); and Benjamin Page and Lawrence Jacobs, *Class War? What Americans Really Think About Economic Inequality* (Chicago: University of Chicago Press, 2009).

10. Steve Fraser and Gary Gerstle, eds., *The Rise and Fall of the New Deal Order, 1930–1980* (Princeton, NJ: Princeton University Press, 1989), ix; and Ira Katznelson, *Fear Itself: The New Deal and the Origins of Our Time* (New York: Liveright, 2015).

11. Arthur Schlesinger Jr., *The Cycles of American History* (Boston: Houghton Mifflin Harcourt, 1999); and Peter Novick, *That Noble Dream: The "Objectivity Question" and the American Historical Profession* (Cambridge: Cambridge University Press, 1989).

12. Fraser and Gerstle, *Rise and Fall of the New Deal Order*, xi; on the origins of the *New Deal Order* volume, see Gary Gerstle, "America's Neoliberal Order," in *Beyond the New Deal Order*, ed. Gary Gerstle, Nelson Lichtenstein, and Alice O'Connor (Philadelphia: Pennsylvania University Press, 2019), 257–278. For uses of the concept, see Romain Huret, *American Tax Resisters* (Cambridge, MA: Harvard University Press, 2014); Jason Scott Smith, *Building New Deal Liberalism: The Political Economy of Public Works, 1933–56* (New York: Cambridge University Press, 2009); David Kennedy, *Freedom from Fear* (New York: Oxford University Press, 1996); and Lichtenstein, *State of the Union*, chap. 1; Eric Foner, *The Story of American Freedom* (New York: Norton, 1998).

13. Suzanne Mettler, *Dividing Citizens: Gender and Federalism in New Deal Public Policy* (Ithaca: Cornell University Press, 1998), 96; Dorothy Sue Cobble, *The Other Women's Movement* (Princeton, NJ: Princeton University Press, 2004). About 80 percent of women were excluded from the National Labor Relations Act and Social Security Act, but the number was even higher with the Fair Labor Standards Act, which covered only 14 percent of working women and only 20 percent of the overall workforce; Alice Kessler-Harris, *In Pursuit of Equity: Women, Men and the Quest for Economic Citizenship in 20th-Century America* (New York: Oxford University Press, 2003), 95–105; Alan Brinkley, *The End of Reform* (New York: Knopf, 1994); Gwendolyn Mink, *The Wages of Motherhood: Inequality in the Welfare State, 1917–1942* (Ithaca, NY: Cornell University Press, 1995), 127; Vanessa H. May, *Unprotected Labor: Household Workers, Politics, and Middle-Class Reform in New York, 1870–1940* (Chapel Hill: University of North Carolina Press, 2011); Alice Kessler-Harris, *Out to Work: A History of Wage-Earning Women in the United States* (New York: Oxford University Press, 1982); and Eileen Boris, *Home to Work: Motherhood and the Politics of Industrial Homework in the United States* (New York: Cambridge University Press, 1994).

14. Robert Self, "Matthew Countryman's Up South and Urban Political History," *Pennsylvania Magazine of History and Biography* 130, no. 4 (October 2006): 398; Martha Biondi, *To Stand and Fight: The Struggle for Civil Rights in Postwar New York City* (Cambridge, MA: Harvard University Press, 2006); Matthew Countryman, *Up South* (Philadelphia: University of

Pennsylvania Press, 2006); Robert Self, *American Babylon: Race and the Struggle for Postwar Oakland* (Princeton, NJ: Princeton University Press, 2003); Paul D. Jones, *The Selma of the North: Civil Rights Insurgency in Milwaukee* (Cambridge, MA: Harvard University Press, 2009); Gordon K. Mantler, *Power to the Poor: Black-Brown Coalition and the Fight for Economic Justice, 1960–1974* (Chapel Hill: University of North Carolina Press, 2013); Rhonda Williams, *Concrete Demands: The Search for Black Power in the Twentieth Century* (New York: Routledge, 2014); Todd E. Robinson, *A City Within a City: The Black Freedom Struggle in Grand Rapids* (Philadelphia: Temple University Press, 2012); Nikhil Pal Singh, *Black Is a Country: Race and the Unfinished Struggle for Democracy* (Cambridge, MA: Harvard University Press, 2005); Thomas J. Sugrue, *Sweet Land of Liberty: The Forgotten Struggle for Civil Rights in the North* (New York: Random House, 2008); and Jacqueline Hall, "The Long Civil Rights Movement and the Political Uses of the Past," *Journal of American History* 91, no. 4 (March 2005): 1233–1263. For a critique of the long civil rights movement historiography, see Sundiata Keita Cha-Jua and Clarence Lang, "The Long Movement as Vampire," *Journal of African American History* 92, no. 2 (Spring 2007): 265–288.

15. William Jones, *The March on Washington* (New York: Norton, 2013); and Paul LeBlanc and Michael D. Yates, *A Freedom Budget for All Americans: Recapturing the Promise of the Civil Rights Movement in the Struggle for Economic Justice Today* (New York: Monthly Review Press, 2013).

16. Robert Zieger, *For Jobs and Freedom: Race and Labor in America Since 1965* (Lexington: University Press of Kentucky, 2010); Michael Goldfield, "Race and the CIO: The Possibilities for Racial Equalitarianism during the 1930s and 1940s," *International Labor and Working-Class History* 44 (1993): 1–32; Herbert Hill, "The Importance of Race in American Labor History," *International Journal of Politics, Culture and Society* 9 (1995): 317–343, and "The Problem of Race in American Labor History," *Reviews in American History* 24 (1996): 180–208; Gary Gerstle, "Working Class Racism: Broaden the Focus," *International Labor and Working-Class History* 44 (1993): 33–40; Sophia Lee, *The Workplace Constitution: From the New Deal to the New Right* (New York: Cambridge University Press, 2014); Reuel Schiller, *Forging Rivals: Race, Class, Law and the Collapse of Postwar Liberalism* (New York: Cambridge University Press, 2015); Robert Korstad and Nelson Lichtenstein, "Opportunities Found and Lost: Labor Radicals and the Early Civil Rights Movement," *Journal of American History* 75 (1988): 786–811; and Risa Goluboff, *The Lost Promise of Civil Rights* (New York: Cambridge University Press, 2007).

17. Jonathan Levy, *Freaks of Fortune: The Emerging World of Capitalism and Risk in America* (Cambridge, MA: Harvard University Press, 2012); Jeffrey Sklansky, *Sovereign of the Market: The Money Question in Early America* (Chicago: University of Chicago Press, 2017); Scott Reynolds Nelson, *A Nation of Deadbeats: An Uncommon History of America's Financial Disasters* (New York: Knopf, 2012); Edward Balleisen, *Fraud: An American History from Barnum to Madoff* (Princeton, NJ: Princeton University Press, 2017); Sven Beckert, *The Monied Metropolis: New York City and the Consolidation of the American Bourgeoisie, 1850–1896* (New York: Cambridge University Press, 2001); and Richard White, *Railroaded: The Transcontinentals and the Making of Modern America* (New York: Norton, 2011).

18. Naomi Lamoreaux and William Novak, eds., *Corporations and American Democracy* (Cambridge, MA: Harvard University Press, 2017).

19. Meg Jacobs, *Pocketbook Politics: Economic Citizenship in Twentieth-Century America* (Princeton, NJ: Princeton University Press, 2005); Lizabeth Cohen, *A Consumers' Republic: The Politics of Mass Consumption in Postwar America* (New York: Knopf, 2003); and Eric Rauchway, *The Money Makers: How Roosevelt and Keynes Ended the Depression, Defeated Fascism, and Secured a Prosperous Peace* (New York: Basic Books, 2015).

20. Gordon, *The Rise and Fall of American Growth*; Robert Collins, *More: The Politics of Economic Growth in Postwar America* (New York: Oxford University Press, 2000); Michael Bernstein, *The Great Depression: Delayed Recovery and Economic Change in America, 1929–1939* (New York: Cambridge University Press, 1987); and Colin Gordon, *New Deals: Business, Labor, and Politics in America, 1920–1935* (New York: Cambridge University Press, 1994).

21. Philip Scranton, *Endless Novelties: Specialty Production and American Industrialization, 1865–1925* (Princeton, NJ: Princeton University Press, 1997); and Howell John Harris, *Bloodless Victories: The Rise and Fall of the Open Shop in the Philadelphia Metal Trades, 1890–1940* (New York: Cambridge University Press, 2000).

22. Alfred Chandler, *The Visible Hand: The Managerial Revolution in American Business* (Cambridge, MA: Harvard University Press, 1977); Richard Parker, *John Kenneth Galbraith: His Life, His Politics, His Economics* (New York: Farrar, Straus and Giroux, 2005); David Hounshell, *From the American System to Mass Production: The Development of Manufacturing Technology in the United States, 1800–1932* (Baltimore: Johns Hopkins University Press, 1985); Marc Levinson, *The Box: How the Shipping Container Made the World Smaller and the World Economy Bigger* (Princeton, NJ: Princeton University Press, 2006); Jordan Schwarz, *Liberal: Adolf A. Berle and the Vision of an American Era* (New York: Free Press, 1987).

23. Lizabeth Cohen, *Making a New Deal: Industrial Workers in Chicago, 1919–1939* (New York: Cambridge University Press, 1990); David Farber, *Sloan Rules: Alfred Sloan and the Triumph of General Motors* (Chicago: University of Chicago Press, 2002); Nelson Lichtenstein, *The Most Dangerous Man in Detroit: Walter Reuther and the Fate of American Labor* (New York: Basic Books, 1995); and David Stebenne, *Arthur J. Goldberg: New Deal Liberal* (New York: Oxford University Press, 1996); and Joshua Freeman, *Behemoth: A History of the Factory and the Making of the Modern World* (New York: Norton, 2018).

24. Howard Brick, *Transcending Capitalism: Visions of a New Society in Modern American Thought* (Ithaca, NY: Cornell University Press, 2006); John Judis, *William F. Buckley, Jr., Patron Saint of the Conservatives* (New York: Simon and Schuster, 1988); Angus Burgin, *The Great Persuasion: Reinventing Free Markets Since the Depression* (Cambridge, MA: Harvard University Press, 2012); Daniel Stedman Jones, *Masters of the Universe: Hayek, Friedman, and the Birth of Neoliberal Politics* (Princeton, NJ: Princeton University Press, 2012); Jennifer Burns, *Goddess of the Market: A Biography of Ayn Rand* (New York: Oxford University Press, 2012); Nancy MacLean, *Democracy in Chains: The Deep History of the Radical Right's Stealth Plan for America* (New York: Penguin, 2018): Kim Phillips-Fein, *Invisible Hands: The Businessman's Crusade Against the New Deal* (New York: Norton, 2010); and Lawrence Glickman, *Free Enterprise: An American History* (New Haven, CT: Yale University Press, 2019).

25. Howell Harris, *The Right to Manage: Industrial Relations Policies of American Business During the 1940s* (Madison: University of Wisconsin Press, 1982); Mark Wilson,

Destructive Generation: Business and the Winning World War II (Philadelphia: University of Pennsylvania Press, 2016); Jennifer Klein, *For All These Rights: Business, Labor, and the Shaping of America's Public-Private Welfare State* (Princeton, NJ: Princeton University Press, 2003); Shane Hamilton, *Trucking Country: The Road to America's Wal-Mart Economy* (Princeton, NJ: Princeton University Press, 2008); Elizabeth Shermer, *Sunbelt Capitalism: Phoenix and the Transformation of American Politics* (Philadelphia: University of Pennsylvania Press, 2013); Lichtenstein, *Retail Revolution*; Bethany Moreton, *To Serve God and Wal-Mart: The Making of Christian Free Enterprise* (Cambridge, MA: Harvard University Press, 2009); Benjamin Waterhouse, *Lobbying America: The Politics of Business from Nixon to NAFTA* (Princeton, NJ: Princeton University Press, 2014); and Meg Jacobs, *Panic at the Pump: The Energy Crisis and the Transformation of American Politics in the 1970s* (New York: Hill and Wang, 2016).

26. Gerald Davis, *Managed by the Markets: How Finance Reshaped America* (New York: Oxford University Press, 2009); Louis Hyman, *Temp: How American Work, American Business, and the American Dream Became Temporary* (New York: Viking, 2018); David Weil, *The Fissured Workplace: Why Work Became So Bad for So Many and What Can Be Done to Improve It* (Cambridge, MA: Harvard University Press, 2014); Richard Appelbaum and Nelson Lichtenstein, eds., *Achieving Workers' Rights in the Global Economy* (Ithaca, NY: Cornell University Press, 2016); and Jean-Christian Vinel, *The Employee: A Political History* (Philadelphia: University of Pennsylvania Press, 2013).

27. Mark Leff, *The Limits of Symbolic Reform: The New Deal and Taxation, 1933–1939* (Cambridge: Cambridge University Press, 1984); Huret, *American Tax Resisters*; Ajay Mehrotra, *Making the Modern American State: Law, Politics, and the Rise of Progressive Taxation, 1877–1929* (Cambridge: Cambridge University Press, 2013); Isaac Martin, *Rich People's Movement: Grassroots Campaign to Untax the One Percent* (New York: Oxford University Press, 2013); Joseph J. Thorndike, *Their Fair Share: Taxing the Rich in the Age of FDR* (Washington, DC: Urban Institute Press, 2013); Monica Prasad, *Starving the Beast: Ronald Reagan and the Tax Cut Revolution* (New York: Russell Sage Foundation Press, 2018); and Kim Phillips-Fein, *Fear City: New York's Fiscal Crisis and the Rise of Austerity Politics* (New York: Metropolitan Books, 2017).

28. Ira Katznelson, "Was the Great Society a Lost Opportunity?," in Fraser and Gerstle, *Rise and Fall of the New Deal Order*, 191–192.

29. Burgin, *Great Persuasion*; Philip Mirowski and Dieter Plehwe, eds., *The Road from Mont Pèlerin* (Cambridge, MA: Harvard University Press, 2009); Jean Solchany, *Wilhelm Röpke, l'autre Hayek: Aux origines du néolibéralisme* (Paris: Publications de la Sorbonne, 2015); Daniel Stedman Jones, *Masters of the Universe: Hayek, Friedman, and the Birth of Neo-liberal Politics* (Princeton, NJ: Princeton University Press, 2012); and McLean, *Democracy in Chains*.

30. Marion Fourcade-Gourinchas and Sarah L. Babb, "The Rebirth of the Liberal Creed: Paths to Neoliberalism in Four Countries," *American Journal of Sociology* 108, no. 3 (November 2002): 533–579; François Denord, *Le néo-libéralisme à la française: Histoire d'une idée politique* (Paris: Agone, 2016); and Naomi Klein, *The Shock Doctrine: The Rise of Disaster Capitalism* (New York: Metropolitan Books, 2007).

31. Mark Blyth, *Great Transformations: Economic Ideas and Institutional Change in the Twentieth Century* (New York: Cambridge University Press, 2002); David Harvey, *A Brief History of Neo-Liberalism* (New York: Oxford University Press, 2005); and Stephanie Lee Smudge, "What Is Neo-liberalism?," *Socio-Economic Review* 6, no. 4 (October 2008): 703–773.

32. Judith Stein, *Pivotal Decade: How the United States Traded Factories for Finance in the Seventies* (New Haven, CT: Yale University Press, 2010).

33. Brian Balogh, *A Government out of Sight: The Mystery of National Authority in Nineteenth Century America* (New York: Cambridge University Press, 2009); William Novak, *The People's Welfare: Law and Regulation in Nineteenth-Century America* (Raleigh: University of North Carolina Press, 1996); Gary Gerstle, *Liberty and Coercion: The Paradox of American Government from the Founding to the Present* (Princeton, NJ: Princeton University Press, 2015); and Desmond King and Robert Lieberman, "Finding the American State: Transcending the 'Statelessness' Account," *Polity* 40, no 3 (July 2008): 368–378.

34. John Micklethwait and Adrian Wooldridge, *The Right Nation: Conservative Power in America* (New York: Penguin, 2005) is a good example of an approach focusing on the anti-statism of the Right while leaving out state structures and institutional dynamics.

35. Stephen Skowronek, "Taking Stock," in Jacobs and King, *Unsustainable American State*, 334; Brian Glenn and Stephen Teles, *Conservatism and American Political Development* (New York: Oxford University Press, 2009); Theda Skocpol and Paul Pierson, eds., *The Transformation of American Politics: Activist Government and the Rise of Conservatism* (Princeton, NJ: Princeton University Press, 2007); and Richard A. Harris and Sidney Milkis, *The Politics of Regulatory Change* (New York: Oxford University Press, 1996). In the same fashion, Morton Keller has contended that we have for decades "lived in a polity best defined as a lengthened shadow of the New Deal"; see Keller, "The New Deal and Progressivism: A Fresh Look," in Sidney Milkis and Jerome Mileur, eds., *The New Deal and the Triumph of Liberalism* (Amherst: University of Massachusetts Press, 2002), 319.

Chapter 1

1. See, for example, Angus Burgin, *The Great Persuasion* (Cambridge, MA: Harvard University Press, 2012); Kim Phillips-Fein, *Invisible Hands: The Making of the Conservative Movement from the New Deal to Reagan* (New York: Norton, 2009); and Vanessa Williamson and Theda Skocpol, *The Tea Party and the Remaking of Republican Conservatism* (New York: Oxford University Press, 2012).

2. Steve Fraser and Gary Gerstle, eds., *The Rise and Fall of the New Deal Order, 1930–1980* (Princeton, NJ: Princeton University Press, 1989).

3. See, for example, Charles Postel, *The Populist Vision* (Oxford: Oxford University Press, 2009); William Novak, *The New Democracy* (forthcoming); and Ira Katznelson, *Fear Itself: The New Deal and the Origins of Our Time* (New York: Norton, 2013).

4. This chapter is based on arguments further developed in my book, K. Sabeel Rahman, *Democracy Against Domination* (New York: Oxford University Press, 2017).

5. See, for example, Department of the Treasury, *Financial Regulatory Reform: A New Foundation: Rebuilding Financial Supervision and Regulation* (Washington, D.C.: U.S.

Government Printing Office, 2009), 1. See also Barack Obama, speech on financial regulation, Cooper Union, New York, April 22, 2010; transcript, http://www.huffingtonpost.com/2010 /04/22/obamas-wall-street-speech_n_547880.html.

6. See K. Sabeel Rahman, "Envisioning the Regulatory State: Technocracy, Democracy, and Institutional Experimentation in the 2010 Financial Reform and Oil Spill Statues," *Harvard Journal on Legislation* 48 (2011): 555–590.

7. See, for example, Greta Krippner, *Capitalizing on Crisis: The Political Origins of the Rise of Finance* (Cambridge, MA: Harvard University Press, 2011), esp. 145–150 (describing the bureaucratization and depoliticization of financial regulation, sidestepping fundamental moral questions about distribution, democracy, and equity); see also Barry C. Lynn, *Cornered: The New Monopoly Capitalism and the Economics of Destruction* (Hoboken, NJ: Wiley, 2010) (noting the same in the context of antitrust law).

8. See, for example, Simon Johnson and James Kwak, *13 Bankers: The Wall Street Takeover and the Next Financial Meltdown* (New York: Vintage, 2011).

9. See K. Sabeel Rahman, "Conceptualizing the Economic Role of the State: Laissez-Faire, Technocracy, and the Democratic Alternative," *Polity* 43, no. 2 (2011): 264–286; K. Sabeel Rahman, "Domination, Democracy, and Constitutional Political Economy in the New Gilded Age: Towards a Fourth Wave of Legal Realism?," *Texas Law Review* 94 (2016): 1329–1359; Postel, *Populist Vision*; and Alex Gourevitch, *From Slavery to the Cooperative Commonwealth: Labor and Republican Liberty in the Nineteenth Century* (New York: Cambridge University Press, 2014).

10. See generally, Daniel Rodgers, *Atlantic Crossings: Social Politics in a Progressive Age* (Cambridge, MA: Harvard University Press, 1998); Morton Keller, *Regulating a New Society: Public Policy and Social Change in America, 1900–1933* (Cambridge, MA: Harvard University Press, 1994); Shelton Stromquist, *Reinventing "The People": The Progressive Movement, The Class Problem, and the Origins of Modern Liberalism* (Urbana: University of Illinois Press, 2006); and Postel, *Populist Vision*.

11. Louis Brandeis, "Big Business and Industrial Liberty," in *The Curse of Bigness: Miscellaneous Papers of Louis Brandeis*, ed. Osmond Fraenkel (New York: Viking Press, 1935), 38–39, 39.

12. Alex Gourevitch, "Labor Republicanism and the Transformation of Work," *Political Theory* 41, no. 4 (2013): 591–617, 596.

13. Louis Jaffe, "Law Making by Private Groups" (1937), in *American Legal Realism*, ed. William W. Fisher III, Morton Horwitz, and Thomas Reed (New York: Oxford University Press, 1993), 115–120, 116.

14. Guido Marx, "How to Control Public Utilities," *The Nation*, April 1, 1931.

15. Jaffe, "Law Making by Private Groups," 120. As Jaffe argued, such "tolerated, covert monopolies—power exercised indirectly—may be much more difficult to attack or to ameliorate than the edicts of majorities arrived at openly and according to the forms of law."

16. Robert Hale, "Coercion and Distribution in a Supposedly Non-Coercive State" (1923), in Fisher, Horwitz, and Reed, *American Legal Realism*, 101–108, 108.

17. On the development of this critique among economists during this period, see, for example, Herbert Hovenkamp, "The First Great Law and Economics Movement," *Stanford Law Review* 42, no. 4 (1990): 993–1058.

18. See, for example, Barbara Fried, *The Progressive Assault on Laissez Faire: Robert Hale and the First Law and Economics Movement* (Cambridge, MA: Harvard University Press, 1998).

19. See, for example, Novak, *New Democracy*, forthcoming.

20. Franklin Delano Roosevelt, Campaign Address in Columbus, Ohio, August 20, 1932.

21. Ibid.

22. Franklin Delano Roosevelt, Address in Marietta, Georgia, July 8, 1938.

23. See, for example, Krippner, *Capitalizing on Crisis*, 60–62.

24. Joel Seligman, *The Transformation of Wall Street: A History of the Securities and Exchange Commission and Modern Corporate Finance* (Boston: Northeastern University Press, 1995), 41–42, 51–52; Jessica Wang, "Imagining the Administrative State: Legal Pragmatism, Securities Regulation, and New Deal Liberalism," *Journal of Policy History* 17, no. 3 (2005): 257–293; and Jessica Wang, "Neo-Brandeisianism and the New Deal: Adolf A. Berle, Jr., William O. Douglas, and the Problem of Corporate Finance in the 1930s," *Seattle University Law Review* 33 (2010): 1221–1349.

25. See James Kloppenberg, "Deliberative Democracy and Poverty in America," in *Virtues of Liberalism* (New York: Oxford University Press, 1998), 106–108.

26. See Anne Kornhauser, *Debating the American State: Liberal Anxieties and the New Leviathan, 1930–1970* (Philadelphia: University of Pennsylvania Press, 2015), 56–60.

27. Nelson Lichtenstein, *State of the Union: A Century of American Labor* (Princeton, NJ: Princeton University Press, 2002), 27, 34–37.

28. Lizabeth Cohen, *A Consumer's Republic: The Politics of Mass Consumption in Postwar America* (New York: Knopf, 2003), 18–28.

29. Meg Jacobs, *Pocketbook Politics: Economic Citizenship in Twentieth-Century America* (Princeton, NJ: Princeton University Press, 2005); and Meg Jacobs, "'How About Some Meat?' The Office of Price Administration, Consumption Politics, and State Building from the Bottom Up, 1941–1946," *Journal of American History* 84, no. 3 (December 1997): 910–941.

30. Adolf Berle and Gardiner Means, *The Modern Corporation and Private Property* (New Brunswick, NJ: Transaction, 2009 [1932]), esp. 309–310; Dalia Tsuk, "From Pluralism to Individualism: Berle and Means and 20th-Century American Legal Thought," *Law and Social Inquiry* 30 (2005): 193, 207–208; Adolf Berle, "Corporate Powers as Powers in Trust," *Harvard Law Review* 44, no. 1049 (1931).

31. Raymond Moley quoted in Seligman, *The Transformation of Wall Street*, 40.

32. See K. Sabeel Rahman, "Democracy and Productivity: The Glass–Steagall Act and the Shifting Discourse of Financial Regulation," *Journal of Policy History* 24, no. 4 (2012): 612–643.

33. See, for example, David Ciepley, *Liberalism in the Shadow of Totalitarianism* (Cambridge, MA: Harvard University Press, 2006), 98–115.

34. Cohen, *Consumer's Republic*, 24.

35. See Lichtenstein, *State of the Union*, 106–117.

36. For example, unions came to be skeptical of the Robinson-Pateman Act, which limited the ability of firms to create large multibranch chains, in part because of the promise

from the chain giant A&P to engage in bargaining with the union in exchange for labor's opposition to the act. See Marc Levinson, *The Great A&P and the Struggle for Small Business in America* (New York: Hill & Wang, 2011).

37. Alan Brinkley, "The Late New Deal and the Idea of the State," in *Liberalism and Its Discontents* (Cambridge, MA: Harvard University Press, 1998), 37–62, 44–45.

38. Kornhauser, *Debating the American State*, 30–48.

39. James Landis, *The Administrative Process* (New Haven, CT: Yale University Press, 1938).

40. Ibid., 62.

41. Ibid., 99–100.

42. Ibid., 46.

43. This historical account is by now familiar in the administrative law literature. See, for example, Elena Kagan, "Presidential Administration," *Harvard Law Review* 114 (2001): 2245–2385, 2253–2254; Richard Stewart, "The Reformation of American Administrative Law," *Harvard Law Review* 88, no. 8 (1975), 1669–1813; Gerald Frug, "The Ideology of Bureaucracy in American Law," *Harvard Law Review* 97 (1983–1984), 1276–1388; Morton Horwitz, *The Transformation of American Law, 1870–1960* (New York: Oxford University Press, 1992); Reuel Schiller, "Enlarging the Administrative Polity: Administrative Law and the Changing Definition of Pluralism, 1945–1970," *Vanderbilt Law Review* 53, no. 5 (2000): 1390–1453; Reuel E. Schiller, "The Era of Deference: Courts, Expertise, and the Emergence of New Deal Administrative Law," *Michigan Law Review* 106, no. 3 (December2007): 399–441; Peter Strauss, "From Expertise to Politics: The Transformation of American Rulemaking," *Wake Forest Law Review* 31 (1996): 488–526; and Robert Rabin, "Federal Regulation in Historical Perspective," *Stanford Law Review* 38 (1985–1986), 1189–1328.

44. See Horwitz, *Transformation*, 217–240 (recounting a famous debate between James Landis and Roscoe Pound over the legitimacy of modern regulatory agencies).

45. See, for example, *A. L. A. Schechter Poultry Corp. v. United States*, 295 U.S. 495 (1935) (invalidating the National Industrial Recovery Act, holding that "Congress is not permitted to abdicate or to transfer to others the essential legislative functions with which it is vested"); and *Crowell v. Benson*, 285 U.S. 22 (1932).

46. See, for example, Mark Tushnet, "Administrative Law in the 1930s: The Supreme Court's Accommodation of Progressive Legal Theory," *Duke Law Journal* 60 (2011), 1565–1639, 1569–1575; Schiller, "Era of Deference," 399–441, 413–435; Robert Rabin, "Federal Regulation in Historical Perspective," *Stanford Law Review* 38 (1985–1986), 1189–1328, 1254–12561.

47. Daniel Ernst, *Tocqueville's Nightmare: The Administrative State Emerges in America, 1900–1940* (New York: Oxford University Press, 2015).

48. See Walter Gellhorn, "The Administrative Procedure Act: The Beginnings," *Virginia Law Review* 72, no. 2 (1986): 219–233.

49. Horwitz, *Transformation*, 232.

50. See Ciepley, *Liberalism*; and Michael Sandel, *Democracy's Discontent: America in Search of a Public Philosophy* (Cambridge, MA: Harvard University Press, 1998).

51. See, for example, Ciepley, *Liberalism*, 81–98, 146–163; and Sandel, *Democracy's Discontents*, 250–274.

52. See, for example, David Harvey, *A Brief History of Neoliberalism* (New York: Oxford University Press, 2007).

53. S. M. Amadae, *Rationalizing Capitalist Democracy: The Cold War Origins of Rational Choice Liberalism* (Chicago: University of Chicago Press, 2003), 106–117. See also Burgin, *Great Persuasion*.

54. Amadae, *Rationalizing Capitalist Democracy*, 133–155.

55. Ibid., 172–175.

56. Ibid., 176–189. See also Jessica Leight, "Public Choice: A Critical Reassessment," in *Government and Markets: Toward a New Theory of Regulation*, ed. Edward Balleisen and David Moss (New York: Cambridge University Press, 2009), 213–255.

57. Daniel Rodgers, *Age of Fracture* (Cambridge, MA: Belknap Press of Harvard University Press, 2011), 86–89.

58. Ibid., 98.

59. Leight, "Public Choice"; and David Moss and Mary Oey, "The Paranoid Style in the Study of American Politics," in Balleisen and Moss, *Government and Markets*, 365–396.

60. See Leight, "Public Choice"; and Moss and Oey, "The Paranoid Style."

61. Edward A. Purcell Jr., *The Crisis of Democratic Theory: Scientific Naturalism and the Problem of Value* (Lexington: University Press of Kentucky, 1967), 109.

62. Rodgers, *Age of Fracture*, 42.

63. See, for example, Justin Fox, *The Myth of the Rational Market: A History of Risk, Reward, and Delusion on Wall Street* (New York: Harper Business, 2011).

64. See, for example, Herbert Hovenkamp, *The Opening of American Law* (New York: Oxford University Press, 2015), 174–183.

65. Rodgers, *Age of Fracture*, 47–76; and Phillips-Fein, *Invisible Hands*, 13–19.

66. Burgin, *Great Persuasion*; and Phillips-Fein, *Invisible Hands*, 42–56.

67. Phillips-Fein, *Invisible Hands*, 86.

68. Phillips-Fein, *Invisible Hands*, 160–165. See also Lawrence Glickman, *Free Enterprise: An American History* (New Haven, CT: Yale University Press, 2019).

69. See Nancy MacLean, *Democracy in Chains: The Deep History of the Radical Right's Stealth Plan for America* (New York: Viking, 2017).

70. For a good example of the interactions between civil rights movement actors and the federal bureaucracy, and how antisegregation activists and policymakers navigated the internal bureaucratic politics of the federal government to overcome a prior New Deal–era desire to avoid a deep commitment to racial integration, see David Smith, *Power to Heal: Civil Rights, Medicare, and the Struggle to Transform America's Health Care System* (Nashville, TN: Vanderbilt University Press, 2016). For an account of how desegregation efforts became a battleground over the role of the state and an arena incubating new forms of conservative backlash against both the economic inclusion and racial equity commitments of the federal government, see Justin Driver, *The Schoolhouse Gate: Public Education, the Supreme Court, and the Battle for the American Mind* (New York: Pantheon, 2018).

71. Thomas McCraw, *Prophets of Regulation* (Cambridge, MA: Belknap Press of Harvard University Press, 1984), 217–219.

72. Lawrence Lessig, "The New Chicago School," *Journal of Legal Studies* 27, no. 2 (1998): 661–691.

73. See, for example, Jodi Short, "The Paranoid Style in Regulatory Reform," Georgetown Public Law and Legal Theory Research Paper No. 11–10 (2011), 10.

74. Ibid., 23–29.

75. Ibid., 35.

76. See, for example, ibid.

77. Martin Shapiro, *Who Guards the Guardians? Judicial Control of Administration* (Athens: University of Georgia Press, 1988), 14–15; and Sheila Jasanoff, "Constitutional Moments in Governing Science and Technology," *Science Engineering Ethics* 17 (2011): 621–638, 632.

78. Jody Freeman and Adrian Vermeule, "Massachusetts v EPA: From Politics to Expertise," *Supreme Court Review* 2007, no. 2: 51–110, 52; *Massachusetts v. EPA*, 549 U.S. 497 (2007).

79. See Executive Order 12866, *Federal Register* 58, no. 190 (1993), https://www.archives .gov/files/federal-register/executive-orders/pdf/12866.pdf; and Executive Order 13563, January 18, 2011, https://obamawhitehouse.archives.gov/the-press-office/2011/01/18/executive -order-13563-improving-regulation-and-regulatory-review.

80. On the ideological nature of judicial review of agency action through the arbitrary and capricious review doctrine, see Richard Revesz, "Environmental Regulation, Ideology, and the DC Circuit," *Virginia Law Review* 83, no. 8 (1997): 1717–1771; Cass Sunstein, David Schkade, and Lisa Ellman, "Ideological Voting on Federal Courts of Appeals: A Preliminary Investigation," *Virginia Law Review* 90 (2004): 301–354; and Thomas Miles and Cass Sunstein, "The Real World of Arbitrariness Review," *University Chicago Law Review* 75 (2008): 761–814.

81. *Securities Industry Association v. Board of Governors of the Federal Reserve System*, 468 U.S. 207 (1984); *Securities Industry Association v. Board of Governors of the Federal Reserve System*, 807 F.2d 1052 (1986) (upholding the Fed's gradual erosion of Glass–Steagall's separation of investment and commercial banking in the 1980s, out of the "greatest deference" to their regulatory expertise).

82. See, for example, *Business Roundtable and Chamber of Commerce of the USA v. SEC*, No. 10-1305, D.C. Cir. (July 2011), 7 (striking down SEC rules implementing Dodd–Frank's provisions on proxy nomination and election processes for public company boards because the agency had "inconsistently and opportunistically" skewed its cost-benefit analysis by, in the court's view, failing to quantify certain costs or to justify its predictive judgments). Although the agency did cite several studies, the court dismissed these as "unpersuasive," providing "insufficient empirical data." *Business Roundtable*, 11. See also *International Swaps and Derivatives Association v. US*, F. Supp. 2d (D.D.C. 2012) 2012 WL 4466311 (holding that, contrary to the agency's belief, the statutory language permitted but did not require the Commodity Futures Trading Commission (CFTC) to issue the rule as the agency believed—and as a result the agency would have to provide a more reasoned justification for its decision on remand). For the CFTC regulation, see CFTC, Position Limits Rule, 76 F.R. 71626 (November 2011). See also Ben Protess, "Regulator Prepares to Appeal Dodd–Frank Court Ruling," *New York Times, Dealbook,* October 9, 2012, http://dealbook.nytimes.com/2012/10/09 /regulator-prepare-to-appeal-dodd-frank-court-ruling/.

83. See, for example, Kagan, "Presidential Administration."

84. *Free Enterprise Fund v. Public Company Accounting Oversight Board*, 561 U.S. 477 (2010).

85. *Free Enterprise Fund*, 130 S. Ct., 3156.

86. Richard Pildes and Cass Sunstein, "Reinventing the Regulatory State," *University of Chicago Law Review* 62, no. 1 (1995): 1–129.

87. Dodd–Frank Act § 119 (to be codified at 12 U.S.C. § 5329). See Rahman, "Envisioning the Regulatory State."

88. Dodd–Frank Act §§ 962–964 (amending 15 U.S.C. §§ 78d-7 to 78d-9).

89. John Dewey, "Liberty and Social Control," *Later Works of John Dewey, 1925–1953, vol. 11: 1935–1937* (Carbondale: Southern Illinois University Press, 1935), 359–363.

90. John Dewey, *The Public and Its Problems* (Athens: Swallow Press, Ohio University Press, 2004), 208.

91. Ibid., 145.

92. See, for example, Louis Brandeis, "How Far Have We Come on the Road to Industrial Democracy? An Interview," in Fraenkel, *Curse of Bigness*, 43–47; "Efficiency Systems and Labor," in Fraenkel, *Curse of Bigness*, 48–50; "On Industrial Relations," in Fraenkel, *Curse of Bigness*, 70–95, 76, 79. See also Philippa Strum, ed., *Brandeis on Democracy* (Lawrence: University Press of Kansas, 1995), 74–78.

93. See, for example, Brandeis, "Efficiency Systems and Labor," 48–50.

94. *Liggett v. Lee*, 283 U.S. 517 (J. Brandeis, dissenting).

95. *Liggett*, 283 U.S., 545, 548, 550–557.

96. *Liggett*, 283 U.S., 580.

97. See, for example, Gourevitch, *From Slavery to the Cooperative Commonwealth*; James Pope, "Labor's Constitution of Freedom," *Yale Law Journal* 106, no. 4 (1997): 941–1031.

98. Steven Piott, *Giving Voters a Voice: The Origins of the Initiative and Referendum in America* (Columbia: University of Missouri Press, 2003); and Barry Friedman, "The History of the Countermajoritarian Difficulty, Part Three: The Lesson of *Lochner*," *New York University Law Review* 76 (2001): 1383–1455.

99. David Barron, "Reclaiming Home Rule," *Harvard Law Review* 116 (2003): 2257–2386; and Kevin Mattson, *Creating a Democratic Public: The Struggle for Urban Partiicpatory Democracy During the Progressive Era* (University Park· Pennsylvania State University Press, 1997).

100. See, for example, Postel, *Populist Vision*; and Eric Schickler, *Racial Realignment: The Transformation of American Liberalism, 1932–1935* (Princeton, NJ: Princeton University Press, 2016).

101. See, for example, Thomas Merrill, "Capture Theory and the Courts: 1967–1983," *Chicago-Kent Law Review* 72 (1996–1997): 1039–1117; Stewart, "Reformation of American Administrative Law," 1713–1756; and Schiller, "Enlarging the Administrative Polity," 1390–1453, 1415–1443.

102. For several analyses of the positive political effects of the War on Poverty and their implications for democratizing governance today, see, for example, Tara Melish, "Maximum Feasible Participation of the Poor: New Governance, New Accountability, and a 21st Century War on the Sources of Poverty," *Yale Human Rights and Development Law Journal* 13 (2010): 1–134; Noel Cazenave, *Impossible Democracy: The Unlikely Success of the War on Poverty*

Community Action Programs (Albany: State University of New York Press, 2007); and Annelise Orleck and Lisa Hazirjian, *The War on Poverty: A New Grassroots History, 1940–1980* (Athens: University of Georgia Press, 2001).

103. See Mariano-Florentino Cuellar, "Rethinking Regulatory Democracy," *Administrative Law Review* 57, no. 2 (2005): 411–500, 491–497; Daniel Schwarcz, "Preventing Capture Through Consumer Empowerment Programs: Some Evidence from Insurance Regulation," in *Preventing Capture: Special Interest Influence and How to Limit It*, ed. Daniel Carpenter and David Moss (New York: Cambridge University Press, 2013).

104. See Steven Croley, *Regulation and the Public Interest: The Possibility of Good Regulatory Government* (Princeton, NJ: Princeton University Press, 2008), esp. 134–141; and Cuellar, "Rethinking Regulatory Democracy." This same basic approach has also been advanced by other scholars under different rubrics, of "reflexive regulation," "experimentalism," or "pragmatist regulation." See generally, Orly Lobel, "The Renew Deal: The Fall of Regulation and the Rise of Governance in Contemporary Legal Thought," *Minnesota Law Review* 89 (2004): 342–470; Jody Freeman, "Collaborative Governance in the Administrative State," *UCLA Law Review* 45, no. 1 (1997): 1–98; and Michael Dorf and Charles Sabel, "A Constitution of Democratic Experimentalism," *Columbia Law Review* 98 (1998): 267–473.

105. See, for example, Dorf and Sabel, "Democratic Experimentalism"; Lobel, "Renew Deal," 395–396; and Freeman, "Collaborative Governance," 9–14, 96.

106. See, for example, Cynthia Farina et al., "Democratic Deliberation in the Wild: The McGill Online Design Studio and the RegulationRoom Project," *Fordham Urban Law Journal* 41 (2014): 1527.

107. See, for example, "Political Power," Movement for Black Lives platform, https://policy.m4bl.org/political-power/.

108. See Dan Carpenter, *The Forging of Bureaucratic Autonomy: Networks, Reputations and Policy Innovation in Executive Agencies, 1862–1928* (Princeton, NJ: Princeton University Press, 2001); Carpenter and Moss, *Preventing Capture*; Balleisein and Moss, *Government and Markets*; and Gillian Metzger, "Administrative Constitutionalism," *Texas Law Review* 91 (2013): 1897.

Chapter 2

1. Barack Obama, "Remarks by the President on the Economy in Osawatomie, Kansas," December 6, 2011, https://www.whitehouse.gov/the-press-office/2011/12/06/remarks-president-economy-osawatomie-kansas. On the political context for the address, see E. J. Dionne Jr., *Why the Right Went Wrong: Conservatism from Goldwater to the Tea Party and Beyond* (New York: Simon and Schuster, 2016), 336–341.

2. Heather Cox Richardson, *To Make Men Free: A History of the Republican Party* (New York: Basic Books, 2014), 167–168.

3. Obama, "Remarks."

4. Ibid.

5. Theodore Roosevelt, *The New Nationalism* (New York: Outlook Company, 1910), 3.

6. "Mr. Roosevelt's Issue," *New York Times*, September 11, 1910, 10.

7. On the conceptual history of the economy, see Hugo Radice, "The National Economy: A Keynesian Myth?," *Capital & Class* 22 (1984): 111–140; Timothy Mitchell, "Fixing the Economy," *Cultural Studies* 12, no. 1 (1998): 82–101; Margaret Schabas, "Constructing 'The Economy,'" *Philosophy of the Social Sciences* 39, no. 3 (January 2009): 3–19; Quinn Slobodian, "How to See the World Economy: Statistics, Maps, and Schumpeter's Camera in the First Age of Globalization," *Journal of Global History* 10, no. 2 (July 2015): 307–322; Keith Tribe, *The Economy of the Word: Language, History, and Economics* (Oxford: Oxford University Press, 2015); Daniel Hirschman, "Inventing the Economy: Or, How We Learned to Stop Worrying and Love the GDP" (PhD diss., University of Michigan, 2015); Timothy Shenk, "Inventing the American Economy" (PhD diss., Columbia University, 2016); and David Grewal, *The Invention of the Economy: A History of Economic Thought* (Cambridge, MA: Harvard University Press, forthcoming).

8. To borrow from K. Sabeel Rahman's terminology (Chapter 1, this volume), the history of the economy is a quintessential instance of managerialism in action: it developed under the auspices of New Dealers and grew even more imposing in the neoliberal era that followed. For more on the shift toward emphasizing continuities running through either side of the rise and fall of the New Deal order, see Brent Cebul, Lily Geismer, and Mason Williams, "Beyond Red and Blue: Crisis and Continuity in Twentieth-Century U.S. Political History," in *Shaped By the State: Toward a New Political History of the Twentieth Century*, ed. Brent Cebul, Lily Geismer, and Mason Williams (Chicago: University of Chicago Press, 2019), 3–23. On the broader stakes of this project, see Michel Foucault, *Birth of Biopolitics: Lectures at the Collège de France, 1978–1979*, trans. Graham Burchell (Basingstoke: Palgrave Macmillan, 2008), 19–20.

9. Stuyvesant Fish, "Economy," *Arena* 264, no. 35 (March 1906): 264.

10. William Howard Taft, "Message of the President of the United States on Economy and Efficiency in the Government Service" (Washington, DC: Government Printing Office, 1912), 4.

11. Quoted in Sean Wilentz, *The Rise of American Democracy: Jefferson to Lincoln* (New York: Norton, 2005), 44.

12. Agrippa, "On the Present Prosperity," in *The Debate on the Constitution: Federalist and Antifederalist Speeches, Articles, and Letters During the Struggle over Ratification: Part One, September 1787 to February 1788*, ed. Bernard Bailyn (New York: Library of America, 1993), 429.

13. Quoted in Robert Remini, *Andrew Jackson: The Course of American Democracy, 1833–1845* (Baltimore: Johns Hopkins University Press, 1998), 257.

14. Quoted in Michael Holt, *Political Parties and American Political Development from the Age of Jackson to the Age of Lincoln* (Baton Rouge: University of Louisiana Press, 1992), 167.

15. Quoted in Tribe, *Economy of the Word*, 50.

16. John Stuart Mill, *Principles of Political Economy with Some of Their Applications to Social Philosophy* (London: Longmans, Green, Reader, and Dyer, 1871), 421.

17. John Stuart Mill, *A System of Logic, Ratiocinative and Inductive: Being a Connected View of the Principles of Evidence and the Methods of Scientific Investigation* (New York: Harper and Brothers, 1900), 622.

18. Thorstein Veblen, *The Place of Science in Modern Civilisation and Other Essays* (New York: B. W. Huebsch, 1919), 282.

19. Claude Lefort, *The Political Forms of Modern Society: Bureaucracy, Democracy, Totalitarianism*, ed. John Thompson (Cambridge, MA: MIT Press, 1986), 139–236; Foucault, *Birth of Biopolitics*, 291–316; Keith Baker, "Enlightenment and the Institution of Society: Notes for a Conceptual History," in *Main Trends in Cultural History*, ed. Willem Melching and Wyger Velema (Amsterdam: Rodopi, 1994), 95–120; Daniel Gordon, *Citizens Without Sovereignty* (Princeton, NJ: Princeton University Press, 1995), 43–85; David Bell, *The Cult of the Nation in France: Inventing Nationalism, 1680–1800* (Cambridge, MA: Harvard University Press, 2001), 22–49; and Jonathan Sheehan and Dror Wahrman, *Invisible Hands: Self-Organization and the Eighteenth Century* (Chicago: University of Chicago Press, 2015).

20. John Adams, "Thoughts on Government," in *The Political Writings of John Adams*, ed. George Peek Jr. (Indianapolis: Hackett, 2003), 85.

21. Quoted in Sheldon Wolin, *Tocqueville Between Two Worlds: The Making of a Political and Theoretical Life* (Princeton, NJ: Princeton University Press, 2001), 457.

22. See, for example, Fred Fairchild, Edgar Furniss, and Norman Buck, *Elementary Economics*, 2 vols. (New York: Macmillan Company, 1926).

23. Friedrich List, *National System of Political Economy*, trans. Sampson Lloyd (Kitchener, ON: Batoche, 2001), 188.

24. Lindley Keasbey, "The Economic State," *Political Science Quarterly* 8, no. 4 (December 1893): 602.

25. Ibid.

26. "DRAFT AGENDA for Conference called by the Rockefeller Foundation to Consider the Desirability and Feasibility of Encouraging Coordination of Fundamental Economic Research Upon Problems of Economic Change," box 13, series 3, Wesley Clair Mitchell Papers, Rare Book and Manuscript Library, Columbia University.

27. Alfred Marshall, *Principles of Economics* (London: Macmillan, 1920), www.econlib.org/index.html.

28. Richard Ely, *An Introduction to Political Economy* (New York: Hunt & Eaton, 1889), 14, 98.

29. Allyn Young, "Social Economy," 1908, box 2, folder 8, Allyn Abbot Young Papers, Harvard University Archives.

30. Irving Fisher, *Elementary Principles of Economics* (New York: Macmillan Company, 1916), 514, and Irving Fisher, "Principles of Economics, 1909–10," 1910, box 38, folder 525A, series 3, Irving Fisher Papers, Manuscripts and Archives, Yale University Library. "Societology" was the preferred term of Fisher's mentor William Graham Sumner, on which, see A. G. Keller, "William Graham Sumner," *American Journal of Sociology* 15, no. 6 (May 1910): 835.

31. Daniel Rodgers, "An Age of Social Politics," in *Rethinking American History in a Global Age*, ed. Thomas Bender (Berkeley: University of California Press, 2002), 250–273; William Novak, *The People's Welfare: Law and Regulation in Nineteenth-Century America* (Chapel Hill, NC: University of North Carolina Press, 1996), 19–50.

32. Woodrow Wilson, "The Lawyer and the Community," *North American Review* 192, no. 660 (November 1910): 605.

33. Ibid., 612.

34. Ibid., 608.

35. Wesley Mitchell, "Financial Processes in Revival. The Psychological Factor. Construction Enterprises. The Petroleum Industry," January 28, 1928, box 5, series 2, Mitchell Papers.

36. Wesley Mitchell, *Business Cycles: The Problem and Its Setting* (New York: National Bureau of Economic Research, 1927), 58, 180.

37. Frank W. Taussig, Frederick C. Mills, F. B. Garver, Frank H. Knight, R. W. Souter, Lewis L. Lorwin, and Mordecai Ezekiel, "The Theory of Economic Dynamics as Related to Industrial Instability," *American Economic Review* 20, no. 1 (March 1930): 31.

38. Bill Clinton, "Address Before a Joint Session of Congress on Administration Goals," February 17, 1993, http://www.presidency.ucsb.edu/ws/index.php?pid=47232.

39. Robert Caro, *The Passage of Power: The Years of Lyndon Johnson*, vol. 4 (New York: Vintage, 2012), 395–397.

40. Democratic Party Platform of 1960, July 11, 1960, http://www.presidency.ucsb.edu/ws/?pid=29602. This change was part of a broader shift in platforms, which a generation earlier had consisted of sweeping outlines of policy goals, and had by midcentury given way to specific macroeconomic targets. Hirschman, "Inventing the Economy," 106.

41. Walter Lippmann, *The New Imperative* (New York: Macmillan, 1935), 28–29.

42. For instance, see Walter Lippmann, *The Method of Freedom* (New York: Macmillan, 1934) 30, 46, 48.

43. Walter Lippmann, *A Preface to Politics* (New York: Mitchell Kennerley, 1914), 87.

44. Ibid., 126.

45. Clinton Rossiter and James Lare, eds., *The Essential Lipmann: A Political Philosophy for Liberal Democracy* (Cambridge, MA: Harvard University Press, 1982), 92.

46. Lillian Brandt, "Department of Social Economy at St. Louis," *Charities* 12, no. 24 (June 11, 1904): 704.

47. Quoted in Quinn Slobodian, *Globalists: The End of Empire and the Birth of Neoliberalism* (Cambridge, MA: Harvard University Press, 2018), 164.

48. John F. Kennedy, "Commencement Address at Yale University," June 11, 1962, http://www.presidency.ucsb.edu/ws/?pid=29661.

49. U.S. Congress, House of Representatives, The Budget for 1966: Committee on Appropriations and Public Works, 89th Cong., 1st Sess., 1965, 39.

50. Daniel Bell, *The End of Ideology: On the Exhaustion of Political Ideas in the Fifties*, 2nd ed. (Cambridge, MA: Harvard University Press, 2001), 69.

51. Federal Reserve Bank of St. Louis and U.S. Office of Management and Budget, Federal Net Outlays as Percent of Gross Domestic Product, https://fred.stlouisfed.org/series/FYONGDA188S.

52. Sheldon Wolin, "The New Public Philosophy," *Democracy* 1, no. 4 (October 1981): 27.

53. Historians of the New Deal will recognize that much of this interpretation tracks with Alan Brinkley's narrative of liberalism's turn away from "direct intervention in the day-to-day affairs of the corporate world" toward "Olympian manipulation of macroeconomic

levers" over the course of the Depression. Alan Brinkley, *End of Reform* (New York: Vintage Books, 1995), 7. To be sure, it is important to remember—as Samir Sonti (Chapter 4) and Jason Scott Smith (Chapter 3) both demonstrate in this volume—that the ascent of fiscal policy (and later monetary policy) did not rule out more interventionist approaches. But the emergence of a set of tools for managing the economy as a whole, rather than its specific industries or sectors, remains a turning point in modern statecraft.

54. Robert Gordon, *The Rise and Fall of Economic Growth: The U.S. Standard of Living Since the Civil War* (Princeton, NJ: Princeton University Press, 2016), 3.

55. On the corporation's rise, Alfred Chandler's work remains essential, above all *The Visible Hand* and *Scale and Scope: The Dynamics of Industrial Capitalism* (Cambridge, MA: Harvard University Press, 1990). See also Olivier Zunz, *Making America Corporate, 1870–1920* (Chicago: University of Chicago Press, 1992); Charles Perrow, *Organizing America: Wealth, Power, and the Origins of Corporate Capitalism* (Princeton, NJ: Princeton University Press, 2002); Naomi Lamoreaux, Daniel M. G. Raff, and Peter Temin, "Beyond Markets and Hierarchies: Toward a New Synthesis of American Business History," *American Historical Review* 108 (April 2003): 404–433; and Richard White, *Railroaded: The Transcontinentals and the Making of Modern America* (New York: Norton, 2011).

56. On this combination of factors, see Hirschman, "Inventing the Economy," 64–68.

57. Gerald Kramer, "Short-Term Fluctuations in U.S. Voting Behavior, 1896–1964," *American Political Science Review* 65, no. 1 (March 1971): 131–143; Christopher Achen and Larry Bartels, "Blind Retrospection: Why Shark Attacks Are Bad for Democracy," Working Paper 5-2013 (Center for the Study of Democratic Institutions, May 2013), http://www.reed.edu/chinese/chin-hum/claypools09/PDFs/Chicago.pdf; and Andrew Healy and Neil Malhotra, "Retrospective Voting Reconsidered," *Annual Review of Political Science* 16 (May 2013): 285–306.

58. Robert Collins, *More: The Politics of Economic Growth in Postwar America* (New York: Oxford University Press, 2000), 46–47, and David Engerman, *Know Your Enemy: The Rise and Fall of America's Soviet Experts* (New York: Oxford University Press, 2009), 97–128.

59. Suzanne de Brunhoff, *The State, Capital and Economic Policy* (London: Pluto Press, 1978), and Michael Beggs, *Inflation and the Making of Australian Macroeconomic Policy, 1945–85* (New York: Palgrave Macmillan, 2015).

60. Based on data in Ajay Mehrotra, *Making the Modern American Fiscal State: Law, Politics, and the Rise of Progressive Taxation, 1877–1929* (Cambridge: Cambridge University Press, 2013), 7.

61. Carmen Reinhart and Kenneth Rogoff, "Shifting Mandates: The Federal Reserve's First Centennial," paper presented at the American Economics Association Meeting, San Diego, January 5, 2013, 2.

62. On the original justifications for the Federal Reserve, see James Livingston, *Origins of the Federal Reserve System: Money, Class, and Corporate Capitalism, 1890–1913* (Ithaca, NY: Cornell University Press, 1989); Alan Meltzer, *A History of the Federal Reserve: Volume 1, 1913–1951* (Chicago: University of Chicago Press, 2004), 19–126; J. Lawrence Broz, *The International Origins of the Federal Reserve System* (Ithaca, NY: Cornell University Press, 2009); and

Roger Lowenstein, *America's Bank: The Epic Struggle to Create the Federal Reserve* (New York: Penguin Books, 2015).

63. James Lacey, *Keep from All Thoughtful Men: How U.S. Economists Won World War II* (Annapolis, MD: Naval Institute Press, 2011), 32.

64. The crucial work for this period remains Dorothy Ross, *The Origins of American Social Science* (Cambridge: Cambridge University Press, 1991), but on the economics profession and its intellectual context, see also Mary Furner, *Advocacy and Objectivity: A Crisis in the Professionalization* (Lexington: University Press of Kentucky, 1975); Andrew Jewett, *Science, Democracy, and the American University: From the Civil War to the Cold War* (Cambridge: Cambridge University Press, 2012); and Jonathan Franklin, "Irrelevant Genius: A History of Professional Economists and Policymaking in the United States" (PhD diss., University of Maryland, 2016).

65. See, for example, Nancy Cott, *The Grounding of Modern Feminism* (New Haven, CT: Yale University Press, 1987); George Chauncey, *Gay New York: Gender, Urban Culture, and the Making of the Gay Male World* (New York: Basic Books, 1994); George Fredrickson, *Racism: A Short History* (Princeton, NJ: Princeton University Press, 2002); and Samuel Moyn, *The Last Utopia: Human Rights in History* (Cambridge, MA: Harvard University Press, 2010).

66. Such eclecticism is one of the strengths of what is sometimes called historical ontology or historical epistemology, on which, see Arnold Davidson, *The Emergence of Sexuality: Historical Epistemology and the Formation of Concepts* (Cambridge, MA: Harvard University Press, 2001); Ian Hacking, *Historical Ontology* (Cambridge, MA: Harvard University Press, 2002); and Sarah Igo, *The Averaged American: Surveys, Citizens, and the Making of a Mass Public* (Cambridge, MA: Harvard University Press, 2007).

67. Robert Fogel, Enid Fogel, Mark Guglielmo, and Nathaniel Grotte, *Simon Kuznets and the Empirical Tradition in Economics* (Chicago: University of Chicago Press, 2012).

68. Wyatt Wells, *Economist in an Uncertain World: Arthur F. Burns and the Federal Reserve, 1970–1978* (New York: Columbia University Press, 1994).

69. Milton Friedman and Rose Friedman, *Two Lucky People: Memoirs* (Chicago: University of Chicago Press, 1998), 29–31.

70. Milton Friedman and Anna Schwartz, *A Monetary History of the United States, 1867–1960* (Princeton, NJ: Princeton University Press, 1963).

71. Ben Bernanke, *The Courage to Act: A Memoir of a Crisis and Its Aftermath* (New York: Norton, 2015), 30.

72. On technocratic politics, see Gabrielle Hecht, "Technology, Politics, and National Identity in France," in *Technologies of Power: Essays in Honor of Thomas Parker Hughes and Agatha Chipley Hughes*, ed. Michael Allen and Gabrielle Hecht (Cambridge, MA: MIT Press, 2001), 253–294; Timothy Mitchell, *Rule of Experts: Egypt, Techno-Politics, Modernity* (Berkeley: University of California Press, 2002); James Vernon, "The Ethics of Hunger and the Assembly of Society: The Techno-Politics of the School Mean in Modern Britain," *American Historical Review* 110, no. 3 (June 2005): 693–725; and Iginio Gagliardone, "'A Country in Order': Technopolitics, Nation Building, and the Development of ICT in Ethiopia," *Information Technolo-*

gies and International Development 10, no. 1 (Spring 2014): 3–19. Sheila Jasanoff, *Designs on Nature: Science and Democracy in Europe and the United States* (Princeton, NJ: Princeton University Press, 2005) reflects on consequences this shift has had for political theory and democratic practice.

Chapter 3

1. Steve Fraser and Gary Gerstle, eds., *The Rise and Fall of the New Deal Order, 1930–1980* (Princeton, NJ: Princeton University Press, 1989).

2. Quote from Robert A. Lively, "The American System: A Review Article," *Business History Review* 29 (March 1955): 82; see also Oscar Handlin and Mary Flug Handlin, *Commonwealth: A Study of the Role of Government in the American Economy: Massachusetts, 1774–1861* (Cambridge, MA: Harvard University Press, 1947); Louis Hartz, *Economic Policy and Democratic Thought: Pennsylvania, 1776–1860* (Cambridge, MA: Harvard University Press, 1948); George Rogers Taylor, *The Transportation Revolution, 1815–1860* (New York: Harper and Row, 1951); James Willard Hurst, *Law and the Conditions of Freedom in the Nineteenth-Century United States* (Madison: University of Wisconsin Press, 1956); William Novak, *The People's Welfare: Law and Regulation in Nineteenth-Century America* (Chapel Hill: University of North Carolina Press, 1996); Richard R. John, *Spreading the News: The American Postal System from Franklin to Morse* (Cambridge, MA: Harvard University Press, 1995); Harry N. Scheiber, *The Ohio Canal Era: A Case Study of Government and the Economy, 1820–1861* (Columbus: Ohio University Press, 2012 [1969]); John Lauritz Larson, *Internal Improvement: National Public Works and the Promise of Popular Government in the Early United States* (Chapel Hill: University of North Carolina Press, 2001); Edward Balleisen, *Navigating Failure: Bankruptcy and Commercial Society in Antebellum America* (Chapel Hill: University of North Carolina Press, 2001); and Christine Desan, *Making Money: Coin, Currency, and the Coming of Capitalism* (New York: Oxford University Press, 2015).

3. Jordan A. Schwarz, *The New Dealers: Power Politics in the Age of Roosevelt* (New York: Knopf, 1993), xi. See also Jason Scott Smith, *A Concise History of the New Deal* (New York: Cambridge University Press, 2014), and *Building New Deal Liberalism: The Political Economy of Public Works, 1933–1956* (New York: Cambridge University Press, 2006).

4. Hansen, quoted in Alan Brinkley, "The New Deal and the Idea of the State," in Fraser and Gerstle, *Rise and Fall of the New Deal Order*, 85. Brinkley developed his ideas at book-length in his *The End of Reform: New Deal Liberalism in Recession and War* (New York: Knopf, 1995). He later republished the essay, with a title clarifying his chronological focus, "The Late New Deal and the Idea of the State," in Alan Brinkley, *Liberalism and Its Discontents* (Cambridge, MA: Harvard University Press, 1998), 37–62.

5. Steve Fraser and Gary Gerstle's introductory essay in Fraser and Gerstle, *Rise and Fall of the New Deal Order*.

6. Carl Degler, *Out of Our Past: The Forces that Shaped Modern America*, 3rd ed. (New York: Harper and Row, 1984), chap. 13; William E. Leuchtenburg, *Franklin D. Roosevelt and the New Deal* (New York: Harper and Row, 1963), 347.

7. Richard Hofstadter, *The Age of Reform: From Bryan to F.D.R.* (New York: Vintage, 1955); and Eric F. Goldman, *Rendezvous with Destiny: A History of Modern American Reform*, rev. ed. (New York: Vintage, 1977 [1952]). Other analyses of the links between the New Deal and earlier generations of reformers include Otis L. Graham Jr., *An Encore for Reform: The Old Progressives and the New Deal* (New York: Oxford University Press, 1967), and Daniel T. Rodgers, *Atlantic Crossings: Social Politics in a Progressive Age* (Cambridge, MA: Harvard University Press, 1998), esp. 409–484.

8. Brinkley, *End of Reform*. Others who have questioned the commitment of the New Deal to reform include Howard Zinn, Paul Conkin, Barton Bernstein, Ronald Radosh, Gabriel Kolko, and Colin Gordon.

9. For the classic liberal account, see Arthur M. Schlesinger Jr., *The Age of Roosevelt*, 3 vols. (Boston: Houghton Mifflin, 1957–1960).

10. Mark H. Leff, *The Limits of Symbolic Reform: The New Deal and Taxation, 1933–1939* (Cambridge: Cambridge University Press, 1984).

11. Colin Gordon, *New Deals: Business, Labor, and Politics in America, 1920–1935* (Cambridge: Cambridge University Press, 1994).

12. The American Federation of Labor president William Green called section 7(a) the "Magna Carta of Labor of the United States." Quoted in Irving Bernstein, *Turbulent Years: A History of the American Worker, 1933–1941* (Boston: Houghton Mifflin, 1970), 349. For the "counterfeit liberty" reading of the history of labor law, see Christopher L. Tomlins, *The State and the Unions: Labor Relations, Law, and the Organized Labor Movement in America, 1880–1960* (Cambridge: Cambridge University Press, 1985), 326–28.

13. James T. Patterson, "United States History Since 1920," in *The American Historical Association's Guide to Historical Literature*, vol. 2, 3rd ed., ed. Mary Beth Norton (New York: Oxford University Press, 1995), 1455; and James T. Patterson, "Americans and the Writing of Twentieth-Century United States History," in *Imagined Histories: American Historians Interpret the Past*, ed. Anthony Molho and Gordon S. Wood (Princeton, NJ: Princeton University Press, 1998), 185–205. See also Brinkley, "Prosperity, Depression, and War," in *The New American History*, rev. ed., ed. Eric Foner (Philadelphia: Temple University Press, 1997), 134–137; and Leuchtenburg, *Franklin D. Roosevelt*, 346.

14. For a review of the literature suggesting that the range and subtlety of Leuchtenburg's work was one of the reasons that the New Left never really developed a sustained critique of the New Deal, see Brinkley, "Prosperity, Depression, and War," 143–144.

15. Hofstadter, *Age of Reform*, 319.

16. This essay has been republished as "The Limits of the New Deal," in Howard Zinn, *The Politics of History*, 2d ed. (Urbana: University of Illinois Press, 1990), 125.

17. Ibid., 133.

18. Ibid., 134.

19. Barton J. Bernstein, "The New Deal: The Conservative Achievements of Liberal Reform," in *Towards a New Past: Dissenting Essays in American History*, ed. Bernstein (New York: Vintage, 1967), 264. The intellectual genealogy of corporate liberalism can be traced through William Appleman Williams, *The Contours of American History* (New York: New

Viewpoints, 1973 [1961]), esp. 439–469; Gabriel Kolko, *The Triumph of Conservatism: A Rein-terpretation of American History, 1900–1916* (New York: Free Press, 1963); James Weinstein, *The Corporate Ideal in the Liberal State* (Boston: Beacon Press, 1968); Gabriel Kolko, *Main Currents in Modern American History* (New York: Harper and Row, 1976), esp. 111–157; and Martin J. Sklar, *The Corporate Reconstruction of American Capitalism, 1890–1916: The Market, the Law, and Politics* (Cambridge: Cambridge University Press, 1988). See also R. Jeffrey Lustig, *Corporate Liberalism: The Origins of Modern American Political Theory, 1890–1920* (Berkeley: University of California Press, 1982).

20. Bernstein, "New Deal," 281.

21. Brinkley, *End of Reform*, 6, 7.

22. Ellis W. Hawley, *The New Deal and the Problem of Monopoly: A Study in Economic Ambivalence* (New York: Fordham University Press, 1995 [1966]), 57; and Andrew Wender Cohen, *The Racketeer's Progress: Chicago and the Struggle for the Modern American Economy, 1900–1940* (New York: Cambridge University Press, 2004).

23. Thomas K. McCraw, "Review of Alan Brinkley, *The End of Reform: New Deal Liberalism in Recession and War," Journal of American History* 82 (December 1995): 1171. For more on McCraw's work and its importance to historians of capitalism, see Richard R. John and Jason Scott Smith, "Beyond the New Deal: Thomas K. McCraw and the Political Economy of Capitalism," in *Capital Gains: Business and Politics in Twentieth-Century America*, ed. Richard R. John and Kim Phillips-Fein (Philadelphia: University of Pennsylvania Press, 2016), 95–116. Brinkley, to be sure, does acknowledge the achievements of the New Deal's mixed economy (see *End of Reform*, 267–268), only to conclude that while liberalism's "redefinition in the last years of the New Deal made possible many of its later achievements," at the same time "that redefinition also stripped postwar liberalism of its ability to deal with some enduring and inescapable problems" (271).

24. Christina Romer, "What Ended the Great Depression?," *Journal of Economic History* 52 (December 1992): 757, 781; E. Cary Brown, "Fiscal Policy in the 'Thirties: A Reappraisal," *American Economic Review* 46 (December 1956): 857–879; Milton Friedman and Anna Jacobson Schwartz, *A Monetary History of the United States, 1867–1960* (Princeton, NJ: Princeton University Press, 1963); Ben S. Bernanke and Martin Parkinson, "Unemployment, Inflation, and Wages in the American Depression: Are There Lessons for Europe?," *American Economic Review* 79 (May 1989): 210–214; J. Bradford De Long and Lawrence H. Summers, "How Does Macroeconomic Policy Affect Output?," *Brookings Papers on Economic Activity*, no. 2 (1988): 433–480; Barry Eichengreen, *Golden Fetters: The Gold Standard and the Great Depression, 1919–1939* (New York: Oxford University Press, 1992); Gavin Wright, "The New Deal and the Modernization of the South," *Federal History* 2 (2010), http://shfg.org/shfg/wp-content/uploads/2011/01/5-Wright-design5-_Layout-1.pdf; and Alexander J. Field, *A Great Leap Forward: 1930s Depression and U.S. Economic Growth* (New Haven, CT: Yale University Press, 2011). For an interpretation of FDR's presidency that clarifies the role of Keynesian-inspired monetary policy to the New Deal, see Eric Rauchway, *The Money Makers: How Roosevelt and Keynes Ended the Depression, Defeated Fascism, and Secured a Prosperous Peace* (New York: Basic Books, 2015).

25. For these paragraphs, see Smith, *Concise History of the New Deal* and Smith, *Building New Deal Liberalism*.

26. For more on the history of World War II mobilization, see Mark R. Wilson's terrific account, *Destructive Creation: American Business and the Winning of World War II* (Philadelphia: University of Pennsylvania Press, 2016).

27. Smith, *Concise History of the New Deal*, 169.

28. Walter S. Salant, "The Spread of Keynesian Doctrines and Practices in the United States," in *The Political Power of Economic Ideas: Keynesianism Across Nations*, ed. Peter A. Hall (Princeton, NJ: Princeton University Press, 1989), 27–51; and Michael A. Bernstein, *A Perilous Progress: Economists and Public Purpose in Twentieth-Century America* (Princeton, NJ: Princeton University Press, 2001). Kiran Klaus Patel also stresses the importance of World War II in ratifying the New Deal's response to the Great Depression; see his *The New Deal: A Global History* (Princeton, NJ: Princeton University Press, 2016).

29. Chase quoted in Thomas K. McCraw, "The New Deal and the Mixed Economy," in *Fifty Years Later: The New Deal Evaluated*, ed. Harvard Sitkoff (New York: Knopf, 1985), 39.

30. Mira Wilkins, *The Maturing of Multinational Enterprise: American Business Abroad from 1914 to 1970* (Cambridge, MA: Harvard University Press, 1974); Amy L. S. Staples, *The Birth of Development: How the World Bank, Food and Agriculture Organization, and World Health Organization Changed the World, 1945–1965* (Kent, OH: Kent State University Press, 2006); Thomas W. Zeiler, *Free Trade, Free World: The Advent of GATT* (Chapel Hill: University of North Carolina Press, 1999); Michele Alacevich, *The Political Economy of the World Bank: The Early Years* (Stanford, CA: Stanford University Press, 1999); and Albert O. Hirschman, "How the Keynesian Revolution Was Exported from the United States, and Other Comments," in Hall, *Political Power of Economic Ideas*, 347–359. Jason Scott Smith, "The Great Transformation: The State and the Market in the Postwar World," in *Boundaries of the State in US History*, ed. James T. Sparrow, William J. Novak, and Stephen W. Sawyer (Chicago: University of Chicago Press, 2015), 127–151.

31. Michael J. Hogan, *The Marshall Plan: America, Britain, and the Reconstruction of Western Europe, 1947–1952* (Cambridge: Cambridge University Press, 1987); Theodore Cohen, *Remaking Japan: The American Occupation as New Deal*, ed. Herbert Passin (New York: Free Press, 1987); John W. Dower, *Embracing Defeat: Japan in the Wake of World War II* (New York: Norton, 1999); and David Ekbladh, *The Great American Mission: Modernization and the Construction of an American World Order* (Princeton, NJ: Princeton University Press, 2010).

32. Charles S. Maier, "'Malaise': The Crisis of Capitalism in the 1970s," in *The Shock of the Global: The 1970s in Perspective*, ed. Niall Ferguson, Charles S. Maier, Erez Manela, and Daniel J. Sargent (Cambridge, MA: Harvard University Press, 2010), 29.

33. Hirschman, "How the Keynesian Revolution Was Exported."

34. Brinkley, *End of Reform*, 263; and Bernstein, *Perilous Progress*.

35. For an essential critique of the Right's history of the New Deal, see Eric Rauchway, "New Deal Denialism," *Dissent* 57 (Winter 2010): 68–72.

36. Paul Conkin, *The New Deal*, 2nd ed. (Arlington Heights, IL: AHM Publishing, 1975 [1967]), 100; J. Joseph Huthmaker, *Trial by War and Depression: 1917–1941* (Boston: Allyn and Bacon, 1973), 179; David Kennedy, "What the New Deal Did," *Political Science Quarterly* 124

(2009): 252 (this article is an adapted and updated version of the argument advanced in his 2009 work *Freedom from Fear*); and Mary Beth Norton et al., *A People and a Nation: A History of the United States*, 9th ed. (Boston: Cengage Learning 2012), 675.

Chapter 4

1. Alan Brinkley, *The End of Reform: New Deal Liberalism in Recession and War* (New York: Knopf, 1995); Colin Gordon, *New Deals: Business, Labor, and Politics in America, 1920–1935* (Cambridge: Cambridge University Press, 1994); and Ira Katznelson, *Fear Itself: The New Deal and the Origins of Our Time* (New York: Norton, 2014).

2. Howard Brick, *Transcending Capitalism: Visions of a New Society in Modern American Thought* (Ithaca, NY: Cornell University Press, 2006).

3. On the planners in the New Deal USDA, see especially Jess Gilbert, *Planning Democracy: Agrarian Intellectuals and the New Deal* (New Haven, CT: Yale University Press, 2015) and Richard Kirkendall, *Social Scientists and Farm Politics in the Age of Roosevelt* (Columbia: University of Missouri Press, 1966). On the origins of the planning wing in the pre–New Deal USDA, see David E. Hamilton, *From New Day to New Deal: American Farm Policy from Hoover to Roosevelt* (Chapel Hill: University of North Carolina Press, 1991). On the Agricultural Adjustment Administration (AAA) more generally, see Anthony Badger, *The New Deal: The Depression Years* (New York: Ivan R. Dee, 1989), 147–189; Theodore Salutos, *The American Farmer and the New Deal* (Ames: Iowa State University Press, 1982); Arthur M. Schlesinger Jr., *The Coming of the New Deal* (Boston: Houghton Mifflin, 1958), 27–84; and Van L. Perkins, *Crisis in Agriculture: The Agricultural Adjustment Administration and the New Deal, 1933* (Berkeley: University of California Press, 1968).

4. Meg Jacobs, *Pocketbook Politics: Economic Citizenship in Twentieth-Century America* (Princeton, NJ: Princeton University Press, 2004).

5. Anthony Badger, *The New Deal: The Depression Years, 1933–1940* (New York: Hill and Wang, 1989), chap. 5. Simpson quoted in David E. Conrad, *The Forgotten Farmers: The Story of Share Croppers in the New Deal* (Urbana: University of Illinois Press, 1965), 28.

6. See Hamilton, *From New Day to New Deal*, 195–250; Ellis Hawley, "Economic Inquiry and the State in New Era America: Antistatist Corporatism and Positive Statism in Uneasy Coexistence," in *The State and Economic Knowledge: The American and British Experiences*, ed. Mary O. Furner and Barry Supple (New York: Cambridge University Press, 1990), 287–324; Malcolm Rutherford, "The USDA Graduate School: Government Training in Statistics and Economics, 1921–1945," *Journal of the History of Economic Thought* 33, no. 4 (2011): 419–447; and Mordecai Ezekiel, *Jobs for All, Through Industrial Expansion* (New York: Knopf, 1939).

7. Carolyn Goldstein, *Creating Consumers: Home Economists in Twentieth-Century America* (Chapel Hill: University of North Carolina Press, 2012), 63–64.

8. Adolph Berle and Gardiner Means, *The Modern Corporation and Private Property* (New York: Macmillan, 1932); Gardiner Means, *Industrial Prices and Their Relative Inflexibility*, U.S. Senate Document 13, 74th Cong., 1st Sess. (Washington, DC: Government Printing Office, 1935), 1.

9. Means, *Industrial Prices*, 8.

10. Ibid., 10.

11. Ibid.

12. See especially Ellis Hawley, *The New Deal and the Problem of Monopoly* (Princeton, NJ: Princeton University Press, 1966).

13. Means, *Industrial Prices*, 12.

14. On Means and the New Deal, see Frederic S. Lee, "A New Dealer in Agriculture: G. C. Means and the Writing of Industrial Prices," *Review of Social Economy* 46, no. 2 (1988): 180–202, and "From Multi-Industry Planning to Keynesian Planning: Gardiner Means, the American Keynesians, and National Economic Planning at the National Resources Committee," *Journal of Policy History* 2, no. 2 (1990): 186–212. On Means's thought more generally, see Warren J. Samuels and Steven G. Medema, *Gardiner C. Means: Institutionalist and Post-Keynesian* (New York: M. E. Sharpe, 1990) ; Frederic S. Lee and Warren Samuels, eds., *The Heterodox Economics of Gardiner C. Means: A Collection* (Armonk, NY: M. E. Sharpe, 1992); and Mary Furner, "From State Interference to Return of the Market," in *Governments and Markets: Toward a New Theory of Regulation*, ed. Edward J. Balleisen and David A. Moss (New York: Cambridge University Press, 2010), 92–142.

15. See Peter Irons, *The New Deal Lawyers* (Princeton, NJ: Princeton University Press, 1993), esp. Part II.

16. On Pressman, see Gilbert J. Gall, *Pursuing Justice: Lee Pressman, the New Deal, and the CIO* (Albany: State University of New York Press, 1999). After leaving the AAA and before joining the CIO, Pressman served as general counsel for Rexford Tugwell's Resettlement Administration.

17. Ibid., 29–30.

18. Peek, quoted in Schlesinger, *Coming of the New Deal*, 55.

19. Henry Wallace to George Peek, June 10, 1933, box 1, file 1, Donald E. Montgomery Papers, Walter P. Reuther Library of Labor and Urban Affairs, Wayne State University, Detroit, MI (hereafter DEM); Kenneth Miller, *From Progressive to New Dealer: Frederic C. Howe and American Liberalism* (University Park: Pennsylvania State University Press, 2010), 381; and Persia Campbell, *Consumer Representation in the New Deal* (New York: Columbia University Press, 1940), 203. The historical literature on the Consumers' Counsel is scant. The best account remains Campbell, *Consumer Representation*, 194–261. Campbell was a Columbia-trained social scientist and a leader of the emergent working-class consumer movement. See also Jacobs, *Pocketbook Politics*, 122–135; Miller, *From Progressive to New Dealer*, 377–405; Landon Storrs, *The Second Red Scare and the Unmaking of the New Deal Left* (Princeton, NJ: Princeton University Press, 2012), 25; Cohen, *Consumers' Republic*, 29; and Edwin G. Nourse, Joseph S. Davis, and John D. Black, *Three Years of the Agricultural Adjustment Administration* (Washington: Department of Agriculture, 1937), 391–399.

20. Miller, *From Progressive to New Dealer*, 383. See also Jerry N. Hess, "Oral History Interview with Louis H. Bean," September 11, 1970, Harry S. Truman Library and Museum, 24–25.

21. Quoted in George N. Peek, *Why Quit Our Own* (New York: Van Nostrand, 1936). On Howe, see Miller, *From Progressive to New Dealer*.

22. Quoted in Gilbert, *Planning Democracy*, 66, 70. On Jackson, see Donald H. Grubbs, "Gardner Jackson, That 'Socialist' Tenant Farmers' Union, and the New Deal," *Agricultural History* 42, no. 2 (April 1968): 125–137; William H. Riker, *The Firing of Pat Jackson* (Washington, DC: Inter-University Case Program, 1951); and Arthur Schlesinger, "Gardner Jackson, 1897–1965," *New Republic*, May 1, 1965. See also Gardner Jackson, "The Reminiscences of Gardner Jackson," Columbia University Oral History Research Office Collection, May 1959.

23. On Taylor, see Storrs, *Second Red Scare*, 25; and Gladys Baker, "Women in the U.S. Department of Agriculture," *Agricultural History* 50, no. 1 (1976): 190–201. The FBI maintained a file on Taylor, which is reprinted in Storrs, *Second Red Scare*, 279.

24. This point is central to Campbell's analysis in *Consumer Representation*. The other New Deal consumer bodies were the Consumer' Advisory Board of the NRA, the Consumers' Division of the National Emergency Council, and the Consumers' Counsel of the National Bituminous Coal Commission. For a brief history of each, see Richard J. Leighton, "Consumer Protection Agency Proposals: The Origins of the Species," *Administrative Law Review* 25, no. 3 (1973): 269–312.

25. Quoted in Miller, *From Progressive to New Dealer*, 387–388.

26. Quoted in ibid., 388.

27. Quoted in Schlesinger, *Coming of the New Deal*, 56.

28. For a useful historical and geographical analysis of milk production and distribution, see Shane Hamilton, *Trucking Country: The Road to America's Wal-Mart Economy* (Princeton, NJ: Princeton University Press, 2014), 24–34. See also, John D. Black, *The Dairy Industry and the AAA* (Washington, DC: Brookings Institution, 1935).

29. "Text of License for Chicago Milk Sales," *Wall Street Journal*, August 3, 1933.

30. *Consumers Guide*, October 28, 1933; *Consumers Guide*, November 14, 1933; and *Consumers Guide*, November 29, 1933.

31. "Show How Milk Code Fails to Help Farmers," *Chicago Tribune*, November 29, 1933. Around the same time, Wallace rejected a proposed marketing agreement covering the meatpacking industry for its failure to include a provision granting access to corporate books and records. See "Roosevelt Curbs AAA Power As Peek Revolts," *New York Times*, December 7, 1933.

32. "Labor's Platform Urges Expansion of Mayor's Regime," *New York Times*, September 8, 1937.

33. *Consumers Guide*, August 23, 1937.

34. "Consumers Begin Cheap Milk Fight," *New York Times*, November 23, 1937.

35. Archie Wright to Meyer Parodneck, May 22, 1939, box 4, file 8, DEM; and Meyer Parodneck to Donald Montgomery, May 26, 1939, ibid.

36. Richard E. Berlin, August 18, 1939, box 2, file 16, DEM.

37. "Dies Investigator Says Reds Utilize Consumer Groups," *New York Times*, December 11, 1933.

38. Paul Appleby to Milton Eisenhower et al., May 20, 1939, box 2, file 2, DEM.

39. Milton Eisenhower et al. to Paul Appleby, June 30, 1939, box 2, file 1, DEM.

40. Montgomery to Appleby, August 9, 1939, box 2, file 8, DEM; and Appleby to Montgomery, August 10, 1939, box 2, file 8, DEM.

41. *Consumers Guide*, March 15, 1940.

42. *Consumers Guide*, April 1, 1940.

43. On the tensions between structural reform and commercial Keynesianism, see especially Brinkley, *End of Reform*.

44. Michal Kalecki, "The Political Aspects of Full Employment," *Political Quarterly* 14, no. 4 (1943): 326.

45. Michael W. Flamm, "The National Farmers Union and the Evolution of Agrarian Liberalism, 1937–1946," *Agricultural History* 68, no. 3 (1994): 74, esp. n90. See also Gary Mucciaroni, *The Political Failure of Employment Policy, 1945–1982* (Pittsburgh: University of Pittsburgh Press, 1990); and Margaret Weir, *Politics and Jobs: The Boundaries of Employment Policy* (Princeton, NJ: Princeton University Press, 1993).

46. Mucciaroni, *Political Failure*, 22–25.

47. The only book-length treatment of the Employment Act of 1946 is Stephen Bailey, *Congress Makes a Law: The Story of the Employment Act of 1946* (New York: Columbia University Press, 1950).

48. Jacobs, *Pocketbook Politics*, 179–261; Allen J. Matusow, *Farm Policies and Politics in the Truman Years* (Cambridge, MA: Harvard University Press, 1967), chap. 3.

49. Montgomery, "Statement Before New York State Joint Legislative Committee on Nutrition," December 15, 1943, box 6, file 1, DEM.

50. See House Committee on Agriculture, *General Farm Program, Including Joint Hearings with the Senate Committee on Agriculture and Forestry*, 81st Cong., 1st Sess., pt. 2 (Washington, DC: Government Printing Office, 1949). The National Farmers' Union also reprinted the Brannan Plan, Charles Brannan, *Farm Price Support Program* (Denver, CO: National Farmers' Union, 1949). On the Brannan Plan, see Virgil W. Dean, *An Opportunity Lost: The Truman Administration and the Farm Policy Debate* (Columbia: University of Missouri Press, 2006); Adam Sheingate, *The Rise of the Agricultural Welfare State* (Princeton, NJ: Princeton University Press, 2003), 128–134; and Matusow, *Farm Policies and Policies*, chap. 9.

51. On this point, see esp. Michael W. Flamm, "National Farmers Union."

52. "Transcript of NBC program—"Should the Agricultural Act of 1948 Be Revised?," box 35, file 5, DEM.

53. Quoted in Bess Furman, "Subsidies Replace Parity to Farmer in Full-Food Plan," *New York Times*, April 8, 1949.

54. "Lourie Denounces Brannan Plan," *New York Times*, May 12, 1949; Dean, *Opportunity Lost*, 153. For a range of perspectives on the Brannan Plan, see House Committee on Agriculture, *General Farm Program, Including Joint Hearings with the Senate Committee on Agriculture and Forestry*, 81st Cong., 1st Sess., pts. 3 (Testimony of farm organizations) and 5 (Testimony of producers' groups) (Washington, DC: Government Printing Office, 1949); and Subcommittee of the Committee on Agriculture and Forestry, United States Senate, *Hearings on S. 1882: A Bill to Amend the Agricultural Adjustment Act of 1938 and S. 1971: A Bill to Stabilize Farm Income and Farm Prices of Agricultural Commodities*, 81st Cong., 1st Sess. (Washington, DC: Government Printing Office, 1949).

55. See esp. Dean, *Opportunity Lost*, chaps. 6–8.

56. Barry Eichengreen and Peter Garber, "Before the Accord: U.S. Monetary-Financial Policy, 1945–1951," in *Financial Markets and Financial Crisis*, ed. R. Glen Hubbard (Chicago: University of Chicago Press, 1991), 175–206.

57. William J. Barber, "The Kennedy Years: A Purposeful Pedagogy," in *Exhortation and Controls: The Search for a Wage Price Policy, 1945–1971* (Washington, DC: Brookings Institution, 1975), 135–191.

58. Benjamin Waterhouse, "Mobilizing for the Market: Organized Business, Wage-Price Controls, and the Politics of Inflation," *Journal of American History* 100, no. 2 (2013): 454–478. On the politics behind the Humphrey–Hawkins Act, see Dean Baker, Sarah Rawlins, and David Stein, "The Fully Employment Mandate of the Federal Reserve: Its Origins and Importance," *Center for Economic and Policy Research* (July 2017), http://cepr.net/images/stories/reports/full-employment-mandate-2017-07.pdf.

59. The author received support from the Washington Center for Equitable Growth for research conducted for this chapter.

Chapter 5

1. In general, see Frances Fox Piven and Richard A. Cloward, *Regulating the Poor: The Functions of Public Welfare* (New York: Pantheon, 1971); Mimi Abramovitz, *Regulating the Lives of Women: Social Welfare Policy from Colonial Times to the Present* (Boston: South End Press, 1988); Linda Gordon, "What Does Welfare Regulate?," *Social Research* 55, no. 4 (1988): 609–630; and Robert Lieberman, *Shifting the Color Line: Race and the American Welfare State* (Cambridge, MA: Harvard University Press, 1998). More recent works on the U.S. welfare state break new ground in many respects, but leave this narrative undisturbed. See, for example, Cybelle Fox, *Three Worlds of Relief: Race, Immigration, and the American Welfare State from the Progressive Era to the New Deal* (Princeton, NJ: Princeton University Press, 2012), 250–280. My 2016 book, on which this chapter draws, is an attempt at revision. Karen M. Tani, *States of Dependency: Welfare, Rights, and American Governance, 1935–1972* (New York: Cambridge University Press, 2016).

2. Jason Scott Smith makes a similar, albeit more triumphalist, argument in Chapter 3 of this volume, where he calls attention to New Deal economic accomplishments that the current historiography elides.

3. I refer here to the need-based income support programs authorized by the Social Security Act of 1935. See Pub. L. No. 74-271, 49 Stat. 620 (1935) (Titles I, IV, and X). The law built on experiments pioneered by the Federal Emergency Relief Administration (FERA) and, before it, the Children's Bureau (through its administration of grants for maternal and infant health). On FERA's policies and programs, see especially Josephine Chapin Brown, *Public Relief, 1929–1939* (New York: Henry Holt, 1940); William R. Brock, *Welfare, Democracy, and the New Deal* (Cambridge: Cambridge University Press, 1988); and Susan Stein-Roggenbuck, *Negotiating Relief: The Development of Social Welfare Programs in Depression-Era Michigan, 1930–1940* (Columbus: Ohio State University Press, 2008). On the work of the Children's Bureau, see Kriste Lindenmeyer, *"A Right to Childhood": The U.S. Children's Bureau and Child Welfare, 1912–1946* (Champaign: University of Illinois Press, 1997).

4. Important and often-cited accounts include Martha F. Davis, *Brutal Need: Lawyers and the Welfare Rights Movement, 1960–1973* (New Haven, CT: Yale University Press, 1993); Premilla Nadasen, *Welfare Warriors: The Welfare Rights Movement in the United States* (New York: Routledge, 2005); Annelise Orleck, *Storming Caesars Palace: How Black Mothers Fought Their Own War on Poverty* (Boston: Beacon Press, 2005); and Felicia Ann Kornbluh, *The Battle for Welfare Rights: Politics and Poverty in Modern America* (Philadelphia: University of Pennsylvania Press, 2007). On the "two-track" account of the U.S. welfare state, classic articulations include Barbara Nelson, "The Origins of the Two-Channel Welfare State: Workmen's Compensation and Mothers' Aid," in *Women, the State, and Welfare*, ed. Linda Gordon (Madison: University of Wisconsin Press, 1990) ; Linda Gordon, "Social Insurance and Public Assistance: The Influence of Gender in Welfare Thought in the United States, 1890–1935," *American Historical Review* 97, no. 1 (1992): 19–54; Theda Skocpol, *Protecting Soldiers and Mothers: The Political Origins of Social Policy in the United States* (Cambridge, MA: Belknap Press of Harvard University Press, 1992); Suzanne Mettler, *Dividing Citizens: Gender and Federalism in New Deal Public Policy* (Ithaca, NY: Cornell University Press, 1998); Robert Lieberman, *Shifting the Color Line: Race and the American Welfare State* (Cambridge, MA: Harvard University Press, 1998); and Alice Kessler-Harris, "In the Nation's Image: The Gendered Limits of Social Citizenship in the Depression Era," *Journal of American History* 86, no. 3 (1999): 1251–1279. On how claims to social resources came to be understood as "charity" and why that label was so difficult to change, see Nancy Fraser and Linda Gordon, "Contract Versus Charity: Why Is There No Social Citizenship in the United States?," *Socialist Review* 22 (1992): 45–68.

5. Roosevelt famously summoned Americans to war by reminding them of cherished "negative" rights (freedom of religion and speech) and declaring newer "positive" ones (government protection against poverty and insecurity). He also employed rights language when, in the midst of the Great Depression, he assured Americans of their "right to live." Tani, *States of Dependency*, 73 (citing examples from Roosevelt's public addresses between 1934 and 1941).

6. The SSB underwent numerous changes during the period I discuss. It began as an independent agency headed by a three-member advisory board. In 1939, as part of a broader reorganization, the SSB became part of the Federal Security Agency (FSA), a subcabinet-level agency that housed various New Deal and war-related programs. In 1946 the SSB was renamed the Social Security Administration and a single commissioner replaced the board at the top of the agency. In 1953 the FSA became a cabinet-level agency and was renamed the Department of Health, Education, and Welfare (HEW). Social Security Administration, "Organizational History," accessed May 15, 2015, http://www.ssa.gov/history/orghist.html. To avoid unnecessary confusion, I often use terms like "the federal agency" and "federal administrators."

7. Jack Tate, "Opportunity for a Fair Hearing," April 27, 1936, box 95, Office of the Commissioner, Chairman's Files, 1935–1942, Records of the Social Security Administration, RG 47, National Archives, College Park, MD (hereafter SSAR).

8. Leonard Calhoun to Louis Resnick, March 10, 1937, box 4, GC Correspondence Relating to Old-Age and Survivors' Benefits, 1935–42, Records of the Department of Health, Education, and Welfare and the Federal Security Agency, RG 235, National Archives, College Park,

MD (hereafter HEWR). For a similar observation, circulated more widely, see A. Delafield Smith, "Citizenship and Family Security," *Social Security Bulletin* 3, no. 5 (1940): 8. On the Social Security Board's efforts to sell Social Security to a skeptical American public, including the now pervasive characterization of Social Security benefits as an "earned right," see John G. Winant, "An Approach to Social Security," *Atlantic Monthly* 158 (July 1936): 69–76; and Jerry R. Cates, *Insuring Inequality: Administrative Leadership in Social Security, 1935–1954* (Ann Arbor: University of Michigan Press, 1983), 30.

9. A. Delafield Smith, "Interrelationship of Education and Practice in the Development of a Profession," January 26, 1939, Richard G. Smith family papers, private collection, notes on file with author.

10. A. Delafield Smith, "The Need for Legal Concepts in the Formulation of Administrative Procedures," *Social Service Review* 15, no. 3 (1941): 451; see also A. Delafield Smith, "Judicial Trends in Relation to Public Welfare Administration," *Social Service Review* 15, no. 2 (1941): 242.

11. Jane M. Hoey, "The Contribution of Social Work to Government," in *National Conference of Social Work* (New York: Columbia University Press, 1941), 13.

12. On why New Deal administrators were so drawn to rights language in these contexts, see Karen M. Tani, "Welfare and Rights Before the Movement: Rights as a Language of the State," *Yale Law Journal* 122 (2012): 314–383.

13. Federal Security Agency in collaboration with Bureau of Accounts and Audits and Office of the General Counsel, *Money Payments to Recipients of Old-Age Assistance, Aid to Dependent Children, and Aid to the Blind* (Washington, DC: Government Printing Office, 1944). Jane Hoey published a very similar document in the *Social Security Bulletin*, where other public welfare administrators presumably read it. Jane M. Hoey, "The Significance of the Money Payment in Public Assistance," *Social Security Bulletin* 7 (1944): 3–5.

14. Charlotte Towle, *Common Human Needs: An Interpretation for Staff in Public Assistance Agencies*, Public Assistance Report no. 8 (Washington, DC: Government Printing Office, 1945); and Agnes Van Driel to Jane Hoey et al., November 1, 1944, box 214, Bureau of Public Assistance, Correspondence Relating to Plans and Programs, 1935–1948, SSAR.

15. Towle, *Common Human Needs*, vii, 23. Another 1944 report, which the bureau distributed to public assistance agencies in 1946, urged similar views on its readers. In *The Nature of Service in Public Assistance Administration*, the author Grace Marcus describes "administering assistance as a right" as the agency's primary responsibility." Grace Marcus, *The Nature of Service in Public Assistance Administration*, Public Assistance Report no. 10 (Washington, DC: Government Printing Office, 1946), 4–5.

16. On state agency documents, see, for example, Richard McEvoy, "State-Federal Public Assistance, 1935–1946" (PhD diss., University of Maryland, 1980), 292–293 (finding in Idaho's 1942 welfare department manual the statement that it was "the legal and democratic right of any person to make application for assistance, to receive equitable consideration of his application and to receive assistance provided he is eligible"); Bureau of Public Assistance, Regional Staff Conference, May 13, 1944, "Personnel," box 193, Mixed Files, Correspondence Relating to Public Assistance Plans and Programs, 1935–1948, SSAR (praising Oklahoma's 1944 orientation materials for its emphasis on "see[ing] that people eligible under the law

get [assistance]," and respecting the client's spending choices); and Margaret Kincaid Bishop, "County Participation in a Public Assistance Program," *Public Welfare* 3, no. 12 (1945): 274 (referring to "the right to assistance" as the program's "fundamental premise").

17. For various views on how welfare applicants and recipients experienced the public assistance system in these decades, see Lisa Levenstein, *A Movement Without Marches: African American Women and the Politics of Poverty in Postwar Philadelphia* (Chapel Hill: University of North Carolina Press, 2009); Kornbluh, *Battle for Welfare Rights*; Ellen Reese, *Backlash Against Welfare Mothers: Past and Present* (Los Angeles: University of California Press, 2005); and Winifred Bell, *Aid to Dependent Children* (New York: Columbia University Press, 1965). Unfortunately, the literature focuses almost exclusively on the Aid to Dependent Children program and thus offers a limited view of the experiences of people who sought relief on the basis of old age, blindness, or, after 1950, "permanent and total" disability.

18. Tani, *States of Dependency*, 113–125.

19. Ibid., 125–141.

20. Joseph McDowell Mitchell, untitled address, ca. 1961, box 1, mss. 800, Elizabeth Wickenden Papers, Wisconsin Historical Society, Madison.

21. On popular enthusiasm for Mitchell and his ideas, see this chapter's section on "The Reinvigoration of Localism."

22. Tani, "Welfare and Rights Before the Movement"; and Karen M. Tani, "States' Rights, Welfare Rights, and 'The Indian Problem': Negotiating Citizenship and Sovereignty, 1935–1954," *Law and History Review* 33, no. 1 (2015): 1–40.

23. Jon C. Teaford, *The Rise of the States: Evolution of American State Government* (Baltimore: Johns Hopkins University Press, 2002), 5. Teaford devotes little attention to New Deal public assistance, other than to say that during the Depression, states shouldered responsibility for many local functions (120–121). He draws most of his evidence from the policy areas of transportation infrastructure (highways) and education.

24. There are some notable exceptions. The most important is Martha Derthick's work on Massachusetts. Martha Derthick, *The Influence of Federal Grants: Public Assistance in Massachusetts* (Cambridge, MA: Harvard University Press, 1970). See also William Pickens, "The New Deal in New Mexico," in *The New Deal: The State and Local Levels*, ed. John Braeman, Robert H. Bremner, and David Brody (Columbus: Ohio State University Press, 1975), 331 ("Far from usurping authority from the states, federal officials begged them to assume more responsibilities"); and James R. Leiby, "State Welfare Administration in California, 1930–1945," *Southern California Quarterly* 55, no. 3 (1973): 303–318. For a different perspective, see Margaret Weir, "States, Race, and the Decline of New Deal Liberalism," *Studies in American Political Development* 19 (Fall 2005): 157–172, 165 (using evidence of the unreformed nature of state-level politics to argue that states "resisted federal efforts to build state capacities").

25. Historians who have written about these conditions have tended to frame them as deeply inadequate and a lost opportunity to implement truly meaningful reform. They lament, for example, Congress's failure to place a national "floor" on the benefits that states promised to their poor citizens. I am asking scholars to turn their gaze from the conditions that might have been to the conditions that actually were, and to think about the implications of these conditions for broader structures of government.

26. The former federal administrator Blanche D. Coll provides a useful overview of many of these changes in *Safety Net: Welfare and Social Security, 1929-1979* (New Brunswick, NJ: Rutgers University Press, 1995).

27. In general, see Weir, "States, Race, and the Decline of New Deal Liberalism," 165 (describing state governments on the eve of the New Deal as remaining "highly decentralized" and having "little capacity to promote state-wide social or economic perspectives"). State-level studies bear out Weir's general observations. See, for example, Pickens, "New Deal in Mexico," 322 ("State government [in the early 1930s in New Mexico] touched the lives of few people. . . . Many departments did little except draw up budgets").

28. By 1935, many states had some kind of state-level social welfare board or agency, but few exercised meaningful authority over the day-to-day administration of relief for the poor. Some states—such as Arkansas, Idaho, Mississippi, Nevada, and Utah—had no state-level welfare department of any kind. Robert E. Moran Sr., "Public Relief in Louisiana from 1928 to 1960," *Louisiana History* 14, no. 4 (1973): 369–385, 376. For a contemporary perspective on the radical transformations that the Social Security Act appeared to require at the state level, see W. Brook Graves, "The Future of the American States," *American Political Science Review* 30, no. 1 (1936): 24–50, 28.

29. See, for example Charles McKinley and Robert W Frase, *Launching Social Security: A Capture-and-Record Account, 1935-1937* (Madison: University of Wisconsin Press, 1970); Robert Lansdale et al., *The Administration of Old Age Assistance* (Chicago: Public Administration Service, 1939); Marietta Stevenson, *Public Welfare Administration* (New York: Macmillan, 1938); and William Haber, "Problems of State Administration," in *National Conference of Social Work* (Chicago: University of Chicago Press, 1937): 445–451. A number of secondary accounts have also explored this phenomenon, in varying degrees of depth. See, for example, James Patterson, *The New Deal and the States: Federalism in Transition* (Princeton, NJ: Princeton University Press, 1969); McEvoy, "State-Federal Public Assistance"; Coll, *Safety Net*; Derthick, *Influence of Federal Grants*; and Stein-Roggenbuck, *Negotiating Relief*.

30. Margaret Leahy, "Intake Practices in Local Public Assistance Agencies," *Social Security Bulletin* 4, no. 10 (1941): 3–4.

31. In general, see Tani, *States of Dependency*; and Derthick, *Influence of Federal Grants*.

32. Derthick, *Influence of Federal Grants*, 35–36; see also Daniel I. Cronin, "Impact of Federal Welfare Grants on Municipal Governments," *Boston University Law Review* 40 (1960): 531–543. The exception to this statement is for "general relief"—that is, relief of needy people who did not qualify for one of the federally subsidized categories of aid. In many places, local authorities retained control over this program. General relief was a relatively small fiefdom, however, especially after the creation in 1950 of federally subsidized Aid to the Permanently and Totally Disabled.

33. Weir, "States, Race, and the Decline of New Deal Liberalism," 166, 169.

34. A. Delafield Smith, "Community Prerogative and the Legal Rights and Freedom of the Individual," *Social Security Bulletin* 9 (1946): 6–10, 7. For more evidence, see the discussion in Karen M. Tani, "Administrative Equal Protection: Federalism, the Fourteenth Amendment, and the Rights of the Poor," *Cornell Law Review* 100 (2015): 825–899, 846–850, 852.

35. Paul Molloy, "Relief Chiselers Are Stealing Us Blind," *Saturday Evening Post*, September 8, 1951, 32–33, 142–44.

36. In general, see Jennifer Mittelstadt, *From Welfare to Workfare: The Unintended Consequences of Liberal Reform, 1945–1965* (Chapel Hill: University of North Carolina Press, 2005); Reese, *Backlash Against Welfare Mothers*; and Molly C. Michelmore, *Tax and Spend: The Welfare State, Tax Politics, and the Limits of American Liberalism* (Philadelphia: University of Pennsylvania Press, 2012).

37. See Bureau of Public Assistance, State Letter no. 46, March 5, 1945, box 1, State Letters, Policies, and Regulations Relating to Public Welfare Programs, 1942–1971, SSAR (recommending that "suitable home" provisions be omitted from state public assistance laws and "that the protective purpose" of such provisions be incorporated into states' generally applicable public laws). The observations about state-level trends come from Bell, *Aid to Dependent Children*, 51, 57–58.

38. Tani, *States of Dependency*, 209–211.

39. News Bureau, Florida State University, untitled press release on Florida Suitable Home study, September 25, 1962, box 2, Robert T. Lansdale Collection, SW 169, Social Welfare History Archives, University of Minnesota, Minneapolis. The study was published as Robert T. Lansdale, *The Florida Suitable Home Law: A Statistical Analysis of 17,999 Aid to Dependent Children Cases Affected* (Tallahassee: Florida State University, 1962).

40. W. L. White, "'On the County'—Then and Now," *Reader's Digest*, March 1952, 110–113.

41. Thomas Sugrue, "All Politics Is Local: The Persistence of Localism in Twentieth-Century America," in *The Democratic Experiment*, ed. Meg Jacobs, William J. Novak, and Julian E. Zelizer (Princeton, NJ: Princeton University Press, 2003), 302; Daniel Scroop, "Local and National Identities in the Politics of Consumption: The Anti-Chain Store Movement Reconsidered," *History Compass* 6, no. 3 (2008): 947–968; and Lizabeth Cohen, *A Consumers' Republic: The Politics of Mass Consumption in Postwar America* (New York: Knopf, 2003).

42. Alan Brinkley, *Voices of Protest: Huey Long, Father Coughlin, and the Great Depression* (New York: Vintage Books, 1982), 261–262.

43. See, for example, Meg Jacobs, *Pocketbook Politics: Economic Citizenship in Twentieth-Century America* (Princeton, NJ: Princeton University Press, 2005) (on the National Recovery Administration and Agricultural Adjustment Administration).

44. On the ADC program's changing demographics in the 1940s and 1950s, see Bell, *Aid to Dependent Children*; Reese, *Backlash Against Welfare Mothers*; and Levenstein, *A Movement Without Marches*. These scholars also document the perception that welfare motivated African Americans' migration, employment, and reproductive choices.

45. "New Rash of Public Welfare Investigations," *Survey* 87, no. 5 (1951): 230.

46. On the relief scandal in Baltimore, see, in general, Benjamin H. Lyndon, "Relief Probes: A Study of Public Welfare Investigations in Baltimore, New York, and Detroit; 1947–1949" (PhD diss., University of Chicago School of Social Services Administration, 1953), 13–102. On the controversy over *Common Human Needs*, see Wendy B. Posner, "Common Human Needs: A Story from the Prehistory of Government by Special Interest," *Social Service Review* 69, no. 2 (1995): 188–225.

47. The Newburgh incident received ample journalistic coverage. For more recent scholarly interpretations, see Lisa Levenstein, "From Innocent Children to Unwanted Migrants and Unwed Moms: Two Chapters in the Public Discourse on Welfare in the United States, 1960–1961," *Journal of Women's History* 11, no. 4 (2000); and Elisa Minoff, "The Rise of the Toxic Politics of Migration," *Bulletin of the GHI* (Spring 2014): 91–108, http://test2.ghi-dc.org/files/publications/bulletin/bu054/bu54_091.pdf.

48. Minoff, "Rise of the Toxic Politics of Migration," 106.

49. On waivers and other state-level innovations in this period, see Lucy A. Williams, "The Abuse of Section 1115 Waivers: Welfare Reform in Search of a Standard," *Yale Law and Policy Review* 12, no. 1 (1994): 8–37; Robert C. Lieberman and Greg M. Shaw, "Looking Inward, Looking Outward: The Politics of State Welfare Innovation Under Devolution," *Political Research Quarterly* 53, no. 2 (2000): 215–240; Yvonne Zylan and Sarah A. Soule, "Ending Welfare As We Know It (Again): Welfare State Retrenchment, 1989–1995," *Social Forces* 79, no. 2 (2000): 623–652; and Joe Soss, Richard C. Fording, and Sanford F. Schram, *Disciplining the Poor: Neoliberal Paternalism and the Persistent Power of Race* (Chicago: University of Chicago Press, 2011): 115–120. For historical accounts of changes to welfare policy in the last four decades of the twentieth century, see Sanford F. Schram, Joe Soss, and Richard C. Fording, *Race and the Politics of Welfare Reform* (Ann Arbor: University of Michigan Press, 2003); Marisa Chappell, *The War on Welfare: Family, Poverty, and Politics in Modern America* (Philadelphia: University of Pennsylvania Press, 2011); and Julilly Kohler-Hausmann, *Getting Tough: Welfare and Imprisonment in 1970s America* (Princeton, NJ: Princeton University Press, 2017). Felicia Kornbluh and Gwendolyn Mink extend their account into the twenty-first century. Felicia Kornbluh and Gwendolyn Mink, *Ensuring Poverty: Welfare Reform in Feminist Perspective* (Philadelphia: University of Pennsylvania Press, 2019).

50. Soss, Fording, and Schram, *Disciplining the Poor*, 120–140.

51. I do not mean to imply that decentralization was a myth or that local administrators became mere functionaries of the state and federal governments. Social scientists have documented the powerful effects local administrators have on the lives of welfare state beneficiaries and the significant ways in which experiences can vary from locality to locality. See, for example, Joe Soss, *Unwanted Claims: The Politics of Participation in the U.S. Welfare System* (Ann Arbor: University of Michigan Press, 2000); Soss, Fording, and Schram, *Disciplining the Poor*, 153–175; and Jamila Michener, *Fragmented Democracy: Medicaid, Federalism, and Unequal Politics* (New York: Cambridge University Press, 2018). What I aim to show in this section is that there is a difference between the politically appealing rhetoric of localism and reality; to characterize today's welfare workers as the functional equivalents of nineteenth-century overseers of the poor is to lose sight of a robust apparatus of state and federal control.

52. See, for example, K. Sabeel Rahman, Chapter 1 in this volume.

Chapter 6

1. Thomas Snyder, *120 Years of American Education: A Statistical Portrait* (Washington, DC: U.S. Department of Education, Office of Educational Research and Improvement, 1993), http://nces.ed.gov/pubs93/93442.pdf; and Camille Ryan and Curt Bauman, *Educational*

Attainment in the United States: 2015 (Washington, DC: U.S. Census Bureau, 2015), https://www.census.gov/content/dam/Census/library/publications/2016/demo/p20-578.pdf.

2. Katie Lobosco, "The Case for Canceling All Student Debt," CNN Money, February 15, 2018, http://money.cnn.com/2018/02/15/pf/college/canceling-student-debt/index.html; and Elizabeth Tandy Shermer, "The Student Debt Crisis and Its Deniers," *Public Books*, March 15, 2017, http://www.publicbooks.org/the-student-debt-crisis-and-its-deniers/.

3. Nelson Lichtenstein, *State of the Union: A Century of American Labor* (Princeton, NJ: Princeton University Press, 2002), 20–97.

4. Jason Scott Smith, *A Concise History of the New Deal* (New York: Cambridge University Press, 2014), 183–200; Ira Katznelson, *When Affirmative Action Was White: An Untold Story of Racial Inequality in Twentieth-Century America* (New York: Norton, 2005); Sanford Jacoby, *Modern Manors: Welfare Capitalism Since the New Deal* (Princeton, NJ: Princeton University Press, 1997); Jennifer Klein, *For All These Rights: Business, Labor, and the Shaping of America's Public–Private Welfare State* (Princeton, NJ: Princeton University Press, 2003); Lewis Hyman, *Debtor Nation: The History of America in Red Ink* (Princeton, NJ: Princeton University Press, 2011); Judith Stein, *Pivotal Decade: How the United States Traded Factories for Finance in the Seventies* (New Haven, CT: Yale University Press, 2010); Alyssa Fetini, "A Brief History of the 401(k)," *Time*, October 16, 2008, http://content.time.com/time/magazine/article/0,9171,1851124,00.html; Jonathan Levy, *Freaks of Fortune: The Emerging World of Capitalism and Risk in America* (Cambridge, MA: Harvard University Press, 2012); and Rick Wartzman, *End of Loyalty: The Rise and Fall of Good Jobs in America* (New York: Public Affairs, 2017).

5. Elizabeth Tandy Shermer, "From Educator to Creditor in Chief: The American Presidency, Higher Education, and the Student Loan Industry," in *The President and American Capitalism since 1945*, ed. Mark Rose and Roger Biles (Gainesville: University of Florida Press, 2017), 123–150.

6. Geiger, *To Advance Knowledge: The Growth of American Research Universities, 1900–1940* (New York: Oxford University Press, 1986), 94–139; David Levine, *The American College and the Culture of Aspiration, 1915–1940* (Ithaca, NY: Cornell University Press, 1986), 39–60; and Laurence Veysey, *Emergence of the American University* (Chicago: University of Chicago Press, 1970), 263–341.

7. D. Bruce Johnstone, *New Patterns for College Lending: Income Contingent Loans* (New York: Columbia University Press), 1–2; Levine, *American College*, 188; Ernest Victor Hollis, *Philanthropic Foundations and Higher Education* (New York: Columbia University Press, 1938), 188–190; and Dorothy Woolf, "Loans to Students on Business Basis," *New York Times*, November 22, 1931, 77.

8. Hollis, *Philanthropic Foundations*, 186–190, quote on 190; Levine, *American College*, 188.

9. Levine, *American College*, 185–209, quote on 193.

10. Dorothy Woolf, "Loans to Students on Business Basis," *New York Times*, November 22, 1931, 77; Geiger, *Advance Knowledge*, 246–268; and Levine, *American College*, 185–209.

11. Paula Fass, "Without Design: Education Policy in the New Deal," *American Journal of Education* 91, no. 1 (November 1982): 36–64; David Labaree, "A System Without a Plan: Emergence of an American System of Higher Education in the Twentieth Century," *Bildungsge-*

schichte 3, no. 1 (2013): 46–59; and Ronald Story, "The New Deal and Higher Education," in *The New Deal and the Triumph of Liberalism*, ed. Sidney Milkus and Jerome Mileur (Amherst: University of Massachusetts Press, 2002), 272–296.

12. Smith, *Concise History of the New Deal*.

13. Lichtenstein, *State of the Union*, 20–97; Klein, *For All These Rights*, 78–115; and Hyman, *Debtor Nation*, 45–97.

14. Fass, "Without Design"; Larabee, "A System Without a Plan"; Story, "New Deal and Higher Education"; and Richard Novak and David Leslie, "A Not So Distant Mirror: Great Depression Writings on the Governance and Finance of Public Higher Education," *History of Higher Educational Annual* 20 (2000): 59–78.

15. Story, "New Deal and Higher Education."

16. Morris Appell, "Franklin Delano Roosevelt and Education" (PhD diss., Ohio State University, 1947), 29–91.

17. Fass, "Without Design"; Story, "New Deal and Higher Education."

18. Christopher Loss, *Between Citizens and the State: The Politics of American Higher Education in the 20th Century* (Princeton, NJ: Princeton University Press, 2012), 53–90; Story, "New Deal and Higher Education"; Fass, "Without Design"; and Richard Reiman, *New Deal and American Youth: Ideas and Ideals in a Depression Decade* (Athens: University of Georgia Press, 1992, 97–109.

19. Reiman, *New Deal and American Youth*, 97–109; Smith, *Concise History of the New Deal*; and James Patterson, *Congressional Conservatism and the New Deal: The Growth of the Conservative Coalition in Congress, 1933–1939* (Lexington: University of Kentucky Press, 1967).

20. Reiman, *New Deal and American Youth*, 120–123; and Katznelson, *Fear Itself*, 133–224.

21. Reiman, *New Deal and American Youth*, 120–129; Palmer Johnson and Oswald Harvey, *The National Youth Administration* (New York: Arno, 1974), 8–22; John Salmond, *Southern Rebel: The Life and Times of Aubrey Willis Williams, 1890–1965* (Chapel Hill: University of North Carolina Press, 1983), 121–136; National Advisory Committee, *Report of the National Advisory Committee of the National Youth Administration to the President of the United States* (Washington, DC: Government Printing Office, 1942), 38–39; and Franklin Delano Roosevelt, Executive Order 7086, June 26, 1935, American Presidency Project, http://www.presidency.ucsb.edu/ws/?pid=15092.

22. Salmond, *Southern Rebel*, 7–42, quote on 32.

23. Levine, *American College*, 197–203; Johnson and Harvey, *National Youth Administration*, 96; National Advisory Committee, *Report*, 63–68; and Betty Lindley and Ernest Lindley, *A New Deal for Youth: The Story of the National Youth Administration* (New York: Viking, 1938), 158–183.

24. Levine, *American College*, 200–205, quote on 204; Salmond, *Southern Rebel*, 154–157; and Reiman, *New Deal and American Youth*, 123–140.

25. National Advisory Committee, *Report*, 63–68; and Lindley and Lindley, *New Deal for Youth*, 158–183.

26. Lindley and Lindley, *New Deal for Youth*, 158–183; Levine, *American College*, 197–207; "NYA Students Do Well," *New York Times*, June 20, 1938, 10; National Advisory Committee, *Report*, 63–68.

27. Salmond, *Southern Rebel*, 96–104; *Congressional Conservatism and the New Deal*; and Reiman, *New Deal and American Youth*, 158–181.

28. Katznelson, *Fear Itself*, 365–466; G. C. Altschuler and S. M. Blumin, *The GI Bill: A New Deal for Veterans* (Oxford: Oxford University Press, 2009); Story, "New Deal and Higher Education," 280–283; Loss, *Between Citizens and the State*, 91–120; Robert Serow, "Policy as Symbol: Title II of the 1944 G.I. Bill," *Review of Higher Education* 27, no. 4 (Summer 2004): 481–499; Suzanne Mettler, *Soldiers to Citizens: The G.I. Bill and Making of the Greatest Generation* (New York: Oxford University Press, 2005); and Frydl, *The GI Bill* (New York: Cambridge University Press, 2009).

29. Keith W. Olson, "The G.I. Bill and Higher Education: Success and Surprise," *American Quarterly* 25, no. 5 (December 1973): 596–610, quote on 600.

30. Altschuler and Blumin, *GI Bill*, 11–34; Frydl, *GI Bill*, 36–99; Story, "New Deal and Higher Education," 280–283.

31. Olson, "G.I. Bill and Higher Education."

32. Ibid., 601–605, quotes 601, 602, 603, 604; and Altschuler and Blumin, *GI Bill*, 51–84;

33. Altschuler and Blumin, *GI Bill*, 51–84; and David Nasaw, *The Chief: The Life of William Randolph Hearst* (New York: Houghton Mifflin, 2000), 576–603.

34. Altschuler and Blumin, *GI Bill*, 51–84.

35. Altschuler and Blumin, *GI Bill*, 85–116; Frydl, *GI Bill*, 301–351; and Christopher Kiernan, "Federal Aid to Higher Education: The Pell Grant Program in Historical Perspective" (PhD diss., Boston College, 1992), 155–157.

36. Mettler, *Soldiers to Citizens*, 41–86; Tod Ottman, "Forging SUNY in New York's Political Cauldron," in *SUNY at Sixty: The Promise of the State University of New York*, ed. John Clark, W. Bruce Leslie, and Kenneth O'Brien (Albany: State University of New York Press, 2010), 15–28.

37. Mettler, *Soldiers to Citizens*, 41–58; Frydl, *GI Bill*, 303–351, quoted 338; and Olson, "G.I. Bill and Higher Education," 600–606, quotes on 604, 605.

38. Mettler, *Soldiers to Citizens*, 1–14, 59–86, 163–176; Olson, "G.I. Bill and Higher Education"; and Shermer, "From Educator to Creditor in Chief."

39. Shermer, "From Educator to Creditor in Chief."

40. Ibid.; Wayne Urban, "James Bryant Conant and the Limits of Educational Planning in California and New York," in Clark, Leslie, and O'Brien, *SUNY at 60*, 190–198; and Paddy Riley, "Clark Kerr: From the Industrial to the Knowledge Economy," in *American Capitalism: Social Thought and Political Economy in the Twentieth Century*, ed. Nelson Lichtenstein (Philadelphia: University of Pennsylvania Press, 2006), 71–87.

41. Shermer, "From Educator to Creditor in Chief"; Theodore Thompson, *The National Defense Education Act of 1958* (Ithaca, NY: Project One Publication Office, 1964); and Barbara Gale, "The National Defense Student Loan Program: Its History, Significance, and Problems" (PhD diss., George Washington University, 1974).

42. Shermer, "From Educator to Creditor in Chief."

43. Ibid.; Loss, *Between Citizens and the State*, 165–213; Graham, *The Uncertain Triumph: Federal Education Policy in the Kennedy and Johnson Years* (Chapel Hill: University of North Carolina Press, 1984), xiii–xxiv, quoted xv; and Lyndon Baines Johnson, "Remarks on Signing the Higher Education Act," November 8, 1965, http://www.txstate.edu/commonexperience /pastsitearchives/2008-2009/lbjresources/higheredact.html.

44. Shermer, "From Educator to Creditor in Chief."

45. Ibid.

46. Ibid.

47. Ibid.

48. Ibid.

49. Ibid.

50. Ibid.; Lawrence Gladieux and Thomas Wolanin, *Congress and the College: The National Politics of Higher Education* (Lexington, MA: Lexington Books, 1976); Patrick Mungovan, "The Role of the U.S. Federal Government in the Student Loan Industry" (masters thesis, MIT Sloan School of Management, 2005), 22–44; Erin Dillon, *Leading Lady: Sallie Mae and the Origins of Today's Student Loan Controversy* (Washington, DC: Education Sector, 2007); and John Dean, Saul Moskowitz, and Karen Cipriani, "Implications of the Privatization of Sallie Mae," *Journal of Public Budgeting, Accounting & Financial Management* 11, no 1 (Spring 1999): 56–80.

51. Michael Mumper, "The Student Aid Industry," in *Financing a College Education: How It Works, How It's Changing*, ed. Jacqueline King (Phoenix, AZ: American Council on Education Oryx Press, 1999), 64–77; Susan Hannah, "Higher Education Act of 1992: Skills, Constraints, and the Politics of Higher Education," *Journal of Higher Education* 67, no. 5 (Sept–Oct 1996): 498–527; Derek Price, *Borrowing Inequality: Race, Class, and Student Loans* (Boulder, CO: L. Rienner, 2004), 27–44; Francis Keppel, "Higher Education Acts Contrasted, 1965–1986: Has Federal Policy Come of Age?," *Harvard Education Review* 57, no. 1 (February 1987): 49–67; Dillon, *Leading Lady*, 4; and Mungovan, "Role of the U.S. Federal Government in the Student Loan Industry," 9–10.

52. Shermer, "From Educator to Creditor in Chief"; and Shermer, "Student Loan Crisis and Its Deniers."

53. Mumper, "The Student Aid in Industry," 64–77.

54. Shermer, "From Educator to Creditor in Chief"; and Elizabeth Tandy Shermer, "How Tax Policy Made College Unaffordable," *Washington Post*, December 21, 2017, https:// www.washingtonpost.com/news/made-by-history/wp/2017/12/21/how-tax-policy-broke-the -american-university-system/?utm_term=.24ca9bfda23b.

55. Shermer, "From Educator to Creditor in Chief"; Kristin Conklin, *Federal Tuition Tax Credits and State Higher Education Policy: A Guide for State Policy Makers* (San Jose, CA: National Center for Public Policy and Higher Education, 1998); Bridget Long, "Impact of Federal Tax Credits for Higher Education Expenses," in *College Choices: The Economics of Where to Go, When to Go, and How to Pay for It*, ed. Caroline Hoxby (Chicago: University of Chicago Press, 2004), 101–168; A. Clayton Spencer, "New Politics of Higher Education," in King,

Financing A College Education, 101–119; and Kristin Conklin and Joni Finney, "State Policy Response to the Taxpayer Relief Act of 1997," in King, *Financing A College Education*, 151–164.

56. Shermer, "From Educator to Creditor in Chief," quote on 163.

Chapter 7

1. Service Employees International Union (SEIU) Executive Office files: George Hardy collection, Wayne State University, box 93, folder 5.

2. Isaac William Martin, *The Permanent Tax Revolt: How the Property Tax Transformed American Politics* (Stanford, CA: Stanford University Press, 2008), 109; John Kingdon, *Agendas, Alternatives, and Public Policies* (New York: Pearson, 1995), 97; Monica Prasad, *The Politics of Free Markets: The Rise of Neoliberal Economic Policies in Britain, France, Germany, and the United States* (Chicago: University of Chicago, 2006), 46; Brian Steensland, *The Failed Welfare Revolution: America's Struggle over Guaranteed Income Policy* (Princeton, NJ: Princeton University Press, 2008), 213; and Peter Schrag, *Paradise Lost: California's Experience, America's Future* (Berkeley: University of California Press, 1999).

3. Steve Fraser and Gary Gerstle, eds., *The Rise and Fall of the New Deal Order, 1930–1980* (Princeton, NJ: Princeton University Press, 1990). On the contradictions of the New Deal order, see Ira Katznelson, *City Trenches: Urban Politics and the Patterning of Class in the United States* (Chicago: University of Chicago Press, 1981); Robert O. Self, *American Babylon: Race and the Struggle for Postwar Oakland* (Princeton, NJ: Princeton University Press, 2005); and Theda Skocpol, "The Limits of the New Deal System and the Roots of Contemporary Welfare Dilemmas," in *The Politics of Social Policy in the United States*, ed. Margaret Weir, Ann Shola Orloff, and Theda Skocpol (Princeton, NJ: Princeton University Press, 1988), 293–311.

4. See Todd Swanstrom, *The Crisis of Growth Politics: Cleveland, Kucinich, and the Challenge of Urban Populism* (Philadelphia: Temple University Press, 1985); Martin, *Permanent Tax Revolt*, 69–70, 98–104; and Arkansas Community Organizations for Reform Now, "ACORN Cites Developments in Its Campaign for Pulaski Tax Equalization," June 21, 1974, Wisconsin State Historical Society, Movement for Economic Justice Records, box 21, folder 4.

5. See Angus Burgin, *The Great Persuasion: Reinventing Free Markets Since the Depression* (Cambridge, MA: Harvard University Press, 2012); Nancy MacLean, *Democracy in Chains: The Deep History of the Radical Right's Stealth Plan for America* (New York: Viking, 2017); and Kim Phillips-Fein, *Invisible Hands: The Making of the Conservative Movement from the New Deal to Reagan* (New York: Norton, 2009).

6. Michael R. Hyman, "Taxation, Public Policy, and Political Dissent: Yeoman Dissatisfaction in the Post-Reconstruction Lower South," *Journal of Southern History* 55, no. 1 (1989): 49–76; and J. Mills Thornton III. "Fiscal Policy and the Failure of Radical Reconstruction in the Lower South" in *Region, Race, and Reconstruction: Essays in Honor of C. Vann Woodward*, ed. J. Morgan Kousser and James M. McPherson (New York: Oxford University Press, 1982), 349–394.

7. William Warren Rogers, *The One-Gallused Rebellion: Agrarianism in Alabama, 1865–1896* (Baton Rouge: Louisiana State University Press, 1970), 41–42; Eric Foner, *Reconstruction: America's Unfinished Revolution, 1863–1877* (New York: Harper Collins, 1988), 552–553;

Allen Going, *Bourbon Democracy in Alabama, 1874-1890* (Montgomery: University of Alabama Press, 1951), 18–22; and Price, quoted in Malcolm Cook McMillan, *Constitutional Development in Alabama, 1798-1901: A Study in Politics, the Negro, and Sectionalism* (Chapel Hill: University of North Carolina Press, 1955), 181.

8. McMillan, *Constitutional Development*, 189. Walker's speech is in *Journal of the Constitutional Convention of the State of Alabama, Assembled in the City of Montgomery, September 6th, 1875* (Montgomery: W. W. Screws, 1875), 5–6; and see *McCulloch v. Maryland*, 17 U.S. 316, at 432.

9. McMillan, *Constitutional Development*, 203.

10. *Constitution of the United States of America*, art. 1, § 9; cf. *Constitution of the Confederate States*, art. 1, § 9. See the discussion in *State of Lousiana v. Jumel*, 107 U.S. 711, at 719–720.

11. McMillan, *Constitutional Development*, 203.

12. *Constitution of the State of Alabama* (1875), art. 10, §§ 5 and 7. On special legislation establishing tax rates for Alabama cities and counties, see, for example, *Journal of the Session of 1872-73 of the Senate of Alabama* (Montgomery: Arthur Bingham, 1873), 167, 349, 434, 472, 608; and, more generally, Scott Allard, Nancy Burns, and Gerald Gamm, "Representing Urban Interests: The Local Politics of State Legislatures," *Studies in American Political Development* 12 (1998): 267–302.

13. Montgomery *Advertiser*, quoted in McMillan, *Constitutional Development*, 211, and in Harvey H. Jackson III, "White Supremacy Triumphant: Democracy Undone," in *A Century of Controversy: Constitutional Reform in Alabama*, ed. Bailey Thomson (Tuscaloosa: University of Alabama Press, 2002), 17.

14. McMillan, *Constitutional Development*, 234, 329–330; and Jackson, "White Supremacy Triumphant."

15. *Journal of the Constitutional Convention*, 5.

16. Thomas M. Milling, "Tax Limitations," in *Proceedings of the Annual Conference on Taxation under the Auspices of the National Tax Association* 18 (November 9–13, 1925), 39; Mabel Newcomer,"The Growth of Tax Limitation Legislation," in *Property Tax Limitation Laws*, ed. Glen Leet and Robert M. Paige (Chicago: Public Administration Service, 1936), 38; Daniel R. Mullins and Kimberly A. Cox, *Tax and Expenditure Limits on Local Governments* (Washington, DC: Advisory Commission on Intergovernmental Relations, 1995); and Foner, *Reconstruction*, 588. On the role of borrowing in Western states' constitutional conventions, see Christian G. Fritz, "The American Constitutional Tradition Revisited: Preliminar Observations on State Constitution-Making in the Nineteenth-Century West," *Rutgers Law Journal* 25, no. 4 (1994): 945–998.

17. Jens P. Jensen, "Tax Limitation," *Proceedings of the Annual Conference on Taxation under the Auspices of the National Tax Association* 28 (October 14–17, 1935): 340–356; Harley L. Lutz, "Motives Behind the Tax Limitation Movement," in Leet and Paige, *Property Tax Limitation Laws*, 17; and Clifton Yearley, *The Money Machines: The Breakdown and Reform of Governmental and Party Finance* (Albany: State University of New York Press, 1969).

18. Clarence E. Ridley and Orin F. Nolting, "Tax Reduction Through Efficient Management," in Leet and Paige, *Property Tax Limitation Laws*, 33; Herbert U. Nelson, "The Case

for Tax Limitation," in Leet and Paige, *Property Tax Limitation Laws*, 11; Jensen, "Tax Limitation Laws"; Martin, *Permanent Tax Revolt*, 29–30; and David Beito, *Taxpayers in Revolt: Tax Resistance During the Great Depression* (Chapel Hill: University of North Carolina Press, 1989).

19. The so-called Riley–Stewart amendment of 1933 shifted public utility property from the state to the local property tax rolls, and imposed a limitation of 5 percent on the annual growth of local budgets for the next two years so that local governments could not simply treat the increase in the tax base as a revenue windfall. The result was a constitutionally required cut in local property tax rates. The amendment also authorized the state legislature to limit local property tax rates by statute. See California Senate Constitutional Amendment 30 (1933), accessed August 31, 2015, http://repositoryuchastings.edu/ca_ballot_props/303; and James E. Hartley, Steven M. Sheffrin, and J. David Vasche, "Reform During Crisis: The Transformation of California's Fiscal System During the Great Depression," *Journal of Economic History* 56, no. 3 (1996): 657–678; see also Newcomer, "Growth of Tax Limitation Legislation," 38.

20. Jensen, "Tax Limitation"; Lutz, "Motives," 20; and Raymond D. Thomas, Edward P. Doyle, T. Levron Howard, Jens P. Jensen, Melvin B. McPherson, R. W. Nelson, J. A. Scott, Don C. Sowers, George G. Tunnel, and Lent D. Upson, "Report of the Committee on Property Tax Limitation and Homestead Exemption," *Proceedings of the Annual Conference on Taxation Under the Auspices of the National Tax Association* 31 (October 24–28, 1938), 796.

21. Jensen, "Tax Limitation," 340; and Lutz, "Motives," 20.

22. On the New Deal contribution to the language of economic rights and conflicts over localism, see Karen M. Tani, Chapter 5 in this volume; and on the transformation of property tax administration, see Martin, *Permanent Tax Revolt*, 44–73.

23. Philip E. Watson, "Tax Reform and Professionalizing the Los Angeles County Assessor's Office," oral history interview with Steven Edgington and Richard Candida Smith (Los Angeles: Oral History Program of the University of California–Los Angeles, 1989), 85–86, 95, 109, 304–305; John D. Allswang, *The Initiative and Referendum in California, 1898–1998* (Stanford, CA: Stanford University Press, 1998), 96; and California Proposition 9 (1968), *Taxation, Limitations on Property Tax Rate*, accessed August 31, 2015, http://repositoryuchastings.edu/ca_ballot_props/707; California Proposition 14 (1972) *Property Tax Limitations*, accessed August 31, 2015, http://repositoryuchastings.edu/ca_ballot_props/765.

24. Milton Friedman papers, box 100, folder 100.7, Hoover Institution Archives; and Lewis K. Uhler, "Remarks at UCLA Symposium: The California Tax Limitation Amendment: Wisdom or Folly?," July 10, 1973. On the Virginia school, see MacLean, *Democracy in Chains*, and Chapter 9 in this volume.

25. See California Proposition 1 (1973), *Tax and Expenditure Limitations*, accessed August 31, 2015, http://repositoryuchastings.edu/ca_ballot_props/776.

26. See California Proposition 1 (1973); Allswang, *Initiative and Referendum*, 97; and Garin Burbank, "Governor Reagan's Only Defeat: The Proposition 1 Campaign in 1973," *California History* 72, no. 4 (1993): 360–373.

27. Watson, "Tax Reform," 425–426; Howard Jarvis and Robert Pack, *I'm Mad as Hell* (New York: New York Times, 1979), 39; and Isaac William Martin, *Rich People's Movements: Grassroots Campaigns to Untax the One Percent* (New York: Oxford University Press, 2013), 161. Watson later insisted that Proposition 13 retained the marks of his authorial hand, but when pressed for details about which provisions of his first draft Jarvis and Gann had retained, he admitted that it was perhaps only "the definitions" (Watson, "Tax Reform," 425). Proposition 13 notoriously did not include any definitions. Jarvis clearly got the general idea of property tax limitation from Watson—before joining forces with the latter, he had been fixated instead on a quixotic campaign to abolish the property tax—but there is no textual evidence that he borrowed any policy specifics from either of Watson's previous measures.

28. California Proposition 13 (1978), *Property Tax Limitation*, accessed August 31, 2015, http://repositoryuchastings.edu/ca_ballot_props/850.

29. A Maryland statute of 1957 was the only previous state law to limit the increase of assessed values. They could increase by no more than 6 percent per year, a generous limitation that would affect the distribution of tax burdens only in extreme cases. This statutory limitation was not widely known even to experts at that time, or generally classed among property tax limitations. It is unlikely that Jarvis or Gann knew of it. See Mullins and Cox, *Tax and Expenditure Limitations*, 39; cf. Advisory Commission on Intergovernmental Relations (ACIR), *State Limitations on Local Taxes and Expenditures* (Washington, DC: ACIR, 1977), 20.

30. Watson, "Tax Reform," 427.

31. Robert Kuttner, *Revolt of the Haves: Tax Rebellions and Hard Times* (New York: Simon and Schuster, 1980), 75; and David Sears and Jack Citrin, *Tax Revolt: Something for Nothing in California* (Cambridge, MA: Harvard University Press, 1985), 191–192.

32. Arthur O'Sullivan, Terri A. Sexton, and Steven M. Sheffrin, *Property Taxes and Tax Revolts: The Legacy of Proposition 13* (New York: Cambridge University Press, 1995); and Mark DiCamillo, "Californians' Views of Proposition 13 Thirty Years After Its Passage," in *After the Tax Revolt: California's Proposition 13 Turns 30*, ed. Jack Citrin and Isaac William Martin (Berkeley, CA: Berkeley Public Policy Press, 2009), 11–28.

33. Lindley H. Clark Jr., "Monetary Maverick: Milton Friedman, Man of Many Roles, Now Is a Tax Revolutionary," *Wall Street Journal*, July 17, 1978; and Geoffrey Brennan and James Buchanan, The Reason of Rules: Constitutional Political Economy (Indianapolis: Liberty Fund, 2000 [1985]), 82, 91; cf. Jon Elster, "Ulysses and the Sirens: A Theory of Imperfect Rationality," Social Science Information 16, no. 5 (1977): 469–526.

Chapter 8

1. Among the many published accounts of these events, the discussion I have found most insightful is that of Theda Skocpol, *Obama and America's Political Future* (Cambridge, MA: Harvard University Press, 2012), 49. For an engaging exploration of the deeper tradition, which opens with this protest, see Isaac William Martin, *Rich People's Movements: Grassroots Campaigns to Untax the One Percent* (New York: Oxford University Press, 2013).

On grassroots activism, see Kate Zernike, *Boiling Mad: Behind the Lines in Tea Party America* (New York: St. Martin's Griffin, 2010).

2. David Kirby and Emily Ekins, "Libertarian Roots of the Tea Party," [Cato Institute] *Policy Analysis*, no. 705 (August 6, 2012): 1.

3. For an illuminating effort to solve the puzzle, see Philip Mirowski, *Never Let a Serious Crisis Go to Waste: How Neoliberalism Survived the Financial Meltdown* (New York: Verso, 2013).

4. For a fuller version of the George Mason University (GMU) story, see Nancy MacLean, *Democracy in Chains: The Deep History of the Radical Right's Stealth Plan for America* (New York: Viking, 2017); for national media exposure of the continuing corruption of academic integrity and normal governance by Koch-funded operations on the campus, owing to the work of UnKoch My Campus, see https://www.unkochmycampus.org/charles-koch-foundation -george-mason-mercatus-donor-influence-exposed/.

5. Tyler Cowen, "Why Does Freedom Wax and Wane? Some Research Questions in Social Change and Big Government," Mercatus Center, GMU, 2000. The piece was reprinted online in 2015. The original has no page numbers, so my subsequent paragraphs do not repeat the citation, but all quotes are from it.

6. Cowen, "Why Does Freedom Wax and Wane?" For Charles Koch's version of the same research agenda, see Charles G. Koch, "Koch Industries, Market Process Analysis, and the Science of Liberty," *Journal of Private Enterprise* 22 (Spring 2007), esp. 4–6. For research grants to fund the project from Koch's Institute for Humane Studies, see Tyler Cowen and David Nott memorandum, May 13, 1997, Buchanan House Archives (hereafter cited as BHA). Cowen has also been the general director of what was originally the James M. Buchanan Center for Political Economy and has been the Mercatus Center since 1998. The Buchanan archive has since been moved to the Special Collections Research Center at George Mason, which is now processing the Buchanan papers. Archive staff later discovered more than 30 additional boxes of material, most of it covering the formative era of the 1970s and early 1980s.

7. Calling voters who do not share the cause's economics "a public nuisance," one of Cowen's Mercatus colleagues said it would be wise "to reduce or eliminate efforts to increase voter turnout." Bryan Caplan, *The Myth of the Rational Voter: Why Democracies Choose Bad Policies* (Princeton, NJ: Princeton University Press, 2007), 197, 199. For the importance of guardrails, see Steven Levitsky and Daniel Zimblatt, *How Democracies Die* (New York: Crown, 2018).

8. Cowen here echoed José Piñera, who shifted from the Pinochet regime to the staff of Koch's Cato Institute, where he taught would-be emulators of Chile's "radical reform" that "there is also a political economy motive for swift action" that enlists the "element of surprise" and "advances on all fronts simultaneously." It was quite simple: "giving a reform's opponents time to adjust also gives them time to orchestrate a political counterattack." José Piñera, "Chile," in *The Political Economy of Policy Reform*, ed. John Williamson (Washington, DC: Institute for International Economics, 1994), 228.

Ironically, the first attack on *Democracy in Chains* (of more than ninety by early 2018 from Koch-funded faculty and operatives who failed to admit their conflicts of interest until after exposure by a Greenpeace researcher) was on the passage in this paragraph from Tyler Cowen. Russ Roberts, then of the Hoover Institution, wrote a piece saying: "Nancy MacLean Owes Tyler Cowen an Apology," in which he claimed I had misrepresented Cowen. I replied that, no, in fact, Tyler Cowen owes the country an apology (Roberts did not print that): https://medium.com/@russroberts/nancy-maclean-owes-tyler-cowen-an-apology-e6277ee75eb3. I stood by my interpretation and still do. I was doing exactly what historians do, not rote transcription but interpretation in context and in light of other sources. Indeed, subsequent events have rendered my case not just an accurate representation of the past but a veritable prediction of what the Koch network has done since the book came out.

Here is the amusing coda: a series of Freedom of Information Act requests by anti-Koch students revealed corrupt hiring agreements at George Mason. And the worst of the large group was the hiring of Russ Roberts: he was chosen by a donor for a tenured position in a deal signed off on by . . . Tyler Cowen. See https://www.unkochmycampus.org/charles-koch-foundation-george-mason-mercatus-donor-influence-exposed/. One more thing Roberts did not inform his readers of was his participation in Koch donor summits. Seeing how lacking in scruple the libertarian professors are, I stopped paying attention to their criticisms, which, I learned from environmentalist researchers, follow the exact method of climate science deniers—not surprising, since Koch is the top funder of that enterprise as well. My final response can be found at https://www.chronicle.com/article/Nancy-MacLean-Responds-to-Her/240699.

9. For the complaint about feminism, see Henry Manne to James Buchanan, "Draft Program Synopsis for Mont Pelerin Society Meeting in Washington, DC, September 1998," BHA; on the Independent Women's Forum, see Joan Walsh, "Meet the 'Feminists' Doing Koch Dirty Work," *Nation*, August 18, 2016; and Lisa Graves, "The Independent 'Women's' Voice'? Most Known Donors Are Men," *PR Watch*, August 24, 2016.

10. For more, see Nancy MacLean, "'Since We Are Greatly Outnumbered': Why and How the Koch Network Uses Disinformation to Thwart Democracy," in *The Disinformation Age: How We Got Here*, ed. Lance Bennett and Steven Livingston (New York: Cambridge University Press, 2020).

11. Colleen Kearney Rich, "The Wonderful World of Masonomics," *Mason Spirit*, November 1, 2010. On Limbaugh as a pioneer and key exemplar of the genre, see Yochai Benkler, Robert Faris, and Hal Roberts, *Network Propaganda: Manipulation, Disinformation, and Radicalization in American Politics* (New York: Oxford University Press, 2018), 20 and passim thereafter.

12. For more on disinformation, including alliances with the Tobacco Institute and climate science denial, see MacLean, "Since We Are Greatly Outnumbered"; Jeff Nesbit, *Poison Tea: How Big Oil and Big Tobacco Invented the Tea Party and Captured the GOP* (New York: St. Martin's Press, 2016); and Calvin Sloan, "Koch Brothers Are Watching You: And New Documents Reveal Just How Much They Know," *PR Watch*, November 5, 2018.

13. David Leonhardt, "Washington's Invisible Hand," *New York Times Magazine*, September 26, 2008; for more detail on both Gramms, see Patricia Kilday Hart, "John McCain's Gramm Gamble," *Texas Observer*, May 30, 2008. The act partially repealed the New Deal's Glass–Steagall Act. On the CSE's role, see Lisa Graves, "ALEC Exposed: The Koch Connection," *Nation*, July 12, 2011; Nouriel Roubini and Stephen Mihm, *Crisis Economics: A Crash*

Course in the Future of Finance (New York: Penguin Press, 2010), 199; and Roger Lowenstein, *The End of Wall Street* (New York: Penguin Press, 2010), 61.

14. For reckoning of the overall toll, see Joseph E. Stiglitz, *The Price of Inequality: How Today's Divided Society Endangers Our Future* (New York: Norton, 2012).

15. Kenneth S. Baer, *Reinventing Government: The Politics of Liberalism from Reagan to Clinton* (Lawrence: University Press of Kansas, 2000), 255; and Sean Wilentz, *The Age of Reagan: A History, 1974–2008* (New York: Harper Perennial, 2008), 371, 407. For earlier refutation of Buchanan's theory, see Kevin F. Forbes and Ernest M. Zampelli, "Is Leviathan a Mythical Beast?," *American Economic Review* 79 (June 1989): 568–577.

16. For this foundational story, see MacLean, *Democracy in Chains*, esp. chaps. 8–9 and 11.

17. "A surprising number of the people we met [in Tea Party groups] dated their first political experience to the Goldwater campaign in 1964," comment Theda Skocpol and Vanessa Williamson, *The Tea Party and the Remaking of Republican Conservatism* (New York: Oxford University Press, 2012), 41. On the transition from the CSE to the AfP, the explanation in Nesbit, *Poison Tea*, is unsurpassed.

18. Charles G. Koch, *Creating a Science of Liberty* (Fairfax, VA: Institute for Humane Studies at George Mason University, 1997).

19. Skocpol and Williamson, *Tea Party*, 9.

20. Biography on the site of the Independent Women's Forum, the Koch-funded organization that appointed Pfotenhauer president in 2001, http://web.archive.org/web /20041214151602/www.iwf.org/about_iwf/pfotenhauer.asp. On Gramm as McCain's top economic adviser, see Lisa Lerer, "McCain Guru Linked to Subprime Crisis," *Politico*, March 28, 2008.

21. Jim Rutenberg, "How Billionaire Oligarchs Are Becoming Their Own Political Parties," *New York Times Magazine*, October 17, 2014; and "Timothy R. Phillips," Century Strategies, ca. 2003, Wayback Machine, http://web.archive.org/web/20040603164236/http://www .censtrat.com/staffbio.cfm?staff_id=13.

22. The Right's most strategic coalition builder, Grover Norquist, offered essential guidance for the effort in a timely 2008 book that enlisted public-choice thinking to frame the threat (the "takings coalition") and cobble together a team identity with enough voting power to move the agenda of massive rules change (the "leave us alone coalition"). See Grover G. Norquist, *Leave Us Alone: Getting the Government's Hands off Our Money, Our Guns, and Our Lives* (New York: HarperCollins, 2008).

23. Skocpol and Williamson, *Tea Party*, 105. See also Nesbit, *Poison Tea*, on Koch and wider corporate Right underwriting and organizing of purportedly grassroots mobilizations.

24. Skocpol and Williamson, *Tea Party*; on the role of white reaction, see the unrivaled study by Christopher S. Parker and Matt A. Barreto, *Change They Can't Believe In: The Tea Party and Reactionary Politics in America* (Princeton, NJ: Princeton University Press, 2013).

25. Michael Sokolove, "The Outside's Insider," *New York Times*, November 8, 2009; and Dick Armey and Matt Kibbe, *Give Us Liberty: A Tea Party Manifesto* (New York: Harper-Collins, 2010). See also Jane Mayer, "Covert Operations: The Billionaire Brothers Who Are

Waging a War on Obama," *New Yorker*, August 30, 2010; and Skocpol and Williamson, *Tea Party*, 4.

26. Armey and Kibbe, *Give Us Liberty*, chap. 7.

27. Amity Shlaes, "The New PC," *Forbes*, August 3, 2009; on her Mercatus ties and support for the team's policy agenda, see Shlaes, "Phil Gramm Is Right," *Washington Post*, July 12, 2008. The breakout book, mentioned in the text as shaped by Virginia School thought, was *The Forgotten Man: A New History of the Great Depression* (New York: HarperCollins, 2009).

28. Kevin Robillard, "James O'Keefe Agrees to Pay $100,000 Settlement," *Politico*, March 8, 2013. The most comprehensive history of the organization and the campaign against it is John Atlas, *Seeds of Change: The Story of ACORN, America's Most Controversial Antipoverty Community Organizing Group* (Nashville: Vanderbilt University Press, 2010). See also the chilling account of the deceit that characterized the wider Right's attacks on ACORN, in Lori C. Minnite, *The Myth of Voter Fraud* (Ithaca, NY: Cornell University Press, 2010), 94–99, 267n20. The two young libertarian perpetrators of the sting, James O'Keefe and Hannah Giles, had been trained in yet another Koch-funded project, the Leadership Institute, founded in 1979: https://www.leadershipinstitute.org/aboutus/morton.cfm. Far from being scorned as a fabricator thereafter, O'Keefe became a well-paid operative and headline speaker at Koch-linked conferences, where he tutored others in his techniques. See, for example, Rhett Forman, "Restoring NC to Greatness: Conservative Leadership Conference," *Civitas Capitol Connection*, February 2013, 1.

29. Muriel Kane, "Conservatives' 25-Year Goal of 'Defunding the Left' Revealed by ACORN Controversy," *Raw Story*, October 30, 2009; see also Capital Research Center website, https://capitalresearch.org.

30. Brian Tashman, "Live Action Gives Planned Parenthood the ACORN Treatment," Right Wing Watch, posted February 1, 2011; and "The Right-Wing Dough Supporting the 'Stings' at Planned Parenthood," Alternet, posted July 23, 2012.

31. James T. Bennett, *Tax-Funded Politics* (New Brunswick, NJ: Transaction, 2004), 9, 194; and https://economics.gmu.edu/people/jbennett.

32. Ed Pilkington and Suzanne Goldenberg, "State Conservative Groups Plan US-Wide Assault on Education, Health and Tax," *Guardian*, December 5, 2013. For the superb report, see Center for Media and Democracy, "SPN: The State Policy Network," 5.

33. John J. Miller, "Fifty Flowers Bloom," *National Review*, November 19, 2007; Ed Pilkington and Suzanne Goldenberg, "State Conservative Groups Plan US-Wide Assault on Education, Health and Tax," *Guardian*, December 5, 2013; and Center for Media and Democracy, "Exposed: The State Policy Network," November 2013, esp. 6, http://www.alecexposed.org /w/images/2/25/SPN_National_Report_FINAL.pdf. Graves has since co-created an incredibly valuable clearinghouse of information for researchers and journalists called "Koch Docs: Hard to Find Documents about Charles Koch and His Agenda All in One Place" (https:// kochdocs.org). In a related project, DeSmog Blog, which exposes climate denial, has made the tracking of individuals and organizations in this network easier for researchers with its Koch Network Database (https://www.desmogblog.com/koch-network-database#ilist-F).

34. Tracie Sharp, "SPN Remembers Whitney Ball," State Policy Network, https://spn .org/spn-remembers-whitney-ball; James Piereson, "Whitney Ball Knew the Landscape of the Conservative Movement Unlike Any Other," *National Review*, August 18, 2015; and "In Memoriam: Whitney Ball," Atlas Network, August 17, 2015. The Mercatus Center at GMU launched a "State and Local Policy Project" to inform the partner organizations. Tyler Cowen to Richard M. Larry, president, Sarah Scaife Foundation, October 2, 1998, BHA.

35. For an explanation of how the changes enable "no-cost extremism," see Thomas Schaller, "55–45 Politics in a 50–50 Country," *American Prospect*, October 28, 2015.

36. Gordon Brady to Bob Tollison et al., February 5, 1997, BHA. In 1987, Koch's Institute for Humane Studies elected Art Pope to its board; John Blundell to All Board Members and close friends of the Institute, November 1988, BHA.

37. Max Borders, "Getting Greed Out of Government," Civitas Institute, October 6, 2008.

38. Jane Mayer, "State for Sale," *New Yorker*, October 10, 2011.

39. Mayer, "State for Sale"; Mayer, *Dark Money: The Hidden History of the Billionaires Behind the Rise of the Radical Right* (New York: Doubleday, 2016), 240–267, 263.

40. David Daley, *Ratf**ked: The True Story Behind the Secret Plan to Steal America's Democracy* (New York: Liveright, 2016), 110. A longtime colleague of Buchanan's, W. Mark Crain, led in redistricting work while on the GMU economics faculty, winning recognition from the two Republican governors associated with the Koch base camp at George Mason. For Crain's CV, see https://policystudies.lafayette.edu/wp-content/uploads/sites/41/2016 /02/Mark-Crain-CV.pdf.

41. Robert E. Mutch, *Buying the Vote: A History of Campaign Finance Reform* (New York: Oxford University Press, 2014), 170–171; and Koch, *Creating a Science of Liberty.*

42. Jeffrey Toobin, "Money Unlimited: How Chief Justice Roberts Orchestrated the *Citizens United* Decision," *New Yorker*, May 21, 2012. See also the superb discussion by Senator Sheldon Whitehouse, with Melanie Wachtell Stinnett, *Captured: The Corporate Infiltration of American Democracy* (New York: New Press, 2017), and his ongoing online clearinghouse, "Captured Courts," https://medium.com/captured-court.

43. Toobin, "Money Unlimited." In its tenets as well as its lineage, the *Citizens United* ruling, too, had its roots in the cause. The Law and Liberty Project of Charles Koch's Institute for Humane Studies had been making the case for "free speech for corporations" in elections since the early 1970s with leadership from Henry Manne, Koch's longtime Law and Economics grantee. The Cato Institute and other libertarian outfits thereafter fought spending limits for decades. James C. Miller provided new aid to the cause in *Monopoly Politics*, a 1999 book published by the Hoover Institution and touted widely on the Right. Miller argued that incumbents enjoyed unfair advantages from those they had favored with government largesse. By creating "political markets" akin to economic markets, open to new private investment and free of regulation, incumbents would lose their "monopoly power." One of Miller's "refreshingly novel arguments," said an allied reviewer, was that revealing the names of corporate donors restrains political competition and is therefore wrong. Apparently, the Supreme Court's majority agreed, unleashing the flow of dark, untraceable money. See Institute for Humane Studies, "The Law and Liberty Project" [n.d., but in 1971–1976 file], box 118, Gordon Tullock Papers, Hoover Institution Archives; Ron Scherer, "Nobel Prize Winner Focuses on

Government Self-Interest," *Christian Science Monitor*, October 20, 1986, 5; James C. Miller III, *Monopoly Politics* (Stanford, CA: Hoover Institution Press, 1999); Andrew Siff, "A Real Contribution to the Campaign Finance Debate," *Federalist Society, Free Speech & Election Law Practice Group Newsletter*, no. 3 (Winter 2000); and Mutch, *Buying the Vote*, 179.

44. Michael Cooper and Megan Thee-Brenan, "Majority in Poll Back Employers in Public Unions," *New York Times*, March 1, 2011, A1, 16; "The Hollow Cry of Broke" (editorial), *New York Times*, March 3, 2011, A22; Roger Bybee, "After Proposing Draconian Anti-Union Laws, Wis. Gov. Walker Invokes National Guard," *In These Times*, February 15, 2011. In his later autobiography, Walker notes that his approval rating fell to 37 percent because the act was so unpopular. Calling collective bargaining "a racket, not a right," he admitted he had aimed to end it "permanently." Scott Walker, *Unintimidated: A Governor's Story and a Nation's Challenge* (New York: Sentinel, 2013), 75, 82, 225. Why? "Organized labor is the skeletal frame and muscle of the left," explains the ever-strategic Norquist in *Leave Us Alone*, 68.

45. Dan Kaufman, "Land of Cheese and Rancor," *New York Times Magazine*, May 27, 2012, 30, 32; Dan Kaufman, "Fate of the Union," *New York Times Magazine*, 55. Walker later bragged that the furor over the bill enabled his team "to pass a raft of other measures" that usually would have set off "protests and controversy" but "went virtually unnoticed" in the wake of its big bang; Walker, *Unintimidated*, 215.

46. Mona Charen, "What Madison Revealed," *National Review*, February 22, 2011 ("Teachers are rent seekers" appeared in the online edition, not the hard copy; its version read, "public employees in many states are classic rent seekers"). The new governor "had to break the power of unions," the head of a Wisconsin affiliate of the State Policy Network argued, quoting the character Omar Little in the acclaimed television series *The Wire*: "If you come at the King, you best not miss." Richard Esenberg, "Walker Had No Choice," *WI Magazine*, March 2012.

47. Kaufman, "Land of Cheese and Rancor," 30, 32; and "Political Money Talks" (editorial), *New York Times*, May 29, 2012. See also Cato's Roger Pilon, "Scott Walker and Public-Sector Unions," *Cato at Liberty*, May 14, 2012, http://www.cato.org/blog/scott-walker-public-sector-unions. For a fuller treatment of the Wisconsin events, see Dan Kaufman, *The Fall of Wisconsin: The Conservative Conquest of a Progressive Bastion and the Future of American Politics* (New York: Norton, 2018).

48. Trip Gabriel, "Teachers Wonder, Why the Heapings of Scorn?," *New York Times*, March 3, 2011, A1, 18.

49. Kevin D. Williamson, "Socialism Is Back," *National Review*, January 19, 2011.

50. See also the steady spate of books from right-wing activists that bear titles like *The Worm in the Apple: How the Teacher Unions Are Destroying American Education*, by Peter Brimelow (New York: Harper, 2004); Myron Lieberman, *The Teachers' Unions: How the NEA and AFT Sabotage Reform and Hold Students, Parents, Teachers, and Taxpayers Hostage to Bureaucracy* (New York: Free Press, 1997); and Clint Bolick, *Voucher Wars: Waging the Legal Battle Over School Choice* (Washington, DC: Cato, 2003).

51. A case in point cites the Virginia segregationist turned market-fundamentalist mantra about "the freedom not to associate"; Matt Kibbe (the president and CEO of Freedom-Works), *Hostile Takeover: Resisting Centralized Government's Stranglehold on America* (New York: HarperCollins, 2012), 238, 252.

52. Eric Lichtblau, "Challenge to Health Overhaul Puts Obscure Think Tank in Spotlight," *New York Times*, March 5, 2015.

53. Ibid.; Michael S. Greve CV, http://www.law.gmu.edu/assets/files/faculty/cv/greve.pdf; Michael S. Greve, "The Originalism That Was, and the One That Will Be," *Yale Journal of Law and the Humanities* 25 (2013): 110; and Adele M. Stan, "Who's Behind Friedrichs?," *American Prospect*, October 29, 2015.

54. Jeffrey Rosen, "The Unregulated Offensive," *New York Times Magazine*, April 17, 2005.

55. Robert O'Harrow Jr. and Shawn Boburg, "A Conservative Activist's Behind-the-Scenes Campaign to Remake the Nation's Courts," *Washington Post,* May 21, 2019: Matthew Barakat, "George Mason Tightens Rules After Uproar over Koch," *AP,* April 26, 2019. To read the donor agreements and related emails, see "Donor Influence at George Mason Finally Exposed," UnKoch My Campus. See also the bracing analysis of Senator Sheldon Whitehouse, once a prosecutor and state attorney general: "Whitehouse Remarks on the Federalist Society and Leonard Leo," May 22, 2019, https://www.whitehouse.senate.gov/news/speeches/whitehouse-remarks-on-the-federalist-society-and-leonard-leo.

56. Linda Greenhouse, "Is Anyone Watching?," *New York Times*, February 23, 2011; and Ari Berman, *Give Us the Ballot: The Modern Struggle for Voting Rights in America* (New York: Farrar, Straus and Giroux, 2015), 280–281.

57. It was apparently not enough for the Koch Right that turnout was already extremely low among poor Americans of all backgrounds. Alec MacGillis, "Who Turned My Blue State Red?," *New York Times*, November 22, 2015, SR1, 4. On threats from the Right to the youth vote and a cutting-edge litigation strategy for its defense, see Yael Bromberg, "Youth Voting Rights and the Unfulfilled Promise of the Twenty-Sixth Amendment," *University of Pennsylvania Journal of Constitutional Law* 21 (May 2019), 1105–1166.

58. Berman, *Give Us the Ballot*, 299.

59. No one has explained that strategy and its impact better than Ian Haney López, *Dog-Whistle Politics: How Coded Racial Appeals Have Reinvented Racism and Wrecked the Middle Class* (New York: Oxford University Press, 2014).

60. Kenneth P. Vogel, "The Koch ATM," *Politico*, November 17, 2015. It, too, was presided over by GMU-trained operatives, in this case Wayne Gable and Kevin Gentry: "Wayne Gable," SourceWatch; http://www.sourcewatch.org/index.php/Wayne_Gable.

61. "Ryan's Kinetic Rise, Perhaps to a Spot with Romney," *New York Times*, April 30, 2012, A14. On Ryan's budget as the dream of the Tea Party's billionaire funders, not its rank and file, see Skocpol and Williamson, *Tea Party*, 210–211; also Zernike, *Boiling Mad*, 201–202, 208.

62. "The New Republican Landscape" (editorial), *New York Times*, April 18, 2011, A20; Walker, *Unintimidated*, 195–196; Morton Kondracke and Fred Barnes, *Jack Kemp: The Bleeding-Heart Conservative Who Changed America* (New York: Sentinel, 2015), 252–253, 322, https://www.sourcewatch.org/index.php/Citizens_for_a_Sound_Economy. For Cato enthusiasm, see Chris Edwards, "Paul Ryan's Fiscal Framework," *Cato.org*, posted May 11, 2012. For Americans for Prosperity support, see Skocpol and Williamson, *Tea Party*, 105–106, quote on 174.

63. Charles J. Sykes, *A Nation of Moochers: America's Addiction to Getting Something for Nothing* (New York: St. Martin's, 2012); Skocpol, *Obama*, 54–57, 60 (see also 153–156 on how

the new right-wing media helped systematically misinform them); Skocpol and Williamson, *Tea Party*, 55, 60–61, 63; see also Zernike, *Boiling Mad*, 181, 193. On the feelings of lost racial dominance that animate Tea Party activists and the prominence of conspiratorial beliefs about President Obama, see Parker and Barreto, *Change They Can't Believe In*.

64. "The New Republican Landscape" (editorial), *New York Times*, April 18, 2011, A20; Paul Ryan, "A Roadmap for America's Future," http://www.wispolitics.com/1006/_080521 _Ryan_roadmap.pdf. On the budget priorities Ryan laid out as "further to the right than at any time since the modern federal government began taking shaped nearly eight decades ago," see Jackie Calmes, "A Conservative Vision, with Bipartisan Risks," *New York Times*, April 6, 2011, A17.

65. Paul Krugman, "Trillion Dollar Fraudsters," *New York Times*, March 20, 2015, A27; among many in this vein, see also Paul Krugman, "Republicans and Medicare," *New York Times*, February 14, 2010, A27.

66. Martin, *Rich People's Movements*.

67. On Armey and Forbes, see Michael Sokolove, "The Outside's Insider," *New York Times*, November 8, 2009.

68. Alexandra Forter Sirota, "Public Investment Falls, Tax Responsibility Shifts," in NC Policy Watch, *Altered State: How Five Years of Conservative Rule Have Redefined North Carolina* (Raleigh: NC Policy Watch, 2015), 4–5.

69. The measure reaches back to the tax limitation constitutional amendment on which Buchanan and one of his students had advised Governor Reagan's team in California in the early 1970s. Two veterans of that effort, Lewis K. Uhler and Ed Meese III, carried the baton into the new era, where it has been taken up by Americans for Prosperity and the State Policy Network. See Alexander Gourse, "The Politics of Enforced Austerity," chap. 5 of "Restraining the Reagan Revolution: The Lawyer's War on Poverty and the Durable Liberal State" (PhD diss., Northwestern University, 2015), 234–279; see also Martin, *Rich People's Movements*, 24, 168–71, 177, 181.

70. Rob Christensen, "Problems with NC Legislation to Cap Taxes, Reduce Spending," Raleigh *News & Observer*, August 11, 2015.

71. See, for example, Andrew Burstein and Nancy Isenberg, "GOP's Anti-School Insanity: How Scott Walker & Bobby Jindal Declared War on Education," *Salon*, February 9, 2015; and Richard Fausset, "Ideology Seen as Factor in Closings at University," *New York Times*, February 20, 2015.

72. Matthew J. Flynn, "Gov. Scott Walker Is Vandalizing UW System," *Journal Media Group*, March 22, 2016. See also Steve Mims's superb documentary *Starving the Beast: The Battle to Disrupt and Reform America's Public Universities* (2016), http://www .starvingthebeast.net.

73. Eric Lipton, "In G.O.P., a Campaign Takes Aim at Tea Party," *New York Times*, November 6, 2013, A12. Rather, the Koch network has built, in the words of a careful team of Harvard researchers, "a massive cadre-directed operation capable of leveraging the Republican Party and pulling agendas of American politics further toward the right" to achieve ends counter to "majority citizen preferences." Theda Skocpol and Alexander Hertel-Fernandez, "The Koch Effect: The Impact of a Cadre-Led Network on American Politics," prepared for

the Inequality Mini-Conference, Southern Political Science Association, San Juan, Puerto Rico, January 8, 2016.

74. Thomas E. Mann and Norman Ornstein, *It's Even Worse Than It Looks: How the American Constitutional System Collided with the New Politics of Extremism* (New York: Basic Books, 2012).

75. Quoted in MacLean, *Democracy in Chains*, 244n27.

Chapter 9

1. Franklin D. Roosevelt, "Acceptance Speech for the Renomination for the Presidency, Philadelphia, June 27, 1936, at the website of the UCSB American Presidency Project.

2. Theodore Roosevelt, "New Nationalism Speech," August 31, 1910, delivered at Osawatomie, Kansas, found at TeachingAmericanHistory.org. In *Private Government: How Employers Rule Our Lives (and Why We Don't Talk About It)* (Princeton, NJ: Princeton University Press, 2017), the philosopher Elizabeth Anderson makes a similar point by revisiting the critique offered by the Roosevelts and other reformers to explain how the market, which in the seventeenth and eighteenth centuries had been useful to those advocating a republican egalitarianism, became in the late nineteenth and early twentieth centuries a weapon wielded by a new private tyranny.

3. For legal scholarship on the structure of corporations and state efforts to shape and regulate them, see many of the essays collected in Naomi Lamoreaux and William Novak, *Corporations and American Democracy* (Cambridge, MA: Harvard University Press, 2017), especially Daniel Crane, "The Disassociation of Incorporation and Regulation in the Progressive Era and the New Deal," 109–138; Margaret Blair and Elizabeth Pollman, "The Supreme Court's View of Corporate Rights: Two Centuries of Evolution and Controversy," 245–285; and William Novak, "The Public Utility Idea and the Origins of Modern Business Regulation," 329–358.

4. Scholars of labor, both at home and abroad have been among the first to recognize the disconnect between Wagner-era labor law and the structure of contemporary corporations and supply chains. See, Craig Becker, "Labor Law Outside the Employment Relation," *Texas Law Review* 74 (June 1996): 1527–1562; Kate Andrias, "The New Labor Law," *Yale Law Journal* 126, no. 1 (2016): 2–100; and Richard Appelbaum and Nelson Lichtenstein, eds., *Achieving Workers' Rights in the Global Economy* (Ithaca, NY: Cornell University Press, 2016), which considers the failures of "corporate social responsibility" in twenty-first-century international supply chains.

5. David Weil, *The Fissured Workplace: Why Work Became So Bad for So Many and What Can Be Done to Improve It* (Cambridge, MA: Harvard University Press, 2014).

6. Richard S. Tedlow, *New and Improved: The Story of Mass Marketing in America* (New York: Basic Books, 1990) for studies of Sears and A&P; and Frank Ernest Hill and Allan Nevins, *Ford: Expansion and Challenge, 1915–1933* (New York: Charles Scribner's Sons, 1957).

7. Ronald Coase, "The Nature of the Firm," *Economica*, November 1937, 338; and Peter Drucker, *Concept of the Corporation* (New York: John Day, 1946). See also R. H. Coase, "The Acquisition of Fisher Body by General Motors," *Journal of Law and Economics* 43 (April 2000):

15–31. The purchase by General Motors in 1926 of the car body supplier Fisher Body is the paradigmatic example of vertical integration, much debated among economists.

8. For a collection of papers on the influence of Ronald Coase, see Oliver Williamson and Sidney Winter, *The Nature of the Firm: Origins, Evolution, and Development* (New York: Oxford University Press, 1991); and see Alfred Chandler, *The Visible Hand: The Managerial Revolution in American Business* (Cambridge, MA.: Harvard University Press, 1977).

9. Ellis W. Hawley, *The New Deal and the Problem of Monopoly* (Princeton, NJ: Princeton University Press, 1966); Robert Wiebe, *The Search for Order, 1877–1920* (New York: Hill and Wang, 1966); Martin Sklar, *The Corporate Reconstruction of American Capitalism, 1890–1916* (New York: Cambridge University Press, 1988); Thomas McCraw, *Prophets of Regulation: Charles Frances Adams; Louis D. Brandeis; James M. Landis; Alfred E. Kahn* (Cambridge, MA: Harvard University Press, 1986); Alan Brinkley, *The End of Reform: New Deal Liberalism in Recession and War* (New York: Knopf, 1995); Morton Keller, *Regulating a New Economy: Public Policy and Economic Change in America, 1900–1933* (Cambridge, MA: Harvard University Press, 1998); Barbara Fried, *The Progressive Assault on Laissez Faire: Robert Hale and the First Law and Economics Movement* (New York: Cambridge University Press, 2001); and K. Sabeel Rahman, *Democracy Against Domination* (New York: Oxford University Press, 2016).

10. Many of the insights in this section of the essay are drawn from Thomas K. McCraw, "In Retrospect: Berle and Means," *Reviews in American History* 18 (1990): 578–596. The quotes above are from page 582. In *The Great Merger Movement in American Business, 1895–1904* (New York: Cambridge University Press, 1988), Naomi Lamoreaux offers the most comprehensive analysis of the wave of corporate consolidation that would for a long generation become such an object of regulatory ideas and praxis.

11. As quoted in Jordan Schwarz, *Liberal: Adolf A. Berle and the Vision of an American Era* (New York: Free Press, 1987), 60.

12. Howard Brick, *Transcending Capitalism: Visions of a New Society in Modern American Thought* (Ithaca, NY: Cornell University Press, 2006), 65, 74; and see Brian Cheffins and Steven Bank, "Is Berle and Means Really a Myth?," *Business History Review* 83 (Autumn 2009): 443–474.

13. McCraw, "In Retrospect," 590.

14. Jason Scott Smith, "The Liberal Invention of the Multinational Corporation: David Lilienthal and Postwar Capitalism," in *What's Good for Business: Business and American Politics since World War II*, ed. Kim Phillips-Fein and Julian Zelizer (New York: Oxford University Press, 2012), 114.

15. Roland Marchand, "Where Lie the Boundaries of the Corporation? Explorations in 'Corporate Responsibility' in the 1930s," *Business and Economic History* 26 (Fall 1997): 80, 83.

16. Meg Jacobs, *Pocketbook Politics: Economic Citizenship in Twentieth-Century America* (Princeton, NJ: Princeton University Press, 2005), 95–135; Lizabeth Cohen, *A Consumers' Republic: The Politics of Mass Consumption in Postwar America* (New York: Knopf, 2003), 18–61; Steve Fraser, *Labor Will Rule: Sidney Hillman and the Rise of American Labor* (New York: Free Press, 1991), 282–288; and Theda Skocpol and Kenneth Finegold, "State Capacity

and Economic Intervention in the Early New Deal," *Political Science Quarterly* 97 (Summer 1982): 255–278.

17. I discuss much of this at greater length in Nelson Lichenstein, *State of the Union: A Century of American Labor* (Princeton, NJ: Princeton University Press, 2013), 98–140. See also Timothy Noah, *The Great Divergence: America's Growing Inequality Crisis and What We Can Do About It* (New York: Bloomsbury Press, 2012), 10–27.

18. William Lazonick, "Innovative Business Models and Varieties of Capitalism: Financialization of the U.S. Corporation," *Business History Review* 84 (Winter 2010): 675–702.

19. Berle and Means, *Corporation and Private Property*, 356.

20. Peter Drucker, *Post-Capitalist Society* (New York: HarperCollins, 1993), 43. Although this quote is taken from one of Drucker's later books, his views on the managerial transition to postcapitalism have been consistent since he wrote *Concept of the Corporation* in 1945.

21. Mark Mizruchi, "Berle and Means Revisited: The Governance and Power of Large U.S. Corporations," *Theory and Society* 33 (2004): 583; and also Mark Mizruchi and Daniel Hirschman, "The Modern Corporation as Social Construction," *Seattle University Law Review* 33, no. 4 (2010): 1065–1108; C. A. Harwell Swells, "The Cycles of Corporate Social Responsibility: An Historical Retrospective for the Twenty-First Century," *Kansas Law Review* 51 (November 2002): 77–140.

22. Milton Friedman, "The Social Responsibility of Business is to Increase Profits," *New York Times Magazine*, September 13, 1970, 17–19.

23. Angus Burgin, *The Great Persuasion: Reinventing Free Markets since the Depression* (Cambridge, MA: Harvard University Press, 2012), 186–213.

24. Louis Hyman, "Rethinking the Postwar Corporation: Management, Monopolies, and Markets," in Phillips-Fein and Zelizer, *What's Good for Business*, 195–211.

25. Donald Woutat, "GM Chairman Stempel Resigns Under Pressure," *Los Angeles Times*, October 27, 1992, A1.

26. Mizruchi, "Berle and Means Revisited," 599.

27. As quoted in Tom Frank, *One Market Under God: Extreme Capitalism, Market Populism, and the End of Economic Democracy* (New York: Anchor Books, 2000), 211.

28. As quoted in Dalia Tsuk, "From Pluralism to Individualism: Berle and Means and Twentieth-Century American Legal Thought," *Law and Social Inquiry* 30 (Winter 2005): 215. See also Kenneth Lipartito and Yumiko Morii, "Rethinking the Separation of Ownership from Management in American History," *Seattle University Law Review* 33, no. 4 (2010): 1025–1063. In their conclusion, Lipartito and Morii write, "The original message of *The Modern Corporation* was lost when commentators shifted their reading of the book to principal-agent conflict and reduced corporate responsibility to just one issue—maximizing shareholder value" (1057).

29. David Bensman, "Keep on Truckin': The Supply Chain Motors Down the Low Road," *New Labor Forum* 17 (Spring 2008): 27–33.

30. Josh Eidelson, "Labor Board Alleges Repeated Retaliation at Walmart's Top US Warehouse," *The Nation*, March 20, 2013.

31. David Weil, "Examining the Underpinnings of Labor Standards Compliance in Low Wage Industries," *Report to the Russell Sage Foundation*, May 31, 2012, 15.

32. Jeremy Peters, "Delphi in Court to Void its Union Contracts," *New York Times*, May 10, 2006, C3.

33. Richard Langlois, "The Vanishing Hand: The Changing Dynamics of Industrial Capitalism," *Industrial and Corporate Change* 12 (2003): 373. See also Nitin Nohria, Davis Dyer, and Frederick Dalzell, *Changing Fortunes: Remaking the Industrial Corporation* (New York: Wiley, 2002).

34. Gerald F. Davis, "After the Corporation," *Politics and Society* 41 (June 2013): 283–308.

35. Tian Luo, Amar Mann, and Richard Holden, "The Expanding Role of Temporary Help Services from 1990 to 2008," *Monthly Labor Review* (August 2010): 3–16.

36. E. Mazareanu, "Franchising in the U.S.—Statistics & Facts," *Statista*, November 26, 2019.

37. U.S. Census, "Census Bureau's First Release of Comprehensive Franchise Data Shows Franchises Make Up More Than 10 Percent of Employer Businesses," September 14, 2010, www.census.gov/newsroom/releases/archives.

38. Nelson Lichtenstein, *The Retail Revolution: How Wal-Mart Created a Brave New World of Business* (New York: Picador, 2010), 211.

39. Erin Hatton, *The Temp Economy: From Kelly Girls to Permatemps in Postwar America* (Philadelphia: Temple University Press, 2011), 27.

40. George Gonos, "The Contest over 'Employer' Status in the Postwar United States: The Case of Temporary Help Firms," *Law and Society Review* 31 (1997): 90.

41. Ibid., 102.

42. Louis Hyman, *Temp: How American Work, American Business, and the American Dream Became Temporary* (New York: Viking, 2018), 2–3.

43. As quoted in Hatton, *Temp Economy*, 74.

44. Gonos, "Contest over 'Employer' Status," 86–87.

45. Ibid., 105; see also Katherine V. W. Stone, "Legal Protections for Atypical Employees: Employment Law for Workers without Workplaces and Employees without Employers," *Berkeley Journal of Employment and Labor Law* 27, no. 2 (2006): 253–270.

46. Josh Eidelson, "Finally Paying for Wal-Mart's Sins: Wage Theft Settlement Yields Millions," *Salon*, December 16, 2013.

47. Weil, *Fissured Workplace*, 66.

48. Lydia DePillis, "Why Franchises Are Such a Huge Obstacle to Higher Wages," *Washington Post*, December 6, 2013.

49. Annette Bernhardt, "Making Sense of the New Government Data on Contingent Work," UC Berkeley Center for Labor Research and Education, June 10, 2018. For an overview of how the emergence of contingent or "precarious" work has influenced the sociological study of employment, see Arne Kalleberg, "Precarious Work, Insecure Workers: Employment Relations in Transition," *American Sociological Review* 73, no. 1 (February 2009): 1–22.

50. Emily Nelson, "Retailing: Why Wal-Mart Sings, 'Yes, We Have Bananas!'" *Wall Street Journal*, October 6, 1998, B1.

51. Constance Hays, "What They Know About You," *New York Times*, November 14, 2004, 1.

52. Sarah Ellison, Ann Zimmerman, and Charles Forelle, "Sales Team—P&G's Gillette Edge: The Playbook It Honed at Wal-Mart," *Wall Street Journal*, January 31, 2005

53. Langlois, "The Vanishing Hand"; and Gary Gereffi, John Humphrey, and Timothy Sturgeon, "The Governance of Global Value Chains," *Review of International Political Economy* 12 (February 2005): 79–82.

54. Immanuel Wallerstein, "The Rise and Future Demise of the World-Capitalist System: Concepts for Comparative Analysis," *Comparative Studies in Society and History* 16, no. 4 (1974): 387–415; the quote is taken from Terence K. Hopkins and Immanuel Wallerstein, "Commodity Chains in the World-Economy Prior to 1800," *Review* 10, no. 1 (Summer 1986): 159.

55. For an overview of this literature see Jennifer Bair, "Global Capitalism and Commodity Chains: Looking Back, Going Forward," *Competition and Change* 9, no. 2 (June 2006): 129–156; Frederick H. Abernathy, John T. Dunlop, Janice Hammon, and David Weil, *A Stitch in Time: Lean Retailing and the Transformation of Manufacturing—Lessons from the Apparel and Textile Industries* (New York: Oxford University Press, 1999); Gary Gereffi and Miguel Korzeniewicz, eds., *Commodity Chains and Global Capitalism* (Westport, CT: Praeger, 1994), 95–122; Misha Petrovic and Gary G. Hamilton, "Making Global Markets: Wal-Mart and Its Suppliers," in *Wal-Mart: the Face of Twenty-First Century Capitalism*, ed. Nelson Lichtenstein (New York: New Press, 2006), 107–142; and the author's telephone interview with a former Bain and Company consultant, November 15, 2005.

56. Gary Gereffi, John Humphrey, and Timothy Sturgeon, "The Governance of Global Value Chains," *Review of International Political Economy* 12 (February 2005): 79–82; and Nelson Lichtenstein, "The Return of Merchant Capitalism," *International Labor and Working-Class History*, no. 81 (Spring 2012): 8–27.

57. Hong Xue, "Outsourcing in China: Wal-Mart and Chinese Manufacturers," in *Wal-Mart in China*, ed. Anita Chan (Ithaca, NY: Cornell University Press, 2011).

58. James A. Schmiechen, *Sweated Industries and Sweated Labor: The London Clothing Trades 1860–1914* (Urbana: University of Illinois Press, 1984); Sheila Blackburn, "'Between the Devil of Cheap Labour Competition and the Deep Sea of Family Poverty?' Sweated Labour in Time and Place, 1840–1914," *Labour History Review* 71, no. 2 (August 2006): 99–121.

59. Andrew Wender Cohen, *The Racketeer's Progress: Chicago and the Struggle for the Modern American Economy, 1900–1940* (New York: Cambridge University Press, 2004); Shane Hamilton, *Trucking Country: The Road to America's Wal-Mart Economy* (Princeton, NJ: Princeton University Press, 2008); and Philip Scranton, *Endless Novelty: Specialty Production and American Industrialization, 1865–1925* (Princeton, NJ: Princeton University Press, 1997).

60. Steve Fraser, *Labor Will Rule: Sidney Hillman and the Rise of American Labor* (New York: Free Press, 1991), 26.

61. Emil Schlesinger, *The Outside System of Production in the Women's Garment Industry in the New York Market* (New York: ILGWU, 1951), 5–6.

62. Louis Stark, "Garment Industry Nears Agreement," *New York Times*, July 22, 1933, 20.

63. Jennifer Bair, "The Limits to Embeddedness: Triangular Bargaining and the Institutional Foundations of Organizational Networks," *Institute of Behavioral Science Working Paper*, University of Colorado, August 2012, 8.

64. Ibid., 10.

65. Mark Anner, Jennifer Bair, and Jeremy Blasi, "The Relevance of Twentieth-Century New York Jobbers' Agreements for Twenty-First Century Global Supply Chains," in Appelbaum and Lichtenstein, *Achieving Workers' Rights*, 247.

66. Ibid., 251–252; and Scott Nova and Chris Wegemer, "Outsourcing Horror: Why Apparel Workers Are Still Dying One Hundred Years After Triangle Shirtwaist," in Appelbaum and Lichtenstein, *Achieving Workers' Rights*, 17–31.

67. In "The New Labor Law," Andrias discusses efforts to curb subcontracting, including a 2015 NLRB decision in Browning-Ferris, holding a company and its subcontractor "joint employers." It is likely that the NLRB appointed by President Donald Trump will reverse this decision. Natalie Kitroeff, "Labor Department Walks Back Obama-era Guidance on 'Joint Employers' and Gig Workers," *Los Angeles Times*, June 7, 2017.

Chapter 10

1. Quoted in Karen W. Arenson, "A 'Hot' Offering Retrospective," *New York Times*, December 30, 1980, D1.

2. "The End of the Trail: Snapshots from One Night in November," *Washington Post*, November 5, 1980, F17. On the emergence of entrepreneurial capitalism, see Nicholas Lemann, "New Tycoons Reshape Politics," *New York Times*, June 8, 1986, sec. M.

3. Philip Shenon, "Investment Climate Is Ripe for Offering by Apple Computer," *Wall Street Journal*, August 20, 1980, 24.

4. Carl E. Whitney, "Wall Street Discovered Microcomputers," *InfoWorld* 2, no. 18 (October 13, 1980): 4–5.

5. Steve Fraser and Gary Gerstle, *The Rise and Fall of the New Deal Order, 1930–1980* (Princeton, NJ: Princeton University Press, 1989), ix.

6. Ronald Reagan: "Remarks and a Question-and-Answer Session with the Students and Faculty at Moscow State University," May 31, 1988, in Gerhard Peters and John T. Woolley, *The American Presidency Project*, accessed December 14, 2014, http://www.presidency.ucsb.edu/ws/?pid=35897.

7. "A Different Scenario: Personal Computers in the 80's," *InfoWorld* 2, no. 6 (April 14, 1980): 11. Box 1, Liza Loop Papers, M1141, Stanford University Special Collections, Stanford, CA.

8. Elizabeth Drew, "The Democrats," *New Yorker*, March 22, 1982, 130.

9. House Democratic Caucus, *Rebuilding the Road to Opportunity: Turning Point for America's Economy* (Washington, DC: Government Printing Office, 1982).

10. Judith Stein, *Pivotal Decade: How the United States Traded Factories for Finance in the Seventies* (New Haven, CT: Yale University Press, 2010).

11. Gary M. Fink and Hugh Davis Graham, *The Carter Presidency: Policy Choices in the Post-New Deal Era* (Lawrence: University Press of Kansas, 1998); Bruce J. Schulman, *The Seventies: The Great Shift in American Culture, Society, and Politics* (New York: Free Press, 2001); Jefferson Cowie, Joseph Heathcott, and Barry Bluestone, eds., *Beyond the Ruins: The Meanings of Deindustrialization* (Ithaca, NY: Cornell University Press, 2003); Jefferson Cowie,

312 Notes to Pages 203–204

Stayin' Alive: The 1970s and the Last Days of the Working Class (New York: New Press, 2010); Stein, *Pivotal Decade*; and Daniel T. Rodgers, *Age of Fracture* (Cambridge, MA: Belknap Press of Harvard University Press, 2011).

12. The few who have written on the subject have provided compelling insights into gender and class (Glenna Matthews, *Silicon Valley, Women, and the California Dream: Gender, Class, and Opportunity in the Twentieth Century* [Stanford, CA: Stanford University Press, 2003]), race (Steve Pitti, *The Devil in Silicon Valley: Northern California, Race, and Mexican Americans* [Princeton, NJ: Princeton University Press, 2003]), political realignment (Lily Geismer, *Don't Blame Us: Suburban Liberals and the Transformation of the Democratic Party* [Princeton, NJ: Princeton University Press, 2014]), corporate structure and geography (Stephen B. Adams, "Growing Where You Are Planted: Exogenous Forces and the Seeding of Silicon Valley," *Research Policy* 40, no. 3 [April 2010]: 368–379), as well as the broader cultural and social milieu of the tech industry (Leslie Berlin, *The Man Behind the Microchip: Robert Noyce and the Invention of Silicon Valley* [New York: Oxford University Press, 2006]).

13. For a recent review of this rightward swing, see Julian E. Zelizer, "Reflections: Rethinking the History of American Conservatism," *Reviews in American History* 38, no. 2 (2010): 367–392. See also Benjamin C. Waterhouse, "Mobilizing for the Market: Organized Business, Wage-Price Controls, and the Politics of Inflation, 1971–1974," *Journal of American History* 100, no. 2 (September 2013): 454–478. Both Zelizer and Waterhouse observe that there were many conservative movements, and that modern conservatism is best understood as a plural noun. The "incomplete" conservative revolution and the sustained activism and influence of liberal social movements in the 1970s is explored in Bruce J. Schulman and Julian E. Zelizer, eds., *Rightward Bound: Making America Conservative in the 1970s* (Cambridge, MA: Harvard University Press, 2008) and in a special section on "Reconsidering the 1970s" in the *Journal of Contemporary History* 43, no. 4 (October 2008): 617–700. Liberals take center stage in recent work, which includes Bruce Miroff, *The Liberals' Moment: The McGovern Insurgency and the Identity Crisis of the Democratic Party* (Lawrence: University Press of Kansas, 2007); Guian A. McKee, *The Problem of Jobs: Liberalism, Race, and Deindustrialization in Philadelphia* (Chicago: University of Chicago Press, 2008); Jonathan Bell and Timothy Stanley, eds., *Making Sense of American Liberalism* (Urbana: University of Illinois Press, 2012); and Geismer, *Don't Blame Us*.

14. The mechanical punch-card tabulator—IBM's first marquee product—resulted from an early 1880s U.S. Census Bureau competition to invent a machine capable of rapidly calculating vital statistics for a growing, urbanizing nation. Herman Hollerith, "The Electrical Tabulating Machine," *Journal of the Royal Statistical Society* 57 (1894): 678–689. See also James W. Cortada, *Before the Computer: IBM, NCR, Burroughs, and Remington Rand and the Industry They Created, 1865–1956* (Princeton, NJ: Princeton University Press, 1993).

15. "I.B.M. Machines Adapted to Need for Keeping New Social Security Records," *Wall Street Journal*, October 19, 1936, 10; and David Stebenne, "Thomas J. Watson and the Business-Government Relationship, 1933–1956," *Enterprise and Society* 6, no. 1 (February 2005): 48.

16. Fritz Machlup, *The Production and Distribution of Knowledge in the United States* (Princeton, NJ: Princeton University Press, 1962), 311, 9.

17. W. Stuart Leslie, *The Cold War and American Science: The Academic-Military-Industrial Complex at MIT and Stanford* (New York: Columbia University Press, 1993); Bruce Schulman, *From Cotton Belt to Sunbelt: Federal Policy, Economic Development, and the Transformation of the South, 1938–1980* (Durham, NC: Duke University Press, 1994); Janet Abbate, *Inventing the Internet* (Cambridge, MA: MIT Press, 1999); and Margaret Pugh O'Mara, *Cities of Knowledge: Cold War Science and the Search for the Next Silicon Valley* (Princeton, NJ: Princeton University Press, 2005).

18. Dallas was home to Texas Instruments (TI), a leading transistor innovator and manufacturer since the early 1950s, and whose Jack Kilby had been one of the inventors of the integrated circuit. TI engineers had gone on to found a number of companies in the Dallas area, including the semiconductor success story Mostek (founded 1969), giving the region the moniker "Silicon Prairie" by the early 1980s.

19. Terman, quoted in O'Mara, *Cities of Knowledge*, 122; and Daniel Holbrook, "Government Support of the Semiconductor Industry: Diverse Approaches and Information Flows," *Business and Economic History* 24, no. 2 (Winter 1995): 133–177.

20. Government money was also responsible for a wave of university-based research and teaching in science, math, and the emerging academic discipline of computer science, seeding ideas and educating human capital. See O'Mara, *Cities of Knowledge*, chap. 1.

21. Reid Dennis, interview with the author, May 26, 2015, Palo Alto, CA.

22. U.S. Department of Commerce, Bureau of Economic Analysis, "Value Added by Industry in Current Dollars, Quantity Indexes by Industry, and Price Indexes by Industry, 1947–1997; and Value Added by Industry, Gross Output by Industry, Intermediate Inputs by Industry, and the Components of Value Added by Industry, 1987–1997."

23. U.S. Department of Commerce, Bureau of Economic Analysis, "Private Nonfarm Employment by Metropolitan Statistical Area: San Jose-Sunnyvale, 1969–2000."

24. Gene Bylinsky, *The Innovation Millionaires: How They Succeed* (New York: Charles Scribner's Sons, 1976), 6. See also AnnaLee Saxenian, *Regional Advantage: Culture and Competition in Silicon Valley and Route 128* (Cambridge, MA: Harvard University Press, 1996).

25. Gene Bylinsky, "California's Great Breeding Ground for Industry," *Fortune* (June 1974): 128–135.

26. I thank Kathie Maxfield for this observation, drawn from her personal experience. Bob and Katherine Maxfield, interview with the author, May 28, 2015, Saratoga, CA.

27. Gordon Moore, "Cramming More Components onto Integrated Circuits," *Electronics* 38, no. 8 (April 19, 1965), 114–117. For discussion of this technological transition, see Paul E. Ceruzzi, *A History of Modern Computing* (Cambridge, MA: MIT Press, 1998).

28. Katherine Maxfield, *Starting Up Silicon Valley: How ROLM Became a Cultural Icon and a Fortune 500 Company* (Austin, TX: Emerald Book, 2014), 78.

29. Ben Rosen, "Government Accelerates Funding for Technology," *Rosen Electronics Letter*, February 29, 1980, 1–7. Catalog no. 102661121, Computer History Museum Archives.

30. Don C. Hoefler, "Silicon Valley U.S.A.," *Electronic News*, January 11, 1971. This banner headline ran over a three-part series written by the insider electronics journalist, and is the first known instance of the term being used in print.

31. Bylinsky, "California's Great Breeding Ground," reprinted in Bylinsky, *Innovation Millionaires*, 55.

32. Quoted in Margaret Comstock Tommervik and Craig Stinson, "Women at Work with Apples," *Softalk*, March 1981, 49. Box 2, Liza Loop Papers, M1141, Stanford University Special Collections.

33. As both Fred Turner and John Markoff have shown, the confluence of hippies and techies in the Bay Area—especially in the suburban and semirural areas around Stanford—was not simply a moment of happenstance community comingling but of extraordinary intellectual fusion, shaping ideas and technology-industry practices into the Internet age. Fred Turner, *From Counterculture to Cyberculture: Stewart Brand, the Whole Earth Network, and the Rise of Digital Utopianism* (Chicago: University of Chicago Press, 2006); and John Markoff, *What the Dormouse Said: How the Sixties Counterculture Shaped the Personal Computer Industry* (New York: Penguin Books, 2006). Lee Felsenstein is quoted in Turner, *From Counterculture to Cyberculture*, 114.

34. Joseph A. Schumpeter, *Capitalism, Socialism, and Democracy* (New York: Harper and Brothers, 1947); and William H. Whyte, *The Organization Man* (New York: Doubleday, 1957). Ironically, Whyte's *Fortune* magazine became an important house organ for the high-technology industry in the 1970s; by the 1980s, newer business periodicals like *Inc.* joined in this venture.

35. Venture capitalists who backed these companies often brought in "adult supervision" when entrepreneurs were particularly young and unseasoned, while keeping founders as the public face of the company. Two prominent examples were Apple, where the venture investor Arthur Rock recruited the seasoned marketing executive and investor Mike Markkula to oversee the young Steve Jobs and Steve Wozniak in their first year of operation, and Google, where the industry veteran Eric Schmidt came in as chief executive officer in 2001 at the behest of the venture investors John Doerr and Michael Moritz. See Walter Isaacson, *Steve Jobs* (New York: Simon and Schuster, 2011), 75–78; and Ken Auletta, *Googled: The End of the World as We Know It* (New York: Penguin Press, 2015), 55.

36. "Hewlett Co-Founder Retiring from Post," *New York Times*, January 20, 1987, B1.

37. Packard quoted in Jim Collins, Foreword to David Packard, *The HP Way: How Bill Hewlett and I Built Our Company* (New York: HarperBusiness, 2005 ed.). For a discussion of amenities at HP, see John Findlay, *Magic Lands: Western Cityscapes and American Culture Since 1940* (Berkeley: University of California Press, 1992), 138–139.

38. Marty Goldberg and Curt Vendel, *Atari Inc.: Business Is Fun* (Carmel, NY: Syzygy Press, 2012), 101–102.

39. "Space-Age Pinball," *Time*, April 1, 1974; Leonard Herman, "Company Profile: Atari," in *The Video Game Explosion: A History from PONG to Playstation and Beyond*, ed. Mark J. P. Wolf (Westport, CT: Greenwood Press, 2008), 53–61; and Elizabeth Rourke, Paul S. Bodine, and Howard A. Jones, "Atari Corporation," in *International Directory of Company Histories*, ed. Tina Grant and Miranda H. Ferrara (Detroit, MI: St. James Press, 2005), 66:16–20.

40. As Jennifer Klein has shown, this system for achieving economic security and income redistribution was a public-private hybrid through which benefits like health care were tied to work. Union pressure was critical to keeping benefit levels robust. Jennifer Klein, *For*

All These Rights: Business, Labor, and the Shaping of America's Public-Private Welfare State (Princeton, NJ: Princeton University Press, 2004).

41. David Olmos, "Computer Industry Resists Organized Labor," *Computerworld*, September 10, 1984, 113. On white-collar organizing, see "Why White Collar Workers Can't Be Organized," *Harper's Magazine* 215, no. 1287 (August 1, 1957): 45–50. Labor unions gained more traction among public-sector white-collar workers than in the private sector, a pattern seen both in the United States and Great Britain; see Clive Jenkins and Barrie Lawson, *White-Collar Unionism: The Rebellious Salariat* (London: Routledge and Kegan Paul, 1979).

42. Matthews, *Silicon Valley*.

43. Women were particularly vulnerable. In one industry-sponsored study, women workers in fabrication plants were found to have a rate of miscarriages 40 percent above those of non-manufacturing workers (William Glaberson with Julia Campbell, "Ailing Computer-Chip Workers Blame Chemicals, Not Chance," *New York Times*, March 28, 1996, B1). On the effect of high tech on both environmental and human health, see Margaret O'Mara, "The Environmental Contradictions of High-Tech Urbanism," in *Now Urbanism: The Future City Is Here*, ed. Jeffrey Hou, Ben Spencer, Thaisa Way, and Ken Yocum (New York: Routledge, 2015), 26–42.

44. Quoted in David Bacon, "Organizing Silicon Valley's High-Tech Workers," accessed August 21, 2015, http://dbacon.igc.org/Unions/04hitec1.htm (archived at http://perma.cc /QSR2-RY46).

45. Kenneth B. Noble, "Union Plans Drive to Organize I.B.M.," *New York Times*, July 16, 1985, A16. The textile manufacturer J. P. Stevens was the target of a prolonged and ultimately successful unionization drive in the 1970s.

46. Olmos, "Computer Industry Resists Organized Labor."

47. Ibid.; and Bacon, "Organizing Silicon Valley's High-Tech Workers." See also Donna K. H. Walters, "High-Tech Boosts Profile as Lobbying Intensifies," *Los Angeles Times*, April 6, 1986, E1.

48. For a rare critique, see Lenny Siegel and John Markoff, *The High Cost of High Tech: The Dark Side of the Chip* (New York: Harper and Row, 1985).

49. Thomas Byrne Edsall, "The Changing Shape of Power," in Fraser and Gerstle, *Rise and Fall of the New Deal Order*, 269–293.

50. Charles Elkind, "Riding the High-tech Boom: The American Electronics Association Story, 1943–1990," unpublished manuscript, ca. 1990, 27. FF1, MISC 333, Stanford University Special Collections.

51. Ralph Landau, "Technology, Economics, and Public Policy," February 1985, box 49, FF "Conference on Economic and Technology Policy," Ed Zschau Papers, Hoover Institution Archives.

52. Gary Klott, "Venture Capitalists Wary of Tax Plan," *New York Times*, January 9, 1985, D1; Burton J. McMurtry, "Tax Policy Influence on Venture Capital (Presentation to Conference on Technology and Economic Policy)," February 4, 1985, box 49, FF "Conference on Economic and Technology Policy," Ed Zschau Papers, Hoover Institution Archives.

53. David Morgenthaler and Reid Dennis, interview with the author, May 26, 2015, Palo Alto, CA. On the "Boys' Club," see John W. Wilson, *The New Venturers: Inside the High-Stakes Game of Venture Capital* (Reading, MA.: Addison-Wesley, 1985), 49.

54. "The Capital Blues," *Princeton Alumni Weekly*, February 12, 1979, 14; and David Morgenthaler, interview with the author, March 18, 2015, Palo Alto, CA.

55. Ed Zschau, interview with the author, June 24, 2015, Stanford, CA; and *Capital Gains Tax Bills: Hearings Before the Subcommittee on Taxation and Debt Management Generally of the Committee on Finance*, United States Senate, 95th Cong., 2nd Sess., June 28 and 29, 1978, 269.

56. Jimmy Carter, "Tax Reduction and Reform Message to the Congress," January 20, 1978, Gerhard Peters and Woolley, *American Presidency Project*, accessed March 2, 2015, http://www.presidency.ucsb.edu/ws/?pid=31055.

57. Paul "Pete" McCloskey, interview with the author, Rumsey, CA, February 18, 2016.

58. The Securities Industry Association, for example, Jack Egan, "SIA Sees Tax Cuts Aiding Economy," *Washington Post*, March 3, 1978, B8.

59. Barry Sussman, "Surprise: Public Backs Carter on Taxes: Roper Survey Shows Fairness Rated Above Tax Cut," *Washington Post*, August 6, 1978, D5.

60. Clayton Fritchey, "Today's 'Forgotten Man': The Investor," *Washington Post*, August 5, 1978, A15; Art Pine, "A Tax Break for the Rich in an Election Year?," *Washington Post*, May 21, 1978, A2; and "Rich, Poor, and Taxes," *Washington Post*, June 2, 1978, A16.

61. Art Pine, "Capital Gains Remarks by Carter Draw Hill Fire," *Washington Post*, June 29, 1978, D12. Blumenthal later relented a bit, only to be undercut by the White House's Georgia Mafia, with the press secretary Jody Powell telling reporters that "no one in the treasury" was authorized to speak about possible compromises on the capital gains issue (Hobart Rowen, "If Only Blumenthal Could Join the Team," *Washington Post*, August 10, 1978, A28).

62. For a comprehensive account of the bill's passage, see Robert Wolcott Johnson, "The Passage of the Investment Incentive Act of 1978: A Case Study of Business Influencing Public Policy" (MA thesis, Harvard University, 1980). For a broader assessment of shifting political economy occurring on Carter's watch, see Fink and Graham, *Carter Presidency*, especially the contributions by Bruce J. Schulman ("Slouching Toward the Supply Side," 51–71) and Melvyn Dubofsky ("Jimmy Carter and the End of the Politics of Productivity," 95–116).

63. Ann Crittenden, "Talking Business with Morton Collins," *New York Times*, December 9, 1980, D2; and Michael Schrage, "Nation's High-Tech Engine Fueled by Venture Capital," *Washington Post*, May 20, 1984), G1. Venture capitalists have pointed to this ever since as evidence that supply-side economics fueled the high-tech boom. Tax cuts certainly made a difference, but other factors fueled the fire: Paul Volcker's Fed finally putting the brakes on inflation, the introduction of faster microchips, the boosts to consumer and Wall Street confidence created by big exits like Apple and Genentech. Subsequent analyses have indicated that the liberalization of the "prudent man" rule actually had a far greater influence, pointing out that investments subject to capital gains make up only a minority fraction of overall investment. The biggest boon that the 1978 tax cut provided may have been a psychic one, giving both venture capitalists and entrepreneurs more confidence to risk starting up new companies. See in particular James M. Poterba, "Venture Capital and Capital Gains Taxation," *Tax Policy and the Economy* 3 (1989): 47–67.

64. "How Washington Spurs the High-Tech Companies," *Business Week* 2662 (November 10, 1980): 98.

65. Their numbers were further bolstered after 1976. For a discussion of the "Watergate Babies" and their influence, see Julian E. Zelizer, *On Capitol Hill: The Struggle to Reform Congress and Its Consequences, 1948–2000* (Cambridge, MA.: Cambridge University Press, 2004). On the weakening of the Democrats' labor–liberal coalition before 1980, see Nelson Lichtenstein, "Labor, Liberalism, and the Democratic Party: A Fruitful but Vexed Alliance," in Bell and Stanley, *Making Sense of American Liberalism*, 229–248; and Jonathan Reider, "The Rise of the 'Silent Majority,'" in Fraser and Gerstle, *Rise and Fall of the New Deal Order*, 243–268.

66. For example, leaders like Steve Jobs and Bill Gates studiously avoided Washington, DC, and its politicians for a good chunk of their careers, only engaging when their enterprises had reached a size and influence that bumped up uncomfortably against limits on monopolism. Gates's painful political indoctrination came in the 1990s with the antitrust battles between Microsoft and the Department of Justice. See Ken Auletta, *World War 3.0: The Microsoft Trial and the Battle to Rule the New Economy* (New York: Random House, 2000).

67. Gary Hart, *Right from the Start: A Chronicle of the McGovern Campaign* (New York: Quadrangle, 1973), 330.

68. Kevin S. Price, "The Partisan Legacies of Preemptive Leadership: Assessing the Eisenhower Cohorts in the U.S. House," *Political Research Quarterly* 55, no. 3 (September 1, 2002): 609–631; and David Stebenne, *Modern Republican Arthur Larson and the Eisenhower Years* (Bloomington: Indiana University Press, 2006).

69. For further discussion of the 1978 tax acts and tax expenditures generally, see Christopher Howard, *The Hidden Welfare State: Tax Expenditures and Social Policy in the United States* (Princeton, NJ: Princeton University Press, 1999), 139–160, 175–192.

70. Leslie Wayne, "Designing a New Economics for the 'Atari Democrats,'" *New York Times*, September 26, 1982.

71. Interview, July 5, 1985, quoted in Hedrick Smith, *The Power Game: How Washington Works* (New York: Random House, 1988), 135. The term began to appear frequently in Washington reportage starting in the spring of 1982; its origination with Matthews is referenced in Martin Tolchin, "Working Profile: Christopher J. Matthews; He Who Speaks for the Speaker," *New York Times*, June 21, 1985, A14.

72. House Democratic Caucus, *Rebuilding the Road to Opportunity: Turning Point for America's Economy* (Washington, DC: General Printing Office, 1982).

73. Mark Bloomfield, "Memorandum to Capital Gains Coalition," December 14, 1984, box 51, FF "Capital Gains II," Ed Zschau Papers, Hoover Institution Archives; "Statement of Burton J. McMurtry, President, NVCA, Before the Senate Committee on Small Business, June 4, 1986," n.d., box 51, FF "Capital Gains II," Ed Zschau Papers, Hoover Institution Archives.

74. Thomas W. Lippman, "Designating Shultz as the Next Secretary of State Adds to Bechtel's Strong Administration Links," *Washington Post*, June 26, 1982, D8.

75. U.S. Department of Commerce, International Trade Administration, "An Assessment of U.S. Competitiveness in High Technology Industries" (Government Printing Office, February 1983), 60; and Paul Tsongas, "Meeting the Japanese Challenge," n.d., box 2A, FF 37, Tsongas Collection, Center for Lowell History, University of Massachusetts Lowell. On

Japanese policy, see Chalmers A. Johnson, *MITI and the Japanese Miracle: The Growth of Industrial Policy, 1925–1975* (Stanford, CA: Stanford University Press, 1982).

76. Walters, "High-Tech Boosts Profile."

77. William D. Marbach and Christopher Ma, "High Hopes for High Tech," *Newsweek*, February 14, 1983, 61.

78. Hobart Rowen, "Entire Data Processing Industry Target of Japanese Companies: TI Gains A Foothold In Japan West Coast Firms Miss Big Question," *Washington Post*, March 23, 1980, E1.

79. The fullest and most incisive account of the SIA and Bob Noyce's "political entrepreneurship" is found in Berlin, *Man Behind the Microchip*, 257–280.

80. Rowen, "Entire Data Processing Industry."

81. Ben Rosen, "Jerry Sanders' Humor," *Rosen Electronics Letter*, August 25, 1982, 14–15, Cat. no. 102661121, Computer History Museum Archives, Mountain View, CA.

82. "High-Tech Jobs Going Overseas as Costs Rise."

83. The chief banner waver for the movement was the *Washington Monthly* publisher Charles Peters, who in 1983 published "A Neoliberal's Manifesto" in that magazine, which laid out some basic philosophical precepts very similar to Reich, Tsongas, and others, but with a more emphatic push for turning away from old industries and toward new. Charles Peters, "A Neoliberal's Manifesto," *Washington Monthly* (May 1983).

84. David S. Broder, "The Campaign's Best—and Worst," *Washington Post*, November 7, 1984, A15.

85. Haynes Johnson, "Silicon Valley's Satisfied Society; Search for Stability Steering Sunnyvale Voters to Reagan; Disaffection With Traditional Democrats Guides Choice," *Washington Post*, October 10, 1984, A5.

86. Calvin Sims, "Silicon Valley Takes a Partisan Leap of Faith," *New York Times*, October 29, 1992, B1.

87. PriceWaterhouseCoopers, "Global Top 100 Companies by Market Capitalization," March 31, 2015, accessed August 18, http://www.pwc.com/gx/en/audit-services/capital-market /publications/assets/document/pwc-global-top-100-march-update.pdf (archived at http:// perma.cc/S7GP-VK3F). Only the financial industry has a larger combined market cap, its swollen coffers resulting in large part from three decades of post-Reagan deregulation but also from more recent market euphoria over tech.

88. Shane Hamilton, *Trucking Country: The Road to America's Wal-Mart Economy* (Princeton, NJ: Princeton University Press, 2008), 4.

Chapter 11

1. "CIO Unions to Open Organizing Drives," *New York Times*, April 22, 1946; and "Double Campaign," *Businessweek* (May 4, 1964): 80.

2. Barbara S. Griffith, *The Crisis of American Labor: Operation Dixie and the Defeat of the CIO* (Philadelphia: Temple University Press, 1988), xvi; and Nelson Lichtenstein, "From Corporatism to Collective Bargaining: Organized Labor and the Eclipse of Social Democ-

racy in the Postwar Era," in *The Rise and Fall of the New Deal Order, 1930-1980*, ed. Steve Fraser and Gary Gerstle (Princeton, NJ: Princeton University Press, 1989), 122. On Operation Dixie, see Timothy Minchin, *What Do We Need a Union For? The TWUA in the South, 1945-1955* (Chapel Hill: University of North Carolina Press, 1997); Robert H. Zieger, *The CIO, 1935-1955* (Chapel Hill: University of North Carolina Press, 1995), 227-252; and William P. Jones, "Black Workers and the CIO's Turn Toward Racial Liberalism: Operation Dixie and the North Carolina Lumber Industry, 1946-1953," *Labor History* 41, no. 3 (2000): 279-306. For an emerging literature on public-sector unions, see Joseph A. McCartin, "Bringing the State's Workers In: Time to Rectify an Imbalanced US Labor Historiography," *Labor History* 47, no. 1 (2006): 73-94. See also Joseph A. McCartin, "'A Wagner Act for Public Employees': Labor's Dream Deferred and the Rise of Conservatism, 1970-1976," *Journal of American History* 95, no. 1 (June 2008): 123-148; Joseph A. McCartin, *Collision Course: Ronald Reagan, the Air Traffic Controllers, and the Strike That Changed America* (Oxford: Oxford University Press, 2011); Clarence Taylor, *Reds at the Blackboard: Communism, Civil Rights, and the New York City Teachers Union* (New York: Columbia University Press, 2011); Philip F. Rubio, *There's Always Work at the Post Office: African American Postal Workers and the Fight for Jobs, Justice and Equality* (Chapel Hill: University of North Carolina Press, 2010); Leon Fink and Brian Greenberg, *Upheaval in the Quiet Zone: A History of Hospital Workers' Union, Local 1199* (Urbana: University of Illinois Press, 1989); Karen Brodkin Sacks, *Caring by the Hour: Women, Work, and Organizing at Duke Medical Center* (Urbana: University of Illinois Press, 1988); Francis Ryan, *AFSCME's Philadelphia Story: Municipal Workers and Urban Power in the Twentieth Century* (Philadelphia: Temple University Press, 2011); and Ruth Milkman, *L.A. Story: Immigrant Workers and the Future of the U.S. Labor Movement* (New York: Russell Sage Foundation, 2006). On the broader lack of scholarship on public employee unions, see Robert Shaffer, "Where Are the Organized Public Employees? The Absence of Public Employee Unionism from U.S. History Textbooks, and Why It Matters," *Labor History* 43, no. 3: 315-334.

3. Richard B. Freeman, "Unionism Comes to the Public Sector," *Journal of Economic Literature* (March 1986): 41.

4. Michael B. Katz, Mark J. Stern, and Jamie J. Fader, "The New African American Inequality," *Journal of American History* 92, no. 1 (June 2005): 77.

5. Nelson Lichtenstein, "Bashing Public Employees and Their Unions," in *A Contest of Ideas: Capital, Politics, and Labor* (Urbana: University of Illinois Press, 2013), 201.

6. "Defying Predictions, Union Membership Isn't Dropping Post-Janus," *Governing* (December 10, 2018); and Jonathon Berlin and Kyle Bentle, "What Wisconsin Says About What Could Happen to Illinois Unions After Janus," *Chicago Tribune*, June 29, 2018.

7. Jake Rosenfeld, *What Unions No Longer Do* (Cambridge, MA: Harvard University Press, 2014), 31-67.

8. Milton MacKaye, "The CIO Invades Dixie," *Saturday Evening Post* (July 20, 1946): 12; "UPWA Leaders Arrested for Protesting Atlantic City Restaurant Discrimination," *Public Record* (May 1946); and "New Union Urges Wider Labor Law," *New York Times*, April 26, 1946.

9. "Public Bears Burden of Low Wages in High Welfare Load," *Public Record* (April 1946); Analysis of UPW Locals from *Public Record*"; "City Hospital Organizing Plan," box 9, folder 9, Ewart Guinier Papers, Schomburg Center for Research in Black Culture, New York.

10. "New Union Urges Wider Labor Law," *New York Times*, April 26, 1948; Max Krochmal, "An Unmistakably Working-Class Vision: Birmingham's Foot Soldiers and Their Civil Rights Movement," *Journal of Southern History* 76, no. 4 (November 2010): 923–960; UPWA, "Analysis of UPW Locals from Public Record," AFSCME Secretary Treasurers Office, GCEOC, box 1, folder 5; "Settled Out of Court," *Atlanta Daily World*, January 4, 1949, 6; "Teachers Sue School Board," *Chicago Defender*, February 15, 1947, 2; "Alabama State University Memorial Honors Dr. Ruby J. Gainer," *Jet* (January 15, 1976): 16; and "Howard University Profs Vote for Unionism," *Amsterdam News*, February 15, 1947, 3.

11. "Canal Zone Workers in Union," *New York Times*, August 26, 1946; "UPW Officers Present Petition to White House Urging End of Discrimination on Canal Zone," *Public Record* (June 1948); and on the Silver/Gold system, see Julie Greene, *The Canal Builders: Making America's Empire at the Panama Canal* (New York: Penguin Press, 2009), 270–272.

12. "City's Garbage Piles Up as 175 Here Walk Out," *Atlanta Constitution*, July 23, 1941, 1; W. A. Florence to Arnold Zander, July 24, 1941, Zander to Florence, July 30, 1941, Florence to Gordon Chapman, September 17, 1941, box 42, folder 2, AFSCME President Zander Papers, Walter P. Reuther Library; Hub Miller, "Report on AFSCME Organizing in Detroit," June 8, 1945, box 79, folder 2, AFSCME President Zander Papers, Reuther Library, "Public Employee Unionization in County Growing," *Los Angeles Times*, March 17, 1945, 9; and Jewel Bellush and Bernard Bellush, *Union Power and New York: Victor Gotbaum and District Council 37* (New York: Praeger, 1984), 9–10.

13. "Scientists in Group Discharged at Aberdeen," *Washington Post*, July 19, 1946, 1.

14. Jules DuBois, "Eye Red Union for Danger to Panama Canal," *Chicago Daily Tribune*, February 26, 1947, 6; and Ralph De Toledano, "Stalin's Hand in the Panama Canal," *Plain Talk* (November 1947): 31–39.

15. "Atomic Board Serves Notice on Two Unions," *Los Angeles Times*, October 9, 1948, 4; and Geoffrey R. Stone, *Perilous Times: Free Speech in Wartime from the Sedition Act of 1798 to the War on Terrorism* (New York: Norton, 2004), 347–348.

16. "Factions Vie as UPW Cast Votes Today," *Washington Evening Star*, May [n.d.] 1946; "Postal Union Quits UPW," *New York Times*, January 5, 1947, 9; Build the Union Committee, "Open Letter to Members of the United Public Workers of America, CIO," [n.d.], box 1, folder 8, AFSCME S-T, GCEOC Records; "Union Drops Six Officers," *New York Times*, March 10, 1948, 54; "Quill Heads Drive on Leftists in CIO," *New York Times*, May 25, 1948, 22; "City CIO Workers Plan Rival Union," *New York Times*, June 17, 1948, 9; "Anti-Communists Seek Charter," *New York Times*, July 1, 1948, 24; Lawrence E. Davies, "Murray Sourges CIO Left-Wingers," *New York Times*, November 23, 1948, 1; and "CIO Leftist Count Forced in Showdown," *Los Angeles Times*, November 24, 1948, 2

17. John Cramer, "New Anti-Commie CIO Union Gaining Members from UPW," *Washington Daily News*, August 8, 1948, 2; "Conference to Organize Public Employees in the CIO," September 9, 1949, box 1, folder 13, AFSCME S-T, GCEOC Records; William Mirengoff and Morton Lifton, "To All Local Unions, Government Workers Union," February 2, 1950, box 1,

folder 14, AFSCME S-T, GCEOC Records; Ruth Wiencek, "Response to Inquiry about Membership of GCEOC," March 22, 1954, box 2, folder 12, AFSCME S-T, GCEOC Records; and Steve Rosswurm, ed., *The CIO's Left-Led Unions* (New Brunswick, NJ: Rutgers University Press, 1992).

18. Carey Haigler to Milton Murray, August 31, 1950, box 2, folder 11, AFSCME S-T, GCEOC Records; "More than 300 Street, Garbage Workers Go out on Strike Again," *Birmingham News*, August 26, 1951; "Garbage Workers, Morgan to Meet," *Birmingham News*, September 12, 1952; "George Westerman to Milton Murray, May 15, 1950, box 3, folder 3, AFSCME S-T, GCEOC Records "Transport Union Leader in Panama," *New York Amsterdam News*, May 20, 1950, 5; "Union Program to Aid Canal Zone Workers," *Pittsburgh Courier*, August 12, 1950, 11; and Milton Murray to Irwin DeShelter, June 14, 1951, box 5, folder 13, AFSCME S-T, GCEOC Records.

19. Joseph C. Goulden, *Jerry Wurf: Labor's Last Angry Man* (New York: Atheneum, 1982); and Daniel Bell, "Labor: What's Behind the News and What's Ahead," *Fortune* (May 1955): 59.

20. Bell, "Labor," 59.

21. Daniel Di Salvo, *Government Against Itself: Public Union Power and Its Consequences* (Oxford: Oxford University Press, 2015), 48–49; William G. Weart, "Philadelphia Signs with a Union to Represent Most City Workers," *New York Times*, February 14, 1957, 1; Goulden, *Jerry Wurf*, 52; "Union Shop Out for City," *Milwaukee Journal*, November 7, 1956; and Bellush and Bellush, *Union Power and New York*, 68, 71.

22. Arnold Zander, "A Union Grows in Dixie," *Municipal South* (February 1959): 24; "Business Week Sees AFSCME as 'The Union of the Future,'" *Public Employee* (May 1959): 8; and Jack Stieber, *Public Employee Unionism: Structure, Growth, Policy* (Washington, DC: Brookings Institution, 1973).

23. "The Workers' Rights and the Public Weal," *Time*, March 1, 1968.

24. AFSCME District 37, "Tentative Agreement on Merger," December 2, 1956, box 27, folder 8, AFSCME S-T, GCEOC Records; "New Group to Aid Negroes in South," *New York Times*, March 1, 1956, 28; and "Wurf, Zimmerman to Head CORE Labor Committee," *Public Employee Press*, March 29, 1963.

25. Bellush and Bellush, *Union Power and New York*, 99.

26. John P. Caldwell to Professor Joseph A. Von Arx, June 15, 1956, box 51, folder 2, AFSCME President's Office, Arnold Zander Collection, Wisconsin Historical Society; W. A. Rowe to Arnold Zander, July 28, 1956, box 96, folder 7, AFSCME President Zander Papers, Walter Reuther Library; Dick Young, "Garbage Strike Over, Trucks Roll," *Charlotte News*, September 2, 1959; and Robert Rogers, "Strikes, Alabama," May 7, 1960, box 96, folder 6, AFSCME President Zander Collection, Reuther Library.

27. Elinor Glenn, "SEIU Organizer," Oral History Interview, May 23–September 9, 2002, UCLA Oral History Program; "Union Opens Drive for City Workers," *Los Angeles Times*, April 5, 1955, 4; "County Workers Will Seek Pay Boosts," *Los Angeles Times*, April 22, 1958; "Two Hospitals, 16 Clinics Face Strike," *Los Angeles Times*, August 9, 1957; and "Kaiser Hospital Pact Ratified by Union Vote," *Los Angeles Times*, September 31, 1957.

28. Daniel Bell, "The Next American Labor Movement," *Fortune*, April 1953, 206; and Stieber, *Public Employee Unionism*, 28.

29. King, quoted in Honey, *Going Down Jericho Road: The Memphis Strike, Martin Luther King's Last Campaign* (New York: Norton, 2008), 300, 298; and Lucy, quoted in Michael Keith Honey, *Black Workers Remember: An Oral History of Segregation, Unionism, and the Freedom Struggle* (Berkeley: University of California Press, 1999), 317–318.

Chapter 12

This work is derived from an article originally published in the *Yale Law Journal*. See Kate Andrias, "The New Labor Law," *Yale Law Journal* 126, no. 1 (October 2016): 57–69.

1. See Jake Rosenfeld, *What Unions No Longer Do* (Cambridge, MA: Harvard University Press, 2014), 10–30; cf. Richard B. Freeman and James L. Medoff, *What Do Unions Do?* (New York: Basic Books, 1984) (describing, as of the mid-1980s, the role of trade unions in the United States). See also "Union Members—2017," Bureau of Labor Statistics, U.S. Department of Labor, 2017, https://www.bls.gov/news.release/pdf/union2.pdf (providing data about union membership). Despite recent declines, unions still represent about 35 percent of public-sector workers; the unionization rate in the private sector is about 6 percent. "Union Members—2017."

2. Rosenfeld, *What Unions No Longer Do*, 4–8; see Jacob S. Hacker and Paul Pierson, "Winner-Take-All Politics: Public Policy, Political Organization, and the Precipitous Rise of Top Incomes in the United States," *Politics and Society* 38, no. 2 (June 2010): 152–204.

3. Thomas Piketty, *Capital in the Twenty-First Century* (Cambridge, MA: Harvard University Press, 2014), 23–24.

4. See Larry M. Bartels, *Unequal Democracy: The Political Economy of the New Gilded Age* (Princeton, NJ: Princeton University Press, 2008), 2, 285; Martin Gilens, *Affluence and Influence: Economic Inequality and Political Power in America* (Princeton, NJ: Princeton University Press, 2012), 79–81, 157–158; Rosenfeld, *What Unions No Longer Do*, 170–181; Kay Lehman Schlozman, Sidney Verba, and Henry E. Brady, *Unheavenly Chorus: Unequal Political Voice and the Broken Promise of American Democracy* (Princeton, NJ: Princeton University Press, 2012), 69–95; Thomas Byrne Edsall, "The Changing Shape of Power: A Realignment in Public Policy," in *The Rise and Fall of the New Deal Order, 1930–1980*, ed. Steve Fraser and Gary Gerstle (Princeton, NJ: Princeton University Press, 1989), 269; and Hacker and Pierson, "Winner-Take-All Politics," 152–204.

5. National Labor Relations (Wagner) Act, 29 U.S.C. §§ 151–169 (2012).

6. National Labor Relations (Wagner) Act § 7, 29 U.S.C. § 157.

7. Karl E. Klare, "Judicial Deradicalization of the Wagner Act and the Origins of Modern Legal Consciousness, 1937–1941," *Minnesota Law Review* 62, no. 3 (March 1978): 265.

8. See Mark Barenberg, "Democracy and Domination in the Law of Workplace Cooperation: From Bureaucratic to Flexible Production," *Columbia Law Review* 94, no. 3 (April 1994): 961; and Mark Barenberg, "The Political Economy of the Wagner Act: Power, Symbol, and Workplace Cooperation," *Harvard Law Review* 106, no. 7 (May 1993): 1389.

9. 79 Congressional Record 7565 (1935), reprinted in NLRB, *Legislative History of the National Labor Relations Act (Wagner Act) 1935*, vol. 2 (1959), 2321.

10. On the American Federation of Labor's (AFL) embrace of private enterprise bargaining, see William E. Forbath, *Law and the Shaping of the American Labor Movement* (Cambridge, MA: Harvard University Press, 1991), 128–130; and William E. Forbath, "The Shaping of the American Labor Movement," *Harvard Law Review* 102, no. 6 (April 1989): 1125.

11. 29 U.S.C. §§ 158, 159(b).

12. National Labor Relations (Wagner) Act (NLRA) § 2, 29 U.S.C. § 152(3) (2016); and Introduction, 4–6.

13. Nelson Lichtenstein, "From Corporatism to Collective Bargaining: Organized Labor and the Eclipse of Social Democracy in the Postwar Era," in Fraser and Gerstle, *Rise and Fall of the New Deal Order*, 122–123; and Klare, "Judicial Deradicalization," 286–287. For a history of the early years of the internal workings of the NLRB, including the agency's transformation from a tripartite body designed to conciliate disputes between employers and unions to a quasi-judicial entity, see James Gross, *The Making of the National Labor Relations Board: A Study in Economics, Politics, and the Law 1933–1937*, vol. 1 (Albany: State University of New York Press, 1974).

14. Klare, "Judicial Deradicalization," 292–293, 301–310, 322–325, 327–334, 337; James B. Atleson, *Values and Assumptions in American Labor Law* (Amherst: University of Massachusetts Press, 1983), 19; and Matthew W. Finkin, "Labor Policy and the Enervation of the Economic Strike," *University of Illinois Law Review*, no. 3 (1990): 549–567.

15. Labor Management Relations (Taft–Hartley) Act, 29 U.S.C. § 141 (2012) (amending the National Labor Relations Act of 1935). See Kim Phillips-Fein, *Invisible Hands: The Businessmen's Crusade Against the New Deal* (New York: Norton, 2010), 31–32; and Archibald Cox, "The Evolution of Labor-Management Relations," in *Law and the National Labor Policy* (Berkeley: University of California Press, 1960), 13–14. For a discussion of how the late New Deal more generally embraced a managerial view of political economy and moved away from a more progressive and democratic approach, see Sabeel Rahman, Chapter 1 in this volume.

16. Labor historians disagree over whether the Taft–Hartley was a codification and consolidation of preexisting legal restriction or a turning point. See Nelson Lichtenstein, "Taft–Hartley: A Slave-Labor Law?," *Catholic University Law Review* 47, no. 3 (1998): 763–765 (reviewing the debate); and Christopher L. Tomlins, *The State and the Unions: Labor Relations, Law, and the Organized Labor Movement in America, 1880–1960* (New York: Cambridge University Press, 1985), 250–251 (discussing the extent to which reorientation was present in prior NLRB and Supreme Court decisions).

17. 29 U.S.C. § 151 (2012).

18. 29 U.S.C. § 158(b)(4) (2012).

19. Lichtenstein, "Taft–Hartley," 766.

20. Nelson Lichtenstein, *Walter Reuther: The Most Dangerous Man in Detroit* (New York: Basic Books, 1995), 271–298 (describing "The Treaty of Detroit"); and Mark Anner, Jennifer Bair, and Jeremy Blasi, "Learning from the Past: The Relevance of Twentieth-Century New York Jobbers' Agreements for Twenty-First-Century Global Supply Chains," in *Achieving Workers' Rights in the Global Economy*, ed. Richard P. Appelbaum and Nelson Lichtenstein

(Ithaca, NY: Cornell University Press, 2013), 239 (describing jobbers' agreements negotiated among workers, garment manufacturers, and purchasers in the U.S. garment sector in the early and mid-twentieth century). Industry-wide bargaining persists in some industries, including the arts and professional sports. See, for example, Catherine Fisk, *Writing for Hire: Unions, Hollywood, and Madison Avenue* (Cambridge, MA: Harvard University Press, 2016) (describing industry-wide bargaining in Hollywood).

21. Union density and pattern bargaining were by no means the only drivers of this relative economic equality. A range of other factors, including a growing economy, technological changes, the enactment of the GI Bill, comparatively low executive pay, robust financial regulation, a progressive tax system, and the entrance of women into the workforce all contributed to the rise of the American middle class and the period of relative economic egalitarianism. See Jefferson Cowie, *The Great Exception: The New Deal & the Limits of American Politics* (Princeton, NJ: Princeton University Press, 2016), 153; Jacob S. Hacker and Paul Pierson, *Winner-Take-All Politics: How Washington Made the Rich Richer—And Turned its Back on the Middle Class* (New York: Simon and Schuster, 2010), 88–90; Michael Lind, *Land of Promise: An Economic History of the United States* (New York: Harper, 2012), 329–362; and Suzanne Mettler, *Soldiers to Citizens: The G.I. Bill and the Making of the Greatest Generation* (New York: Oxford University Press, 2007).

22. William P. Jones, Chapter 11 in this volume; Joseph Slater, *Government Employee Unions, the Law and the State, 1900–1962* (Ithaca, NY: Cornell University Press, 2004), 193–195; and Leon Fink and Brian Greenberg, *Upheaval in the Quiet Zone* (Chicago: University of Illinois Press, 1989).

23. David Weil, *The Fissured Workplace: Why Work Became So Bad for So Many and What Can Be Done to Improve It* (Cambridge, MA: Harvard University Press, 2014). See also James C. Cobb, *The Selling of the South: The Southern Crusade for Industrial Development, 1936–1990* (Chicago: University of Illinois Press, 1993), 96–121, 209–228; and Craig Becker, "Labor Law Outside the Employment Relation," *Texas Law Review* 74, no. 7 (June 1996): 1527 and n1. For a discussion of this transformation and of similar problems faced in the pre–New Deal era, see Nelson Lichtenstein, Chapter 9 in this volume.

24. See Joseph A. McCartin, *Collision Course: Ronald Reagan, the Air Traffic Controllers, and the Strike That Changed America* (New York: Oxford University Press, 2011); Jefferson Cowie, *Stayin' Alive: The 1970s and the Last Days of the Working Class* (New York: New Press, 2010), 362–364; and Rosenfeld, *What Unions No Longer Do*, 86–88.

25. Phillips-Fein, *Invisible Hands*, 89–90; Becker, "Labor Law Outside the Employment Relation," 1528–1530; Kate Bronfenbrenner, "No Holds Barred: The Intensification of Employer Opposition to Organizing," *E.P.I. Briefing Paper* no. 235, 1, 10, table 3 (2009); and Kate L. Bronfenbrenner, "Employer Behavior in Certification Elections and First-Contract Campaigns: Implications for Labor Law Reform," in *Restoring the Promise of American Labor Law*, ed. Sheldon Friedman et al. (Ithaca, NY: Cornell University Press, 1994).

26. See, for example, *First National Maintenance Corp. v. NLRB*, 452 U.S. 666 (1981); and *Textile Workers Union v. Darlington Manufacturing Co.*, 380 U.S. 263 (1965); see also Becker, "Labor Law Outside the Employment Relation," 1527; Terry Collingsworth,

"Resurrecting the National Labor Relations Act—Plant Closings and Runaway Shops in a Global Economy," *Berkeley Journal of Employment and Labor Law* 14, no. 1 (1993): 76, 101–104; and Katherine Van Wezel Stone, "Labor and the Corporate Structure: Changing Conceptions and Emerging Possibilities," *University of Chicago Law Review* 55, no. 1 (1988): 90–91.

27. See Rosenfeld, *What Unions No Longer Do*, 96.

28. Paul Weiler, "Promises to Keep: Securing Workers' Rights to Self-Organization Under the NLRA," *Harvard Law Review* 96, no. 8 (June 1983): 1769–1827.

29. See, for example, Dale L. Belman and Kristen A. Monaco, "The Effects of Deregulation, De-Unionization, Technology, and Human Capital on the Work and Work Lives of Truck Drivers," *Industrial and Labor Relations Review* 54, no. 2A (March 2001): 508.

30. See, for example, Stone, "Labor and the Corporate Structure," 73–173; Weil, *Fissured Workplace*, 4; and Mark Barenberg, "Widening the Scope of Worker Organizing: Legal Reforms to Facilitate Multi-Employer Organizing, Bargaining, and Striking," Roosevelt Institute, 2015, 3, http://rooseveltinstitute.org/wp-content/uploads/2015/10/Widening-the-Scope-of-Worker-Organizing.pdf (archived at https://perma.cc/JWN2-DS57).

31. Lawrence Mishel, Elise Gould, and Josh Bivens, "Wage Stagnation in Nine Charts," *Economic Policy Institute*, January 6, 2015, http://www.epi.org/files/2013/wage-stagnation-in-nine-charts.pdf (archived at https://perma.cc/R2C5-QAH5).

32. Richard B. Freeman and Joel Rogers, *What Workers Want* (Ithaca, NY: Cornell University Press, 1999); and Lichtenstein, Chapter 9 in this volume.

33. Julius G. Getman, "Explaining the Fall of the Labor Movement," *St. Louis University Law Journal* 41, no. 2 (1997): 578–584; Michael H. Gottesman, "In Despair, Starting Over: Imagining a Labor Law for Unorganized Workers," *Chicago-Kent Law Review* 69, no. 1 (1993): 61–62; and Weiler, "Promises to Keep," 1769–1770, 1774–1804.

34. House Subcommittee on Labor-Management Relations of the House Committee on Education and Labor, 98th Cong., *The Failure of Labor Law: A Betrayal of American Workers* (Comm. Print, 1984), 1.

35. Weiler, "Promises to Keep," 1770. For accounts by human rights organizations' and political officials, see, for example, Lance Compa, *Unfair Advantage: Workers' Freedom of Association in the United States Under International Human Rights Standards* (Ithaca, NY: Cornell University Press, 2002); Dunlop Commission on the Future of Worker-Management Relations, U.S. Department of Labor, *Final Report* (1995); and for a historian's perspective, see, for example, Cowie, *Great Exception*, 25–26.

36. See, for example, Michael L. Wachter, "The Striking Success of the National Labor Relations Act," in *Research Handbook on the Economics of Labor and Employment Law*, ed. Cynthia L. Estlund and Michael L. Wachter (Cheltenham: Edward Elgar, 2012), 427–462 (arguing that the NLRA has achieved its most important goal: industrial peace).

37. See Weiler, "Promises to Keep," 1769–1770. For a summary of reform failures, see Benjamin I. Sachs, "Despite Preemption: Making Labor Law in Cities and States," *Harvard Law Review* 124, no. 5 (March 2011): 1163–1164; and Cynthia L. Estlund, "The Ossification of American Labor Law," *Columbia Law Review* 102, no. 6 (October 2002): 1611–1612. There was one significant reform in the post–Taft–Hartley era: The Landrum–Griffin Act of 1959

imposed a regime for the regulation of internal union affairs and union democracy, while tinkering with some elements of Taft–Hartley. See Labor-Management Reporting and Disclosure (Landrum–Griffin) Act of 1959, Pub. L. No. 86-257, 73 Stat. 519 (codified as amended in scattered sections of 29 U.S.C.).

38. See Stone, "Labor and the Corporate Structure," 73–173; and Samuel Estreicher, "Labor Law Reform in a World of Competitive Product Markets," *Chicago-Kent Law Review* 69, no. 1 (1993): 5n5. Notably, other industrialized countries experienced similar trends of globalization, the fissuring of the traditional employment relationship, and the use of automation. But unions in these countries did not experience the same collapse as U.S. unions; in some countries, union density has remained steady or even increased, while income distribution remained relatively constant. Hacker and Pierson, *Winner-Take-All Politics*, 57–58; and Kathleen Thelen, *Varieties of Liberalization and the New Politics of Social Solidarity* (New York: Cambridge University Press, 2014), 35–37; cf. Jonas Pontusson, David Rueda, and Christopher R. Way, "Comparative Political Economy of Wage Distribution: The Role of Partisanship and Labour Market Institutions," *British Journal of Political Science* 32, no. 2 (April 2002): 307 ("While market forces have tended to generate more inequality, there is nonetheless no uniform or universal trend towards more overall wage inequality among full-time employees across the OECD").

39. See Weil, *Fissured Workplace*; and Barenberg, "Widening the Scope of Worker Organizing."

40. See Weil, *Fissured Workplace*, 58–59, 68–69, 160; and Barenberg, "Widening the Scope of Worker Organizing."

41. Weil, *Fissured Workplace*, 26, 102, 128, 159–168, 173–177.

42. Brishen Rogers, "Employment Rights in the Platform Economy: Getting Back to Basics," *Harvard Law and Policy Review* 10, no. 2 (2016): 480 (defining the "platform economy" as "companies such as Uber, Lyft, TaskRabbit, Postmates, and Handy, all of which provide online platforms that match consumers with workers for short-term tasks").

43. But see, for example, *Berwick v. Uber Technologies Inc.*, No. 11-46739 EK, at 10 (Cal. Labor Commissioner, June 3, 2015) (holding that Uber drivers qualify as employees under California law); and *Razak et al. v. Uber Technologies Inc. et al.*, 2018 WL 1744467 (E.D. Pa. 2018) (holding that drivers for Uber's luxury car service are statutory employees under the Fair Labor Standards Act).

44. National Labor Relations Act § 2(3), 29 U.S.C. § 152(3) (2012).

45. For example, the NLRB is widely thought to lack authority to sanction or punish lawmakers or business-funded antiunion organizations for retaliating against workers for organizing. See Amanda Becker, "Legal Challenge to VW Union Election Could be 'Uncharted Territory,'" *Reuters*, February 14, 2014, http://uk.reuters.com/article/autos-vw-legal -idUKL2N0LJ1IT20140214 (archived at https://perma.cc/J8RT-A7KZ) (describing the efforts of Tennessee elected officials to dissuade Volkswagen workers from unionizing, including by threatening retaliation).

46. The NLRB's position changed with *Browning-Ferris Industries of California, Inc.*, 362 N.L.R.B. No. 186 at 2 (August 27, 2015). However, following several new appointments by President Trump, the NLRB soon overturned *Browning-Ferris*, in *Hy-Brand Industrial Con-*

tractors, 365 NLRB No. 156 (2017). That decision was vacated after the NLRB's inspector general held that one member should have recused himself from the case due to a conflict of interest. "Board Vacates Hy-Brand Decision," NLRB Office of Public Affairs, February 26, 2018, https://www.nlrb.gov/news-outreach/news-story/board-vacates-hy-brand-decision. In the meantime, the D.C. Circuit issued an opinion upholding, in part, the *Browning-Ferris* standard. *Browning-Ferris Industries of California v. NLRB*, 911 F.3d 1195 (D.C. Cir. 2018). Nonetheless, the board has proposed a new rule that would make it more difficult to demonstrate joint employment status. The Standard for Determining Joint-Employer Status, 83 Fed. Reg. 46681 (proposed September 14, 2018).

47. *Artcraft Displays, Inc.*, 262 N.L.R.B. 1233 (1982), *clarified*, 263 N.L.R.B. 804 (1982); see Barenberg, "Widening the Scope of Worker Organizing," 11.

48. Lichtenstein, *Walter Reuther*, 271–298 (describing "The Treaty of Detroit"); and Anner, Bair, and Blasi, "Learning from the Past," in Appelbaum and Lichtenstein, *Achieving Workers' Rights*, 239 (describing jobbers' agreements negotiated among workers, garment manufacturers, and purchasers in the U.S. garment sector in the early and mid-twentieth century). Industry-wide bargaining persists in some industries, including the arts and professional sports. See, for example, Fisk, *Writing for Hire* (describing industry-wide bargaining in Hollywood).

49. National Labor Relations Act § 8(b)(4), 29 U.S.C. § 158(b)(4) (2012).

50. *See International Longshoremen's Association v. Allied International, Inc.*, 456 U.S. 212, 226 (1982); and *NLRB v. Retail Store Employees Union, Local 1001*, 447 U.S. 607, 616 (1980).

51. See, for example, *Gimrock Construction, Inc.*, 344 N.L.R.B. 934 (2005); NLRA § 8(e) (prohibiting so-called hot cargo agreements except in the garment and construction industries). For further discussion, see Barenberg, "Widening the Scope of Worker Organizing," 21.

52. See Rosenfeld, *What Unions No Longer Do*, 168–173, 180–181; and Benjamin I. Sachs, "The Unbundled Union: Politics Without Collective Bargaining," *Yale Law Journal* 123, no. 1 (October 2013): 153–154, 178–179.

53. The country's history of privately provided health and pension benefits and the two-party political system, with no tradition of a labor party, also help explain, and are in part explained by, the comparatively apolitical orientation of labor unions. See Nelson Lichtenstein, *State of the Union: A Century of American Labor* (Princeton, NJ: Princeton University Press, 2013), 126, 143–144, 146.

54. See Clyde W. Summers, "Worker Participation in the U.S. and West Germany: A Comparative Study from an American Perspective," *American Journal of Comparative Law* 28, no. 3 (1980): 385–388; and Steven J. Silvia, *Holding the Shop Together: German Industrial Relations in the Postwar Era* (Ithaca, NY: Cornell University Press, 2013), 38–41.

55. Thelen, *Varieties of Liberalization*, 58.

56. Ibid., 65–67.

57. Franz Traxler and Martin Behrens, "Collective Bargaining Coverage and Extension Procedures," *EurWORK*, December 17, 2002, http://www.eurofound.europa.eu/observatories /eurwork/comparative-information/collective-bargaining-coverage-and-extension -procedures (archived at https://perma.cc/2PWM-4HHP); see also Silvia, *Holding the Shop Together*, 27–28 (discussing the German system of contract extension and its limitations).

58. *Eastex, Inc. v. NLRB*, 437 U.S. 556 (1978); see also "Memorandum from Ronald Meis-burg, General Counsel, NLRB to All Regional Directors, Officers-in-Charge, and Resident Officers, Memorandum GC 08-10," July 22, 2008 (providing guidelines for how to handle unfair labor practice charges involving political activity arising out of immigration rallies).

59. See *Citizens United v. FEC*, 558 U.S. 310 (2010) (declaring restrictions on independent corporate and union political expenditures unconstitutional).

60. But see James J. Brudney, "Collateral Conflict: Employer Claims of RICO Extortion Against Union Comprehensive Campaigns," *Southern California Law Review* 83, no. 4 (May 2010): 731–795 (describing how unions' ability to pressure employers to enter organizing framework agreements through the use of political pressure has been somewhat chilled by RICO suits brought by employers).

61. See Sachs, "Unbundled Union," 152, 168–171 (describing successful political efforts of unions); and Rosenfeld, *What Unions No Longer Do*, 170–173.

62. See, for example, Lichtenstein, *State of the Union*, 58–59, 76–85, 262–264. But see ibid., 95–96 (describing how racial and gender assumptions of unionists and policymakers shaped even broadly inclusive and beneficial national legislation); and Alice Kessler-Harris, *In Pursuit of Equity* (New York: Oxford University Press, 2001), 17–18, 100–111, 141–143, 171–177 (detailing how a deeply embedded set of gender beliefs shaped seemingly neutral social legislation to limit the freedom and equality of women).

63. See Lichtenstein, *State of the Union*, 186 (describing the structure of unions and its relationship to their political activity); Sachs, "Unbundled Union," 153–154 (emphasizing how the decline in union membership reduces workers' influence in politics); and Kate Andrias, "Separations of Wealth: Inequality and the Erosion of Checks and Balances," *Journal of Constitutional Law* 18, no. 2 (2015): 436–456 (summarizing research on government's responsiveness to wealthy interests).

64. James J. Brudney, "Reflections on Group Action and the Law of the Workplace," *Texas Law Review* 74, no. 7 (June 1996): 1570.

65. As one treatise declared in 1994, "A mere thirty years ago, there was no such thing as employment law." Mark A. Rothstein, Charles B. Craver, Elinor P. Schroeder, Elaine W. Shoben et al., *Employment Law* (St. Paul, MN: West, 1994), v. See Cynthia Estlund, *Regoverning the Workplace: From Self-Regulation to Co-Regulation* (New Haven, CT: Yale University Press, 2010), 52–74; and Theodore J. St. Antoine, "Labor and Employment Law in Two Transitional Decades," *Brandeis Law Journal* 42, no. 3 (2004): 526–527.

66. See Nancy MacLean, *Freedom Is Not Enough: The Opening of the American Workplace* (Cambridge, MA: Harvard University Press, 2006), 67–113 (tracing the struggle to pass and implement Title VII and analyzing the statute's influence).

67. See Samuel R. Bagenstos, "Employment Law and Social Equality," *Michigan Law Review* 112, no. 2 (November 2013): 230 and nn18–21.

68. See Benjamin I. Sachs, "Employment Law as Labor Law," *Cardozo Law Review* 29, no. 6 (May 2008): 2687–2693.

69. For leading accounts of the tension between collective and individual rights, see, for example, Lichtenstein, *State of the Union*, x, 141, 171; Brudney, "Reflections on Group Ac-

tion," 1563–1599; Cynthia Estlund, "Rebuilding the Law of the Workplace in an Era of Self-Regulation," *Columbia Law Review* 105, no. 2 (March 2005): 319–404; Reuel Schiller, *Forging Rivals: Race, Class, Law and the Collapse of Post War Liberalism* (New York: Cambridge University Press, 2015), 3, 5, 12; Reuel E. Schiller, "From Group Rights to Individual Liberties: Post-War Law, Liberalism, and the Waning of Union Strength," *Berkeley Journal of Employment and Labor Law* 20, no. 1 (1999): 4; and Katherine Van Wezel Stone, "The Legacy of Industrial Pluralism: The Tension Between Individual Employment Rights and the New Deal Collective Bargaining System," *University of Chicago Law Review* 59, no. 2 (1992): 575–644. Other historians complicate the divide between individual and collective rights; see Sophia Z. Lee, *Workplace Constitution: From the New Deal to the New Right* (New York: Cambridge University Press, 2014), 5–6, 73–75.

70. See Annette Bernhardt, Ruth Milkman, Nik Theodore, et al., *Broken Laws, Unprotected Workers: Violations of Employment and Labor Laws in America's Cities*, 2009, 50, https://www.nelp.org/wp-content/uploads/2015/03/BrokenLawsReport2009.pdf; Kim Bobo, *Wage Theft in America: Why Millions of Working Americans Are Not Getting Paid—And What We Can Do About It*, rev. ed. (New York: New Press, 2011), 6–22; and Weil, *Fissured Workplace*, 214–222.

71. See Alexander J. S. Colvin, "Mandatory Arbitration and Inequality of Justice in Employment," *Berkeley Journal of Employment and Labor Law* 35, nos. 1–2 (2014): 71–90; and Judith Resnik, "Diffusing Disputes: The Public in the Private of Arbitration, the Private in Courts, and the Erasure of Rights," *Yale Law Journal* 124, no. 8 (June 2015): 2804–2939. See also *Epic Systems Corp. v. Lewis*, 584 U.S. (2018) (holding that mandatory arbitration agreements prohibiting class proceedings must be enforced notwithstanding the NLRA's protection of concerted activity).

72. See Rachel Arnow-Richman, "Just Notice: Re-Reforming Employment at Will," *UCLA Law Review* 58, no. 1 (October 2010): 4n9, 5n10, 8; and Cynthia L. Estlund, "How Wrong Are Employees About Their Rights, and Why Does It Matter?," *New York University Law Review* 77, no. 1 (April 2002): 8.

73. See Congressional Budget Office, Pub. No. 4856, *The Effects of a Minimum Wage Increase on Employment and Family Income* (2014), 11; Kathryn J. Edin and H. Luke Shaefer, *$2.00 a Day: Living on Almost Nothing in America* (New York: Houghton Mifflin Harcourt, 2015); and David Cooper, "The Minimum Wage Used to Be Enough to Keep Workers out of Poverty—It's Not Anymore," Economic Policy Institute, December 4, 2013, http://www.epi.org/publication/minimum-wage-workers-poverty-anymore-raising/ (archived at http://perma.cc/MT9L-ZVFR).

74. Mishel, Gould, and Bivens, "Wage Stagnation in Nine Charts," 4 fig. 2, 7 fig. 5; and Lichtenstein, *State of the Union*, 12–16.

75. Employee Free Choice Act of 2007, H.R. 800, 110th Cong. (2007). Although the House of Representatives passed the Employee Free Choice Act in 2007, the bill died after a threatened senatorial filibuster. See, for example, Steven Greenhouse, "Democrats Drop Key Part of Bill to Assist Unions," *New York Times*, July 17, 2009, http://www.nytimes.com/2009/07/17/business/17union.html (archived at https://perma.cc/6QAN-UWNT).

76. See Sachs, "Despite Preemption," 1163–1164; and Benjamin I. Sachs, "Labor Law Renewal," *Harvard Law and Policy Review* 1, no. 2 (2007): 376.

77. See James J. Brudney, "Neutrality Agreements and Card Check Recognition: Prospects for Changing Paradigms," *Iowa Law Review* 90, no. 3 (March 2005): 837–838; and César F. Rosado Marzán, "Organizing with International Framework Agreements: An Exploratory Study," *UC Irvine Law Review* 4, no. 2 (May 2014): 770–771.

78. See, for example, Eileen Boris and Jennifer Klein, *Caring for America: Home Health Workers in the Shadow of the Welfare State* (New York: Oxford University Press, 2012); and Linda Delp and Katie Quan, "Homecare Worker Organizing in California: An Analysis of a Successful Strategy," *Labor Studies Journal* 27, no. 1 (2002): 6.

79. Janice Fine, *Worker Centers: Organizing Communities at the Edge of the Dream* (Ithaca, NY: Cornell University Press, 2006); Jennifer Gordon, *Suburban Sweatshops: The Fight for Immigrant Rights* (Cambridge, MA: Harvard University Press, 2005); Ruth Milkman, Introduction to Ruth Milkman et al., eds., *Working for Justice: The L.A. Model of Organizing and Advocacy* (Ithaca, NY: Cornell University Press, 2010), 1; Janice Fine, "New Forms to Settle Old Scores: Updating the Worker Centre Story in the United States," *Journal of Industrial Relations* 66, no. 4 (2011): 606–609; and Kati L. Griffith, "Worker Centers and Labor Law Protections: Why Aren't They Having Their Cake?," *Berkeley Journal of Employment and Labor Law* 36, no. 2 (2015): 331.

80. Fine, "New Forms to Settle Old Scores," 609–611.

81. Cynthia L. Estlund, "The Death of Labor Law?," *Annual Review of Law and Social Science* 2, no. 1 (December 2006): 117.

82. Benjamin I. Sachs, "Enabling Employee Choice: A Structural Approach to the Rules of Union Organizing," *Harvard Law Review* 123, no. 3 (January 2010): 713–727.

83. Samuel Estreicher, "'Easy In, Easy Out': A Future for U.S. Workplace Representation," *Minnesota Law Review* 98, no. 5 (May 2014): 1615; and Michael M. Oswalt, "Automatic Elections," *UC Irvine Law Review* 4, no. 2 (May 2014): 801.

84. Richard D. Kahlenberg and Moshe Z. Marvit, *Why Labor Organizing Should Be a Civil Right: Rebuilding a Middle-Class Democracy by Enhancing Worker Voice* (New York: Century Foundation Press, 2012).

85. Ellen Dannin, *Taking Back the Workers' Law: How to Fight the Assault on Labor Rights* (Ithaca, NY: Cornell University Press, 2006); Cynthia L. Estlund, "Labor, Property, and Sovereignty After *Lechmere*," *Stanford Law Review* 46, no. 2 (January 1994): 305–359; Catherine L. Fisk and Benjamin I. Sachs, "Restoring Equity in Right-to-Work Law," *UC Irvine Law Review* 4, no. 2 (May 2014): 858–859; Charles J. Morris, *The Blue Eagle at Work: Reclaiming Democratic Rights in the American Workplace* (Ithaca, NY: Cornell University Press, 2005); and Marion Crain and Ken Matheny, "Beyond Unions, Notwithstanding Labor Law," *UC Irvine Law Review* 4, no. 2 (May 2014): 605.

86. Marion Crain and John Inazu, "Re-Assembling Labor," *University of Illinois Law Review* 2015, no. 5 (2015): 1791; Charlotte Garden, "*Citizens, United* and *Citizens United*: The Future of Labor Speech Rights?," *William & Mary Law Review* 53, no. 1 (October 2011): 1–53; and Charlotte Garden, "Labor Values Are First Amendment Values: Why Union Comprehensive Campaigns Are Protected Speech," *Fordham Law Review* 79, no. 6 (May 2011): 2617.

87. James J. Brudney, "Envisioning Enforcement of Freedom of Association Standards in Corporate Codes: A Journey for Sinbad or Sisyphus?," *Comparative Labor Law and Policy Journal* 33, no. 4 (2012): 555–556, 598; and Estlund, *Regoverning the Workplace*, 77–128.

88. See Ian Ayres and John Braithwaite, *Responsive Regulation: Transcending the Deregulation Debate* (New York: Oxford University Press, 1992); Estlund, *Regoverning the Workplace*; Orly Lobel, "The Renew Deal: The Fall of Regulation and the Rise of Governance in Contemporary Legal Thought," *Minnesota Law Review* 89, no. 2 (December 2004): 342–470; and Estlund, "Rebuilding the Law of the Workplace," 319.

89. See James Brudney, "Decent Labour Standards in Corporate Supply Chains: The Immokalee Workers Model," in *Temporary Labour Migration in the Global Era*, ed. Joanna Howe and Rosemary Owens (Oxford: Hart, 2016), 551.

90. Brudney, "Envisioning Enforcement," 567–574; and Weil, *Fissured Workplace*, 262–264.

91. For the most famous of the many recent accounts of the rise in inequality, see Piketty, *Capital*.

92. See Rosenfeld, *What Unions No Longer Do*, 10–30; cf. Freeman and Medoff, *What Do Unions Do?* (describing, as of the mid-1980s, the role of trade unions in the United States). See also "Union Members—2017" (providing data about union membership). Despite recent declines, unions still represent about 35 percent of public-sector workers; the unionization rate in the private sector is about 6 percent. "Union Members—2017."

93. Gilens, *Affluence and Influence*; Hacker and Pierson, "Winner-Take-All Politics," 152–204; and Phillips-Fein, *Invisible Hands*.

94. Harold Meyerson, "Under Obama, Labor Should Have Made More Progress," *Washington Post*, February 10, 2010, http://www.washingtonpost.com/wp-dyn/content/article/2010/02/09/AR2010020902465.html (archived at https://perma.cc/M8T2-YAR2) (describing the Senate's inability to pass the EFCA as "devastating and galling" for the unions).

95. "Minimum Wage Tracker," Economic Policy Institute, 2018, http://www.epi.org/minimum-wage-tracker (archived at https://perma.cc/HTG4-QHZQ); "State Minimum Wages," National Conference of State Legislatures, 2018, http://www.ncsl.org/research/labor-and-employment/state-minimum-wage-chart.aspx (archived at https://perma.cc/UQ4E-MYMC); and "City Minimum Wage Laws: Recent Trends and Economic Evidence," National Employment Law Project, 2015, http://www.nelp.org/content/uploads/City-Minimum-Wage-Laws-Recent-Trends-Economic-Evidence.pdf (archived at https://perma.cc/VS5C-D3AX).

96. See S.B. 3, 2016 Leg., Reg. Sess. (Cal. 2016); "City Minimum Wage Laws," National Employment Law Project; Press Release, "Governor Cuomo Signs $15 Minimum Wage Plan and 12 Week Paid Family Leave Policy into Law," New York Governor's Press Office, April 4, 2016, http://www.governor.ny.gov/news/governor-cuomo-signs-15-minimum-wage-plan-and-12-week-paid-family-leave-policy-law (archived at https://perma.cc/NYP6-UCQC); and Katherine Landergan and Rebecca Rainey, "Blue States' $15 Minimum Wage Push Gets a Jump-Start," *Politico*, February 16, 2019.

97. See "State and Local Laws Advancing Fair Work Scheduling," National Women's Law Center, 2018, https://nwlc-ciw49tixgw5lbab.stackpathdns.com/wp-content/uploads/2018/04/state-and-local-fair-scheduling.pdf; and "Paid Sick Leave," National Conference of State Legislatures, 2018, http://www.ncsl.org/research/labor-and-employment/paid-sick-leave.aspx.

98. On the distinction between employment law and labor law, see Sachs, "Employment Law as Labor Law," 2688–2689; see also St. Antoine, "Labor and Employment Law," 526–527.

99. See Patrick McGeehan, "Push to Lift Minimum Wage Is Now Serious Business," *New York Times*, July 23, 2015, http://www.nytimes.com/2015/07/24/nyregion/push-to-lift -hourly-pay-is-now-serious-business.html (archived at https://perma.cc/S7M8-9VPH); and Jenny Brown, "Fast Food Strikes: What's Cooking," LaborNotes.org, June 24, 2013, http:// www.labornotes.org/2013/06/fast-food-strikes-whats-cooking (archived at https://perma.cc /A739-Y6CQ).

100. More precisely, the campaign demands fifteen dollars an hour and the right to a union "free of intimidation." See Arun Gupta, "Fight for 15 Confidential: How Did the Biggest-Ever Mobilization of Fast-Food Workers Come About, and What Is Its Endgame?," *In These Times*, November 11, 2013, http://inthesetimes.com/article/15826/fight_for_15 _confidential (archived at https://perma.cc/Y5V6-SNKS); see also Josh Eidelson, "Fast Food Strikes to Massively Expand," *Salon*, August 14, 2013, http://www.salon.com/2013/08/14/fast _food_strikes_massively_expanding_theyre_thinking_much_bigger (archived at https:// perma.cc/N9J2-6M3P); and Lydia DePillis, "It's Not Just Fast Food: The Fight for $15 is for Everyone Now," *Washington Post*, December 4, 2014, https://www.washingtonpost.com/news /storyline/wp/2014/12/04/its-not-just-fast-food-the-fight-for-15-is-for-everyone-now (archived at https://perma.cc/Z7GV-GJ6M).

101. See Andrias, "The New Labor Law."

102. Andrew M. Cuomo, Opinion, "Fast Food Workers Deserve a Raise," *New York Times*, May 6, 2015, http://www.nytimes.com/2015/05/07/opinion/andrew-m-cuomo-fast -food-workers-deserve-a-raise.html. As Cuomo noted, the New York Legislature had rejected his proposal to raise the minimum wage statutorily. NY Labor Law § 654 (McKinney 2016); Ibid. § 655(1); and Mario J. Musolino, acting commissioner of labor, "Determination Regarding Adequacy of Wages," New York Department of Labor, May 7, 2015, http://www.governor .ny.gov/sites/governor.ny.gov/files/atoms/files/Determination_wages_050715.pdf.

103. "Fast Food Wage Board," New York Department of Labor, 2015, http://labor.ny.gov /workerprotection/laborstandards/wageboard2015.shtm.

104. "Report of the Fast Food Wage Board to the NYS Commissioner of Labor," Fast Food Wage Board, New York Department of Labor, 2015, 10 11, https://www.labor.ny.gov /workerprotection/laborstandards/pdfs/Fast-Food-Wage-Board-Report.pdf.

105. McGeehan, "Push to Lift Minimum Wage."

106. However, in the negotiations over the statewide minimum, employers successfully mobilized to strip the commissioner's authority to establish higher minimums for particular occupations. Thus, the ultimate compromise bill curtailed the powers of future tripartite wage boards. N.Y.L. 2016, chapter 54, part K, § 4. Existing wage orders remain in effect and New York law still allows the commission to act regarding hours. See ibid. § 5; *National Restaurant Association v. Commissioner of Labor*, 34 N.Y.S.3d 232, 235–236 (N.Y. App. Div. 2016) (discussing legislative history).

107. See Karl Klare, "The Horizons of Transformative Labour and Employment Law," in *Labour Law in an Era of Globalization: Transformative Practices and Possibilities*, ed. Joanne Conaghan et al. (New York: Oxford University Press, 2002), 3, 23.

108. For an analysis of how law encouraged the earlier U.S. labor movement's embrace of private ordering over statism, see Forbath, "Shaping of the American Labor Movement," 1109–1256; and Forbath, *Law and the Shaping of the American Labor Movement.*

109. Nelson Lichtenstein, "The Demise of Tripartite Governance and the Rise of the Corporate Social Responsibility Regime," in Appelbaum and Lichtenstein, *Achieving Workers' Rights*, 95 (noting that the system was "often denominated as 'corporatism' in Europe, 'tripartism' in the United States").

110. The current phenomenon is markedly different from previous efforts to blur the distinction between employment law and labor law. Those tended to use employment law to achieve NLRA aims, see Sachs, "Employment Law as Labor Law," 2687 (documenting how "workers and their lawyers are turning to employment statutes like the Fair Labor Standards Act (FLSA) and Title VII of the Civil Rights Act of 1964" to facilitate "their efforts to organize and act collectively"), or abandoned a system of unionization in favor of self-regulation with elements of worker voice, see Estlund, *Regoverning the Workplace*, 52–74 (describing the fall of collective bargaining and the proliferation of substantive mandates).

111. Interview with Judy Scott, general counsel, SEIU, April 10, 2016.

112. Justin Miller, "In New York City, Fast-Food Workers May Soon Have a Permanent Voice," *American Prospect*, June 15, 2017, http://prospect.org/article/new-york-city-fast-food -workers-may-soon-have-permanent-voice.

113. City of Seattle, Ordinance 125627 (2018), to be codified at Seattle Municipal Code, chapter 14.23.

114. See Andrias, "The New Labor Law," 89–95.

115. See William P. Jones, Chapter 11 in this volume; Slater, *Government Employee Unions*, 193–195; and Fink and Greenberg, *Upheaval in the Quiet Zone*. See also Kate Andrias, "An American Approach to Social Democracy: The Forgotten Story of the Fair Labor Standards Act," *Yale Law Journal* 128, no. 3 (January 2019): 616–709; Leon Fink, *The Long Gilded Age: American Capitalism and the Lessons of a New World Order* (Philadelphia: University of Pennsylvania Press, 2015), 96; David Montgomery, *The Fall of the House of Labor: The Workplace, the State, and American Labor Activism, 1865–1925* (New York: Cambridge University Press, 1987); Tomlins, *State and the Unions*; and Lichtenstein, Chapter 9 in this volume.

116. See, for example, Thelen, *Varieties of Liberalization* (examining labor market institutions in the United States, Germany, Denmark, Sweden, and the Netherlands).

117. See Barenberg, "Democracy and Domination," 961 (describing the prospects for a union default rule as in the "political ozone").

118. See Lance Compa, "Not Dead Yet: Preserving Labor Law Strengths While Exploring New Labor Law Strategies," *UC Irvine Law Review* 4, no. 2 (May 2014): 610–612 (arguing that a labor and employment law system cannot be "wrenched from its historical moorings"). See also Estlund, "Ossification of American Labor Law," 1527–1612 (discussing obstacles to labor law reform). But see Matthew Dimick, "Productive Unionism," *UC Irvine Law Review* 4, no. 2 (May 2014): 679–724 (emphasizing the importance of labor union structure to centralized bargaining and suggesting that unions can, on their own, move toward a more industrial system).

119. See David Madland, "The Future of Worker Voice and Power," Center for American Progress, 2016, https://cdn.americanprogress.org/wp-content/uploads/2016/10/06051753

/WorkerVoice2.pdf; Brishen Rogers, "Libertarian Corporatism is Not an Oxymoron," *Texas Law Review* 94, no. 7 (June 2016): 1624; David Rolf, "Toward a 21st Century Labor Movement," *American Prospect*, April 18, 2016, http://prospect.org/article/toward-21st-century -labor-movement (archived at http://perma.cc/DFV5-RRMU); David Rolf, *The Fight for Fifteen* (New York: New Press, 2016), 253–258; and Lawrence Mishel, president, Economic Policy Institute Policy Center, "Raise America's Pay: Testimony Delivered Before the Democratic National Convention Platform Drafting Hearing," June 9, 2016, https://www.epi.org/files/pdf /108654.pdf.

120. Kate Andrias, "Social Bargaining in States and Cities: Toward a More Egalitarian and Democratic Workplace Law," *Harvard Law and Policy Review Online* (2018), https:// harvardlpr.com/wp-content/uploads/sites/20/2018/01/Andrias-Social.pdf.

Kate Andrias is a professor of law at the University of Michigan, where she teaches and writes in the areas of labor law, constitutional law, and administrative law. Her work has appeared in the *Yale Law Journal*, the *Harvard Law Review*, the *Texas Law Review*, and other journals and edited volumes.

Romain Huret is a professor at the School of Advanced Studies in the Social Sciences in Paris. He has published many books and articles on poverty and inequality in the United States, including *American Tax Resisters* (2014) and *The Experts' War on Poverty* (2018).

William P. Jones is a professor of history at the University of Minnesota and an author, most recently, of *The March on Washington: Jobs, Freedom and the Forgotten History of Civil Rights* (2013). He is writing a book on race and public-sector employment in the twentieth-century United States.

Nelson Lichtenstein is a Distinguished Professor of History at the University of California, Santa Barbara, where he directs the Center for the Study of Work, Labor, and Democracy. He contributed an essay on labor to *The Rise and Fall of the New Deal Order, 1930–1980* (1989, edited by Steve Fraser and Gary Gerstle). He has written or edited more than a dozen books on labor, politics, and political economy.

Nancy MacLean is the William H. Chafe Professor of History and Public Policy at Duke University and the author of *Democracy in Chains: The Deep History of the Radical Right's Stealth Plan for America* (2017), a finalist for the National Book Award. Her previous books include *Behind the Mask of Chivalry: The Making of the Second Ku Klux Klan* (1994) and *Freedom Is Not Enough: The Opening of the American Workplace* (2008).

Isaac William Martin is a professor in the Department of Urban Studies and Planning at the University of California, San Diego. He is the author of

Foreclosed America (2015, with Richard Niedt); *Rich People's Movements* (2013); and *The Permanent Tax Revolt* (2008).

Margaret O'Mara is the Howard & Frances Keller Professor of History at the University of Washington and the author of *The Code: Silicon Valley and the Remaking of America* (2019).

K. Sabeel Rahman is an associate professor of law at Brooklyn Law School and the president of Demos, a think-and-do tank focused on issues of democracy, inequality, and racial justice. He is the author of *Democracy Against Domination* (2017), which won the Dahl Prize at the American Political Science Association; and *Civic Power: Rebuilding American Democracy in an Era of Crisis* (2019, with Hollie Russon Gilman).

Timothy Shenk is a fellow at New America, a visiting scholar at Johns Hopkins University, and coeditor of *Dissent*. He is the author of *Maurice Dobb: Political Economist* (2013)

Elizabeth Tandy Shermer is an associate professor of history at Loyola University Chicago. The author of *Sunbelt Capitalism: Phoenix and the Transformation of American Politics* (2013), she is currently finishing a history of the student loan industry. In 2019–2020 she was a fellow at Stanford's Center for Advanced Study in the Behavioral Sciences.

Jason Scott Smith is a professor of history at the University of New Mexico. He is the author of *Building New Deal Liberalism: The Political Economy of Public Works, 1933–1956* (2006) and *A Concise History of the New Deal* (2014). In 2017–2018 he was a Fulbright scholar and was the Mary Ball Washington Professor of American History at University College Dublin, Ireland.

Samir Sonti is an assistant professor in the School of Labor and Urban Studies at the City University of New York. He edits the books and arts section of *New Labor Forum* and is writing a book on the politics of inflation in the twentieth-century United States.

Karen M. Tani is a professor of law at the University of California, Berkeley. She is the author of *States of Dependency: Welfare, Rights, and American Governance, 1935–1973* (2016).

Jean-Christian Vinel teaches American history at the University of Paris Diderot. He is the author of *The Employee: A Political History* (2013) and coeditor of *Postwar Conservatism: A Transnational Investigation* (2017).

INDEX

ACKNOWLEDGMENTS

This book is the product of longstanding exchanges between the three editors. We are most grateful to our respective institutions—the Center for the Study of Work, Labor, and Democracy at the University of California at Santa-Barbara, the Centres d'études nord américaines at the Ecole des hautes études en sciences sociales, and the Laboratoire de recherche sur les cultures anglophones at Paris Diderot for supporting these exchanges. Over the years, Gary Gerstle has been an outstanding intellectual comrade, and without the many discussions we have had on both sides of the Atlantic about the New Deal order, this book would not exist. Special thanks are also owed to Alice O'Connor, Steven Fraser, Eileen Boris and Kit Smemo for helping organize the "Beyond the New Deal Order conference" in Santa-Barbara in 2015, which proved the perfect testing ground for most of the contributions included in this anthology.

Working with Robert Lockhart at Penn has again been a pleasure. With a supporting ear and a critical eye, Bob has helped us make this anthology a more coherent book while understanding our argument that not every book on 20th century US history needs to be pitched, let alone framed, as an explanation for the Trump Presidency. Two anonymous readers also offered very useful insights. At Penn Press, Zoe Kovacs and Noreen O'Connor-Abel helped get the manuscript in final form, and Erin Davis, production editor at Westchester Book Services, skillfully coordinated the editing and proofreading of the book. Jim O'Brien indexed this book in superb fashion.

Finally, we'd like to thank our families and children. They know why.